# Relational Christianity

"Reading this manuscript was a needed breath of Spirit-forming education and edification."

—LARS KIERSPEL
Shiloh University

"Wow. Relishing every word of this revelation!"

—STEPHEN ANTHONY LAUDISE
Pastor, Hawaii

"Very impressive. Fascinating! A revelatory word on the meaning of Christianity."

—STEPHANIE PENNIMAN
Shiloh University

"I loved this piece on relational Christianity—it truly is God inspired and anointed."

—PETER VAN BREDA
The New International University

"If you are an instructor in a seminary and you are dissatisfied with the outcomes of your classroom recipe, this book will help you to produce fresh bread. . . . It was so meaningful and timely for me to read this."

—JOHN MCKENDRICKS
Multnomah University Reno-Tahoe

"Pinkham and Gruenberg give us a unique gift by showing how God's way of being is not only practical but absolutely essential for every aspect of life. . . . The triune God, who is eternally relational, makes humanity in God's image and likeness, so it follows that fullness of humanity is found and experienced only in interpersonal being. Readers will be challenged, awed, stretched, and surprised by a love beyond comprehension—by the hug that changes everything!"

—ANA ("CHIQUI") WOOD
Co-pastor, Table of Friends Church

"This morning, I sat in the parking lot and made myself read this . . . until I was done. Boy, did the Father scoop me up in his arms and take a load off my shoulders. It is not about performance. It is about being drawn into the communion relationship of the Father, the Son, and the Holy Spirit. I'm going to use my influence to give this gift to others in church today. Yeah, Father God!"

—**DOUG PAUL RICHARDSON**
Inactive president, Reinvent Ministries

"Dr. Pinkham demonstrates an intuitive grasp of reality that underlies the lifetime of thought and research supporting the thesis that it is all about relationships—with God and one another. With the depth of a Trinitarian scholar, the passion of a relational preacher, and the heart of a father connecting others to Abba Father, Dr. Pinkham blazes a trail to reimagining what it means to 'know and be known.'"

—**MARK GLENN**
Shiloh University

"Dr. Pinkham bores deep below the surface and examines the bedrock of Christianity—namely, the relational way of being of the triune God. Only as we understand who he is—a God of love—can we understand how to relate to him and how to build churches that reflect his true nature. This is essential for all of us, and especially those under the influence of Western culture, to contemplate and to implement in our lives."

—**FRED W. POSTON**
Southeast Missouri State University

"If we do not receive this revelation, we will continue to misdiagnose what is needed in our culture and in our churches. The gospel message is . . . that personal human identity can be caught up and inextricably bound up in the interpersonal oneness of the triune God. This authentic message will resonate within honest, 'longing' hearts."

—**GREGG GALAN**
Pastor, Edmonton, Alberta

# Relational Christianity

A Remarkable Vision of God

WESLEY M. PINKHAM
*with* JEREMIAH GRUENBERG

*Foreword by Marty Folsom*

WIPF & STOCK · Eugene, Oregon

RELATIONAL CHRISTIANITY
A Remarkable Vision of God

Copyright © 2022 Wesley M. Pinkham and Jeremiah Gruenberg. All rights reserved. Except for brief quotations in critical publications or reviews, no part of this book may be reproduced in any manner without prior written permission from the publisher. Write: Permissions, Wipf and Stock Publishers, 199 W. 8th Ave., Suite 3, Eugene, OR 97401.

Wipf & Stock
An Imprint of Wipf and Stock Publishers
199 W. 8th Ave., Suite 3
Eugene, OR 97401

www.wipfandstock.com

PAPERBACK ISBN: 978-1-6667-3175-0
HARDCOVER ISBN: 978-1-6667-2462-2
EBOOK ISBN: 978-1-6667-2463-9

12/21/22

All Scripture quotations, unless otherwise indicated, are taken from *The Message: The New Testament in Contemporary Language* (MSG). Copyright ©1993 by Eugene H. Peterson. Used by permission of NAVPRESS, P.O. Box 35001, Colorado Springs, Colorado 80935.

Scripture quotations marked NIV are taken from the Holy Bible, New International Version®, NIV®, copyright © 1973, 1978, 1984, 2011 by Biblica, Inc.® Used by permission of Zondervan. All rights reserved worldwide. www.zondervan.com

Scripture quotations marked NASB are taken from the New American Standard Bible®, NASB®, copyright © 1977, 1995, 2020 by The Lockman Foundation. Used by permission.

Scripture quotations marked NKJV are taken from the New King James Version®, copyright © 1982 by Thomas Nelson. Used by permission. All rights reserved.

# Contents

*List of Figures* | ix
*Foreword by Marty Folsom* | xi
*Preface* | xvii
*Acknowledgements* | xxi
*Some Introductory Notes* | xxiii
*Introduction: A Unifying Center* | xxv

**Part I: What Is Reality?** | 3

1 Holistic Thinking and God's Relational Priority | 5
    Introduction | 6
    The Greatest Holistic Story | 8
    That's Where His Mercy Begins | 15
    The Interconnectivity of Love | 17
    Holism and Human Reality | 22
    Holism and Christian Reality | 27
    Holism and Theological Thinking | 28
    Conclusion | 33
    Reflection | 34

2 The Interpersonal Nature of God | 35
    Introduction | 35
    Personhood of God | 36
    Christology and Pneumatology | 44

      Reciprocal Kenosis and Dynamic Communion | 47
      Christ's Church | 51
      Personal Dynamic Communion that Characterizes
        Leaders in the Church | 54
      Conclusion | 56
      Reflection | 57

3   Culture and the Principles of Christianity | 58
      Introduction | 58
      Historical and Cultural Pitfalls | 62
      Stages of Growth in Relating to the Word of God | 69
      A Relational, Interpersonal, Communal Culture | 72
      Conclusion | 78
      Reflection | 79

4   Education, Learning, and Growth toward Wholeness | 80
      Introduction | 80
      1. Teach Relationally | 81
      2. Implement Two Models of Relational Ways of Being | 83
      3. Directly Emphasize Interpersonal Oneness | 84
      Conclusion | 88
      Reflection | 89

## Part II: Why Is It Important to Define Reality? | 91

5   Trinitarian Thinking | 93
      Introduction | 93
      The Nature of Reality | 94
      The Practical Implications of the Trinity | 97
      Conclusion | 100
      Reflection | 101

6   Interpersonal Oneness | 102
      Introduction | 102
      Interpersonal Oneness Is Father-Led | 102
      Interpersonal Oneness Is a Christological Hermeneutic | 106
      Interpersonal Oneness Is the Reconciliation of Jesus | 113
      Conclusion | 115
      Reflection | 116

7   A Relational View of Christ's Covenant | 117
      Introduction | 117
      Covenant | 117

  Contract | 124
  Conclusion | 130
  Reflection | 131

8  Incarnational Paradigms for Transforming the Church | 132
  Introduction | 132
  The Abba Paradigm | 137
  The Paraclete Paradigm | 140
  The Relational Oneness Paradigm | 142
  Conclusion | 145
  Reflection | 146

9  The Defining Relationship of Christianity | 147
  Introduction | 147
  1. What Is the New Testament View of God? | 149
  2. What Is the Mission of the Abba Relationship? | 155
  3. How Do We Live in the Abba Relationship? | 158
  Conclusion | 160
  Reflection | 161

**Part III: How Do We Experience Reality?** | 163

10  Releasing Interpersonal Oneness through Interest Satisfaction | 165
  Introduction | 165
  The Parable of the Orange | 165
  A Practical Theology of Interest Satisfaction | 166
  Interest Satisfaction in Church Leadership | 169
  The Kenotic Interest Satisfaction Model | 173
  Conclusion | 178
  Reflection | 179

11  Living in Interpersonal Oneness | 180
  Introduction | 180
  Realize the Importance of Listening | 180
  Understand the Biblical View of Listening | 182
  Find a Pathway for Interest and Need | 184
  Expand the Power Base for Those with Inner Conflict | 187
  Build Relationships in Reverse | 188
  Ventilate, Then Validate | 189
  Nuke It | 190
  Listen Responsively and Generously | 192
  Conclusion | 193
  Reflection | 194

12  The Study of Being | 195
    Introduction | 195
    A Story of Revival | 195
    The Ontological Truth of Christianity | 198
    The I-AM Ontology | 202
    The Nature of the Church as Derived
        from the Nature of God | 206
    Conclusion | 208
    Reflection | 208

13  Signs of Interpersonal Oneness | 209
    Introduction | 209
    1. Through Interpersonal Oneness Indicators | 212
    2. Through Conversation | 216
    3. Through Avoiding the Pitfalls of Attempting to Measure | 217
    Conclusion | 224
    Reflection | 224

14  The Heart of Christianity | 225
    1. Recapitulated | 225
    2. Reinforced | 227
    Conclusion | 236
    Reflection | 237

*Resources* | 239
*About the Authors* | 241
*Bibliography* | 243
*Subject Index* | 263
*Scripture Index* | 275

# List of Figures

Figure 1: Statute at the Crystal Cathedral in
    Orange County, California | 11

Figure 2: An Optical Illusion | 23

Figure 3: Visual Depiction of the Holistic Discipleship Model | 29

Figure 4: Cultural Perspectives | 62

Figure 5: Steps toward Truthfulness | 176

Figure 6: The Process of Change | 178

Figure 7: Perichoresis | 232

# Foreword

THE TIME HAS COME to give the term "relational" proper theological dignity. Relationality is in the fabric of reality. "Relational" does not imply a fixed meaning. As with all good science, it is a term pointing the way to discover the dynamics of the world in which we live. In the case of this book, we are referring to the source of all relating, the triune God, and the persons God creates for relationship. *Relational Christianity* deals with the possible ways of relating among persons when courageously and fearlessly starting with God. We need proper method in our discovery. This book is an invitation to explore how relational thinking impacts living in response to other persons, but especially the triune God.

We need direction in the quest to reintegrate the life of humanity within God's life. God has never turned away, but humanity seems stuck in a long roller-coaster ride of distractions. In a culture of individualism, the way to creative stability in relationships has been fraught with fear. Control over one's life regularly trumps love of one's neighbor.

Individualism has become the new colonialism. It shows up as a disrespectful domination of the other, denying their dignity to the point of depersonalization. In the end, relational distance starves all friendships. Skills of hospitality and service falter when replaced by the quest for power, possession, and pleasure. Relationships go to hell, meaning they take on the character of an essential separation, marked by despair, depression, anxiety, and fear when considering the other. We develop a spiritual narcissism in our insecurity, a mask of competence. But this becomes a self-absorption that even floods churches. Spiritual growth takes a form of self-fulfillment, instead of relational connection. We need to rediscover the relationality of the God who made us and holds us as beloved children. We are a family of misfits, who in God's eyes are each uniquely wonderful and gifted. This is the healing discovery of *Relational Christianity*.

*Relational Christianity* is the fruit of relational theology, which has occupied most of my academic and professional life. Being rooted in the life of the triune God, relational theology reveals and confirms that God is not passive, abandoning us to work out a relational plan, but is active and involved. God goes before us and is still with us. God is still speaking; we need to learn how to listen. We need guides to point to the reality into which God invites us. Words like "participation" and "union," which open a possible touch point, must be snatched from the realms of abstraction. To grow in relational Christianity, we need to indwell God's always-already abiding with us. Then, we must translate that being embraced into embracing others in a life of sharing meals, nurturing conversations, and caring for others in times of need. We must learn to celebrate all that enriches our daily walking with God and others in friendship. That is *Relational Christianity*.

In the 1970s, Bruce Larson introduced the term "relational theology" to me.[1] His proposal thrived at the local church level in the United States, but not so in the academy. *Christianity Today* published a pushback response, "Relationalism: Principle or Slogan?"[2] Relational theology was seen as a product of the age, a fad manifestation that did not have an objective or intrinsic quality but defaulted to a love ethic that was sure to pass. That caution has been an emergency brake that is still engaged as smoke pours out of the wheels of struggling churches. Only love, properly directed, will get us back on the gas pedal, and that is in the world of relationships.

Relational thinking in theology still meets resistance. The main problem is the appearance of preferring human experience over genuine engagement with God. This is an appropriate concern. However, it ought to be met with clarifying conversations, not exclusion and diminishing. We need proposals that affirm a form of Christianity that really

---

1. Larson, *No Longer Strangers*.
2. Kuhn, "Relationalism," 49–50.

looks like a reflection of the glory of God's love. That would be called *Relational Christianity*.

It is appropriate to recognize that relational theology, and the practiced forms of relational Christianity, may take on forms that need correction. For example, relational thinking has been embraced by process theology, which has value, but questions the constancy and persistence of God's love for us. Its appeal is in making more room for God and humans to process life together. Many contemporary schools of thought may gather under this umbrella of relational theology.[3] These many forms of theology may be over-oriented to the human experience but must still be at the table for mutual learning and finding a theologically and biblically sound way forward.

A more intense resistance has been flaming in the debate around social Trinitarian thinking. The main objection here is that any social thinking will *necessarily* begin with human experience and create God in the form of our relatedness, family life, or human forms of connection. This is a clear possibility, but not a necessity. Social Trinitarian thinking has been invitational, as well as imperfect (like the disciples). We need doors into the church, not barricades. We need tables filled with food and laughter, not just stained-glass windows illuminated for those on the inside. We need a form of Christianity to invite the non-traditional to consider a God who lives beyond Christianity's institutional and intolerant forms. Those systems have their time and place but bring other problems as they become depersonalized and controlling. We need doctors to revitalize the patient, meaning the humanity created by God for relationships.

There is hope. God is still at work in lovingly sustaining his world and his creatures. Some important thinkers have been calling us home. In recent times, Karl Barth,[4] the Torrances,[5] and those who follow in their tracks have provided a more robust theology that is relational. They begin with the revelation of God in Christ as the ground and grammar of all relational thinking. This is where I have found resources for relational theology, and this present book is an extension of that community of explorers. The relational revival is committed to starting again at the beginning, with the triune God revealed in Jesus.

---

3. Oord, *Relational Theology*.

4. Barth, *Church Dogmatics* and *The Humanity of God*.

5. T. F. Torrance, *Christian Doctrine of God*; J. Torrance, *Worship, Community*; A. Torrance, *Persons in Communion*.

The Trinitarian God is relational. By that, I mean the one God exists in the form of three persons who live and love with an inseparable unity. Relational Christianity must never depart from this ever-present embracing by the God who speaks and calls us home.

The Bible itself is relational. By that, I mean that the God revealed in the Old and New Testaments is a covenantal God who creates and lives within a story of a relationship. This begins with Adam and Eve, continues with Noah, Abraham, and the patriarchs, finds rich expression in Israel, and then expands to include all humanity through the work of Jesus. This God, who exists with and for the other, is made known by the revelation of God in Jesus. By the ongoing work of the Spirit, we may live in intimate connection to the Abba of Jesus, with Jesus himself, and experience God's embrace within the community, who connect relationally to the point that they are called the "body of Christ." The great command is to love God, neighbor, and self. The Bible does not just talk about relationships but is intended means to facilitate this dynamic connection (if read as intended by God).

Church history has been an ongoing battle regarding relationships. The story is replete with battles between humans living in isolation and those in relationship. God is not to blame. Humans create dysfunctional organizations; God works to redeem them. *Individualized forms* of Christianity have focused on an interiorized, intellectualized, emotionalized, or performance-based Christianity. *Externalized forms* of Christianity, expressed through a social gospel or a pietistic form of spiritual formation, easily slip away from connecting with the living, triune God. *Relational Christianity* offers hope as a thoughtful, passionate, and engaging adventure in mutually serving friendships that begins with God's mission of love in the world, which includes reinvigorating God's church.

When done well, relational Christianity develops a proper confidence with persons that is other centered. Confidence is a relationship of trust that takes time to develop.[6] The search for certainty has been a destabilizing quest in science and faith that needs rethinking.[7] In its search for proofs and control of knowledge, it has made the human a judge in a world, afraid of being wrong. We become wary observers. We are more concerned about right thinking and not getting hurt than investing in the reality of trust and friendship required for healthy, everyday life together.

---

6. Newbigin, *Proper Confidence*.
7. D. Taylor, *Myth of Certainty*.

*Foreword*

Relational Christianity must begin with a relational God who all along the way has been coming to meet us. As I have contended elsewhere, "God exists in relationship and all that God does is for the purpose of relationships."[8] This must become our DNA. We must exist in relationships and do everything to nurture our relationships.

Renewal begins by rediscovering the triune God revealed in Jesus. In him, we have our basis for relating to God and to the world given space to exercise its relativity. This is not the world of relativism, where there is no truth, only opinions. This relativity echoes the Einsteinian discovery that changed science. We must understand the particularity of each thing as it is known in relation to other elements within its field of relations. We can better understand gravity, light, space, and time because we see them as interrelated. Newton broke the world apart to look at the separated pieces. Once again, we are returning to see how all reality works together in a holistic manner. The kingdom of God is the sphere of God's relating, which includes all his creation. We are invited to participate in God's manner of relating and acts of love. This is the actuality of the relational. This is the space and sphere of relating in which we find the meaningful life, and into which we now go on an adventure with *Relational Christianity*.

Wess Pinkham has been my boss, colleague, and student. Most of all, he is a friend who has journeyed with me in the adventure of indwelling the heart of the Father, embracing the dynamic life of the Son, and catching the creative wind of the Spirit. He is ever a student and a mentor at the same time, as you will discover in this book, which invites us to live in wonder of our relational God and discover that changes everything.

**Marty Folsom, PhD**
Extraordinary Days in Ordinary Time
August 2021

---

8. Folsom, *Face to Face*, 3:382.

# Preface

Jack W. Hayford, Chancellor of The King's University, has a unique hobby. In his world travels he has collected many apothecary dishes. An apothecary was a pharmacist who ground or mixed drugs or spices with a stone tool called a pestle.

> The earliest apothecaries are identified in 2600 BC in Babylon. But they appear in every culture. Most cases, these are "wise men," "mid wives," practitioners/perfumers who create compounds, oils, and perfumes, or natural folk healers, who understand the intricacies of herbs, spices, oils, and methods of healing–emotional, spiritual, and physical.[1]

At our farewell luncheon in honor of our retiring from The King's University, Chancellor Hayford did not give us a gold watch. Instead, he gave us his favorite colorful apothecary dish with a pestle from his private collection. He said to me that the colorful dish reminded him of my wife's ever-smiling presence. He also said that the pestle reminded him of me as a grinder and mixer of different potions, producing new medicines for faculty, staff, and students in my fifteen years at The King's as Dean of Institutional Effectiveness and Dean of Doctoral Studies. I trust I was following in Jesus' footsteps:

---

1. Glenn, "To Know and Be Known," abstract, iii.

> In Medieval and Renaissance times, Jesus was frequently depicted in art as not just a healer, but specifically as an apothecary. For Catholics, Jesus was the source for the "prescriptive life," doling out medicaments, such as humility and charity for ailments, such as gluttony, pride, avarice, and other sins. For others, Jesus was the source of spiritual and physical healing, wisdom, comfort, and the dispenser of God's mercy, grace, and restoration.[2]

Pastor Jack also surprised me by describing me as one of the most unusual persons he had met, a sort of silent servant, and said that he often wondered what I was thinking when listening to his teachings and sermons.

Well, here I share a culmination of my many years of engaging with God and his Word. My dominant interest has been ontological (a way of being). And now Pastor Jack will no longer wonder how I am thinking!

This work centers on one idea: reality is relational. I argue that God has created human existence in this way, and that Christianity can only be properly understood in this context. Father-led interpersonal oneness is the theological river that runs through the landscape of biblical revelation. I see this as one of the first works of practical theology written from a Trinitarian paradigm that suggests an entirely distinctive way of conceiving the relation between the Father, Son, Spirit, with the church as their love-gifted community. I have endeavored to make this book holistically oriented, biblically normed, historically informed, and culturally relevant. I hope to focus on the most important thing to get right in the Christian life, and then pull it through in joyful directions.

In the words of Marcel Proust: "The real voyage of discovery consists not in seeing new sights, but in looking with new eyes." Or, as the most popular version has it: "The real voyage of discovery consists not in seeking new landscapes but in having new eyes."[3] Apparently, Proust meant that "The only true voyage of discovery, the only fountain of Eternal Youth, would be not to visit strange lands but to possess other eyes, to behold the universe through the eyes of another ... [and] fly from star to star."[4] I believe that this book will be a journey for you in this

---

2. Glenn, "To Know and Be Known."

3. See Proust's seven-volume work *Remembrance of Things Past* (or *In Search of Lost Time*). The quotation above is a paraphrase of text in volume 5—*The Prisoner*—originally published in French, in 1923, and first translated into English by C. K. Moncrief.

4. Proust, *Remembrance of Things Past*. Thompson, "What Marcel Proust Really Said": "In chapter 2 of *The Prisoner*, the narrator is commenting at length on art, rather than travel. Listening for the first time to a work by the composer Vinteuil, he finds

Proustian sense. If we can see reality with new eyes, our actions and way of life will follow. This book offers a new paradigm of the Christian faith. When owned by a group of people—a community—a paradigm becomes a vision of reality. This vision becomes the basis on which a community can reshape and reorganize its life.[5] Vision is the basis for change. A Trinitarian community will maintain a love-based paradigm as a vision of reality. Karl Barth, Emil Brunner, and Dietrich Bonhoeffer maintain that Trinitarian personhood is the key to understanding the image of God (*Imago Dei*) in humanity.[6]

I believe that the paradigm on offer here contributes to a proper biblically based Trinitarian paradigm, "the central and substantial content of our doctrine of God," and our "point of departure" for an ontological view of the Trinity.[7] As Stephen Seamands puts it: "I am convinced that no doctrine is, in fact, more relevant to our identity and calling as ministers than the Trinity."[8]

Thank you for reading this work. I truly mean it and cannot express how much I appreciate you choosing to spend your time with what I pray are formational words! May they bring revelation, impartation, connection, and transition. Thank you for trusting me with your time. It is the most valuable resource a person has.

**Dr. Wess Pinkham**

---

himself transported not to a physical location, but to a wonderful "strange land" of the composer's own making. "Each artist," he decides, "seems thus to be the native of an unknown country, which he himself has forgotten . . ." "These artists include composers, such as Vinteuil, and painters, such as the narrator's friend, Elstir."

5. See Kuhn, *Structure of Scientific Revolutions* for an extensive discussion on paradigms and paradigm shifts.

6. Seamands, *Ministry in the Image of God*, loc. 295–97.

7. Awad, "Personhood as Particularity," 2.

8. Seamands, *Ministry in the Image of God*, 11.

# Acknowledgements

*Amicus certus in re incerta cernitur.*
A sure friend is known in unsure times.

GRATITUDE IS ONE OF the hardest emotions to express. Until we get to that world where our thoughts can be adequately expressed in words, "Thank you" will have to do.

Special thanks to Chris Reeves, MEd, VP of Operations of Shiloh University, who leaned into my car window upon leaving our condo in Coronado and said: "Write the book, Wess." He has that special gift of encouragement and bringing the best out of people with whom he works.

To Marty Folsom, PhD, friend and colleague for twenty-five years, I cannot begin to express the respect and admiration I have for this theologian, professor, author, relational, and gold-standard leader. He has been so influential in reframing my Christian worldview so that I could see an entirely distinctive way of conceiving the relation between the Father, Son, and Holy Spirit.

Heartfelt thanks to Dr. Lars Kierspel, PhD, Adjunct Professor of Biblical Studies at Shiloh University, for suggesting edits and adding contributions, and still loving the project and offering high praise: "reading your manuscript was a needed breath of Spirit-forming education and edification."

To my friend Mark H. Glenn, DMin, PhD, President and CAO of Shiloh University, Kalona, IA, thanks for your friendship and inspiration, for insightful conversations, important notes on napkins, and encouragement to complete the vision with passion.

To my dear friend Dr. David S. Edery, DMin, Professor of Hebrew at The King's University. Thanks for your significant Hebrew inputs so that this piece could appeal to both Jewish and Christian readers!

Thank you to Lewis Brown, who helped Jeremiah by reviewing his edits and providing detailed feedback.

I am indebted to Jeremiah Gruenberg, PhD, for his editorial service. He is top notch, a master at clarifying what is on point and on offer in Christ.

A very special thankyou to Chiqui Wood, DMin, author of *The Abba Foundation*, for edits and contributions.

Finally, thanks to Dr. Peter van Breda, President of The New International University, for his constant encouragement to complete what he feels is "a God-inspired and anointed" book.

# Some Introductory Notes

I first heard Wesley Pinkham speak at a graduate commencement as the keynote speaker. I distinctly remember being impressed with his weaving together of a multitude of ideas, images, and quotes to deliver a complete, holistic presentation on the love of God. A few times in the course of the speech, I remember thinking that he was going off topic, only to be proven wrong a minute later when he connected his ideas together in ways that were unexpected but illuminating. A few years later, when I ran into him again, I told him that I hoped to collaborate with him at some point. So, when he emailed me a manuscript a few days later, asking for my feedback, I was just happy that I was able to work with him in some capacity. Well, eventually, that "feedback" ended up turning into a collaborative writing process, which has resulted in this book.

The thesis and main ideas of this book all belong to Wess. The book's purpose and structure were already established long before I became involved. What I have primarily done is attempted to collaborate with Dr. Pinkham in presenting his ideas in the greatest possible clarity. There were a few occasions in which I added a new concept as a result of synthesizing what Dr. Pinkham had already put on paper, but ultimately everything herein is a reflection of Wess's connective and holistic research already on display.

It may at times seem as though topics in this work are discussed in a somewhat idiosyncratic order. However, this is simply what naturally occurs when addressing a holistic theme in a holistic manner. For example, the chapter on the foundational theological importance of the Trinity as a definition of reality is found at the beginning of part II (in satisfaction of its aim in answering the question: "Why is it important to define reality?") even though its details are assumed throughout the first part of the book. For this, we apologize to the linearly minded among us. However, Christian theology is inescapably, holistically recursive in that it folds in on itself as all major themes lead back to each other in a multitude of ways. I find it best to embrace this, albeit in as structurally sound a manner as possible.

I think it is no coincidence that a book such as this, which focuses so much on the significance of relationships and interconnectedness, would end up being the product of relationship and interconnectedness! I am grateful for the opportunity to work with a man who has studied and pondered the things of God on a personal and academic level for his entire life. I see this work as the culmination of Dr. Pinkham's many years of embracing, teaching, and enacting the Word of God. I hope that it challenges and nurtures your relationship with God as much as it has mine.

**Jeremiah Gruenberg, PhD**
Los Angeles, California

# Introduction
## A Unifying Center

Is it possible to state the meaning of Christianity in a simple sentence? Can we reach a level where we can operate with "a set of ultimate concepts and relations as few as possible, but with the greatest conceivable unity"?[1] Let us explore together the necessity for finding such a center, as well as a possible candidate, by answering two questions.

### 1. IS THERE A NEED FOR A SHIFT?

There is a lack of self-understanding in the world right now. The West is facing a crisis of meaning, and Christianity is uniquely positioned to

---

1. Palmer, *Elements of a Christian Worldview*, 24. However, "As Einstein, Polanyi, and others have shown us [e.g., Einstein, "Physics and Reality," 290–323; and Polanyi, *Study of Man*, 46, 93], the stratified structure of scientific knowledge usually comprises three different levels of thought coordinated with one another: the primary or basic level, which is the level of our ordinary day-to-day experience and the loosely organized natural cognitions it involves; the secondary level of scientific theory with its search for a rigorous logical unity of empirical and conceptual factors; and the tertiary level where we develop a more refined and higher logical unity with a minimum of refined concepts and relations. Theoretically this process of raising our thought form from one level to a higher level is indefinite: it goes on until we reach a level where we can operate with a set of ultimate concepts and relations as few as possible, but with the greatest conceivable unity. *In actual practice, however, three levels are normally sufficient to enable us to reach a unified conceptual grasp of the reality in the field of our investigation*" (84, emphasis added).

provide a creative answer. However, in order to do so, Christianity must find its defining, unifying center. To respond to the overarching crisis of meaning, Christian believers must first understand the true nature of their belief.

Today, people are not finding wholeness. Samuel Miller, former Dean of Harvard Divinity School, sees the evidence of this crisis in the world of art, noting the works of Picasso, De Kooning, Kafka, and Camus, who depict humanity as living in a world in which "man feels he amounts to exactly nothing."[2] The sense of disillusionment and dissociation in the West has only deepened since the times of these artists' great works.

There are deep structural and cultural shifts that have taken place throughout the world that have left many in confusion.[3] In this complex, pluralistic, and increasing secular age, the former primary meaning generators, such as Christianity, have been shunned and undervalued.[4]

This, in turn, has led to an identity crisis. The fracturing of community in preference to individualism and the pursuit of money, fame, and success have left us hollow and disconnected from what truly makes us fulfilled. The rise of smartphones and social media has exacerbated this, as they often replace face-to-face relationships with virtual relationships based on counterfeit narratives and little personal honesty or accountability. Some of the crisis of meaning is due to the breaking down of community relationships. A Harvard study of adult development over seventy-five years discovered three important lessons about human relationships: 1) those who are socially connected are happier, 2) the quality of such relationships matters more than the quantity, and 3) relationships are healthy for both body and mind.[5] The nature of contemporary West-

---

2. Miller, *Dilemma of Modern Belief*, 62–63.

3. Montuori, "Transformative Leadership," 2. "Alfonso Montuori is an educator, consultant, and musician. His transdisciplinary research has focused on the application of creativity research and complexity to better understand how to live in a complex, pluralistic, uncertain world. He has focused particularly in the areas of creativity, leadership, future studies, cultural pluralism, transdisciplinarity, and creative inquiry. A graduate of the University of London, the Monterey Institute of International Studies, and the Saybrook Institute, he has been Distinguished Professor in the School of Fine Arts at Miami University of Ohio, and in 1985–86 taught at the Central South University in the People's Republic of China."

4. Montuori, "Transformative Leadership," 2.

5. Waldinger, "What Makes a Good Life?," https://www.ted.com/talks/robert_waldinger_what_makes_a_good_life_lessons_from_the_longest_study_on_happiness.

ern society endangers all three of these principles. Intimate relationships have been lost to many, and the consequences are great. Further, the coronavirus pandemic and its variants have exacerbated this disconnected social landscape by banishing most relationships to the virtual space.

The crisis of meaning is not limited to the secular culture but is also found in Christianity itself. For example, in 2010, in her book *Almost Christian*, Kenda Creasy Dean, Associate Professor of Youth, Church, and Culture at Princeton, highlighted "tectonic rumblings" when sharing what the faith of teenagers is telling the American church:

> After two and a half centuries of shacking up with 'the American dream,' churches have perfected a dicey codependence between consumer-driven therapeutic individualism and religious pragmatism. These theological proxies gnaw, termite-like, at our identity as the Body of Christ, eroding our ability to recognize that Jesus' life of self-giving love directly challenges the American gospel of self-fulfillment and self-actualization.[6]

Replacing basic Christian ethics such as selflessness and giving with the self-generated and self-centered attempt at fulfillment through the attainment of worldly goods has damaged the church's self-understanding.

Further, the church's theological viewpoint has been severely weakened due to contemporary philosophical influences. Postmodernism has popularized the idea that truth is relative, whereas Christ states that he is the truth. Christ himself is not relative. Textual criticism has at times rendered the biblical text impotent, stripping it of its authority as the Word of God. The efforts of demythologization make God impersonal and non-miraculous. There is no doubt that the worldview of the Western church has shifted radically in the last two centuries. This shift has measurable consequences to the Christian faith: "Of an estimated 176 million American adults who identify as Christian, just 6% or 15 million of them actually hold a biblical worldview, a new study from Arizona Christian University shows."[7]

In addition, turmoil and division within the church have contributed greatly to it becoming a waning influence in the world. A deep structural transformation predicated upon a return to the basic meaning and message of Christianity is needed, or the church will continue to become destitute of meaning. As the Latin saying goes, *intra si recta, ne*

---

6. Dean, *Almost Christian*, 5.
7. Blair, "Most Adult US Christians Don't Believe."

*labora*, or "if right within, trouble not." The church is not right within. Thus, we must be troubled to find a way forward.

The generation of Christians currently in their twenties are leaving the church in large numbers. The church is not meeting their needs. This, too, is partially due to a crisis of self-understanding and lack of relationships. In *You Lost Me*, Kinnaman and Hawkins discuss their findings on this generation's attitude toward the church.[8] Younger people do not feel understood or heard by the older generation, which contributes to the breakdown in family and church relationships. They state that the younger generation knows about Jesus on an informational level but are less likely to know about him relationally. Relationships in the church are failing to equip the next generation of Christians to reconcile both their inherent desires and the prevailing cultural worldview with their Christian faith. Many pastors are opting out of vocational ministry, preferring bivocational ministry opportunities.[9] Interpersonal relationships must therefore become a higher priority for the church, or successive generations will continue to feel disconnected from the Christian faith.

What is needed is a revolutionary shift in our conception of the Christian worldview, similar to how our understanding of the physical, created world has been dramatically revised over the last century or so. With the discovery of the atomic structure, our model of physical reality transitioned from seeing matter as being purely solid to seeing it as made up of vibrant interconnectedness. Electrons and protons whirl around the atomic nucleus in constant motion. Connection after connection is required in the configuration of even the most basic forms of matter. Advancements in quantum physics have shifted our understanding of the world as being four dimensions (height, width, depth, and time) to being vastly more multidimensional. Physicists affirm that for the Creator to have created the universe, God would need to operate in at least eleven to twenty-six dimensions of space and time.[10] While we cannot naturally perceive these dimensions, nor the quantum nature of the atomic structure, our ability to make sense of reality is deepened by this knowledge.

These scientific paradigm shifts mirror the need for a fundamental change in the Christian understanding of spiritual reality. Christian self-understanding must move from a limited, linear dimensionality to

---

8. Kinnaman, *You Lost Me*.
9. Leake, "Why Pastors Are Stepping Down," 3.
10. Ross, *Creator and the Cosmos*, 71–73.

a multidimensional, holistic view of life. The Western Christian view of God rarely soars above the four-dimensional realm. Our linear understanding of life reduces the godly lifestyle to a set of rules. While the church should be like an interconnected organism, we often function more like an organized corporation. Holistic relationships are rejected in favor of social order.

Just as our physical reality is made up of numerous levels and dimensions of relationships, theological reality is made up of holistic, connective and interpersonal relationships. This is seen in such truths as the oneness of the members of the Trinity, Christ's invitation that we be in him and he in us, and the resulting divine connections between members of the Christian community. What can instigate such a transformation in the Christian faith? We must rediscover and reclaim the essence of the Christian faith.

## 2. WHAT IS THE ESSENCE OF CHRISTIANITY?

This book seeks to answer the question: "What is the essence of Christianity?" Another way to ask this question would be: What is the unifying heart of Jesus' life and teachings, and how can we live accordingly?

We suggest that the essence of Christianity is *interpersonal oneness*. This idea is multifaceted and requires nuance in both explanation and understanding.

The Trinity is quintessentially interpersonal and indivisibly one (Deut 6:4; 1 John 5:7). Further, the interpersonal Creator has created interpersonal beings after his kind, having made humans in his image (Gen 1:26). We suggest that the center of Christianity reflects the very nature of God—the Trinity—himself: living in interpersonal oneness. If we do not recognize this and live accordingly, then his image in us is easily distorted, leading to an identity crisis resulting in detachment, distortion, dysfunction, and damage.

One of my professors who was highly influential on my theological perspective was Francis A. Schaeffer (1912–1984). He was an American Evangelical Christian theologian, philosopher, and Presbyterian pastor who saw the experience of interpersonal relationships to be so fundamental to human life that it served as an argument for the nature of God. Schaeffer asserts that only two formulas explain creation: (1) [inter] personal + creation + time = [inter] personal; or the illogical and senseless alternative, (2) non-personal [god or universe] + raw chance + time = [inter] personal.[11] The God presented in the Bible is personal and interactive. The incarnate Christ was personal and interactive. These Christian facts resist the alternative of meaninglessness.

As the architect of human existence, God's nature is of pivotal importance in determining both the nature of reality and the essence of Christianity. The Christian view of the human being—that is, our anthropology—will be incomplete if it is not defined by its Godward orientation. What might be the theological equivalent of the discovery of the interconnectivity of the atomic structure, or the exploration of the relational nature of quantum physics? What Christian truth can fundamentally change our Christian perspective from being limited and linear to being multidimensional and holistic? The Trinity as relational reality, resulting in interpersonal oneness.

However, this concept is not always easy to understand or implement, partially due to the hyper-individualized Western view of life. Westerners tend to see the individual as being of supreme importance, and that our existence is primarily individual in nature. Because of this, they tend to view God as an individual. However, this pervasive perspective runs counter to the nature of the Trinity. The self-revelation of God as Father, Son and Holy Spirit is obscured by an unconscious mythologizing of his Person which flows from the West's essentialist individualization of the person. The theological depth of the Trinity cannot be understood if examined through the lens of individualism. If we attempt to do so, we end up seeing God as simply a bigger and badder version of our own individual ideals.

What would happen to our Christian perspective if we were to take God's relational, interpersonal, and unified being as our point of departure? What would Christian theology look like if it rested upon a true Trinitarian view of God and of Christ?[12] Dallas Willard laments the alternative:

> Much of the problem is *not*, as is often said, that we have failed to get what is in our head down in our heart. Much of what hinders

---

11. Schaeffer, "Christianity and the Humanities." Taped lectures by the Media Department of Wheaton College, Wheaton, Il., 1967.

12. Granted, the Trinity is a great mystery and cannot be blueprinted on the church. James B. Torrance, however, contends that the Trinity speaks to us in three areas: (1) The Trinity and the worship of the church, (2) The Trinity and the doctrine of God, and (3) The Trinity and the human person (Torrance, *Doctrine of the Trinity*; lecture given at Seattle Pacific University, Spring 1986).

> us is that we have had a lot of mistaken theology in our head and it *has* gotten down into our heart. And it is controlling our inner dynamics so that the head and heart cannot, even with the aid of the Word and the Spirit, pull one another straight.[13]

If we misidentify the nature of God's image in us, the rest of our theology will be at best incomplete, and at worst resistive of Christ's truth. However, if we incorporate the ramifications of God as Trinity into the understanding of what it means to be made in his image, it is more likely we will be on the right path.

The concept of interpersonal oneness, as presented in this book, is made up of individual topics that function together in a holistic way. Firstly, it involves *personhood*. One cannot be interpersonal without first being a person. In this way, interpersonal oneness acknowledges the fundamental importance of each human being, for the person is the building block of the interpersonal. As D. A. Carson writes, "individualism that is sold out to Christ *can* be of the very essence of godly self-sacrifice and faithful service to the gospel."[14] Secondly, interpersonal oneness is integrally dependent upon the spiritual understanding of *relationship*. Relationships are the points of connection between persons, thereby taking us from the personal to the interpersonal. Thirdly, the *unity of the Trinity*—and their invitation to us to participate in that unity—forms the basis of oneness. Oneness does not entail the erasure of differences, nor does it require conformity. Rather, oneness is based on mutual love in an unbreakable relationship. Fourthly, the means by which interpersonal oneness is achieved is through the *imitation of Christ*. Christ was interpersonal in his ministry, toward both God and humanity. He maintained his oneness with the Father and Holy Spirit throughout his life. He also maintained at least twelve deep, interpersonal relationships with people. He was relationally intelligent! Christlikeness therefore leads to interpersonal oneness, and genuine interpersonal oneness results in increased Christlikeness for believers. Fifthly, interpersonal oneness functions both *vertically* (with God) and *horizontally* (with others in community). The nature and function of the church must be based on the interpersonal oneness on offer in Christ. These interconnected concepts will appear and reappear throughout this book in various contexts and combinations.

---

13. Willard, *Great Omission*, 61.
14. Carson, "Contrarian Reflections on Individualism."

However, they all build toward the main point of this book, which is to investigate interpersonal oneness as the essence of Christianity.

The Trinity is really the heart of the theological perspective of this book. The nature of the Trinity constructs and illuminates every principle comprising interpersonal oneness. The inextricable unity of the Trinity illustrates oneness. Their thoroughgoing love delineates human love for neighbor. The nearly paradoxical interworking of their individual personhood with boundaryless connection ushers us into genuine spiritual community. C. S. Lewis's famous insight could here be applied to the Trinity: "I believe in [the Trinity], as I believe the sun has risen not because I see it, but because by it I see everything else."

This view addresses the theological problem of the nature of God. As R. Kendall Soulen states: "As the vestiges of the Constantinian age melt away, the question 'Who is God?' moves increasingly to the center of Christian theology."[15] Trinitarian theology is the most relevant subject by which to answer this question. God is one. God is three. God is personal.[16]

---

15. Soulen, "YHWH the Triune God," 25. See Schumacher, "Doctrine of the Holy Spirit," 1–2. "The present discussion can be helpfully framed with reference to Karl Rahner's magisterial work on The Trinity, which initiated a revival of interest in Trinitarian theology in our time. In this work, Rahner assesses how Trinitarian theology has been affected by the modern rise of a concept of personhood that diverged quite significantly from preceding philosophical and theological tradition." See Rahner, *Trinity*, 43 for a history of the concept of "person" and its use in Trinitarian theology. See Perez, "Trinitarian Concept of Person," 123–24 on "The Psychological Turn of Modern Philosophy."

16. Craig, *Kalām Cosmological Argument*. Dr. William Lane Craig popularizes the *kalam* cosmological argument (*kalam* is the Arabic word for medieval theology), which contends that God is personal. This argument, "largely forgotten since the time of Kant, is once again back at center stage."

> Ghazali argued that this Uncaused First Cause must also be a personal being. It's the only way to explain how an eternal cause can produce an effect with a beginning like the universe.
>
> Here's the problem: If a cause is sufficient to produce its effect, then if the cause is there, the effect must be there, too. For example, the cause of water's freezing is the temperature's being below 0 degrees Celsius. If the temperature has been below 0 degrees from eternity, then any water around would be frozen from eternity. It would be impossible for the water to *begin* to freeze just a finite time ago. Now the cause of the universe is permanently there, since it is timeless. So why isn't the universe permanently there as well? Why did the universe come into being only 14 billion years ago? Why isn't it as permanent as its cause?
>
> Ghazali maintained that the answer to this problem is that the First Cause must be a personal being endowed with freedom of the will. His creating the universe is a free act which is independent of any prior determining

God is relational. If God is fundamentally personal and relational, as the Trinity certainly is, then the way we approach God must be personal and relational. The way we speak about God to others must be interpersonal and relational. The way we attempt to solve the problems in our lives must be interpersonal and relational.

The Trinity's importance in theology has not always been given the proper attention, however. T. F. Torrance goes so far as to say that a true understanding of the Trinity is a required foundation for the development of all other Christian doctrine. Torrance writes,

> It is not just that the doctrine of the Holy Trinity must be accorded primacy over all the other doctrines, but that properly understood it is the nerve and centre of them all, [*"a first-order doctrine"*] configures them all and is so deeply integrated with them that when they are held apart from the doctrine of the Trinity, they are seriously defective in truth and become malformed.[17]

Regardless of whether one agrees that interpersonal oneness is the essence of Christianity, the implications of the Trinity must nevertheless be wrestled with if we are to build and interact with a Christian theology that is reflective of the nature of God. This is also true when it comes to ecclesial matters. Is it possible that many of the weaknesses and shortcomings of the church today can be traced back to the lack of Trinitarian foundations in preaching, mission, and organization? Colin Gunton states that "the manifest inadequacy of the theology of the church derives from the fact that it has never seriously and consistently been rooted in a conception of the being of God as triune."[18] What would theories of the church look like if built upon the foundation of the Trinity? This is

---

conditions. So, his act of creating can be something spontaneous and new. Freedom of the will enables one to get an effect with a beginning from a permanent, timeless cause. Thus, we are brought not merely to a transcendent cause of the universe but to its Personal Creator. This is admittedly hard for us to imagine. But one way to think about it is to envision God existing alone without the universe as changeless and timeless. His free act of creation is a temporal event simultaneous with the universe's coming into being. Therefore, God enters into time when he creates the universe. God is thus timeless without the universe and in time with the universe.

Ghazali's cosmological argument thus gives us powerful grounds for believing in the existence of a beginningless, uncaused, timeless, spaceless, changeless, immaterial, enormously powerful, Personal Creator of the universe.

17. Torrance, *Christian Doctrine of God*, 6. In this magisterial work he concurs that the Trinity is a first-order doctrine.

18. Gunton, *Promise of Trinitarian Theology*, 56.

one of the questions this book explores. Accordingly, a remarkable vision of God is the antidote to the ills of the contemporary church. As Pastor Edward Suh puts it:

> The lack of a clear vision of God's heart is at the root of why so many believers are trapped in performance-oriented relationships with God; why so many suffer burnout in their attempts to meet God's holy standards; and why the Church has lost so many of the next generation to an unremarkable vision of God.[19]

We are in desperate need of a massive reboot, a remarkable vision of God, a paradigm shift to "the divine life of love"[20] that causes a deep restructuring of human life and saves this pale blue planet in "the throes of an epochal change" as it shifts, slithers, slides, and spirals toward cataclysm. That remarkable vision of God is found in interpersonal oneness.

## REFLECTION

1. A recent survey of two thousand American respondents found that less than one-fifth of Americans believe life's purpose is knowing and loving God.[21] Does the American church currently have a biblical/theological measure for its mission and message that counters this current deemphasis on the divine/human relationship as a generator of meaning?

2. What is your current personal response to the idea that the essence of Christianity is living from interpersonal oneness with God and others? How does your understanding of the Trinity interact with your view of interpersonal oneness?

---

19. Suh, "Inherent Goodness of God," 5.

20. Rempel used this powerful phrase in his review of Malcolm B. Yarnell's *God the Trinity: Biblical Portraits* (2016).

21. Casanova, "Less than 1/5 of Americans Believe," https://www.christianheadlines.com/blog/less-than-1-5-of-americans-believe-lifes-purpose-is-knowing-loving-god-survey-finds.html.

Trinitarian Relationship

# PART I

## What Is Reality?

"God is love"[1]

—1 John 4:8

"... the revelation of God as Father, Son, and Holy Spirit is the center and absolute of all human reality."[2]

—J. Scott Horrell

"the doctrine of the Three-in-One provides a macro-structure of reality that makes sense of life, one that gives a remarkable basis for our perception of ourselves as persons, for our relationships in marriage, family, the local church and community and, in point, the role of the local church in mission."[3]

—J. Scott Horrell

---

1. David S. Edery, email to author, September 2017: "The Hebrew verb אהב (a.h.v) love, appears twice in Exodus, twice in Leviticus, and 23 times in the book of Deuteronomy. Christianity quotes the two most important Jewish commandments of love from Leviticus and Deuteronomy as the basis for their *'agape'* in the Western world. It is misleading to believe that Christianity is the religion of unconditional love, while Judaism is the religion of Law, and retribution. The philosopher Simon May, in his book *Love: A History*, 14, says: *'If love in the Western world has a founding text, that text is Hebrew.'*"

2. Horrell, "Self-Giving Triune God," 119.

3. Horrell, "Self-Giving Triune God."

"That God IS love [as Trinity] is descriptive of who he is and how he lives in eternity, how he interacts with other persons."[4] Father-led interpersonal oneness as the heart of Christianity provides "a macro structure of reality" that gives life the meeting of meaning. The church, then, as an actual, visible community, "is called to be the kind of reality at the finite level that God is in eternity."[5]

—Colin E. Gunton

"... we live in a Trinitarian universe; one where infinite energy of a personal nature is the ultimate reality"[6]

—Dallas Willard

Paul in Ephesians 3:1–21, "reveals that the Spirit gives us his power, his ability, his wisdom and his revelation for one purpose and one purpose only—it's to help us know how much God loves us . . . not to help us to love God, but to help us discover the inestimable nature of God's love–for you and me. *Remarkable*."[7]

—Keith Warrington

"Happiness is a direction; not a destination!"

—unknown

---

4. Morrison, "Theology," https://www.gci.org/articles/an-introduction-to-trinitarian-theology/. David S. Edery, email to author, April 15, 2017: "*In Jewish tradition, God created the world in love and gave us a model of forgiveness, so that we may love one another and forgive one another. We must interact with one another in the same manner we interact with him. When we learn to forgive one another then he forgives us. It is indeed Father-led* InterPersonal *way, because he wants us to relate to him in love and intimacy, awe and reverence.*"

5. Gunton, *Promise*, 78, 80.

6. Willard, *Divine Conspiracy*, 254.

7. Warrington, *Ephesians*, 14.

# 1

# Holistic Thinking and God's Relational Priority

Luke 15:11–32

**The Story of the Lost Son**

<sup>11-12</sup> Then he said, "There was once a man who had two sons. The younger said to his father, 'Father, I want right now what's coming to me.'

<sup>12-16</sup> "So the father divided the property between them. It wasn't long before the younger son packed his bags and left for a distant country. There, undisciplined and dissipated, he wasted everything he had. After he had gone through all his money, there was a bad famine all through that country and he began to hurt. He signed on with a citizen there who assigned him to his fields to slop the pigs. He was so hungry he would have eaten the corncobs in the pig slop, but no one would give him any.

<sup>17-20</sup> "That brought him to his senses. He said, 'All those farmhands working for my father sit down to three meals a day, and here I am starving to death. I'm going back to my father. I'll say to him, Father, I've sinned against God, I've sinned before you; I don't deserve to be called your son. Take me on as a hired hand.' He got right up and went home to his father.

<sup>20-21</sup> "When he was still a long way off, his father saw him. His heart

pounding, he ran out, embraced him, and kissed him. The son started his speech: 'Father, I've sinned against God, I've sinned before you; I don't deserve to be called your son ever again.'

**22-24** "But the father wasn't listening. He was calling to the servants, 'Quick. Bring a clean set of clothes and dress him. Put the family ring on his finger and sandals on his feet. Then get a grain-fed heifer and roast it. We're going to feast! We're going to have a wonderful time! My son is here—given up for dead and now alive! Given up for lost and now found!' And they began to have a wonderful time.

**25-27** "All this time his older son was out in the field. When the day's work was done, he came in. As he approached the house, he heard the music and dancing. Calling over one of the houseboys, he asked what was going on. He told him, 'Your brother came home. Your father has ordered a feast—barbecued beef!—because he has him home safe and sound.'

**28-30** "The older brother stalked off in an angry sulk and refused to join in. His father came out and tried to talk to him, but he wouldn't listen. The son said, 'Look how many years I've stayed here serving you, never giving you one moment of grief, but have you ever thrown a party for me and my friends? Then this son of yours who has thrown away your money on whores shows up and you go all out with a feast!'

**31-32** "His father said, 'Son, you don't understand. You're with me all the time, and everything that is mine is yours—but this is a wonderful time, and we had to celebrate. This brother of yours was dead, and he's alive! He was lost, and he's found!'"

## INTRODUCTION

A CHRISTIAN LEADER IN China stood before me in Hong Kong as I awarded her doctoral degree diploma. I was Dean of Doctoral Studies for The King's University, and it was a touching moment. I always enjoy the feeling of vicarious accomplishment as I congratulate students for their completion of such a lengthy endeavor as earning a doctorate. But that feeling was nothing compared to what was to come.

Later that day, at a restaurant overlooking Victoria Harbor in downtown Hong Kong, my friend leaned over and whispered, "I did not get up at 4:00 a.m. this morning, leave my daughter, who could give birth to my grandchild at any moment, fly halfway across China, endure the three-hour border crossing, taking a long taxi ride to our classroom to receive this diploma. *I came to be with you!*"

I felt tears on my cheeks. Her words touched me. She had gone through so much just to be around me—to hug me, to look me in the eyes, to speak face to face. As a leader in the Abba Father movement in China, she viewed me as a father to herself and other leaders of the underground church in China. She knew what it meant to receive and give a hug from the Heavenly Father. I hate to admit it, but it is rare for me to really feel someone's love. The little orphan-hearted boy inside still needs healing. But this was one of those moments in which God's love was powerfully conveyed to me through a human being.

Her story of weathering the difficulties of travel just to be with a father figure is very similar to the story of the prodigal son. The "pearl of parables" is about two lost sons who did not know their father and could not feel his love.

The story of the prodigal son has genuinely changed the mission and quality of my life. In the first half of my life, I was not thinking about the story from the big picture—partially because I had been trained by Western theologians. Before I was ambushed by the love of Abba as my true Father, I would try to explain love by dissecting it. I would define the eight Hebrew and four Greek words for love and go through their uses in a systematic, propositional, and non-personal manner. That is all illuminating information, but it is very different than living from love. Now my experience of love is to simply release God's love for people in my life.

The parable at hand is about the nature of our Father's personality and perspective, not just about the sin of humanity and its need for repentance, nor the manner of God's restitution and justice.[1] It is a Christian failing that we often do not to allow God to define himself. But here, this is precisely what Jesus is doing. If we do not understand the true emphasis of this parable and what it represents regarding the Father's approach to humanity, we will miss the God of Jesus.

This parable aids in clarifying Jesus' use of the term *abba*, which is a Hebrew term of endearment for "father." The relationship between Jesus and his Father is characterized as tender and loving. Without this

---

1. Galen, "Dynamic of the New Birth." Repentance is about being "born of the atoning love of the triune God" and it "opens the door to the atonement of human identity and growth within this identity."

element, we will settle for a gospel of self-help, self-generation, self-actualization, and self-fulfillment, the trap of Western culture.[2] We can examine our own worldviews by looking at the two perspectives of life as described by this parable. What is at stake? Our view of God, the quality of our lives, and our mission.

In many ways, this story of the two lost sons is this book's anchor. It is a Father-centered ontological view of God, given to us by Jesus, the Son. It describes a gut-wrenched, compassionate, loving Father who values the person. As Robert Schuller concludes, "The classical error of historical Christianity is that we have never started with the value of the person. Rather, we have started from the 'unworthiness of the sinner,' and that starting point has set the stage for the glorification of human shame in Christian theology."[3] The story of the prodigal son reveals a Father for whom love and intimate relationships are the guiding priorities of life. It tells the story of overcoming shame and sin not by human effort or religious repentance (sin management), but by humility and a return to relationship (transformation). It establishes for us the big-picture view of the Christian life.

In this chapter, we will contrast two types of thinking about this parable, and their end results. One may view it from the big-picture perspective (the Father's all-encompassing transforming love) or one can view it as a set of parts (the need for repentance and restitution or justice). One paradigm views the world through the holistic lens of relationships, love, and interconnection, while the other views the world as a set of details to be manipulated. We will then discuss the consequences of each perspective for the mission and quality of the life of a Christian. We will also briefly highlight the cause of this book—to recognize the value of a person formed in community and make the case for relational intelligence. Such holistic thinking is a relational priority. Accordingly, we can appreciate Jesus' view of God as the big truth of the "pearl of parables" by examining its holistic dynamics.

## THE GREATEST HOLISTIC STORY

Charles Dickens said the tale of the prodigal son was "the greatest story in all of history." Thomas Aquinas wrote that it was "the entire Bible in a

---

2. Highfield, *God, Freedom, and Human Dignity*, 91–93.
3. Schuller, *Self Esteem*, 162.

few sentences." Theologian Helmut Thielicke concluded that it contains "the very meaning of the universe itself."

In this famous story, a son asks his father for his inheritance, and the father grants it. The son squanders his inheritance on wine and women, and soon he finds himself destitute and eating from a pig's trough. He decides to take the risk of going home, where his father accepts him with open arms. The father's eldest son, however, is offended and distraught that the father would accept the prodigal son back so easily. Jesus' ends the story with the father explaining to the second son that, contrary to his sour perspective, this is a wonderful time. As *The Message* Bible reads, "His father said, 'Son, you don't understand. You're with me all the time, and everything that is mine is yours—but this is a wonderful time, and we had to celebrate. This brother of yours was dead, and he's alive! He was lost, and he's found!'" (Luke 15:31–32). Brennan Manning suggests any alternative conclusion we offer would upstage Jesus' ending:

> Come up with any other ending to the story of the Prodigal than the one given by Jesus, and you have just destroyed the noblest picture of redeeming grace ever given by Christ to the human family. And, you have just reduced the Abba of Jesus to the level of human virtue. Sad to say, there are many churches, many preachers and many so-called prophets today who are furnishing [a wrong-headed ending]. And so many of God's people are living in the house of fear and not in the house of love.[4]

In a sense, Jesus did not really share the outcome of the conflict. The greatest story ever told by the greatest person in the world leaves us wondering what happened to the two lost sons. Did they ever come to know and love their father? Did they reconcile with one another? But perhaps asking these questions is the wrong way to approach this story. Perhaps we should recognize that the restoration of the parent/child relationship, and the celebration of that restoration, were Jesus' concluding thoughts. The parable is illustrative of Jesus' prioritization of relationship. As C. Baxter Kruger asserts, this story reveals that the worst aspect of sin is that it keeps us from knowing the Father.[5] The son(s) did not know "the divine Life of

---

4. Manning, recording of conference at Alderwood Vineyard, October 1989, Tape 1.

5. Kruger, *Across All Worlds*, loc. 388: "Sin goes way beyond disobedience. The deepest problem of sin is that it makes us utterly incapable of knowing the Father. It afflicts us with such a dastardly wrong-headedness; we cannot know the Father's heart. It makes us so blind; it is impossible for us to see the Father's face. And without knowing the Father's heart, we have no basis for real assurance or hope in our lives at all. If

Love."⁶ Jesus' storytelling reveals an Abba who loves extravagantly, but also points to children who are largely blind to it. Brennan Manning examines our response in the face of such extensive lovingkindness:

> Shouldn't such a view of God call for a joyous response from us? Such an image of God assaults modern standards of justice, our sense of fair play, and the search for rectitude. It comes against the foundations of religious faith. We cannot understand how a young and depraved, good-for-nothing prodigal can be preferred to an older hard-working brother. The idea of celebration rather than punishment in this case blows our minds. We see insane justice that replaces sacred standards, "*reverses all order of rank, makes the last first, the first last, and in the end—all get the same reward?*"⁷

The point of this story is not about human faithlessness, but about the faithfulness of a father who runs toward the lost and lonely. It is a parable about the Father who, in Christ, is the Father of us all. The holistic view of this story focuses on God and his all-encompassing love. The atomized view of the story would reflect the attitude of the elder brother, who reacted to the father's love and acceptance with divisive offense and demanded punishment out of a misguided sense of justice.⁸

One of the challenges of this story is how exuberant the prodigal son was in his sinfulness. He sold his inheritance and birthright in order to fund his debauched, decadent, or depraved lifestyle. His dedication to a lifestyle of bad choices is so strong that he does not return home after running out of money. Rather, it takes a widespread famine in the land to finally get him to relent. Certainly, we can say that the character of the

---

we cannot see his face, we have no possibility of living in the freedom of his abounding love, and in the security and joy of his lavish and eternal embrace." See Keller, *Reason for God*, 168. He defines sin as "the despairing refusal to find your deepest identity in your relationship and service to God. Sin is seeking to become oneself, to get an identity, apart from him."

6. Brent Rempel used this powerful phrase in his review of Yarnell's *God the Trinity*.

7. Manning, recording of conference at Alderwood Vineyard, October 1989, Tape 1.

8. Pinnock, *Flame of Love*, 11. "While offering a relational Spirit Christology, I do not intend here to deny truth in the penal substitutionary model of atonement. Grace has to deal with sin, and the law's just condemnation of us must be silenced. Family room cannot altogether displace courtroom in our theological analogies. Still, the amazing thing is that the judge in this case actually loves us and desires our friendship. The two insights can be merged."

prodigal son illustrates the gleeful pursuit of extreme sinfulness over and above a godly lifestyle. We must understand, however, that such extreme sinfulness pales in comparison to the power of the father's love and acceptance. That sinfulness is no match for the Father's deep valuation of his children. As John the Beloved puts it:

> This is how much God loved the world: he gave his Son, his one and only Son. And this is why: so that no one need be destroyed; by believing in him, anyone can have a whole and lasting life. God didn't go to all the trouble of sending his Son merely to point an accusing finger, telling the world how bad it was. He came to help, to put the world right again. Anyone who trusts in him is acquitted; anyone who refuses to trust him has long since been under the death sentence without knowing it. And why? Because of that person's failure to believe in the one-of-a-kind Son of God when introduced to him. (John 3:16–18)

When the prodigal limps back home, he rehearses his "poor me" script: "Father, I have messed up and am no longer worthy to be called your son." It is obvious that the son did not know how his father felt about him. His father had been keeping his eyes open, scanning the horizon every day for his lost son. Until one day the father saw him—a mere speck on the horizon. The father's heart pounds, and he sprints for his son, and with compassion flings his arms around him! This is movingly depicted in Robert Schuler's statue:

**Figure 1: Statute at the Crystal Cathedral in Orange County, California**

Jesus says that the father felt compassion for his lost son. Jesus' compassion surges from the depths of his being: "his father saw him and felt compassion . . ." (Luke 15:20). Compassion defies human understanding. It cannot be imitated. The Latin root of "compassion" means to suffer, endure, be partakers of the hunger, nakedness, loneliness, pain, and broken dreams of humanity. As Brennan Manning defines it:

> The Greek verb, "*splagchnizomai*" (translated "moved with compassion," in Matthew 9:35–36), is derived from the noun, splanchnon which means intestines, bowels, or heart. Its Hebrew counterpart is *rachamim*, referring to the womb of Yahweh. The Greek word refers to a gut reaction, the inward part of our being from which strong emotion arises. It could be translated, "a movement or impulse wallowing up from one's entrails." A Hebrew would say, "I love you from my liver, from the gut, from the deepest place I feel something!"
>
> English translators fail to capture the physical and emotional flavor of the Greek word for compassion in Mark 6:34. They feebly resort to expressions like, "he was moved with compassion" (KJV), or "he felt sorry" (Jerusalem Bible), or "his heart went out of him" (New English Bible). These phrases fail to give the drama and depth of emotional force that moved and compelled Jesus to act.[9]

Do you hear a compassionate or gut-wrenched Abba Father in this passage? No one goes through life without making mistakes and getting hurt. Those of us who have been deeply wounded in life must accept Jesus' view of the Father as presented in this parable. He sees us as we are, but still has a gut-wrenching love for us. We must accept his acceptance! The true Christian life does not really develop until we believe that. Whatever our hearts are tied to will be our identity. May our hearts be tied to Jesus' view of the ever-loving Father. Keith Warrington adds that in Ephesians 3:1–21 Paul "reveals that the Spirit gives us his power, his ability, his wisdom and his revelation for one purpose and one purpose only—it's to help us know how much God loves us . . . not to help us to love God, but to help us discover the inestimable nature of God's love—for you and me. Remarkable."[10] In Luke 15:20 we find the glory of God's love which goes beyond human expectation and surpasses human understanding (Eph 3:19). "For God did not send his Son into the world

---

9. Manning, "What it Means to Be Cool in Christ Jesus."
10. Warrington, *Ephesians*, 14.

to condemn the world, but that the world through him might be saved" (John 3:17 NKJV). Or as Paul amplifies:

> With the arrival of Jesus, the Messiah, that fateful dilemma is resolved. Those who enter into Christ's being-here-for-us no longer have to live under a continuous, low-lying black cloud. A new power is in operation. The Spirit of life in Christ, like a strong wind, has magnificently cleared the air, freeing you from a fated lifetime of brutal tyranny at the hands of sin and death. (Rom 8:1–2)
>
> How blessed is God! And what a blessing he is! He's the Father of our Master, Jesus Christ, and takes us to the high places of blessing in him. Long before he laid down earth's foundations, he had us in mind, had settled on us as the focus of his love, to be made whole and holy by his love. Long, long ago he decided to adopt us into his family through Jesus Christ. (What pleasure he took in planning this!) He wanted us to enter into the celebration of his lavish gift-giving by the hand of his beloved Son.
>
> Because of the sacrifice of the Messiah, his blood poured out on the altar of the Cross, we're a free people—free of penalties and punishments chalked up by all our misdeeds. And not just barely free, either. *Abundantly* free! He thought of everything, provided for everything we could possibly need, letting us in on the plans he took such delight in making. He set it all out before us in Christ, a long-range plan in which everything would be brought together and summed up in him, everything in deepest heaven, everything on planet earth. (Eph 1:3–10)

This prayer by Ruth Harms Calkin summarizes Paul's experience and ours:

> God, I may fall flat on my face; I may fail until I feel old and beaten and done in. Yet your love for me is changeless. All the music may go out of my life, my private world may shatter to dust. Even so, you will hold me in the palm of your steady hand. No turn in the affairs of my fractured life can baffle you. Satan with all his braggadocio cannot distract you. Nothing can separate me from your measureless love—pain can't, disappointment can't. Anguish can't. Yesterday, today, tomorrow can't. The loss of my dearest love can't. Death can't. Life can't. Riots, war, insanity, hunger, neurosis, disease—none of these things nor all of them heaped together can budge the fact that I

am dearly loved, completely forgiven, and forever free through Jesus Christ your beloved Son."[11]

This is a great everyday prayer. Why? Because things in the present cannot disarm us. Paul asked, "If God is for us, who can be against us?" (Rom 8:31) And Jesus said, "All authority has been given to me" (Matt 28:28).

Jesus shares the gut-wrenching nature of love that his Father is/has, and it drove him to the cross for the purpose of reconciling all of humanity. There he died for all our future sins. His sacrifice communicates to us the intensity of the Father's desire for intimacy with us, because Jesus' earthly activity is directly reflective of God's intent. After all, Jesus is "the image of the invisible God" (Col 1:15 ESV), "And he is the radiance of His glory and the exact representation of his nature and upholds all things by the word of his power" (Heb 1:3a NASB). Christ's entire incarnation, ministry, and sacrifice were motivated by God's desire for us to return to him. Those who are loved the most are changed and release the most!

The story of the prodigal son contains one of the most moving lines in the Bible: "*his father ran.*" This is the only time in the whole Bible that it says God ran. Can we picture this scene? No questions are asked, and no conditions are imposed. Instead, we see the running father coming up to his delinquent kid with a joyous welcome, hugging and kissing him, clasping his hand over the mouth. His sorrowful son is about to ruin the moment with a confession or repentance rooted in self-hatred and shame. His father's heart is so much larger than the boy's darkness. He commands the best robe, a ring, and sandals for tired feet. His voice sounds out, "Where's the beef? Let's party with the best food, music, and dancing!"

Here we have Jesus' picture of the Father as a divine sprinter who welcomes us to him with open arms. It does not matter where we have come from or what we have done. When the wounded return home, it is time to celebrate! It is banquet time! Jesus does not see his Father as one who tabulates sin. There are no spreadsheets documenting our failures. God even loves *bad* people! All he wants is for his kids to be with him. God will never stop being a Father, regardless of our poor choices. Jacob lied to his father and yet found an honored place in Jesus' bloodline. David committed adultery and yet was known as a man after God's own heart. On point, Jesus prayed that everyone would know they are loved

---

11. Jeremiah, *Romans VIII*, 130.

by the Father just like he is loved (John 17:23). Abba knows us best and loves us the most.

## THAT'S WHERE HIS MERCY BEGINS

> Let me share an invitation
> Come join me in this land of rest
> Where we trade our failures
> And gain the Father's best
> Let us turn to him together
> Leaving all our fears behind
> The Father knows your story
> It's mercy you'll find[12]

The prodigal son was expecting to eat humble pie, rather than sweet mercy. His first words to his father was his confession of sin. However, the father did not even respond to that confession. He was simply joyful that the son he loved has returned.

In that moment of reunion, the son could only see his father through his own sin. However, what he needed to learn was how to see his needs through the lens of his father's heart! This shows us the power of our perspective. Do we see ourselves and our relationship to the Father just as the prodigal son did—through the lens of our failings? Or do we see ourselves through the lens of the Father's consummate love and affection? The big-picture view of the God of Jesus sees all the details of our lives from the perspective of an unfailing desire for us to be close with him. It is idolatry to give so much place to our mistakes—in essence, to deify them. According to Brennan Manning, when "Jesus revealed what God is really like, he exposed our projections for the idolatry they are and gave us the way to become free of them."[13] We can be free from the guilt that blocks our feeling of God's love for us and his mission to love others though us.

Elliott R. Ohannes, my college librarian, recalls with a deep sense of satisfaction how his father always used to define him when he messed up, by saying, "Always remember, son, you belong to me!" We are only really free to repent when we know who our Father is! Repentance is about returning to the relationship with our Father. Our daily prayer is,

12. McHugh et al., "That's Where His Mercy Begins."
13. Manning, *Abba's Child*, 16.

"Abba Father, I belong to you!" Repentance must be about a *Who*, not just a *what*. As Ohannes put it:

> The vision of who the Father is, is central to the whole Book of Luke. The prodigal son was with the Father all of the time. Father says to him, *"All that's mine is yours."* They were living in proximity that should have produced an intimate, accurate picture of the Father, but it didn't. It's clear from the son's rehearsal speech that the image of his father was not that of a father, but rather the son's inaccurate understanding of the Father. For whatever reason, the son neither heard nor saw the Father's real personality. In a sense the son refused to permit the Father to define himself. This is idolatry! God says, *"I will be what I will be."* But the son refused to allow God to be God, to allow the Father to be the Father. True, the son had a picture of the Father that seemed pious, but that seeming pious picture was idolatrous because it conformed to the son's vision of his father as one with whom favor was purchased. The son's vision, for all of his piety and pious sorrow, was nothing more than a refined Baal worship, that was based upon the purchase of favor. Christ saw something wrong with the repentance of his day. When we flog ourselves, we think we are pious? How do we become true to whom our Father is if we debase ourselves?
>
> Why do we go through so many years of flogging and failing? One runs out of energy! So, Lord, I'm yours the way I am. The sin of the prodigal son was that he did not know that grace is the truth, not popular piety!
>
> Accordingly, I can't forget the conversation I had with a young mother. She exclaimed, *"I need to see the Father in conditional terms. I need the insecurity and fear to keep me committed in a day-by-day way!"* I wondered how she could see spiritual pathology as a road to discipleship. *"That which is not of faith is sin."*[14]

The prodigal son was unable to see the father's reality because he broke from that relationship in order to be self-focused and independent. Only when the prodigal son came to the dead end of that approach to life could he choose to walk away from his independence. The divine perspective views life as interconnected. It functions properly only in relationship. The prodigal finds true identity when back in connection with the Father. Only in the connective love of the Father can we see ourselves and our lives clearly.

14. Ohannes, personal interview, July 22, 1994.

When the son insisted that his father divide up the inheritance in the first place, he was thinking as if his father had already died and did not really matter to him. But for the father, the relationship was more important than the material goods. The father-son relationship could not be bought or sold. Similarly, God's grace is not a commodity that we earn. God's love is not something we can purchase. There is an acronym sometimes forced onto the word "grace" that transmits bad theology: God's Riches At Christ's Expense. This is false because God is the grace and mercy that he gives. As the psalmist puts it, "Your beauty and love chase after me every day of my life." (Ps 23:6). The relationship with him is the riches. Divine qualities such as grace, mercy, and riches are not commodities. Neither are they ideas, or even things. They are a part of God's very being, and we only interact with them in a relationship with God. To think otherwise is partitioned thinking in which we focus on the parts and allow them to define the whole. Rather, the whole of God must define the parts! This is holistic thinking.

What a paradigm shift! We should no longer look at God through the parts of our lives we see in front of us. Instead, with the help of the Holy Spirit, we should endeavor to see everything through God. If we try to reach God through the individual events, ideas, and feelings in our lives, he will seem unreachable. Similarly, we cannot understand the Word of God unless we approach it in a relationship with the Father. The truth of the Word of God is found by looking at it through the person of God. Christ himself says he is the truth (John 14:6). Our relationship with him is not about what he gives us (the parts), but about who he is within us (the whole).

## THE INTERCONNECTIVITY OF LOVE

One late evening, the red light on my office phone was on. I had seen that red light for fifteen years, but in that moment, I knew something was very wrong. A friend from the University of Washington had left me a message that one of our best students, and our friend for more than twenty years, had committed suicide.

I think I know why. He could not feel love. He was unable to receive the connectivity of love. And for this reason, he could not feel close to God.

His father had been a hardheaded Dutch Calvinist and a lawyer. He demanded perfection, but in an emotionally distant way. His wife, too, had a strained relationship with her father, who had abused her when she was a child. Because both of them never *felt* loved by their parents, they could not love themselves, and they could not accept that they were accepted. They could not accept, on a personal level, the all-encompassing love of Jesus Christ. They could only try to measure up, not treasure up. They could not bond!

When we cannot feel the connection of love, we will feel detached from both God and community. And with this perceived abandonment comes a lack of the sense of belonging. Then our hearts are like orphans and we cannot feel the divine life of love. The truth is that we can only love God in proportion to the amount of love we allow him to give us! Why? Because, as John the Beloved states, we love only because the Father first loved us (1 John 4:19). God's first word is love. His last word is unfailing love (1 John 4:9–10). Are we born to be loved, or are we born to die and live well while able? We were born loved!

Who and what we love, however, shapes us. We are born loved with a love we could not think possible, and only in receiving that relentless love are we able to love others extravagantly. As we love him and what he loves, we are positioned to shape life. We cannot really grow spiritually or be transformed until we live from his love and not for it! Love is God's medium of interconnectivity with us. We are only able to live holistically with him by being made whole and holy by his love.

So, how do we live in the holism of love? First, we accept Jesus' view of God as our own. His compassionate Father must become our Father, and his God our God (John 20:17; Luke 15:20).

Second, we accept that we are defined by Christ's overflowing love—"to know the love of Christ which passes knowledge; that you may be filled with all the fullness of God" (Eph 3:19 NKJV).[15] Accept Christ's overflowing love as the pathway to God's fullness. As Brennan Manning shares:

> Silent solitude makes true speech possible and personal. If I am not in touch with my own belovedness, then I cannot touch the sacredness of others. If I am estranged from myself, I am likewise a stranger to others. Experience has taught me that I connect best with others when I connect with the core of myself.

---

15. The word for "fullness" in the Greek is πλήρωμα (*plērōma*) and is defined as "a full measure, copiousness, plenitude, that which has been completed." The emphasis is on fullness and completion, the idea of being filled to overflowing. So, fullness is not about being filled up but overflowing. See Strong's #4138; Hayford, ed., *Hayford Bible Handbook*, 619.

> When I allow God to liberate me from unhealthy dependence on people, I listen more attentively, love more unselfishly, and am more compassionate and playful. I take myself less seriously, become aware that the breath of the Father is on my face and that my countenance is bright with laughter in the midst of an adventure I thoroughly enjoy.[16]

Third, we live in love's oneness by the Holy Spirit. As we participate in that love, we come to know it. And sometimes we live in that love before we truly experience it. But it will always show up in God's timing. In a sweet moment, he will show up and we will feel it!

That happened for Jerome, a close friend of mine. This may be the best Billy Graham story I have ever heard. It tells more about Billy than do most. On a Saturday morning Jerome went to see his girlfriend and found her in bed with another guy. He was devastated. Later, the daughter of Billy's radio station manager in Montreat, North Carolina, dropped by his home on a lake north of Greensboro. He shared his sadness. She said, "Let's go for a ride." She drove him to Montreat, near Asheville, a two-hour-plus drive. They found one last parking place at the inn across from Lake Susan and Montreat College. They walked into a wedding reception and took a backseat. Billy Graham and some team members were on the dais. Jerome felt that Billy was looking right at him and turning to comment to a team member. This repeated several times. Maybe he thought another wedding was forthcoming? At the end of the reception Billy was accompanied to the elevator by some of his team members. Afterward, Jerome and his friend were walking to the same elevator. Billy saw them and walked over to Jerome and gave him a huge hug. Afterwards Jerome and his friend stopped at the home of Billy's pastor and told him about the hug. He responded, "That's so unbelievable because Billy never, ever, hugs a complete stranger. He can't afford to due to the frequent threats on his life." Jerome's life changed because of that hug!

As Maya Angelou put it, "People will forget what you said, people will forget what you did, but people will never forget how you made them feel."[17] One hug from God and the rest is details! Billy was Jerome's role model. Jerome had attended all his crusades in the Charlotte area. In that one sweet moment, Jerome felt that God truly loved him. His orphan

---

16. Manning, *Abba's Child*, 39–40.

17. https://www.quotespedia.org/authors/m/maya-angelou/ive-learned-that-people-will-forget-what-you-said-people-will-forget-what-you-did-but-people-will-never-forget-how-you-made-them-feel-maya-angelou/.

heart was healed, and he became a pastor. Again, those loved the most are changed the most!

I have my own Billy Graham story. When I was nine, my parents divorced, and with an orphan heart I was sent off to live with my grandma in New Westminster, British Columbia. From my attic bedroom I would look out at all the lights in front of the mighty Fraser River and preach to them, copying my role model, Billy Graham. God evidently heard my sermon. Years later, Billy Graham walked up four flights of stairs to meet me. I kicked myself for six months because I had not said anything profound about the weather. He bought us an Arby's sandwich and forgot the tomato, so I had to forgive him for that. He had an office right above mine in the Billy Graham Center. I went to his home at the end of Mississippi Drive in Montreat, and got my picture taken in his study at his headquarters in Black Mountain. God got on my wavelength and hugged me there. But I did not feel it then.

Divorced, my mother, whom I had not seen in seventeen years, phoned me (her first child) when I was a pastor in Chicago and said she was dying. I said all the right words. But I felt nothing. You see, I was looking at her through the eyes of a hurting nine-year-old and over-expecting her to be where she could not be, given what had happened to her in her life. At her funeral, I stood holding up my sobbing younger brother on one side and my younger sister on the other. I felt nothing. Years later, I hugged my pain until it went away. My concept of home was not a foundation; it had become a detached choice.

Then I was ambushed by the glory of Abba Father's love and began to feel and live from his love. One can (as a pastor, professor, and theologian) go through half a lifetime without feeling love, and God can be trying to hug you all the while. Then the God of Jesus (Luke 15:20) ambushes you and you begin to live from the glory of his love. But we cannot live for love in our past; we get closure by living from his love in our present and future. As Oprah Winfrey put it, "Living in the moment means letting go of the past and not waiting for the future. It means living your life consciously, aware that each moment you breathe is a gift."[18] Life is now. Or as Maya Angelou put it, "If you must look back, do so forgivingly. *If you must look forward, do so prayerfully.* However, the wisest thing you can do is to be present in the present, gratefully."[19]

18. "15 Motivational Quotes for Patients," https://www.caringbridge.org/resources/motivational-quotes-for-patients/.

19. "Maya Angelou Quotes," https://quotefancy.com/maya-angelou-quotes.

Fourth, we love others even though we do not feel it. Feeling is not the engine of our trains; it is the caboose. As Dallas Willard put it, "Feelings are good servants, but they are disastrous masters."[20] God's love in us is the engine that inspires us to release love towards others. "Mostly what God does is love you" (Eph 5:2). Colossians 3:11–15 should always rule our hearts:

> Entering into this fullness is not something you figure out or achieve. It's not a matter of being circumcised or keeping a long list of laws. No, you're already *in*—insiders—not through some secretive initiation rite but rather through what Christ has already gone through for you, destroying the power of sin. If it's an initiation ritual you're after, you've already been through it by submitting to baptism. Going under the water was a burial of your old life; coming up out of it was a resurrection, God raising you from the dead as he did Christ. When you were stuck in your old sin-dead life, you were incapable of responding to God. God brought you alive—right along with Christ! Think of it! All sins forgiven, [past, present, and future] the slate wiped clean, that old arrest warrant canceled and nailed to Christ's cross. He stripped all the spiritual tyrants in the universe of their sham authority at the Cross and marched them naked through the streets.

We cannot forget that God in Christ has provided forgiveness for all our past, present, and future sins. God gave up a whole dimension of time for us. His love has already been bestowed upon us, even before we knew him (Rom 5:8)! It is a gift. We do not need to work for it. We do not need to chase it. If we do that, we act as though we do not have it, and then we will live as though we do not have it—always striving to attain something that God has already accomplished. That mindset believes that we must earn love. That is *works righteousness* via contractual or (if-then) transactional self-help, self-generation, self-actualization, self-achievement, and self-fulfillment. As Campbell writes, "Even observably righteous behavior when it is motivated in extrinsic terms tends to be deeply sinful."[21] It is truly the trap of our times! God as Trinity says we are loved and transformed by his interpersonal way of being toward us. We must simply receive the holistic truth of God's preexisting love by

---

20. Willard, *Renovation of the Heart*, 122.
21. Campbell. "Covenant or Contract in Paul."

believing and releasing it accordingly. The alternative was expressed by Plato: "He whom love touches not walks in darkness."[22]

## HOLISM AND HUMAN REALITY

The holistic interconnectivity of relationships is not just a Christian principle, nor even merely a spiritual principle. It is a central aspect of the nature of human reality.

Robert Hooke was the first to observe and describe plant cells. He did so while looking at a thin slice of cork under a microscope. After drawing what he observed, he dubbed them "cells" because they looked to him like the cells in a monastery. In "Observation XVIII" of his book *Micrographia* (1665), he wrote, "I could exceedingly plainly perceive it to be all perforated and porous, much like a Honey-comb..."[23] Since that time, we have come to realize that all things are made up of smaller, individual parts. There are orders of interconnectedness in all of physical matter, from the parts of the atom to the atoms that make up matter, to the various chemicals and physical structures that come together to make complex objects and organisms. To recognize the importance of such interconnections, and the way in which the relations between parts form the greater whole, is to think holistically.

Atoms are holistic connections of particles and waves. Matter is made up of holistic relationships between atoms. Biomes are a holistic combination of geography, microbiology, plants, and animals that function in holistic patterns. Human bodies are holistic systems of cells and organs. Human beings are holistic creatures of body, soul, and spirit. Communities are holistic organizations of interconnected individuals. Even God himself is holistic as the Trinity of Father, Son, and Holy Spirit. If reality is primarily holistic in nature, then it would behoove us to at least attempt to view ourselves, our lives, our families, and God in a holistic manner. If we cannot see a way out of our long-standing problems, perhaps we should take the time to view things in a new light. Just as with an optical illusion that simultaneously shows two different figures—such as two mirrored faces that form the shape of a cup between them—we can choose to see things in many ways. And how we choose to see something will determine how we react, relate, and respond to it.

22. Plato, *Symposium*.
23. Hooke, *Micrographia*, "Observation XVIII," Schem. 11, Fig. 1.

## Holistic Thinking and God's Relational Priority

Figure 2: An Optical Illusion[24]

Similarly, we cannot truly know the nature of trees and forests without a holistic view. A forest is much more than what we see. In a below-ground web, there is an understory, a "cooperative network" of root systems that reach out to injured or dying trees to give it nutrients, enabling it to "self-heal" and "enhance the resilience of a whole community."[25] Trees are trees more than rugged stems and beautiful crowns. Surprisingly, the connectivity of "mother" and "hub" trees remind us that reality is interconnectional and interdependent. Trees even "nurse their children." So, a holistic view of trees reveals an entire hidden life. They are the visible manifestations of "this other world" underground, "a world of infinite biological pathways that connect trees and allow them to communicate and allow the forest to behave as if it's a single organism. It might remind you of a sort of intelligence . . . Trees can count, can learn, can remember . . . Trees have families."[26] So, the homeless, helpless, and hopeless, or wounded among us need "mother" or "hub trees" to remind them that reality is holistic, interconnectional, and interdependent—that there are those who can reach out to them in their understory to love and nurture them back to whole community.

24. https://openclipart.org/detail/274578/heads-vase-illusion.
25. Toomey, "Exploring."
26. Toomey, "Exploring." View the outstanding YouTube video by Suzanne Simard at https://www.youtube.com/watch?v=Un2yBgIAxYs.

My friend Bruce is a holistic "hub tree" in a forest of the homeless. He was my college academic dean, and later experienced injury to his eyes causing near blindness. On the phone he told me how he packs lunches and almost daily distributes them to the homeless he can barely see in the Seattle area. He spends time with them. How many PhDs take a long bus ride spending the last phases of their lives ministering to the homeless? Apparently, St. Francis of Assisi also lives in Seattle.

Westerners, however, tend not to be interconnected, interdependent, or interpersonal. They tend to think analytically, linearly, or laterally. They tend to break down the whole into the parts in order to understand them. This is not, in itself, a bad thing. In many cases, dissection is an important tool of discovery and identification. However, if they do not take the next step of understanding how the individual parts function together, then their analytical, linear, single-box thought process will misunderstand the nature of reality, and therefore misdiagnose its problems. By breaking down any whole system into its component parts, one can begin to understand it in a greater way, but one's knowledge of it will be limited merely to the parts if one does not also engage a holistic view.[27]

Folsom offers examples that point out that our view of reality is limited due to our linear analytical reasoning:

> It is clear from the history of science, that we often misread reality. We had to learn about the stars to see them as "like our sun" but far away. We had to learn that the sun looks like it goes around the earth, but the opposite is reality. It looks like the earth is flat as we look out the window, but a new point-of-view gives a more faithful understanding of reality. We could pursue this line of discovery about nearly all that we now understand. There is much we do not even begin to understand. Reality is a term for what we indwell, but we are not in an appropriate relation to rightly comprehend what we apprehend.[28]

However, linear thinking can have devastating consequences. If we view Christianity as linear, we will miss out on the multifaceted personality of Christ. Doctrines easily become analytical propositional encapsulations of Christian principles. Even doctrines that are perfectly articulated

---

27. From an ontological perspective, is analytical dissecting and explaining a way of doing in order to be, rather than a way of being from who one is? We can make meaning from the whole or the parts.

28. Folsom, "Trinity and Reality," email to author, October 3, 2018.

must at the very least be explored in relation to other major Christian doctrines. In the words of T. F. Torrance:

> It is not just that the doctrine of the Holy Trinity must be accorded primacy over all the other doctrines, but that properly understood it is the nerve and centre of them all, [a first-order doctrine] configures them all and is so deeply integrated with them that when they are held apart from the doctrine of the Trinity, they are seriously defective in truth and become malformed.[29]

Moreover, if our Christian worldview is not dynamic and interconnected, our relationship with God in Christ will be incomplete at best. What if the best way to live as a Christian is not through the linear limitations of doctrine, but in the holistic freedom of relationship?

The enemy of holism is reductionism. Reductionism reduces complex beings and phenomena down to one primary element. A famous example of reductionism in action is the story of the blind men and the elephant. One touched the side of the elephant and said that an elephant is like a wall. Another touched the trunk and said it is like a hose. Another touched the tail and said it is like a snake. None of them were necessarily wrong, but their descriptions failed to capture the complete truth of an elephant.

Similarly, we may view people as unidimensional. We reduce them down to some personality trait or, even worse, a physical feature. But all humans are complex beings. No one has only one personality trait. If we do not see others as holistic beings, we cannot relate to them in a Christ-like manner. Even if we correctly judge someone's problems, that person should not be defined by their problems if they are in Christ! The corollary of this is that even those we think to be good all have their problems too. If we put someone on a pedestal because we see them as unidimensionally good, then we are sure to be disappointed. Only a multi-linear, interpersonal, and participatory worldview is consistent with Christianity. This is the true conceptual scheme of the Christian faith.

A conceptual scheme is a pattern or arrangement of concepts, ideas, and beliefs by which we consciously or unconsciously interpret and judge reality. A conceptual scheme explains why we see the world as we do, why we often think and act as we do. Further, insight into the worldview of others helps us to understand what makes them tick. We all have our own

---

29. Torrance, *Christian Doctrine of God*, 6. In this magisterial work, he concurs that the Trinity is a first-order doctrine.

conceptual schemes, whether we know it or not. However, we must be sure that the conceptual scheme we subscribe to reflects the true nature of reality, because it provides a comprehensive approach to essential life concerns.

Developing a genuine Christian worldview based on the conceptual scheme of holism and relationship is one of the most important things we can do to enhance self-understanding. The right eyeglasses can put the world into clearer focus, and an appropriate worldview can function in much the same way.

Our priorities are shaped by our worldview, and our worldview is shaped by our beliefs.[30] Our worldview—"a mental model of reality"—is a trajectory decision, for it will aim us in a very particular direction.[31] Therefore, if we want to have the right priorities, we must be sure we have the right worldview. If our worldview does not reflect true reality, we will make bad decisions. We are not what we think we are; we are what we think (Prov 23:7). Our choices, reactions, and responses emerge from our assumptions and beliefs, and if we never question or examine our core assumptions and beliefs, we easily fall into a zombie-like routine of unintentional living.

One of the central aspects of the Christian worldview is the incarnate Jesus, who portrays to us a picture of a relentlessly loving Father. This perspective should shape and interpret all other views!

And this worldview is most readily communicated in the parable of the prodigal son. Luke 15 provides a foundational view of the remarkable God of Jesus, and gives us a multi-linear, interpersonal, and participatory worldview that describes true reality. It begins with the God of Jesus, who makes us whole and holy by his love. It then creates Father-led trajectory decisions for a life of living from love. The point here is that such a perspective is an anchor in the maelstrom of life. Jesus' personal view of God must be a promising part of a Christian's worldview. The relationship that Christ had with the Father is now available to us. But we will not engage in this relationship unless we take on the Christlike worldview.

---

30. Palmer, *Elements of a Christian Worldview*, 24.

31. Wallace, "Three Things," https://www.foxnews.com/opinion/2018/05/20/three-things-wish-someone-had-guts-to-tell-me-when-graduated-from-college.html.

## HOLISM AND CHRISTIAN REALITY

The apostle Paul was rather aware of holism, although that terminology had not yet been developed in his time. When Paul discusses the metaphor of the body of Christ, he is writing about a holistic concept (Rom 12:4–5; Eph 4:16; Col 1:18; 1 Cor 12:12–31). The parts of the human body cannot function independently, and the body itself cannot function properly unless all the parts are in order and connected together in the right way. Similarly, the body of Christ—made up of individual believers—does not function as it should unless all the individual parts are in working order and are properly related to one another. For God's people to function as the body of Christ, we must see the importance of both the individual and interconnected whole. If we only focus on the individual level, we will miss the bigger picture of how Christ moves in his body. If we only focus on the collective form of the body in the church, then we will miss the necessary building blocks of the individual, who must be in good spiritual health and must have healthy relationships with others in the body of Christ. The body of Christ, as a whole, can do much more than individuals can do alone. Individuals, however, must get their proper time and attention for the whole to act according to Christ's headship. The body of Christ is best understood in its relationships and connections. This is what makes it a distinctly holistic reality.

The concept of holism is also revealed in a more spiritual manner in the Trinity. We cannot understand God the Father without also understanding Christ the Son and the Holy Spirit. Further, we will not understand the nature of the three without considering their perichoretic relationships together. The Trinity not only functions holistically—that is, Father, Son, and Holy Spirit in intimate interpersonal connection—but also cannot be genuinely understood except through the lens of holism. Their relationships are outward-bound, in which being is externally defined.

There are two main aspects of how holism functions in the Christian worldview. The first has to do with a way of thinking. Christian theology and experience are best understood as holistic truths. The Bible itself is holistic, in that each book and chapter and verse are interrelated throughout the whole. By the rule of faith (*regula fidei*, in its Protestant usage), scripture interprets scripture. From Genesis to Revelation, God's Word in its various inscripturated forms, by various authors, comments on itself. In this way, the message of the Bible cannot be understood except holistically. Every part relates together to form a whole that goes beyond the mere sum of its parts. Similarly, the doctrines and theology of Christianity cannot be understood individually. For example, the doctrine of salvation cannot be truly examined and internalized without a deep Christology. Nor can the doctrine of ecclesiology be understood apart from the Trinity—the first self-emptying community. A true Christian paradigm will be holistic.

The second way in which holism functions in Christianity is in its lifestyle. Just as the concept of the body of Christ cannot be understood except holistically, the functioning of the body of Christ cannot be enacted except holistically. Our relationship with Christ, the head, and with other believers, must be maintained individually—but with the view that these various interconnections must form a larger whole. Similarly, we cannot begin to interact with the Trinity except holistically. Our relationship with the Holy Spirit affects our relationship with both the Father and the Son. Our relationship with the Father is completely dependent upon our relationship with the Son. In other words, a proper relationship with God in the Christian context involves an ongoing relationship with all members of the Trinity in a holistic fashion. As Folsom writes:

> To be in contact with reality, we must still listen for the voice of Jesus, mediated through the voice of the Spirit who makes contact with the Son, and through him, know the Father, the Creator of Heaven and Earth—all reality.
>
> Once we are opened to the personal reality that speaks the universe into being, we have contact with the context of reality—the Triune God.[32]

Christianity is further holistic in that it must permeate our entire lives. We cannot merely be Christian on Sunday mornings. Christ's love and message must guide what he does within us in the contexts of our family, job, and social life. Christianity is a holistic lifestyle, not just a philosophical outlook or a religious rite.

## HOLISM AND THEOLOGICAL THINKING

How can we apply the principle of holism to Christian theology? One way to understand a holistic system is to see it as a web. When a basketball hits a webbed net, every strand vibrates. A web, with its many points of intersection and interconnectedness, is an excellent real-world illustration of

---

32. Folsom, "Trinity and Reality," email to author, October 3, 2018.

holism.³³ A hierarchical system emphasizes power (or priority) over connection. In a hierarchy, elements are stacked and ranked. However, ideas and principles are at their most powerful when they function together, rather than separated and categorized systematically. Ben Dickson offers a theological model of discipleship based upon the image of a web:

> For an adequate discipleship model to occur it must holistically include elements of connecting people *Upwardly* (Spiritually) with God, enlighten a deeper *Inward* (Personal) connection with who they are created to be, establish them closer *Outwardly* (Communally) with others, and *Downward* (Missional) frees them to respond for God's kingdom by laying down their lives whilst building a theological framework for understanding God's plan and being through it all. The Trinitarian Theologians of Rahner, Pannenberg, Barth, Moltmann, Zizioulas, and LaCugna highlight these very elements within the Triune Godhead himself.³⁴

Let us review these paradigms of Christian discipleship, one by one.

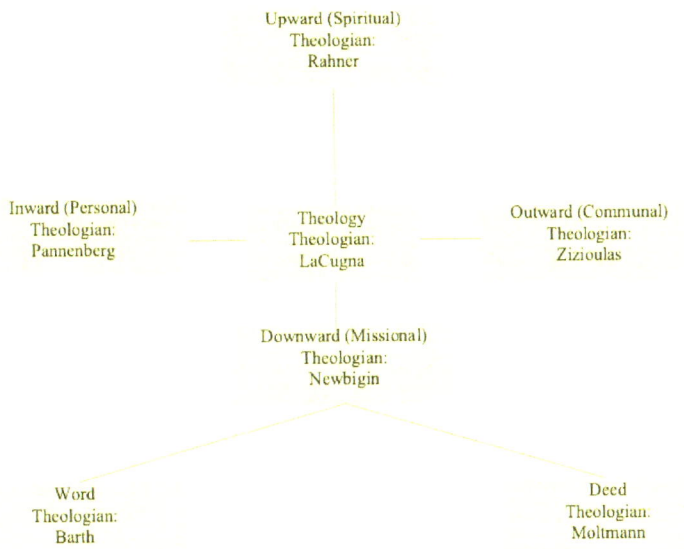

**Figure 3: Visual Depiction of the Holistic Discipleship Model**³⁵

---

33. Murphy, *Beyond Liberalism and Fundamentalism*, 94.
34. Dickson, "Holistic Discipleship," 5.
35. Dickson, "Holistic Discipleship," 6.

### 1. Upward (Spiritual)—Karl Rahner

Rahner (1904–1984), a German Catholic theologian, contended that the Christian spiritual life begins with God's decisive action toward humanity, and that discipleship should be focused on bringing people closer to God in a personal connection. Rather than just focusing on moral behavior, the discipline of discipleship is about knowing God himself. Dickson writes, "A spiritual person therefore becomes someone who bears witness to God's work in salvation, shares in the experiences of God in the world today, values the body of Christ and studies the bible to grow in their knowledge of God. By participating in the Trinity in a daily relationship, the believer is brought into an extraordinary life of divine intimacy. In this sense, the life of the disciple—in Rahner's view—is lived an upward focus toward the Father . . ."

### 2. Inward (Personal)—Wolfhart Pannenberg

"Holistic discipleship also calls the disciple to connect inwardly too."[36] The inward call of discipleship is focused on the human identity as the image of God. This is not a horizontally defined self and worldview focus, a self-centered focus, aimed at independent self-discovery or at satisfying personal desire. Rather, an inward discipleship process partners with the Holy Spirit in the process of the believer discovering his or her true identity in God toward the purpose of living the godly life.

Pannenberg maintains that the Trinity, rather than the Scriptures, is the basis of the Christian life.[37] The Scriptures certainly introduce us to the Trinity and provide the doctrinal basis of the nature of God, but is the relationship with the members of the Trinity of higher priority than the knowledge of the Bible? Is the knowledge of God, in this way, the basis for knowledge of self? The process of this self-knowledge is mediated by the Holy Spirit, a member of the Trinity. Dickson insists that "The Spirit's role has always been the medium of the communion between the Father and the Son and now also is the medium between Christians and Christ, drawing them into his presence and working in their lives to make them

---

36. Dickson, "Holistic Discipleship," 9.

37. Dickson, "Holistic Discipleship," 11. See Pannenberg, *Introduction to Systematic Theology*, vol. 2.

reflect God's glory and dignity."[38] Inward discipleship is therefore directed toward the workings of God in the human interior life.[39]

## 3. Downward (Missional)—Lesslie Newbigin, Karl Barth, Jürgen Moltmann

Discipleship with a downward focus sets its focus on the needs of God's creation. It is distinctly missional in that it places Jesus' salvation—a free gift for the whole world—as its central concern. Dickson clarifies:

> Jesus calls the church to continue on his missional work of making disciples. How? By baptizing them *into* the Trinity (Matt 28:18–20)[40] and carrying his message to the ends of the earth (Acts 1:8). The only reason that there is a church is because there has always been a triune mission of God; the one who is Sender, Sent and Sending. For just as the Father sent the Son into the world (John 3:16–18) and the Father and Son send the Spirit (John 14:26) so too are the Father, Son and Spirit sending his Church into the world to carry on their work (John 17:18). Therefore, a key role in discipleship is to allow Christians to see their role in and partake in the mission of the Triune God.[41]

Theological proponents of this downward discipleship include Newbigin, Barth, and Moltmann. Such discipleship experiences Christlikeness by taking on Jesus' mission to minister to the world. This includes traditional missionary endeavors, as well as the pursuit of social justice—that is, mission in both word and deed.[42] In this way, such a downward discipleship satisfies both the evangelical pursuit of lost souls as well as the focus on aiding the world on practical levels. Perhaps, in

---

38. Dickson, "Holistic Discipleship," 11. Kärkkäinen, *Trinity*, 130.

39. See Tozer, *Pursuit of God*, 37. Tozer writes, "As we focus on God, the things of the Spirit take shape before our inner eyes. Obedience to the word of Christ will bring and inward revelation of the Godhead. It will give accurate perception to see God as promised to the pure of heart. A new God consciousness will seize upon us as we begin to taste, hear and inwardly feel God, who is our life and all."

40. Glenn, "Joy of the Trinity." Note the key phrase, "baptizing them in the name of the Father, and of the Son and of the Holy Spirit." The word "in" is actually a translation of the Greek word *eis*, and that actually means "into," not smoothed out from the original Greek.

41. Dickson, "Holistic Discipleship," 12. Seamands, *Ministry in the Image of God*, 161.

42. Dickson, "Holistic Discipleship," 13.

simpler terms, this approach to discipleship endeavors to share the presence of God in a daily expression of their love of neighbor.[43]

## 4. Outward (Communal)—John Zizioulas

Outward discipleship focuses on the spiritual power of community relationships. As the opposite pole to inward discipleship, this approach focuses primarily on how the community functions together as Christ's disciples. Rather than emphasizing individual responsibility, an outward view recognizes that God has chosen to function within the body of Christ (1 Cor 12:12–14). The gospel cannot be fully realized in a purely individualistic way. To live the gospel in its fullness requires community in which personhood is developed.[44] LaCugna ties it all together and concludes: "the doctrine of the Trinity is ultimately a practical doctrine with radical consequences for Christian life."[45]

## 5. The Holism of the Trinity and the Web of Discipleship

The nature of the Trinity is relational and holistic. The Trinity focuses inward with the relationships between the three members. The Trinity focuses outward with the inclusion of humanity. The Trinity focuses upward with their shared summit of glory. And the Trinity focuses downward with the offer of salvation to the world. The Trinity is therefore the paradigm and the empowering of all discipleship. Dickson summarizes his holistic view of discipleship in this way:

> In regaining an understanding of the Trinity and its practical relationship to Christian life, the call for a holistic discipleship emerges from the inner life of God. This affirms the need for discipleship to connect *Upward* (spiritually) with God, *Inward* (personally) with whom they are created to be, establishes them closer *Outwardly* (communally) with others and calls them to respond by laying their lives *Downward* (missionally) for God's kingdom.[46]

---

43. Dickson, "Holistic Discipleship," 12–13.
44. Dickson, "Holistic Discipleship," 18.
45. Dickson, "Holistic Discipleship," 21. See LaCugna, *God for Us*, 1.
46. Dickson, "Holistic Discipleship," 24.

## CONCLUSION

The prodigal son presents a model of the believer's relationship with God. This "pearl of parables" shows us that the Christian perspective must be one in which relationship, interconnectedness, and love triumph over all other concerns. In other words, it is holistic.

This chapter—and this book as a whole—contends that we must learn to think holistically about Christianity and attempt to see the interconnectedness of God's dynamic activity in human life. Further, we must view the interconnectedness as being personal and relational, not just theoretical. The way we view reality will determine how we live life. If we see reality as a number of disconnected ideas and objects, we will miss the profound breadth and depth of our multidimensional God. Do we relate to God as a Father for whom love motivates his determination to be close with us? Or do we relate to him through the lens of our problems or ambitions?

Both aspects of holism in the Christian context are necessary: in our understanding (knowledge) and in our lifestyle (application). And we must also allow Christ to live the principles of Christianity in us through interconnected relationships with God and community. As Shivers puts it, "The resultant conclusion is that the personal dynamic communion evidenced in the economy of salvation through the person of Christ in relationship with the Father and the Spirit is available in the Church. Through life in the Spirit church leaders are to reflect this personal dynamic communion and reveal the true nature of the Church."[47]

Our view of God, as well as the mission and quality of our lives, are at stake. Accordingly, it is important to probe the elements of one's worldview. We have suggested that we should see reality as holistic, based on the interconnective and interpersonal relationships of the Trinity and with brothers and sisters in Christ. This worldview is reflective of the loving outlook of Jesus and the father-child relationship in the story of the prodigal son. A worldview can be linear or multi-linear. But only a multi-linear, interpersonal, and participatory worldview is true to the Christian view of reality.

---

47. Shivers, "Trinitarian Communion," see esp. abstract.

**REFLECTION**

1. Do you think Jesus' personal view of God is the normative view in Western Christianity? Why or why not?

2. Have you seen or experienced how linear or reductive thinking results in detachment, distortion, dysfunction, and damage in the Christian life? Have you seen or experienced how holistic and relational thinking results in connection, blessing, and intimacy with God?

3. Can you cite examples of holistic or big-picture thinking in the Bible?

4. Do Western Christians tend to be Father-led and Father-centered, just as Jesus was? As Jesus states in John 14:28, "You've heard me tell you, 'I'm going away, and I'm coming back.' If you loved me, you would be glad that I'm on my way to the Father because the Father is the goal and purpose of my life."

# 2

# The Interpersonal Nature of God

## INTRODUCTION

ONE CANNOT ACCURATELY DESCRIBE Christology or Pneumatology outside of the context of the Trinity. The nature of God himself will be misunderstood or mischaracterized if it is examined independently from what Nancy Pearcey calls the "personal dynamic communion of the Godhead."[1] The interpersonal nature of God[2] can begin to be clarified by examining interrelated concepts, such as the personhood of God, Christology, Pneumatology, theology, reciprocal kenosis and dynamic communion, Christ's church, and the personal dynamic communion that must characterize leaders in the church.

---

1. Pearcey, *Total Truth*.

2. Carl, "Against Praxeas": "Tertullian 'coined the word Trinity and solidified the technical terminology that became the standard way of speaking about the being of God in the Trinity and the person of Christ for the Latin church after him . . .'" "Quintus Septimius Florens Tertullianus was born between 150 and 160, believed to be the son of a centurion. Whether or not he was in fact a jurist, his logical argumentation and piercing rhetoric is evident in all of his 31 surviving works. Tertullian flourished in Carthage and Rome where he aligned himself with the Montanist sect. He died between 222 and 225. Tertullian's importance as an apologist and theologian cannot be overestimated. Sellers calls him the 'Origen of the West'" (Sellers, *Council of Chalcedon*, 187; Osborn, *Tertullian*, 116).

## PERSONHOOD OF GOD

There are two concepts that are important to explore if we are to understand the nature of God and the nature of lived Christianity. First, the person of God is relationally dynamic—a truth that is exemplified in the foundational nature of the Trinity. Second, the personhood of God is revealed in the life and character of the incarnate Christ.[3] To explore the person of Jesus is to explore the Trinity. Understanding God in this way allows us to recognize interpersonal nature as a defining characteristic of the Trinity, but also as an invitation into their dynamic relationship through Christ himself. Gordon Fee writes that "it is in salvation history that the three persons and their relationship are revealed."[4]

C. Christopher Shivers describes the interpersonhood of God as "an ontological foundation for being as communion."[5] The nature of God as revealed in Trinity is one of intimate onto-relational connection. However, we cannot think of this communion as something God *does*; we must instead think of it as who God *is*. In other words, the oneness of the Trinity is an ontological way of being—in communion. Their relationships are "communal personal," in contrast to "mechanistic individualism."[6]

---

3. Šijaković, *Ad Orientem*, 151: "Ecclesiology derives its being from God's nature and makes possible a "personal experience of inter-communion with a personal God: A God who is One yet Three, transcendent yet immanent, uncreated yet ecclesially incarnate in history." Shivers, "Trinitarian Communion," ii.5. Shivers contends that "Dynamic personhood is embodied in the Trinity, embodied in the Church, countercultural, and necessary for leadership."

4. Fee, *Pauline Christology*, 313. Fee states in this study of Paul: "the coming of Christ forever marked Paul's understanding of God, so also the coming of Christ forever marked his understanding of the Spirit." And further: "the relationship of the Spirit and Christ in Paul, against those theologians that assert a 'Spirit christology.'"

5. Shivers, "Trinitarian Communion," 9.

6. Shivers, "Trinitarian Communion," 7. Gunton, *One, the Three and the Many*, 214. "... [divine unity's] central concept is that of shared being: the persons do not simply enter into relations with one another but are *constituted by one another in the relations*. Father, Son and Spirit are eternally what they are by virtue of what they are from and to one another. Being and relation can be distinguished in thought but in no way separated ontologically; they are rather part of the one ontological dynamic ... not a blank unity, but a being in communion" (emphasis added). See also Boff, *Trinity and Society*, 123–54. See Gunton, *Promise*, 23. The chief legacy of the Enlightenment was mechanistic individualism. The mechanistic Enlightenment resulted in reducing a person to an impersonal machine, organism, or it.

## The Interpersonal Nature of God

This ontological view of the Trinity, however, exists in stark contrast to the Greek philosophical backdrop of the New Testament.[7] In the Second Temple Greco-Roman perspective, personhood (*prosopon*) was like a mask, a role performed by the individual. Personhood was not ontological, but rather was understood to be merely a response to external stimuli.[8]

The theological reality of the Trinity requires that we see God as irreducibly relational, and thus lays the unbreakable foundation for human relationality. Zizioulas and Gunton, following the Cappadocians,

---

7. Folsom, a paper given at the Evangelical Theological Society Annual meeting in 2016. The theme was *"Advancing Trinitarian Theology."* Marty draws from a basic affirmation by T. F. Torrance who stated, "that theology is formed by hearing the *viva vox* of God as we interpret the Bible, listening to the speaking Voice of the Triune God in a manner true to God and with a careful, critical attentiveness." (Torrance, *Christian Doctrine of God*, 39). "In short, revelation precedes theological reflection and is its critical control." Theology needs to be restored to its InterPersonal character, as opposed to merely "employing selective principles of logic to 'make sense' of God" (Torrance, *Theology in Reconciliation*, 181) and relying on "intellectualized, naturalized and overly historicized horizons of philosophical and theological idealism" (Šijaković, *Ad Orientem*," 147). Gunton insists, "the perennial temptation of the Western mind has been to seek for the unity of things in some deity or divine principle over and above the triune revelation." Gunton, *Father, Son, and Holy Spirit*, i–iii, 55.

Folsom, "Does the Spirit Have a Voice?," email to author, December 3, 2018. Folsom, following T. F. Torrance, contends that we should not look to Latin and Greek renditions because: ". . . both East and West developed into a defensive and definitional mode that missed the Hebrew and Christian mode. The Hebrew mindset within the Bible itself orients theology to listen to God as deeply personal and not built on philosophical presuppositions. The Bible does not begin with the relation of one and three in the Trinity but shows up in person as the unique Word who opens the way to his Father and prepares for the coming of the Spirit who will continue to make Jesus known. The Trinity is discovered through personal encounter." The Latin and Greek church have both missed a proper starting place to this issue. The Hebrew, biblical mode is not focused on the one and three, but begins with voice, especially making room for the Spirit! Marty adds, "Where there is a voice, there is personal presence . . . to begin the task of theology with a philosophical God is to neglect the God revealed in Jesus, . . . any theological task needs correctives to refocus us on the primary task of theological thinking—listening to God and living in faithful response. Doctrine arose out of a defensive stance, not from the intention of revelation. These formulations become philosophically abstract and exclude God's personal Voice from guiding the agenda." Marty insists, "The Hebrew mode of engaging God is one of listening to the God who speaks."

8. Folsom, "Relational Theology," 221–29. "The Trinity as Persons in relation is not about external manifestations of one essence [*essentia*]. That is basically modalism. The basic nature of God is a Being in communion." See C. Christopher Shivers, "Trinitarian Communion," 9–10. See Zizioulas, *Being as Communion*, ch. 1. See also Ury, *Trinitarian Personhood*, 81–99, for a history of the terms related to "person."

contend that the Trinity is "the central and substantial content of the doctrine of God," and that it is the "point of departure" for an ontological view of the Trinity.[9] Zizioulas points to Ignatius of Antioch and Irenaeus (founding fathers of Christian Theology) as the earliest Christian thinkers who extracted Christology from this view. They did so by casting the *Logos* and the life of Christ as ontological. As Folsom puts it, "Zizioulas uses the phrase '*hypostasis* in *ekstasis*,' meaning being in going out to the other who is always coming to meet me. This is the imminent relation, not economic. It is onto-relational, not relationship constituting. The dynamic is always already there, not a secondary movement."[10]

T. F. Torrance contended that the tri-personal God (the Holy Trinity) is revealed to us in Scripture as "one in being." The being and outward-bound acts of the Father and Son are one. For God, his ontology and praxis are unified. Torrance amplifies:

> The one triune Being of God is to be thought of, then, as essentially and intrinsically a mutual movement of loving self-communication between the Father, the Son and the Holy Spirit, an intensely personal Communion, an ever-living ever-loving Being, the Being for Others which the three divine Persons have in common. To say that God is intensely or inherently personal does not mean, of course, that he is a Person in the relational sense of the three particular divine Persons in their otherness or objective relations to one another, but rather that God is a fullness of personal Being within himself, just as he is full of love within himself. He is not less personal, any more than he is less loving, in his one indivisible Being as whole God (ὅλος Θεός, Athanasius' expression) than he is in each Person who is true God of true God and is in himself as the Son or the Spirit whole God (ὅλος Θεός) as well as the Father. He is perfectly One in Three and Three in One. That is the one transcendent personal Being of God who is the creative source of the personal communion which in his outgoing love for others he wants to establish between himself and us. Due to its inherently reciprocal nature, however, we cannot have communion with all three, for they are

---

9. Awad, "Personhood as Particularity," 2. Awad states that Zizioulas and Gunton, following the Cappadocians' perichoretic logic, hold that "the Trinity is the central and substantial *content* of the doctrine of God," and "its point of departure" in order to "revive the relational dimension of the concept of 'person' by the help of a Trinity-based understanding of the patristic ontological statement that 'God is three *hypostases*, not three modes of being.'"

10. Folsom, "Onto-Relational," email to author, October 3, 2021.

who they are precisely as one indivisible Being, three inseparable Persons/three inseparable Persons, one indivisible Being."[11]

Thus, the very truth of the gospel depends on this unity of the Son with the Father. Torrance's key idea[12] was that the function of *homoousion*[13]—a Greek word that combines *homós* (same) with *ousía* (being)—was to affirm that God the Son and God the Father are of the same onto-relational substance. Gunton, following T. F. Torrance, contended that "The function [of *homoousion*] is to establish a new ontological principle: that there can be a sharing in being"—being in relation.[14] So, they concluded that the Nicene theologians created a new biblical category to counter philosophical ones. Here we begin to see the divine interaction of the concepts of being and relationship—both in the Trinity and in Christ's invitation to humanity to participate relationally with the Trinity.

Athanasius of Alexandria, the chief defender of Trinitarianism, was primarily concerned with an ontological paradigm rather than the just the ethical or juridical.[15] The christological approaches of Basil of Caesarea and the Cappadocians advanced the ontological position by introducing the idea that the Father, Son, and Spirit share the same onto-divine substance (*ousia*) in three particular persons (*hypostases*, or natures), or are one in *ousia* and three in *hypostasis* or *persona*.[16] The Cappadocians based "the relational life of the three divine persons on their divine Being and not the opposite."[17] "It is not, as in Western theology, the divine substance which constitutes the persons of the Trinity."[18] What is important

---

11. Torrance, *Christian Doctrine of God*, 133. T. F. Torrance is regarded as one of the finest, most significant, and most challenging Scottish theologians ever. He saw theology as a practical science. While at the University of Edinburg, he published 320 works. After he retired, he added 260 additional publications.

12. T. F. Torrance's major discussions of the *homoousion* appear in three overlapping books on the Trinity: *The Trinitarian Faith* (1988), *Trinitarian Perspectives* (1994), and *The Christian Doctrine of God, One Being Three Persons* (1996).

13. "Homoousios." *Homoousion* was "the key term of the Christological doctrine formulated at the first ecumenical council, held at Nicaea in 325, to affirm that God the Son and God the Father are of the same substance."

14. Gunton, *Promise*, 9. See Schuller, "Colin Gunton on the Trinity," http://schuller.id.au/2005/11/09/colin-gunton-on-the-trinity/.

15. Lytvynenko, "Doctrine of God."

16. Gunton, *Promise*, 9–11. Zizioulas, *Being as Communion*, 37. Ury, *Trinitarian Personhood*, 116, 120.

17. Awad, "Personhood as Particularity," 10.

18. Gunton, "Augustine, the Trinity," 58; see also Gunton, *Promise*, 31–57, and

here is that God exists on account of three particular persons and not due to an impersonal substance or "God stuff." T. F. Torrance argues for an onto-relational understanding of relationship. That is, "substance" can be defined as an onto-relational category:

> ... It will be sufficient to recall that it was due to the development of relational thinking about the activity of God in creation and incarnation that enabled Christian theology to overcome the static container notion of space, and it was out of this relational thinking that there came the concept of *person*, unknown in the world before Christianity, in accordance with which it was held that the relations between persons are of constitutive importance for they enter into what persons really are as persons. Thus, an onto-relational way of understanding persons in community rejected an atomistic way of thinking of them as self-sufficient, independent, separated individuals who may be organised into a society only through their external relations with one another—the very notion into which John Locke disastrously carried European socio-political thought under the impact of Newtonian atomism and action at a distance ... [19]

The term that captures the relational dynamic of the three persons of the Trinity is the Greek word *perichoresis*. This term highlights the interpenetrating and mutual indwelling of the Father, Son, and Holy Spirit. The divine monarchy should not exclusively rest upon the Father's causation alone (classical subordination), but rather by virtue of the perichoresis of the three. T. F. Torrance applies the concept of perichoresis "to highlight the dynamic, spiritual, and intensely personal onto relationships in the Trinity ... Perichoresis refers to that limitless and eternal love between the Father (lover) and the Son (beloved) and the Holy Spirit (Spirit of love that binds both the lover and the beloved)."[20] The Trinity

---

*One, the Three and the Many*. Shivers, "Trinitarian Communion," 10, 12. Moltmann, *Trinity and the Kingdom*, 177: "Gunton [*Promise*, 3–4] argues that Augustine failed to appreciate the achievement of both Athanasius and the Cappadocian Fathers in three ways: 1. He sought patterns of threeness apart from the economy of salvation (e.g., his metaphors). This gives him a rationalist and non-Biblically driven direction (such as anti-material dualism). 2. He over affirms unity and risks losing the distinctives of each person. 3. He muddies the water by treating God uni-personally, rather than one substance in three persons."

19. Torrance, *Christian Theology & Scientific Culture*, 50.
20. Weng, "T. F. Torrance on Perichoresis."

chooses to live in communion, rather than hierarchy.[21] Each person has free relational formation.[22] All three are coeternal, coessential, and coequal.[23] However, within this foundation, Gunton characterizes the Trinity as functioning in "overlapping patterns of relationship," in which "the same person will be sometimes 'subordinate' and sometimes 'superordinate' according to the gifts and graces being exercised."[24] Matthew L. Tinkham agrees, affirming "the ontological and functional equality of the Father, the Son, and the Spirit (while recognizing distinctions of personhood and complementarity of roles and functions)."[25] This is perichoresis in action in the Godhead. As T. F. Torrance puts it:

> When we consider the order of the three divine Persons in this perichoretic way we do indeed think of the Father as first precisely as Father, but not as the Deifier of the Son and the Spirit . . . This does not derogate from the Deity of Son or of the Spirit, any more than it violates the real distinctions within the Triune Being of God, so that no room is left for either a Sabellian modalism or an Arian subordinationism in the doctrine of the Holy Trinity . . . . Since no distinction between underived Deity and derived Deity is tenable, there can be no thought of one Person being ontologically or divinely prior to another or

---

21. Awad, "Personhood as Particularity," 8. "It rather means, as Wolfhart Pannenberg correctly says, that the *monarchia* of the Father is perichoretically affirmed by both the Father's work in creation through the Son and by the Spirit's work in the Son to glorify him with the Father. The Son's and the Spirit's activities serve the monarchy of the Father. But, as Pannenberg adds, "the Father does not have His kingdom or monarchy without the Son and the Spirit, but only through them" (Awad, "Personhood as Particularity," 9). See Pannenberg, *Systematic Theology*, 1:324.

22. Awad, "Personhood as Particularity," 19. Gunton, *One, the Three and the Many*, 164: "Freedom is a substantial attribute of being that produces the "irresistible desire for some ontological account . . . tied to what I am and not simply what I want."

23. See Parker, "Biblical Understanding of the Trinity," 46, for a thorough evaluation. He "emphasizes both the eternal equality of essence and the eternal distinction of persons with regard to the relationships of the Trinity . . . The eternal generation of the Son and the eternal functional subordination of the Son have also been evaluated and shown they are not mutually exclusive and there is biblical validity for affirming both concepts." See also Gordon, "Presence of the Triune God," for a challenging assessment.

24. Gunton, *Promise of Trinitarian Theology*, 78, 80. Gunton contends for "an ecclesiology of Perichoresis" in which "there is no permanent structure of subordination," but rather "overlapping patterns of relationships, so that the same person will be sometimes 'subordinate' and sometimes 'superordinate' according to the gifts and graces being exercised."

25. Tinkham, "Hierarchy or Mutuality," 52.

subsequent to another. Hence while the Father in virtue of his Fatherhood is first in order, the Father, the Son and the Spirit eternally coexist as three fully co-equal Persons in a perichoretic togetherness and in-each-otherness in such a way that, in accordance with the particular aspect of divine revelation and salvation immediately in view, as in the New Testament Scriptures, there may be an appropriate variation in the Trinitarian order from that given in Baptism, as we find in the benediction, 'The grace of the Lord Jesus Christ, and the love of God and the communion of the Holy Spirit be with you all.' Nevertheless, both Athanasius and Basil counseled the Church to keep to the order of the divine Persons given in Holy Baptism, if only to counter the damaging heresy of Sabellianism.[26]

The persons of the Trinity are undefined outside of the fabric of their relationship. Their ontology emerges from their interconnected state. So, "particularity" does not mean that there are three individuals. Rather, "their eternal and characteristic identity can only be seen in relation to each other."[27] As Gunton contends, "Each is only what he is by virtue of what the three give and receive from each other; and yet, by virtue of their mutually constitutive relations each is distinctive and particular."[28] This is the holistic reality of the Trinity. As Folsom summarizes:

> The God of the Bible wants to be known, not locked in philosophical terms. If we emphasize the simplicity and singularity of God, we miss the community. If we emphasize the distinctions in God, we risk advocating three Gods and miss the biblical witness. It is in the unity of the three persons as one God in communion that we find the God acting to reveal God and embrace humanity for a life of participation. We are so often disconnected today from a present, resurrected Jesus, a reconciled Father still embracing, and an awakening Spirit still raising the dead. These three are one, alive, and active.[29]

The Arian and Greek philosophical notion of God's being was non-relational. Arius, a presbyter of Alexandria, contested the eternity of the Son of God. Many branches of Western Christianity label the extreme Arian perspective that God is not Son and Father as the heresy

---

26. Torrance, *Christian Doctrine of God*, 180.
27. Schuller, "Colin Gunton on the Trinity."
28. Gunton, *Promise*, 12.
29. Folsom, "One and Three," email to author, October 3, 2021.

of *modalism*, which asserts that each member of the Trinity is only an expression (or mode) of the same God, and that each member is not a distinct being.

Accordingly, biblical truth need not succumb to philosophical categories that may have made sense in the ancient world but are not genuinely reflective of the biblical perspective. In this case, the concept is that of *perichoretic communion*. This is what best expresses the nature of the Trinity. Barth and T. F. Torrance contend that *perichoresis* is an ontological way of being that is based on the mutual indwelling of the Father, Son and Spirit. One might also frame it as "relationality in being."[30] As Leonardo Boff concludes:

> If God means three divine Persons in eternal communion among themselves, then we must conclude that we also, sons and daughters, are called to communion. We are image and likeness of the Trinity. Hence, we are community beings. Solitude is hell. No one is an island. We are surrounded by persons, things, and beings on all sides. Because of the Blessed Trinity, we are called to maintain relationships of communion with all, giving and receiving, and together building a rich and open shared life, one that respects differences and does good to all.[31]

Understanding the nature of the personhood of God is not a purposeless theological study. For we are exploring the "ultimate originating principle of all reality . . . If God were not personal, God would not exist at all."[32] Establishing the proper view of God's ontology—that is, the being of God—dictates how humans relate to God, and vice versa. Humans were made in God's image, and therefore a greater understanding of the nature of God naturally results in a greater understanding of the nature of humanity.[33] Humans are relational persons, who are able to relate to God

---

30. Schuller, "Colin Gunton on the Trinity."

31. Boff, *Holy Trinity, Perfect Community*, 2.

32. Pava, "Examining Theological Approaches," 6. LaCugna, "God in Communion," 86–87.

33. Cf. Awad, "Personhood as Particularity," 16. Gunton argues that "because God is a community of three particular and inseparable persons, and because the human was created in God's image, it becomes God's creation when it acquires a relational nature where the one and the many are reconciled. Being 'in the image' of God means, for Gunton, having 'a dynamic being in relation' (Gunton, 'Trinity, Ontology and Anthropology,' 47–64). We are human when we reflect in our life, by grace, a relationship of giving and receiving with God and with others."

in their perichoretic personhood.[34] This foundation for communion with God, although perhaps contested, is preserved by the Hebraic biblical tradition. For T. F. Torrance, "the Reformed doctrine of 'communion of the Spirit' is better understood as 'union with Christ through the Communion of the Spirit.' The combination of 'union with Christ' and 'the communion of the Spirit' lies at the foundation of the Church's hope and forms the heart of its eschatology."[35]

## CHRISTOLOGY AND PNEUMATOLOGY

It was suggested in the previous section that the distinct categories of theology, Christology, and Pneumatology cannot be adequately explored without a Trinitarian foundation in place.[36] Given the establishment of onto-Trinitarian personhood as a foundational descriptor of the nature of the Trinity, how does this apply in the study of Christology? Christ himself states that his person reflects the person of the Father (John 14:9).

---

34. Zizioulas, *Being as Communion*, 41–46. "'Zizoulas holds that true personhood is only realised in the *hypostasis of ecclesial existence*... The *hypostasis of biological necessity* is the tragedy of man struggling towards personhood but failing due to never realising the ontological necessity of personhood found in communion. Torrance holds that this view leads to an "over-realised eschatology" and consequently to an "isolationist ecclesiology," 359. It is not in the scope of this work to discuss at what point a human becomes a person or the extent to which the *Imago Dei* is present in believers or non-believers. See Gunton, *Promise*, ch. 6, toward a 'Renewal of the Doctrine of the *Imago Dei*.' Also see Awad, 'Personhood, for a critique of the Trinitarian views of personhood in Zizioulas and Gunton, which make specific references to the *Imago Dei*." Shivers, "Trinitarian Communion," 12, n. 29.

35. Davis, "T. F. Torrance." Torrance, *School of Faith*, cvi.

36. Cf. Šijaković, *Ad Orientem*, 152. "The theology of personhood is a result of several fundamental 'turns' in Orthodox theology. These turns are common ground to a host of Orthodox thinkers of the 20th century" (149). Next to "the (1) divine-human context of orthodox theology, the (2) Trinitarian context of divine-human communion is another essential point of departure for the theology of personhood. Since by communion with the person of Christ one re-discovers his divine-human person, it follows that human personhood is not only Christ-like but also Trinity-like. Christ does nothing alone or by himself: the energies of Christ always entail action in unity with the other two divine Persons (hypostases). This means that the Christology of personhood is discovered to be most immanently connected to a triadology of personhood (for humanity is created as an image of God in Christ by the Spirit). Lastly, this implies that Christian anthropology is to be grounded Christologically and triadologically and, by extension, pneumatologically—all within an ecclesial setting. Consequently, Yannaras calls for an 'ecclesiological anthropology'" (Yannaras, *Elements of Faith*).

In this way, a study of Christ's person as it emerges from the concept of onto-Trinitarian personhood will shed light on not only a relational view of Christology, but also a relational view of theology.

Atkinson defines a "person" as one who potentially maintains a sense of distinct self, but also an ability to relate to a non-self as other.[37] We see Jesus exemplifying this concept in a number of ways. First, he knows who he is and states boldly his sense of distinct self (Matt 9:6; 11:29; Mark 2:10–11; 8:31). Further, he states that he only acts based upon his relationship with the Father (John 8:28–29). Jesus extends this relation to non-self to also include other humans, particularly those who do the will of God (Mark 3:31–35).

However, it is particularly in Jesus' prayer life, as Shivers points out, that the person of Christ is revealed in his relationship to the Father.[38] He teaches others to relate to God as Father, just as he himself relates to God (Luke 11:1–13). Jesus relates with a depth of honesty to the Father, as seen in his dramatic words of intimacy in the garden of Gethsemane (Matt 26:39; Mark 14:36; Luke 22:42), as well as in God's response (John 12:27–28).

Another important aspect of Christ's personhood that speaks to his relation to humanity is his suffering, which was relational in that he accepted it for all of humanity (Heb 2:9). Further, it was an expression of his relationship with the Father in that he chose to suffer and die in obedience to the Father, and it led to his glorification with God (Heb 2:9). The concept behind the Greek word *kenosis* captures Christ's personal choice to empty himself, humble himself, and give himself for others in response to God's plan. Due to that choice, "The personhood of the divine Son cannot be separated from the personhood of the human Jesus of Nazareth."[39] No longer is Jesus only identified as divine, but he is also now and forever identified as human. His personhood reflects both the divine and the human. Humanity, therefore, is already associated with the Trinity via the participation of Christ. Therefore, by virtue of Jesus' humanity, in Christ we participate in his communion and worship of the Father. The Trinitarian relationship exemplified in Christ is now available to all who are in him.

37. Atkinson, "Trinity and Servant-Leadership," 30.

38. Gunton, *Promise*, 97–98, 202; Melissaris, "Challenge of Patristic Ontology," 473. See also Awad, "Personhood as Particularity," 16–17, "for a critique of the point of departure between Gunton and Zizioulas." See Shivers, "Trinitarian Communion," 14.

39. Shivers, "Trinitarian Communion," 15.

Again, although all three are coeternal (eternally generated), co-essential, and coequal,[40] it is also important to recognize Christ's unique quality of humanity. Jesus' humanity is the basis for the human attainment of personhood in relation to the Trinity, as well as the basis of our emulation of Christ by pursuing the Father's indwelling (see John 14:23). Both of these poles—Spirit divinity and humanity—play a role in revealing the nature of the human relationship with God.[41]

Further, the incarnate Christ was just as dependent upon the Holy Spirit as he was upon the Father. Jesus was conceived by the Spirit (Luke 1:35), and his ministry began with the Spirit falling upon him (Luke 3:22). As Shivers states, Luke's narrative shows that "the Spirit is responsible for Jesus' awareness of his relationship with the Father."[42] Therefore, in Christ's incarnate state we see the interpersonal Trinitarian relationship at work in Jesus' ministry and life (e.g., John 16:13–15). The interconnected intimacy of the three persons was not broken with Christ's incarnation.

This reliance upon the Spirit has several implications. First, we must not lose sight of the fact that the acts generally ascribed to the divinity of Jesus were a result of the Spirit's empowering presence. Jesus did not perform miracles independently from the Holy Spirit. Second, there is a clear distinction made in Scripture—and the Gospels in particular—between Jesus and the Holy Spirit. They are persons distinct from each other, even though they functioned in synchronicity. Third, as a human, Jesus was reliant upon the Holy Spirit in the same way that we today are also reliant upon the Spirit.[43] Jesus is our example in his incarnate state and illustrates the average Christian's need (and opportunity) to also rely on the Holy Spirit.

---

40. "See Parker, "Biblical Understanding," 46, for a thorough evaluation. He "emphasizes both the eternal equality of essence and the eternal distinction of persons with regard to the relationships of the Trinity . . . The eternal generation of the Son and the eternal functional subordination of the Son have also been evaluated and shown they are not mutually exclusive and there is biblical validity for affirming both concepts."

41. Shivers, "Trinitarian Communion," 35.

42. Shivers, "Trinitarian Communion," 18.

43. Shivers, "Trinitarian Communion," 18. Amos Yong, *Spirit-Word-Community*, 30, 32: "From what has previously been presented concerning Augustinian dualism, it also holds that the West's deemphasis of the Spirit is a direct result of the deemphasis of Christ's humanity. Can it be coincidence that both of these aspects of Christ and the Spirit are intrinsically linked and yet mutually forgotten?"

## RECIPROCAL KENOSIS AND DYNAMIC COMMUNION

Two related aspects of the Trinitarian dynamic that are applicable to the human Christian life are *reciprocal kenosis* and *dynamic communion*. Both of these ideas first require a proper understanding of individuality and personhood.

In the scriptural context, individuality flies in the face of personhood. This is not intuitive in the standard Western perspective. The relational dynamic of Trinity, however, resists characterizations of individuality. In other words, one cannot treat the Father, Son, or Holy Spirit as separate individuals without irrevocably damaging their identities and personhood. The personhood of Christ is founded upon oneness with the Father and the Holy Spirit (John 5:19–27). Individuality, therefore, as a concept that necessarily involves separateness and the emphasis of distinctives, is antithetical to Trinitarian personhood.

Christ's act of *kenosis*—his self-emptying—reveals the Trinitarian priority of oneness over individualism. The choice to empty oneself is a key departure from the standard Western perspective. It was in his self-emptying that Christ found greater personhood, for it allowed the Father's promise-plan to be fulfilled in his unique earthly ministry. This was accomplished in concert with the activity of the Father and the Holy Spirit. In this way, *kenosis* and personhood are recursively and reciprocally linked. That is, they continually feedback to each other in an ever-expanding spiral.

It should be emphasized that our use of the terms *kenotic* or *kenosis* throughout this book refers to Jesus' servanthood leadership lifestyle rather than a divesting of his divinity. Doros Zachariades challenges "kenotic notions of the Incarnation" contending that they are not faithful to the high-water mark of "Chalcedonianism"—the incarnational "pure picture" that Jesus is "truly and fully a man, while at the same time fully and genuinely God."[44] As Colin Gunton contends, without the appropriate recognition that Jesus is fully God, the result is a view of Jesus as "mythical demi-god that encounters us in Christ."[45] This references a quote by Barth:

> If it is not God, one fully God, but a depotentiated divinity that meets us, then the gospel is void, for that holds that in Christ

---

44. See Zachariades, "Διπλην Επαγγελιαν," 1–2.
45. Zachariades, "Διπλην Επαγγελιαν," 7. See Gunton, *Christ and Creation*, 83.

the fullness of the Godhead dwells bodily. 'God is always God even in his humiliation . . . Any subtraction or weakening of it would at once throw doubt upon the atonement made in him. He humbled himself, but he did not do it by ceasing to be who he is.'[46] If this is salvation being achieved, then it must be the work of God himself, not of some mythical demi-god.[47]

Thus, Gunton contends:

> To recapitulate the articulation of all this by the use of the concept of kenosis, we can therefore say that the self-emptying of the eternal Son in the incarnation and passion is an expression of the love of the triune God worked out in the structures of fallen time and space. On the cross, which clearly represents the climax of the kenosis and is its fulfilment, there takes place the *plerōsis* of the Son's self-emptying to our condition which began with the conception of Jesus in the womb of Mary. The Spirit, the agent of the incarnate Son's relation to the Father who sent him, thus brings it about that the shameful[48] death of the incarnate is the means by which the power of God works in and towards the creation.[49]

Accordingly, we do not endorse kenotic theories of the incarnation that diminish his divinity. In Philippians 2:3–4, Paul states his perichoretic purpose or theme: "in *humility*, think of one another as better than yourselves . . . as in the example of Christ." Paul continues with this theme in 2:5–11, which is a *locus classicus* for incarnational theology, and deals with Christ's self-humiliation and resulting exaltation. As Ralph P. Martin puts it, "The Philippians are here faced with the greatest possible incentive to unity and humility in the picture of the Lord himself whose attitude is described in the noble verses which follow."[50]

---

46. Barth, *Church Dogmatics*, 4.1, p. 179.
47. Gunton, *Christ and Creation*, 83.
48. Gunton, *Christ and Creation*, 89.
49. Gunton, *Christ and Creation*, 89–90.
50. Martin, *Philippians*. Martin, however, interprets the passage: "The eternal Son of God, however, faced with a parallel temptation, renounced what was his by right, and could actually have become his possession by the seizure of it, viz. equality with God, and chose instead the way of obedient suffering as the pathway to his lordship." "Trinitarians take both the active and passive of "harpagmos" (grasped). Martin flat out says that both are possible in the Greek. But either way, the text still teaches that Jesus was either equal to God as a possession or able to be equal with God, as an inherent right that the Father could not refuse." A third position is presented: "He existed

## The Interpersonal Nature of God

What does "empty himself" (v.7) mean? A forfeiture of his divinity? *Impossible theologically*! Jesus never stopped being God. As Thomas Torrance put it:

> Since the relation of the Son of the Father belongs to the union and communion of love which God eternally is in his own Being as Father, Son and Holy Spirit, the Incarnation of the Son in which God gives himself to mankind takes the form of a 'hypostatic union' between divine nature and human nature in his one Person, which is the immediate ground for all Christ's mediatorial and reconciling activity in our human existence. The hypostatic union is grounded in, derived from and is continuously upheld by what is called the 'consubstantial communion' within the Holy Trinity, that is, the mutual indwelling or coinhering of Father, Son and Holy Spirit as three Persons of one and the same Being in God. That is a union in which divine nature and human nature are united in Christ in such a way that there is no diminishing or impairing of his divine nature and no diminishing or impairing of his human nature.[51]

Jesus said, "he who has seen me has seen the Father" (John 14:9). Paul's main point in using *kenosis* does not emphasize that Jesus divested himself of divine attributes. Rather, it was that he lived out a perichoretic, interpersonal, and servanthood lifestyle of humble self-emptying. He exemplified a state of self-giving for others, ultimately and conclusively demonstrated in his choice to die on the cross. So, Paul's main purpose in referring to *kenosis* is to teach that "the community created by the incarnate and enthroned Lord must share his spirit and be controlled by the pattern of self-effacement and humility which his incarnation and cross supremely display."[52] The emphasis is not on Christology but on a model for spirituality that is Christian. It is not about divine divesture of deity but about divine expression ("*because* he existed in the form of God . . . he emptied himself"). Accordingly, Paul writes in Philippians 2:1–6:

> If you've gotten anything at all out of following Christ, if his love
> has made any difference in your life, if being in a community
> of the Spirit means anything to you, if you have a heart, if you

---

in the divine 'condition' or 'rank' as the unique image and glory of God but refused to utilize this favoured position to exploit his privileges and assert himself in opposition to his Father." (https://www.bible.ca/trinity/trinity-Martin.htm).

51. Torrance, *Meditation of Christ*, 64–65.

52. Martin, *Philippians*.

care—then do me a favor: Agree with each other, love each other, be deep-spirited friends. Don't push your way to the front; don't sweet-talk your way to the top. Put yourself aside, and help others get ahead. Don't be obsessed with getting your own advantage. Forget yourselves long enough to lend a helping hand. Think of yourselves the way Christ Jesus thought of himself.

Similarly, James tells us to "Humble yourselves before the Lord, and he will exalt you" (Jas 4:10 NRSV).

To be Christlike will necessarily involve self-emptying in the context of godly relationships.[53] Acts of *kenosis* involve preferring others, the compassionate emptying of self in order to honor another, exalting or filling others, or simply loving otherness. Such acts of *ekstasis* (going out of oneself) will naturally result in interpersonal oneness in reflection of the Trinity. Self-emptying is of particular importance for church leadership, for doing so reflects the prioritization of others over self. Further, the self-emptying of Christ is an illustration of the Trinitarian dynamic that can be pursued and discovered in the relationships that make up the Body of Christ.[54] Reciprocal kenosis is therefore a Christ-centered model of godly relationships. All are called to image Christ in self-emptying and preferring one another (Rom 12:10; Phil 2:3).

*Kenosis* is an integral component to genuine godly love. Since Jesus' provision of salvation was instigated by the love of God (John 3:16), Christ's choice of self-emptying should rightly be seen as an act of love, not only in his relationship with the Father, but also as an expression of love for humanity. Shivers writes, "it must be maintained that the character of God's relationship among the three persons of the Trinity is found in [interpersonal] *kenotic* love."[55] Mutual love expressed in dynamic communion should always show signs of self-emptying as an act of prioritizing the other.

Such kenotic activity naturally leads to *reciprocal communion*, both with God and with others. Reciprocal communion is a state in which both sides of a relationship continually reach out to initiate and maintain intimate connection in a dynamic relationship. Christ's ministry itself is an example of reciprocal communion in that everything he said and

---

53. Atkinson, "Trinity and Servant-Leadership," 31–35, "*kenosis* meaning 'self-emptying.'"

54. Martin, *Hymn of Christ*, 108.

55. Shivers, "Trinitarian Communion," 21.

did emerged from his ongoing relationship with the Father and the Holy Spirit. As C. Christopher Shivers puts it:

> The biblical witness confirms that God is Spirit [John 4:24; 2 Cor 3:17]. If the Spirit of God permeates all creation and as seen above in the life of Christ is the relational link between the Father and the Son, it is not a far leap to understand the Spirit as the "pervasive matrix of divine as well as created life." This reciprocity is also "the *perichoretic* (intra-penetrating) nature of the Persons to *kenotically* give to the other. There is dynamism in the relationships. There is fluidity of persons."[56]

Rather than mechanistic individualism, in which personhood is seen as comprising distinction and separation, reciprocal communion views personhood as emerging from interpersonal and dynamic oneness. As Migliore clarifies:

> The Trinitarian "persons" are not to be understood as separate and autonomous selves. Instead, they have their personal identity in relationship. A Trinitarian understanding of personal life questions modern views of personhood that equate personal existence with the self-consciousness and autonomy of the individual. In such understandings, there is no reference to relationship with others as constitutive of personal life. The Trinitarian persons are precisely not self-enclosed subjects who define themselves from and opposition to others. Rather, in God "persons" are relational realities and are defined by intersubjectivity, shared consciousness, faithful relationships, and the mutual giving and receiving of love.[57]

Reciprocal communion therefore encapsulates a major aspect of Trinitarian personhood, particularly as it may be enjoined by humanity.

## CHRIST'S CHURCH

There is no place more important in which to apply the Trinitarian principles of relationship than in Christ's church. Reciprocal *kenosis* and communion are in fact required acts if the church is to be a reflection of godliness. Relationships in God must reflect the Trinitarian ontology

---

56. Shivers, "Trinitarian Communion," 23.
57. Migliore, *Faith Seeking Understanding*, 77.

of personhood, being formed and maintained in dynamic communion. This forms the basis of any spiritual formation in the Christian church.

What are some obstacles to understanding Christian spirituality as it should be experienced in the church? First, we must examine the term "spiritual." In the West, it is often seen as a substitute for religiousness, and influenced by or confused with New Ageism. When spirituality in the church is overly influenced by non-Christian perspectives, it ends up being about trusting one's own wisdom and promoting it as success for human excellence. In order to find genuine Christian spirituality, we must restore Paul's emphasis on the Holy Spirit as the necessary, sole basis of spirituality. Without this foundation of the Holy Spirit, relationships in the church will not retain the necessary spiritual dimension required to emulate the Trinitarian relationship. Dynamic communion can only function in the church if this proper brand of spirituality is undertaken by genuine Christian persons.[58] Gordon Fee finds it "utterly tragic that most expressions of the Protestant tradition have ended up being trinitarian in name only, but not in practice."[59] Fee refers here to the ignorance of the person and work of the Holy Spirit that leads so much of the Protestant church to be, practically, binitarians (acknowledging only two persons in the Godhead). Christian spirituality, however, cannot be undertaken without the aid of the Holy Spirit.

This leads to the discussion of personhood in the church. Shivers writes, "Just as Christ's personhood is characterised by relationship with others through the power of the Spirit, so human personhood must be characterised by the same."[60] Therefore the recognition of the role of the Holy Spirit is integral to the person of Christ himself, as well as the Christian emulation of Christ. To put it in plain terminology, the question "What would Jesus do?" cannot be answered correctly without reference to the Holy Spirit. The Holy Spirit knows what Jesus would do, for he intimately guided Jesus incarnate actions. Further, Jesus' reliance upon

---

58. Horrell, "Self-Giving Triune God." "Whereas each member of the Godhead was understood as possessing the same nature, the Eastern Church has continually stressed the primacy of the relationships between Father, Son and Holy Spirit." See Prestige, *God in Patristic Thought*, 219–301; Martland, "Study of Cappadocian and Augustinian," 252–63; Rusch, *Trinitarian*, 149–79; and Studer, *Trinity and Incarnation*, 139–53. Eastern Orthodoxy defends the apophatic nature of God, i.e., that divine essence transcends human understanding and can only be spoken of as to what it is not. See Lossky, *In the Image*, 13–29. Shivers, "Trinitarian Communion," 37.

59. Fee, "On Getting the Spirit Back" 43.

60. Shivers, "Trinitarian Communion," 35.

the Holy Spirit also emphasizes that independence is anathema to the relationship with God. Communion and being are inseparable. Persons in the church must therefore refuse to be ontologically separate from God, Christ, the Holy Spirit, and one another.

There are two obstacles in establishing genuine dynamic communion based on the Trinitarian view of God. First, the church must overcome the lack of an ontological foundation for persons in the church. The believer's state of being must become at least as important as the believer's actions. As Shivers contends:

> The danger inherent in a misappropriation of ontology can be seen in the progression of Western thought. If theology cannot sufficiently answer ontological questions, then the church remains vulnerable to misinterpretation on a global scale. Therefore, the Church must rely on the biblical witness of the person of Christ dependent on the Spirit to present the ontological nature of personhood and the nature of the Church.[61]

In other words, if Christ's church cannot display itself as a genuine representation of God's love, oneness, and personhood as displayed in the Trinity, then the church is not representing Christ himself. This is an ontological issue. The misunderstanding of God's way of being leads to a misunderstanding of how God's people in the church should function in personhood.

Second, an incorrect view of the Holy Spirit's role in the church is another obstacle to understand Christian personhood. Christ is Lord, Redeemer, and Head of the church. Without the Holy Spirit's involvement, however, the church does not reflect Christ's own ministry as giver of the Spirit.[62] Just as Jesus himself functioned by the Holy Spirit, he makes the way for his followers to do the same. Without the dependency upon the Holy Spirit, the church is not only lame and ineffective, but also lacking in genuine Christlikeness. Christ's witnesses should be characterized by the power of the Spirit.

---

61. Shivers, "Trinitarian Communion," 29: "It should be understood that Barth did understand God as personal but rejected the idea of three persons of the Trinity or the Cappadocian ontological person of the Father." See Velde, *Doctrine of God*, 360.

62. Volf, "Nature of the Church," 69. See Volf, *After Our Likeness*. See Borysov, *Triadosis*, 141. Holistically, Borysov would see Christ's ministry in the context of the Trinity as the image of God's personhood and redefines transformation into "the likeness of God," which is a transformation into "the likeness of the Trinity." He calls this "*triadosis*."

In 1 Corinthians 12 Paul presents a metaphor that describes the church as the body of Christ. Although it is made of many parts, the body of Christ is unified by the Holy Spirit. This metaphor balances both diversity and unity, as well as the supreme importance of relationships that value otherness. He corrects the misconception the Corinthians have about the reality of the Spirit in their lives so that they can relate kenotically and overcome disunity in their community. Tying this together with concept of spirituality as stemming directly from the Holy Spirit, we recognize that the church's life in the Spirit is relational and unified in Christ.

## PERSONAL DYNAMIC COMMUNION THAT CHARACTERIZES LEADERS IN THE CHURCH

How should church leaders apply these concepts in a practical manner? Trinitarian communion clarifies the nature of church leadership, for it establishes that leadership of persons is above all onto-relational. Dynamic communion gives a model for leading "based on, not just the servant leadership of Jesus, but the Spirit empowered, kenotic form his leadership takes in the Gospels."[63] A model for leadership is needed through the relationship of Christ to his disciples that goes beyond a simple servant-leadership paradigm.[64] Hierarchy and subordination need to be reexamined in light of a renewed view of leadership. The interrelated concepts discussed in this chapter—such as the ontology of God, personhood, *kenosis*, and dynamic communion—are necessary toward establishing a

---

63. Shivers, "Trinitarian Communion," 7.

64. Shivers, "Trinitarian Communion," 52–53. Shivers points to "a leadership model that goes beyond a casual conception of servant leadership. There is nothing wrong with this understanding of leadership per se, except that as a concept it has become saturated in contemporary culture and therefore is open to a host of interpretations. For instance, Robert Greenleaf's book on servant leadership [Greenleaf, *Servant Leadership*], gave prominence to the concept of servant leadership. According to Zscheile [Zscheile, "Trinity, Leadership and Power," 54], it is based on Hermann Hesse's *Journey to the East*. Huizing remarks that Greenleaf's agenda of 'legitimate power and greatness' is perhaps at odds with a Christian servant-leadership paradigm [see Huizing, "Leaders from Disciples," 333]." Shivers adds, "For a look at servant-leadership in Christian circles see Atkinson's recent work on 'The Trinity and Servant Leadership.'" Shivers contends, ". . . service and the servant-leadership of Christ . . . and the necessity of servant-leadership in the Church," however, is tied to kenosis "which underlies Christ's activities and therefore should characterise leader's service" (53).

proper model of church leadership. After all, church leadership must be reflective of Christ's leadership.

Christ's *kenosis* was an act of a servant. Christ's leadership was done in a stance of selflessness, and this should be the stance of how leaders function in service to God and to the church. Reciprocal *kenosis* is inherent to true personhood and is found in a person's capacity to love others in a reflection of the interpersonal nature of God. *Kenosis* should be seen as being synonymous with divine personhood, and it is foundational to Christlike leadership.

Paul views kenotic servanthood as net-mending: ". . . prepare God's people for works of service" (Eph 4:12, *katartismon*;[65] cf. the verb *katartizō* in Matt 4:21, "mending" or "preparing" nets; in Gal 6:1, "restore" for proper use; cf. 2 Cor 13:11; Heb 13:21, perfect or equip). Net-mending is a rich metaphor about equipping people for mutual ministry, which is like repairing broken nets, setting bones, or refitting ships (classical Greek).

Furthermore, church leadership must reflect a true commitment to the lordship of Jesus as the head of the body of Christ. Rather than being influenced by external or secular paradigms of leadership, church leaders must reflect the teachings of the Bible, the person of Christ, and the dynamic of the Trinity. Each leader shapes his or her church. Therefore, what shapes the leader is of utmost consequence.[66] Gordon Fee contends, "I would make a general plea to church leaders to throw away the boxes in which they have kept the Spirit securely under their own control, and to trust the Spirit to guide the whole community to a life in the Spirit that leads to genuine Spirituality in the believers' daily lives."[67] Fee understands that church leaders set the tone for shaping the church and to do so properly requires that they be Spirit-led leaders, just as Christ was Spirit-led.

Leaders cannot claim elite status in the Christian faith as those who have unique access to God that others do not. All Christians are meant

---

65. Michael R. Hawkins. "Net Mending: An Essential Element in Facilitating Perichoretic Community." DMin paper, The King's Seminary, 2008, 65.

66. Shivers, "Trinitarian Communion," 42. "This is in no small part due to the fact that dynamic communion . . . marked by *kenosis*, is not an easy cross to bear. *Kenotic* love is humbling and self-sacrificing. The task set for those attempting to bring modern churches (especially evangelical, market-driven churches) back to a communally oriented ecclesiology is to convince the church to abandon what is easy and comfortable for something that is harder but ultimately life giving."

67. Fee, "Getting the Spirit Back into Spirituality," 43.

to be members of the royal priesthood who have equal access to God through Jesus Christ (1 Pet 2:9). Peter states that elders in the church must be motivated by the will of God, should not seek self-gain, and should not lord their authority over others (1 Pet 5:1–3). Rather, elders should be examples to the church of Christlikeness, and must therefore exercise kenotic love and dynamic communion. Authority comes from God and is mediated through Christ and the Holy Spirit.[68] Therefore, leaders must exercise ecclesial authority under the lordship of Jesus Christ, and under the guidance of the Spirit. This, above all, requires humility, and an attitude that values others as brothers and sisters in Christ.

## CONCLUSION

The interpersonal nature of God can begin to be clarified in terms of interrelated concepts, such as the personhood of God, Christology, pneumatology, theology, reciprocal kenosis, and dynamic communion. This chapter has explored how the relationality of the Trinity forms the foundation for interpersonal relations between God and humanity, as well as between people, with particular attention paid to its application for church leaders. The master metaphor of eternal, reciprocal *kenosis* highlights an incarnational way of reflecting divine love that exalts and fills another. It suggests a rich pathway for discovering underlying ecclesial leadership qualities ("kenotic, humble, self-sacrificing, submissive personhood"[69]) that shape dynamic communion as life in the Spirit. Christianity should reflect the outworking of love displayed by the incarnate Christ. Ecclesiology should derive its way of functioning from the person of Jesus, which necessarily involves the relational dynamism with the Father and the Holy Spirit, as well.[70] The church must promote the accessibility of God through dynamic communion.[71] God may be the

---

68. Gunton, "Authority," 56.

69. Shivers, "Trinitarian Communion," 24.

70. Šijaković, *Ad Orientem*, 151. Ecclesiology derives its being from God's nature and makes possible a "personal experience of inter-communion with a personal God: A God who is One yet Three, transcendent yet immanent, uncreated yet ecclesially incarnate in history."

71. Cf. Šijaković, *Ad Orientem*, 171: "The theology of personhood is not to be understood as a partial 'reconstruction' of Orthodox theology. It is rather a new way of theology itself: vividly marked by a post-apologetic and non-confessionalist attitude. Theology is defended not by recursive confessional deductions, but by witnessing

immanent Creator, but he is a God who makes himself known in Jesus Christ. This approach to the doctrine of the Trinity allows for an onto-relational basis of ecclesiology and practical theology and, therefore, church leadership.

## REFLECTION

1. How does a deeper understanding of the interpersonal dynamic communion of the Trinity affect your personal relationship with Jesus and the Holy Spirit?

2. In what ways does life in the Spirit reclaim an interpersonal dynamic communion in the church?

3. How should interpersonal dynamic communion ("the outworking of love as kenotic, humble, self-sacrificing, submissive personhood"[72]) characterize leaders and leadership development in the church?

4. In what ways would the pursuit of reciprocal *kenosis* affect interpersonal dynamic communion in your church?

---

authentic as much as salvific and beatific prospects for persons in communion with Christ by the Spirit" (cf. John Zizioulas, "Ecumenical Dimensions," 33–40). Šijaković adds: "... communional personhood ... is to being open by the future in Christ and for it ... in which our being is realized in and through 'being for others' (Actually, being for others here coincides with being for Christ, i.e., with a thirsting Christ-bound eros which in loving others loves Christ, and conversely. For instance, such a being-for-an-other is indicated in the cry Maranatha!" ("Our Lord come!"; 1 Cor 16:22).

72. Šijaković, *Ad Orientem*, 151.

# 3

# Culture and the Principles of Christianity

**INTRODUCTION**

ANY ATTEMPT TO ESTABLISH the culture necessary to genuinely experience a Christianity based upon interpersonal oneness requires an examination of how culture promotes or inhibits the principles of Christianity.

In the West, most believers consider themselves to be Judeo-Christian in their thinking, but we are more impacted by the dominant culture that surrounds us than we would like to admit. From the enculturation of media to the indoctrination of schooling to the influence of peers, our view of the world has been defined by a lens crafted for us from the time of our birth. Folsom writes, "Daily decisions about how to use our time, money, and resources are then based on unseen voices of the past, ancient and contemporary. Neatly woven together in our minds, they strongly influence our sense of what is right. They beckon us down culturally acceptable roads."[1]

The Western values of individualism, the pursuit of happiness, the accumulation of wealth, moral relativism, social engineering, systemic racism, and cancel culture prod us in their directions in sometimes

---

1. Folsom, "Relational Theology," 221–29.

invisible ways. Cultural noise needs to be taken out of our understanding of Christianity and the nature of God.

Western values have evolved over centuries, beginning with the Greco-Roman tradition. Christians should not assume, however, that the Western worldview is always compatible with Christianity. We should evaluate the values of the West to determine whether they are commensurate with a biblical worldview. Rather than unthinkingly inherit the cultural worldview we have, we should intentionally sift through it. How much of our understanding of the Bible is accurately reflective of God's perspective, and how much is distorted by our preexisting thought processes? God does not intend to fit into our worldviews as they are; rather, he intends to change our thinking to align to his.

It can be difficult to choose the unfamiliar, because the unfamiliar is usually uncomfortable, or even confounding. However, as God himself states in Isaiah 55:8, "My thoughts are not your thoughts, nor are your ways My ways" (NASB). We must ask whether what we think is true, acceptable, good, beautiful, and rational is, in fact, what God's considers to be true, acceptable, good, beautiful, and rational. As Folsom concludes, "For many, God looks like an American, only much bigger. Definitions of a successful Christian life resonate with the values of the American dream. 'God has blessed me. I have a nice home, good job, well-behaved children, and no pain.' Are these the signs of Kingdom living?"[2] We should not presume that the study of God can possibly begin from our own culturally conditioned perspective. We must stretch ourselves to take on the scriptural worldview as it is.

A biblical (Hebraic) worldview is interpersonal. This stands in contrast to the Greco-Roman cultural perspective, which was predominant in the time of Christ and the early church. This Greco-Roman perspective tended more toward philosophical contemplation and moral pragmatism.

A Greek approach to Christianity emphasizes a philosophical approach centered on the mind and holds the view that everything is predetermined. The Greek view of the Christian God paints him as the ultimate controller of all things. The only way to ensure a good outcome in such a world would be to perfectly follow the proscribed laws of God, for he determines all things according to his fixed set of rules. The idea that this physical world is inherently bad and that the spiritual realm is inherently good is the application of the Greek philosophy of dualism. In this view,

---

2. Folsom, "Relational Theology," 221–29.

the best thing we can hope for is to leave this world and go to heaven. This first requires, however, that we perfectly follow the requirements for attaining heaven. Rather than emphasize a present-day pursuit of a relationship with God, this view emphasizes the avoidance of evil in this life in order to find God in the next world.[3] The Greek approach therefore produces an eccentric valuing of ethics and morality with a view toward *reward*, over and above a relationship with God in the here and now. For this reason, the Greek brand of Christianity is primarily works based, and does not account for the relational aspects of the Scriptural worldview.

Roman pragmatism is seen in its emphasis on authority and objectivity. When adulterated by the Roman viewpoint, God's law is put in place to control us. Punishment is the natural result of this system, and love is only present when the rules are followed. Further, this approach to Christianity emphasizes knowing these rules according to proper doctrines, upon which proscribed thinking and acting are based.[4] Believers stuck in this perspective obsess over their regret for the past and their fear of the future. We should not measure life by what we have lost, but rather by the moments Christ has yet to live in us! This Roman approach is lopsided, exaggerating the consequential aspects of Christianity and ignoring its interpersonal foundations.

However, in opposition to the Roman and Greek approaches to Christianity, the biblical (Hebraic) perspective is interpersonal and prioritizes love. Chiqui Polo-Wood writes that the Hebraic cultural perspective "is a personal society that emphasizes covenant, belonging, and wisdom."[5] The God of the Hebrew people is characterized by covenant. He is defined and revealed by relationship. God's law is therefore a covenantal law, rooted in relationship. It is not a punitive collection of rules and regulations, nor a philosophical enterprise based on mental assent, but rather a relational endeavor toward harmony and oneness between the believer and God, and between believer to believer. In this worldview, "salvation is primarily about restoring relationship, bringing about wholeness in relationship with God and with one another."[6]

Unlike the Greco-Roman perspective, the Hebrew people engaged interpersonally and found their being as persons in the world. The

---

3. Polo-Wood, *Abba Foundation*, 17–18.
4. Polo-Wood, *Abba Foundation*, 17–18.
5. Polo-Wood, *Abba Foundation*, 17–18.
6. Polo-Wood, *Abba Foundation*, 17–18.

Hebrew language of the Bible is rooted in metaphors and imagery. It therefore supports and encourages a holistic way of thinking. Christianity is intended to be the fulfillment of its roots in this Hebraic mindset.[7] It is odd, therefore, that the Western approach to Christianity has moved so far toward concrete language and rigid logic. The prevalent Roman view substitutes relationality with fear and control. Rather than the Hebraic loving God, who functions in intimacy, we have a Roman god who motivates through rules and consequences. The Greek philosophical approach also causes believers to withdraw into individualistic expression, endeavoring to discover meaning through personal exploration. But this is just an attempt to control the world by separating from it and projecting the self onto it. So, the cultural view of Western Christianity often takes an approach of outward control (Roman) or inward contemplation (Greek), rather than interpersonal (Hebraic), which is what God intended us to be. Christianity, from its Hebraic roots, is the original option to which we must return. It predates the Greek and the Roman, and it is the cultural backdrop of the entire Bible—including the person, mission, acts, and teachings of Jesus. These cultural perspectives have been summarized in chart form:[8]

---

7. Glenn, lecture notes.

8. The comparison between Roman, Greek, and Hebrew worldviews appears in the Shiloh University online course "Spiritual and Personal Formation" (DM761), week 4. See Chiqui Polo-Wood's book *The Abba Foundation*, in which she credits these sources: "I owe the foundation of this section to Folsom and Pinkham, *Relational Theology: A Primer*," The King's University, Van Nuys, CA. 73, 113." See also Folsom, *Face to Face*, vol. 3, in the sections "The Birth of Cultural Lenses" (115–19) and "Roman, Greek, Hebrew, and Family" (317–24). This reflects the groundbreaking work that he has done and has led to the wonderful development by The King's University and Shiloh University students; it is his best and most available work on this paradigm as it develops Macmurray's original thoughts. For additional details on the Roman and Greek influences in Western thought and culture, see Macmurray, *Freedom in the Modern World*, 70–79.

|  | Roman | Greek | Hebrew |
|---|---|---|---|
| Type of Society | Pragmatic | Contemplative | Personal |
| Emphasis | Autocratic | Beauty, truth | Covenant, belonging, wisdom |
| God | Law giver who inspires fear | Truth-giver who shapes our minds | Covenanting God of promise and presence |
| Law | System for control | Principle of the universe | Covenant relationship |
| Bible | Rule Book | Book of principles for successful living | The Voice of God who speaks |
| Sin | Breaking the law | Choosing the physical over the spiritual | Loss or injury of relationship; not knowing |
| Salvation | Payment for the penalty of sin | Initiation into a life of good morals and ethics | Restoration to relationship, where there is fullness of life |
| Spiritual Formation | Learning to follow the rules | Learning to live "properly" | Growing in relationship with God with one another |

Figure 4: Cultural Perspectives

## HISTORICAL AND CULTURAL PITFALLS

The Western view of the human person, rooted as it is in the Greco-Roman mindset, is a static concept that we will call "mechanistic individualism." In this mindset, the human being is *mechanistic* (mechanical) in that one must follow rules and function according to a particular logic, and *individualistic* in that the separated individual is valued over and above relational ways of being. As Duane Elmer warns, "Wherever individualism reigns supreme, community is easily sacrificed for personal preferences."[9] Or as James Torrance proposes:

> From the history of Christ thought, we can see that what our doctrine of God is, so is our understanding of humanity and conversely our understanding of the human being reflects our view of God. The counterpart of the rugged individualism of Western culture is the concept of a Sovereign Individual Monad 'out there.' The counterpart of the Protestant 'work ethic' as of much Mediaeval Catholic piety, is the 'contract God' who rewards merit.[10]

Therefore, the Trinity provides not simply an ontological understanding of the Godhead, but the basis for a perichoretic relational

---

9. Elmer, *Cross-Cultural Conflict*, 25.
10. J. Torrance, *Doctrine of the Trinity*, 5.

## Culture and the Principles of Christianity

theology within the framework of Christian community. By centering this perichoretic model in the Godhead itself, Torrance incorporates fellowship with God and man as inextricable components of the same whole. The alternative is an individualism characterized by

> a resultant preoccupation with the self, my rights, my life, my liberty, my pursuit of happiness. Religion then becomes the means towards self-esteem, self-fulfillment, self-identity, the human potential movement, possibility thinking, and leading to the neo-Gnosticism of the New Age movement, which then identifies the self with God. Know yourself. Realize your own identity! Then you will know God in the depths of your own 'spirituality!'[11]

This way of life deemphasizes humanity because it reduces the human being to a computational agent, navigating a world of cold facts. And, since humans cannot help but be anthropocentric, how we conceptualize human personhood will naturally form our view of God's personhood. In the mechanistic individualistic paradigm, God becomes the *Monad*—a philosophical term describing God as the Supreme Being, who is alone in singularity.

This Western view perverts our understanding of the God behind the gospel. The Father of Jesus transcends individualistic perspectives. We may come to Christ one at a time, but Jesus brings us together in his body. If we view God as Monad, whose nature is individualistic and singular, we will miss the significance of Trinitarian community and relationship. God certainly has rules and laws, but his approach to his children is anything but mechanistic. It is covenantal and motivated by love.

The results of the Greco-Roman paradigm are also seen in the valuation of reason as the supreme means of encountering and understanding God. The Roman senator and philosopher Boethius (c. 480–524 AD) defined "person" as an independent, individualistic, autonomous, and self-directed entity whose reasoning was of central importance.[12] If God has made us in his image, and we see ourselves primarily as an independent mind, then we will, in turn, view God as only an independent mind. Similarly, Descartes, in the time of the Enlightenment, identified humans with mind. Descartes may have been a believer, but his philosophical view of the human being has damaged our understanding of

---

11. J. Torrance, *Doctrine of the Trinity*, 5.
12. Boethius, *Liber de Persona*, ch. 3.

Christianity.[13] If being a thinking entity is all that is required of our existence, then the human being is reduced to a mere mind. This approach continues to reinforce the Greco-Roman influences upon Christianity.

The good news, however, is that God reveals himself through more than logic and reason. He reveals himself in love, relationships, revelation, experience, and salvation. While reason may help us to love, to pursue relationships, and to receive salvation, it is not the only—nor even primary—tool by which to do so. Since the Enlightenment, the culture of the West has elevated the human mind as the highest means of human understanding—demoting or even discarding the human spirit, soul, heart, and will. By lionizing the mind, our natural cultural view is necessarily individualistic, because the mind belongs to the individual. There are, however, other ways of knowing God, such as through experience and relationships. As Newbigin suggests, the communication of the gospel is best done in a life that is lived commensurately with God's love and plan. We cannot merely teach about Christ on a mental level, because doing so will miss the nuance of Christ himself, who taught through words, actions, miracles, and demonstrations of love.[14]

A proper delineation must be made between individualism and communitarianism or collectivism. We do not want to make individualism a bogeyman as that would be "naive, biblically and historically short-sighted."[15] There is a place for a Caleb who cries out, "Give me this mountain," and for lonely prophets who speak to their contaminated cultures. As Carson writes, "individualism that is sold out to Christ *can* be of the very essence of godly self-sacrifice and faithful service to the gospel."[16] The church—the community of the new covenant—flows from God's nature. God's community should be a dominant feature of a viable onto-relational theology. Again, as Colin E. Gunton, insisted, "the question of the being of the church is one of the most neglected topics of theology."[17]

---

13. Godway, "Crisis of the Personal," 2.
14. Newbigin. *Trinitarian Doctrine*, 30.
15. Carson, "Contrarian Reflections on Individualism," 380.
16. Carson, "Contrarian Reflections on Individualism," 380.
17. Gunton, *Promise*, 56. See especially ch. 3, "Augustine, The Trinity and the Theological Crisis of the West" and ch. 4, "The Community: The Trinity and the Being of the Church." Gunton maintains that "*the question of the being of the church is one of the most neglected topics of theology.*"

This lack of a relational perspective renders us incapable of forming the basis of ecclesiology and therefore church leadership.[18]

Mechanistic individualism is the egocentric enemy of authentic personhood and true community. It is a slap in the divine face, because the Trinitarian life is not individualistic, but rather dynamic interconnected oneness. Trinitarian relationships are the prototype for the church. Only a community way of being can truly define personhood. In this way, the individual cannot find satisfaction in identity outside of a relationship with God and fellow believers. Certainly, the average human life is interconnected with others, even when viewed only on a naturalistic level. To fail to address the integral role of relationships in human life is to fail to describe human existence. This truth is even more emphatic in consideration of the central importance of the believer's relationship with Christ, and, in turn, Christ's restoration of humanity's relationship to the Father.

The individualistic view of the human being presupposes that there is a consistent, true self within each person that exists in an independent reality, waiting to be discovered. This concept of human ontology began with the writings of Augustine, who championed an inward search for God.[19] This view, however, essentially follows a *substance ontology*, in which the being of a human is of a distinct substance, unique and separate from others.[20] Taylor states that this view emphasizes a first-person

---

18. Shivers, "Trinitarian Communion," 8.

19. Grenz, *Social God and the Relational Self*, 67.

20. Carl, "Against Praxeas," 2–3. "Substance may be the key concept for understanding Tertullian's doctrine of the Trinity. For Tertullian, substance is 'the constitutive material of a thing.' Substance [nature] is that which brings unity to the Trinity. Father, Son, and Holy Spirit may be distinct persons, but they share a common divine substance. Phrases communicating the 'unity of substance' among the members of the Trinity are very common in *Against Praxeas*. Son and Holy Spirit are 'joined with the Father in His substance' and 'members of the Father's own substance.' The Son is derived 'from no other source but from the substance of the Father.' For Tertullian, the phrase 'I and my Father are One' refers to a unity of substance, not a singularity of number. In the incarnation, Jesus consists of two substances [natures], divine and human, not mixed but joined in one person." "Those who share the one substance of the Godhead exist in three *persona* [appears seventy-two times in *Against Praxeas*, who was a modalist]. While *substantia* refers to what joins and unifies the inner life of the Godhead, *Persona* points to what characterizes and distinguishes it." To clarify, we hold that the basic nature of God is a being in communion. "The one transcendent personal Being of God who is the creative source of the personal communion which in his outgoing love for others he wants to establish between himself and us" (Torrance, *Christian Doctrine of God*, 133). Ontology is defined by relationship and being and personhood is determined by relationships with others. Further, being is externally

perspective, which places the human as the definer of the world.[21] The significance of objects, events, and others are filtered through a self-reflexive, self-centered worldview. Whatever we think and experience, however, must not be separate from or outside of a bigger picture of life, or we live in self-delusion. It is not true that our self is separable from what it experiences. Therefore, viewing the self as substantive, distinct, and solo is not only misleading, but damaging to our unavoidable relationships with the world, with others, and with God.

Interestingly, the postmodernist approach rejects the conception that the self is consistent, distinct, and objective, and replaces it with a more relativistic and relational view. While postmodernism is largely incompatible with a biblically centered worldview, it nevertheless offers some intriguing and insightful possibilities in a holistic approach to Christian theology. While the Augustinian/Cartesian conception is still dominant in Western thinking, it may be beneficial to explore the relational aspects of postmodernism.

Having examined the Roman, Greek, and Hebrew cultural lenses, we may also identify two modern cultural filters through which we may interpret Scripture. Each has consequences. They can enhance or retard one's capacity to hear the gospel or shape our culture.

The first is an over/under perspective, which has its roots in the King James translation. The translators of the King James Version spoke sixteenth-century Elizabethan English, which was steeped in an over/under culture. The pope was over the king, the king over the people, and men over women, who were treated like cattle. In Colossians 3:18 the King James translators choose the word "submit," rather than "support" or "partner," for women in relation to their husbands, even though these alternative terms would be acceptable translations. Take another KJV example: Genesis 2:18 could be translated as "I will make a power [or strength] corresponding to man," not "submit" as in the culturally derived KJV translation. R. David Freedman suggests that the second word found in the Hebrew expression in this verse (*kenegdo*) should be rendered

---

defined (*ekstasis*), and therefore there is no genuine ontological life without relationships. Western professionalism defines persons in terms of what they are rather than who they are. "The Hebrew mindset within the Bible itself orients theology to listen to God as deeply personal and not built on philosophical presuppositions" (Folsom, email to author, December 3, 2018).

21. Taylor, *Sources of the Self*, 130.

"equal to him."[22] McFadyen concurs: "Eve's designation as Adam's 'help-meet' must be understood in terms of this dialogical relationship. A helpmeet is not a subordinate assistant, but a help-corresponding-to-him, denoting the closest physical and spiritual mutuality of 'help and understanding, joy, and contentment in each other.'"[23] God made for a man a woman fully his equal and fully his match for the purpose of removing his negative condition—loneliness. This line of reasoning is continued in Genesis 2:23, where Adam sees Eve for the first time and says "This is bone of my bone and flesh of my flesh; she shall be called 'woman,' for she was taken out of man." The idiomatic sense of the phrase "bone of my bone" communicates a "very close relative," "one of us," or in effect "our equal." The woman was never meant to be a "helpmate" to the man. The word "mate" slipped into English as it was close to the old English word "meet," which means "fitting to" or "corresponding to." All that comes from the phrase we are suggesting means "equal to." God intended, therefore, to make a power or a strength that would correspond to Adam, that would be his equal. Why? To remove the negative condition of loneliness. So, is completeness the metamessage (the relational frame), and the gist of the argument—not an over/under message? God created two powers who became complete, one. Both were created strong and equal powers in the image of God! Therefore, we can see how an over/under lens might introduce some interpretational confusion to our reading of the Bible.

The second is a performance-orientation perspective. Western culture tends to be pragmatic and individualistic with a do-in-order-to-be (loved or valued) mindset. This is a performance orientation, a focus on what we do to cause God to love us. This, however, in no way conditions God because this is not how God relates to us. Paul would state, "Mostly what God does is love you" (Eph 5:2). How might one read performance

---

22. Freedman, "Woman, a Power Equal to a Man," 56–58. "However, the customary translation of the two words `ezer kenegdo as helper fit is almost certainly wrong. Recently R. David Freedman has pointed out that the Hebrew word *ezer* is a combination of two roots: `-z-r, meaning 'to rescue, to save,' and g-z-r, meaning 'to be strong.' The difference between the two is the first letter in Hebrew. Today that letter is silent in Hebrew; but in ancient times, it was a guttural sound formed in the back of the throat. The 'g' was a *ghayyin*, and it came to use the same Hebrew symbol as the other sound, `*ayin*. But the fact that they were pronounced differently is clear from such place names which preserve the 'g' sound, such as Gaza or Gomorrah. Some Semitic languages distinguished between these two signs and others did not. For example, Ugaritic did make a distinction between the `*ayin* and the *ghayyin*; Hebrew did not."

23. McFadyen, *Call to Personhood*, 33. See also Westermann, *Genesis 1–11*, 232.

in Colossians 3:22–24? "Do your best. Work from the heart for your real Master, for God, confident that you'll get paid in full when you come into your inheritance." As one layman said in a recent Bible study, "Every day I give my very best, but some days I fail at it." The consequence of our performance-based mindset is a "guilt-ridden, obsessive, and anxious theology,"[24] for one cannot do the Christian life perfectly through human capabilities. We must release Christ's way of being in, through, and for us. The performance-orientation mindset is in direct conflict with a worldview centered on Christ's heart. In the doctrinal section of Colossians, especially 1:27, Paul gives us the hub of his theological wheelhouse, or organizing principle: "Christ in you, the hope of glory." This is the triumph of the gospel established by the person and work of Christ. Everyone will be presented "mature in Christ" (Col 1:28 ESV). "For in him dwells all the fullness of the Godhead bodily; and you are complete in him, who is the head of all principality and power" (Col 2:9–10 NKJV). Spirit formation is about Christ being enabled in us rather than us being self-enabled for him. What will make heaven sing on heaven's judgment day will be what we have released Christ to do through us, not what we did for him. The performance-orientation approach leads merely to filthy rags righteousness. Again, "Even observably righteous behavior when it is motivated in extrinsic terms tends to be deeply sinful."[25] Our actions should not be motivated by the attempt to earn God's love. Rather, our actions should come from being one with Christ. Then we are living from oneness and love. This second perspective is a modern cultural expression of the *self-actualization* approach to Christianity, for it is centered on the human potential for self-improvement rather than Christ's miraculous provision.

It seems now there is more culture in the church than there is church in the culture! If Scripture is read from the wrong pair of glasses, we will fail to hear the gospel and fail to be our mission!

Christians with a Greco-Roman Western mindset who have equated personhood with self-actualization, self-fulfillment, and self-perfection will pay a great price in their relationship with God. Such a humanistic approach values the inherent individuality of the human over and above the potential for onto-relational identity and dynamism. Recent studies of American young people reveal that they tend to be obsessed with "feeling good, happy, secure, at peace." That is, they aim at "subjective

---

24. Campbell, "Covenant or Contract in Paul," 209.
25. Campbell, "Covenant or Contract in Paul," 201.

well-being, being able to resolve problems, and getting along amiably with other people."[26] Self-help, self-perfection, self-generation, self-fulfillment, and self-actualization cannot generate purpose and meaning, as may be assumed. We must not "pervert Christianity into a human potential movement through the power of positive thinking in order to get self-esteem, self-fulfillment, and self-identity. This is essentially a New Age Neo-Gnosticism that identifies the self with God. In such a worldview, if you know yourself, and realize your own identity, then you can know God in the depths of your own spirituality."[27] The pursuit of self, rather than God, is not only a dire mistake, but is an expression of the sin of pridefulness, arrogance, and self-centeredness. It is a "salvation by self-help" (Heb 6:1–3).[28] However, the self cannot attain salvation alone! Inward contemplation will never be a substitute for a genuine relationship with Jesus Christ.

## STAGES OF GROWTH IN RELATING TO THE WORD OF GOD

Aside from historical and cultural lenses, we may also recognize differences in relating to Christianity based upon stages of spiritual growth. We tend to read the Word from where we are in God's natural developmental process.[29] As we enact the Christian life, we progress through several levels of moral reasoning, which informs how and why we make decisions. However, in these various stages, we read Scripture rather differently,

---

26. Beale and Kim, *God Dwells among Us*, 14.

27. J. Torrance, "Doctrine of the Trinity."

28. "So come on, let's leave the preschool fingerpainting exercises on Christ and get on with the grand work of art. Grow up in Christ. The basic foundational truths are in place: *turning your back on 'salvation by self-help'* and turning in trust toward God; baptismal instructions; laying on of hands; resurrection of the dead; eternal judgment. God helping us, we'll stay true to all that. But there's so much more. Let's get on with it! (Heb 6:1–,3 emphasis added).

29. Lawrence Kohlberg, a former Professor in Developmental Psychology at Harvard University, conducted cross-cultural and longitudinal research on moral reasoning. He interviewed respondents over a thirty-year time frame and in a number of cultures. Kohlberg's best-known stages of moral development, which include three levels and six stages, expanded on and revised the ideas of Jean Piaget's previous contribution. We added a fourth or biblical internalized level. Kohlberg indicated that very few people in any culture made most of their decisions on the basis of principles. Christ would be an exception.

and therefore approach the Christian life in differing ways. Friedrich Nietzsche said that "If you know the why, you can live any how."[30] We need a strong sense of *why* for what we do or do not do. Recognizing these stages of growth helps us understand the motivating *why* at distinct levels of spiritual maturity.

The first level of the Christian life tends to be lived out according to the perspective of *consequences*. We do (or do not do) what the Word of God recommends either because we desire reward or because we are afraid of punishment. This is a self-centered view of Christianity because it is focused on how the self is affected by the Word of God. The second level places value in the *commands* of God. In this perspective, we must do (or not do) certain activities because God says so. This is a rules-based view of Christianity and is characterized by legalism. The third level approaches the Word of God as comprising inspired and instructive *concepts*, that is, principles of truth upon which we should build our lives. This perspective finally steps out of a self-focus and begins to see how the Father's community should function according to Christlike principles. The final level of growth in relating to the Word of God recognizes that the principles of Christianity cannot be fully enacted unless they are internalized by the grace of Christ. This level focuses on taking on the *character* of Christ by a Father-led process of transformation.

As an example that is easily visible in these four stages, take the value of tithing. Why might Christians tithe? We can do so for different reasons, each reflecting our process of moral development and effecting our capacity to shape our culture.

In the early stage of our Christian faith, we might tithe because we hear the Word in terms of *consequences* such as reward or punishment. That is, we can tithe to get a hundredfold return on our investment, or we can tithe because we fear that God will zap us if we get out from under the divine umbrella. Children, for example, are literal, concrete, and just do not have the mental tools to abstract to principles. Children begin at a level of dependence. Their trust is in the consequences. They can memorize Scripture to get a gold star, a bag of jelly beans, a bicycle, or a helicopter ride over their city, or due to fear of punishment. This is a focus on self—egocentrism. Obedience is motivated by the kinds of consequences.

Go the next level of why we may do what we do. One can tithe because they hear the Word as *commands* or *demands*. College students can

---

30. Nietzsche, *Twilight of the Idols*.

tithe because their pastor said they should or the Bible says they must (Mal 3:10; 2 Cor 9:6–7). This is a focus on models and rules—legalism. Trust begins to emerge, but it is in the models and rules rather than in the Person behind them.

Go to the next level of why we may do what we do. We can tithe because we hear the Word as *concepts* or *principles*. That is, we can tithe because we love the Lord and others. That is a principle. The focus is not on self or rules but is onto-relational. It is not on it or me, but on we. It is not about dependence or independence, but on interdependence. It is not on egocentrism or legalism, but on liberty or freedom, which springs from a principled basis. However, in this stage, trust is in the external principles rather than in the Person behind the principles.

Finally, we can hear the Word as *character*. That is, we can hear the Word as internalized principles because a Person's (Christ's) character and authority are internalized (attached, bonded) in our lives as reality. Transformation lives in oneness. Trust is in the Person and flowing from his character because of internalizing a biblical principle. This takes us back to Paul's prominent perichoretic focus of "Christ in you, the hope of glory" (*peri* means "with" and *choresis* generates our word "choreography," hence a dance of oneness and withness).

God loves little kids who hear his word as *consequences*, college and young adults who hear his Word as *commands* or rules for the road, adults who hear the Word as external *concepts* or principles, and believers who hear the Word as Christ's *character* which they release. It would be pathological, however, if children were stuck in the first stage for life, for collegians to be embedded in the second stage for life, or worse, for the church to be ministering out of the first two stages for way too long so that transformation is retarded. Revival looks different in the fourth level because it is a return to God's onto-perichoretic life—and his name is Jesus! The church has a weak *why* structure. Its developmental moral reasoning level effects its spiritual formation and the transformation of its culture.

Again, we are not what we think we are; we are what we think (Prov 23:7)! And what or how we think can bring noise that confuses or clarifies our message and mission.

## A RELATIONAL, INTERPERSONAL, COMMUNAL CULTURE

We must allow the Spirit to create a new culture, one that is founded on relationality and interpersonal oneness. This new culture must value the communal aspect of Christianity in a greater way and recognize that true Christianity cannot be undertaken individualistically. What is the proper antidote, however, to mechanistic individualism of the West? One possible answer is illustrated in the African concept of *ubuntu*.

*Ubuntu* is the idea that identity is found in relationships. The only way to find who we truly are is through our connective relationships with others. Interactions with others are necessary to understand what it means to be human. Archbishop Desmond Tutu states that *ubuntu* captures the human condition in his book *No Future Without Forgiveness*:

> *Ubuntu* speaks of the very essence of being human. [We] say "Hey, so-and-so has ubuntu." Then you are generous, you are hospitable, you are friendly and caring and compassionate. You share what you have. It is to say, "My humanity is caught up, is inextricably bound up, in yours." We belong in a bundle of life. We say, "A person is a person through other persons."
>
> A person with *ubuntu* is open and available to others, affirming of others, does not feel threatened that others are able and good, for he or she has a proper self-assurance that comes from knowing that he or she belongs in a greater whole and is diminished when others are humiliated or diminished, when others are tortured or oppressed, or treated as if they were less than who they are.[31]

This sounds very similar to the New Testament cultural outlook that is Christian. One cannot even conceive of personal identity apart from others. Attempting to do so is nonsensical in a Trinitarian worldview. *Ubuntu* captures the idea that personhood is inextricable from interdependence. As Scripture states, we are joyful with others who rejoice, and

---

31. Tutu, *No Future Without Forgiveness*, 1. See Haase, *Living the Lord's Prayer*, 36–37. John Isoka, an African participant in the Shiloh University DMIN course "The Pastor as a Change Agent," posted on January 11, 2019: "Left on its own, the African cultures are very relational and human in the sense that 'I am because we are'. But colonialism and imperialist moves have dented this image. And for Christianity, if effort was made to contextualize it at inception, the syncretistic character that threatens to sell the birth right of the believer would not be prevalent. But the early missionary simultaneously sought to convert the African to the Western culture and to Christianity. The effects of this action still abound."

we weep with those who mourn (Rom 12:5). This speaks to the interconnectedness that guides our personal responses. We are not whole alone. We can only be whole in God together. While *ubuntu* is certainly anthropocentric, it is easily applicable in the Christian context with the addition that the relationships in view must obviously include those of the Trinity.

Another way to establish the culture necessary to the genuine experience of Christianity is presented here by Ray Anderson. He notes four implications of a Christian perception of humanity for a society and culture that shapes practical theology:

> (1) to be human is to be the creature who is free to hear and respond to God, (2) to be human is to be the one who is free to respond to other persons as the counterpart to one's own personhood, (3) to be human is to find and fulfill one's nature and destiny in a symbiotic relationship with the created world and its environment, and (4) to be human is to be concretely this person belonging to these people, while at the same time open to and responsible for the good of all people.[32]

In this view, individuality is primarily defined by responsiveness, and the human being is best understood through interactive dynamism. This responsiveness functions in three directions: toward God, fellow people, and creation.

In the context of the Western view of individuality, seeing oneself as primarily connectively responsive may be jarring, or even offensive. Jesus taught that to find our life, however, we must lose our life for his sake (Matt 6:25; John 12:25). The old life that must die is a life of separateness, self-determination, and self-centeredness. The new life is centered on Christ and his body. Kärkkäinen, following Zizioulas, affirms that "there is no true being without communion." He adds, "Therefore, to be a 'person' in contrast to an 'individual', there needs to be communion, relation, and opening to the Other, or as he often calls it, an *ekstasis* ('going out' of one's self). Human existence, including the existence of the church communion, thus reflects the communal, relational being of God."[33] The distinction made here between being an individual and a person is an important one, for it helps us to contextualize, and perhaps escape, the ingrained individualism of the West. In God, we should aim to be

---

32. Anderson, *Shape of Practical Theology*, 170.
33. Kärkkäinen, *Trinity*, 90.

persons—whole images of God—who find personhood in our relationship with God and others.

The transition from the Western paradigm to a Trinitarian paradigm is one that begins with the rejection of being defined by distinctions and separations. One must exit the worldview of mechanistic individuality, in which atomization reigns. In contrast to the Greco-Roman outlook, the scriptural notion of personhood is grounded in being as relation. Personhood flows out of the Godhead's interpersonal recursive relatedness. What is meant by the term "recursive relatedness"? In his article entitled "Recursion: A Theological Axiom for Relationships," Marty Folsom holds that recursion is the metaphor of choice to help us relationally relate well with God and others:

> Recursion is a descriptor in both divine and human relationships, introduced into theology (Miell, 1989) from the field of social psychology, and especially associated with the metaphor of mental mirrors (Antaki & Lewis, 1986). Picture the effect resulting when two mirrors face each other, generating a corridor of reoccurring images that offer a depth perceived only in the mirrors, and you will have the visual foundation for the relational construct. The image is a metaphor of reoccurring, reflecting back concrete images in multiple dimensions of depth. The closer together the mirrors are placed, the greater the number of recurrences. It is important to note that each mirror is a metaphor for a person's mind, capable of articulating what the other person thinks. Recursion is not to be confused with merely viewing the mirror. The person who stands between mirrors aligned to face each other and looks into one will only see himself or herself repeated. This is not recursion, but only self-reflection. But to stay within the metaphor and portray the model suggested here, one person, like one mirror, accurately reflects and accepts (though not always agreeing with) the thoughts and feelings of another, who is represented by the other mirror. This image can be stated relationally or recursively for persons as, "I know that you know what I know." It is relationally affirming when each of the two accurately receives and considers the thoughts and feeling of the other, a skill far beyond parroting back one's words or reacting in resistant ways to perceived emotions. When a person does not know what his or her spouse thinks or feels about significant issues, both persons experience the loss of recursion as distance and breakdown. The more relationally close a couple is, the more deeply each

confidently knows that the spouse knows them, respecting and honoring the mutual knowing.[34]

I have a story that illustrates the conflict between the mental and relational approaches to Christianity. The culminating experience in a Doctor of Ministry degree program is the defense of a professional applied ministry project in which a candidate demonstrates leadership by managing a problem in his or her ministry setting. At one particular defense, an evaluator opened with a question to create a space for recursion, to hear the candidate's heart, voice, and commitment. He asked, "Does God love you? How does that make you feel right now?" Through these questions, the candidate was given an opportunity to enter an interpersonal space, with the possibility of intimacy, transition, and transformation. In effect, it was a "Loder event." James E. Loder frames it: ". . . when you are encountered by another self-reflecting person whose presence gives evidence that he or she has taken your sense of 'I' and put it into a reflective process of his or her own, then the potentiality of unpacking your own 'I' is awakened."[35]

Our candidate had already accomplished the Greek thing in his thesis. He intellectually demonstrated that he got relational theology informationally, for he was very articulate in explaining and dissecting information in his project report. However, the questioner gifted the candidate, as Christ always did in his interactions, with an opportunity to go beyond doctrine or law. But the candidate responded to the question in a way that stopped further discussion. He stated that he knew God loved him but that he didn't personally feel it.

Later, when he received his "pass with recommendations," he may have felt that he was now a relational theologian. But his response revealed that the mental understanding of God's love does not always result in the experience of God's love. The very core of his thesis was about the impact of theology on relationships, so he could not ignore personal stories or insight. But his own personal story was one rooted in Greco-Roman Christianity. I do not think that he understood that a metaphor had been created in this exchange to lift up what was missing in his seminars, which were designed to prove that participants gained enhanced information. Perhaps to dig a little deeper, the evaluators should have

---

34. Folsom, "Recursion," 163, 201. Recursion is the metaphor of choice to help relationally relate well with God and others.

35. Loder, *Transforming Moment*, 78.

created a pregnant pause at the end of that exchange by asking, "Why was this exchange significant?" If he had been self-aware enough, he could have identified the disconnect between his knowledge and experience.

A gold-standard relational theologian will not stop at a mere informational understanding of God. Instead, relational Christianity uses information to create a recursive space so that a perichoresis can occur. A passionate and capable relational theologian will create spaces for interpersonal connection rather than merely focus on dissecting, explaining, or enhancing information. He or she will interpersonalize, not merely propositionalize, an audience. Relational Christianity experiences ontological moments in which one becomes love, and the interpersonal connectivity flows from it. God's love does not need to be dissected and explained. Rather, it must be accepted and experienced. It must be discovered in the person of Jesus, who is God's unrelenting love. In such an environment of interpersonal oneness, information has an onto-relational context, and the Holy Spirit has more with which to work! Informational exchange is certainly necessary in a church that is Christian, but interpersonal recursive spaces are an invitation that invokes the necessary interpersonal insight that turns information into ontological truth.

That is not to suggest that we devalue a great asset of the Protestant tradition, which is the proclamation of the biblical message. We have a high regard for its delivery and unique nature. As Martin Luther and Calvin,[36] following Heinrich Bullinger, proclaimed, "the Word of God is the Word of God" ("*Predicate verbi dei est verbum dei*"). The basic principle was that "A sermon is the work of Our Lord Jesus Christ, who acts in and through his Word."[37] That is, we must hear Christ's voice in the message. *Praedicatio*, however, means not simply "preaching" but "proclamation." The real presence of the Word is communicated by the process of speech. The church's earliest missionary message proclaimed a particular content, the *kerygma* (the gospel), the message of the cross. In the English Standard Version of Matthew 4:23 this is most clear. Jesus

---

36. Rayburn, "Hearing Sermons." Calvin "said that the preaching of the Word of God *was* the Word of God for three reasons. First because it was an exposition and interpretation of the Bible which is the Word of God; second, because the preacher has been sent and commissioned by God as his ambassador with authority to speak in God's name; and third, because in that preaching God himself speaks, the Holy Spirit using the human words to communicate himself to the soul."

37. Koukoura, "Nature of Luther's Preaching."

went throughout Galilee "teaching [*didasko*] in their synagogues and proclaiming [*kerysso*, κηρύσσω] the gospel." Both are required.

Likewise, today we experience a combination. We announce good news and share what it means relationally. Jesus was interpersonal and communicated "the gospel of the kingdom of God" predominantly through choice metaphors and parables, leaving his audiences with both answers and questions. Even his few long discourses (e.g., the Olivet Discourse and the Sermon on the Mount) contained many metaphors, and metaphors are the medium of holistic thinking. Perhaps we should be more Christlike communicators, combining announcement (declaration), explanation (educational follow-up), and a call for responsiveness in an interpersonal and loving way of being with our audiences.

Jesus' kenotic limitless divine love must define the church that is Christian. "Love," as a term used of God, refers to God's very way of being. We are gifted "to participate in God's self-giving" that provides "a confident, personal knowledge."[38] Personhood in God defines identity.[39] Western professionalism tends to define persons in terms of *what* they are rather than *who* they are. This means that an interpersonal or onto-relational analogy of the Trinity must replace philosophical, psychological,

---

38. Folsom, *Face to Face*, loc. 2521.

39. Torrance, *Christian Doctrine of God*, 133. T. F. Torrance highlights the relational ontology of the Trinity: "The one triune Being of God is to be thought of, then, as essentially and intrinsically a mutual movement of loving self-communication between the Father, the Son and the Holy Spirit, an intensely personal Communion, an ever-living ever-loving Being, the Being for Others which the three divine Persons have in common. To say that God is intensely or inherently personal does not mean, of course, that he is a Person in the relational sense of the three particular divine Persons in their otherness or objective relations to one another, but rather that God is a fullness of personal Being within himself, just as he is full of Love within himself. [The particularity is not a problem as they each are identifiable within the One Communion of love]. He is not less personal, any more than he is less loving, in his one indivisible Being as whole God (ὅλος Θεός, Athanasius' expression) than he is in each Person who is true God of true God and is in himself as the Son or the Spirit whole God (ὅλος Θεός) as well as the Father. He is perfectly One in Three and Three in One. That is the one transcendent personal Being of God who is the creative source of the personal communion which in his outgoing love for others he wants to establish between himself and us. Due to its inherently reciprocal nature, however, we cannot have communion with all three, for they are who they are precisely as one indivisible Being, three inseparable Persons/three inseparable Persons, one indivisible Being."

Barth's definition of "person" is love-based: "The definition of a person—that is, a knowing, willing, acting I—can have the meaning only of a confession of the person of God declared in his revelation, of the One who loves and who as such (living in his own way) is *the* person" (Barth, *Church Dogmatics*, vol. 2, part 1, 284).

and individualistic ones. God's eternal life is profoundly and primarily interpersonal, or relational, covenantal, communal, and formational.[40] As Folsom puts it:

> The God of the Bible wants to be known, not locked in philosophical terms. If we emphasize the simplicity and singularity of God, we miss the community. If we emphasize the distinctions in God, we risk advocating three Gods and miss the biblical witness. It is in the unity of the three persons as one God in communion that we find the God acting to reveal God and embrace humanity for a life of participation. We are so often disconnected today from a present, resurrected Jesus, a reconciled Father still embracing, and an awakening Spirit still raising the dead. These three are one, alive, and active.[41]

Our most basic longings for connection, interpersonal knowledge, and acceptance are reflective of this reality.[42]

## CONCLUSION

We must seek to establish a culture in the church that is commensurate with the scriptural presentation of Christianity. Western Christianity is highly influenced by its historical interactions with Greco-Roman thought and the Enlightenment, as well as the current prevailing cultural worldview. If Christianity is pursued primarily as a religion of the mind, it lacks the formative power of spiritual experience. If Christianity is observed as merely a set of rules and regulations, it lacks the necessary relationality with the Trinity and other believers. And if Christianity is only celebrated as a vehicle for self-actualization in the discovery of

---

40. In taking the opposing view that personhood is relationally, not rationally defined, relational Trinitarians are not advocating social Trinitarianism. This means, according to Marty Folsom, that relational theologians "begin with the being of God and see the human person in the light of the unique revelation of that God . . . Relational Theology not only 'corrects the Social Trinity but sees the impact on human relations all the more as significant to the Triune mission.' . . . Athanasius, Calvin, T. F. Torrance, Barth, and others make this case." Folsom, *Face to Face*, vol. 3, ch. 5. Accordingly, relational Trinitarians "distinguish social Trinitarianism as a label for those who project from the human onto God, without doing all the work of deciding that they need to dismiss Moltmann, Volf, Gunton, etc., who are targeted" by defendants of Western Trinitarianism.

41. Folsom, "One and Three," email to author, October 3, 2021.

42. Beale and Mitchell, *God Dwells among Us*, 17.

*Culture and the Principles of Christianity* 79

independent self, then it lacks the community-centered focus of interpersonal oneness. In order to rediscover and champion the relational center of Christianity, the Western church must identify and replace the non-biblical elements of its worldview.

## REFLECTION

1. Can you give examples of how Western values (e.g., New Age neo-gnosticism that equates personhood with self-help, self-generation, self-actualization, self-fulfillment, and self-perfection) have conditioned our understanding of the gospel? Of ecclesiology?

2. Do you agree that Western Christianity tends to reflect a Greco-Roman as opposed to a Hebraic interpersonal mindset? If so, why?

3. How do you respond to the idea that identity is found in relationships? What would life look like if it were lived in your relationships with Jesus and others, similarly to the *ubuntu* idea that "a person is a person through other persons"?[43] What would your identity be like if it were externally defined by the Heavenly Father, just as Jesus' identity was defined by the Father?

4. How do leaders lead a Christian community away from defining persons in terms of what they are (Western professionalism) rather than who they are (onto-relational Christianity)?

---

43. Tutu, *No Future Without Forgiveness.*

# 4

# Education, Learning, and Growth toward Wholeness

## INTRODUCTION

EDUCATION THAT IS CHRISTIAN should seek to nurture students into a deeper personal relationship with God, as well as a true knowledge of the inscripturated Word of God. The emphasis should be on facilitating teacher-student interaction with foundational knowledge, skills, and interpersonal experiences toward the students' growing relationship with God, his family, and the world surrounding them. If education of any sort does not develop the whole person—including not only the intellectual, physical, and social aspects of being human, but the moral and spiritual dimensions as well—then that education does not address the developing human being as a whole. In other words, education must address the student as a holistic person. A student should not only gain knowledge in the educational process but should also be fundamentally changed by the application of that knowledge.

Recently, efforts towards understanding how to educate for wholeness—incorporating both cognitive and affective learning into higher education—have been applied in the Christian educational context. The purpose of these efforts has been to enable learners to grow both intellectually and spiritually. More work, however, must be done in prioritizing the spiritual and affective facets of the educational process.

We suggest that this may be accomplished through foundational concerted efforts to teach relationally, to model a relational way of being, and to directly emphasize interpersonal oneness. The more that educators view Christian learning as an intermixing of cognitive and affective outcomes, the more their concern for interpersonal relationships will be. Lois E. LeBar illustrates the relational teaching approach in this way:

> Compare the training an athlete gets with that of a spectator at a game. The latter may note the sequence of the plays, may shout and cheer at crucial points, may even learn to appreciate some technical skills. But he is not changed by the process. He couldn't duplicate what he saw if he were to get out on the floor or the field. The players on the other hand must plan each strategic move, be very sensitive to the movements of the other players, exercise judgment, take advantage of openings, practice, and practice techniques. He comes out of the game a different person because every power has been "brought into play." Too long have teachers been the active participants in the game of learning, with the [learners] merely spectators. It's time the [learners] got into the game.[1]

We may prioritize the spiritual and affective facets of the educational process that facilitate education, learning, and growth toward wholeness by emphasizing three foundational elements: teaching relationality, modeling ways of being, and prioritizing interpersonal oneness.

## 1. TEACH RELATIONALLY

If the Trinity, and therefore human reality, is defined by interpersonal oneness, then one of the major domains of human development that must be addressed in an interpersonal way is education—particularly, education that is Christian. The process of education forms what we know and how we act. Education constructs our view of reality. Therefore, the priorities for teaching in the church should take into account the fundamental importance of relationality in Christianity, and engage any educational activity in a onto-relational manner. The relationality of

---

1. LeBar, *Education That Is Christian*, 151. Wess's professor was a master teacher and uniquely interpersonal.

education that is Christian addresses the believer's relationship with self (examining beliefs), with the teacher, and with God.

As Sande K. Woodson[2] argues, the model of teaching established in Jesus occurs within community relationships and emerges from the model of interpersonal oneness found in the Trinity. Their mutual indwelling (*perichoresis*) is the model of harmony to be sought after in Christian relationships and serves as the medium of Christlike teaching. Examining such passages as John 14:16–17; John 17:20–23 and 1 Corinthians 12:12–27, Woodson states that the relationship of oneness between the three members of the Trinity is a beautiful picture of the oneness Christians should have with Christ, the Holy Spirit, the Father, and with other believers. This, then, is the essential functioning environment required in proper Christian education, whether formal or informal, in school or in church.

We maintain that an interpersonal approach in any method is always more effective than a non-interpersonal approach. Studies suggest that there is little difference in measurable outcomes when it comes to particular teaching methods such as lectures, discussion, group work, and research projects.[3] In exploring models of teaching, Mark H. Glenn concludes, "It is relationship, not competency, and presence, not technique that has the most profound effect on facilitating change, forming trust, and satisfying interests."[4] Emphasizing relational connection and connective presence in the act of teaching should be a distinctive of education that is Christian. Examples of mentorship and discipleship found throughout the Bible (e.g., Elijah and Elisha, Jesus and his disciples) provide models for teaching rooted in interpersonal oneness. Further, an interpersonal education should form graduates who will go out and function interpersonally.

If nothing else, education that is Christian cannot avoid the relational aspects of community. As Jesus teaches, loving God and loving brother and sister go hand in hand. Community is an essential aspect of lived Christianity. For this reason, community relationships must be a foundational consideration in the development of educational approaches that are Christian. Further, the development of community

---

2. Woodson, "*Cura Personalis*," 108.

3. Dubin and Taveggia, *Teaching-Learning Paradox*. See Frymier, *Nature of Educational Method*. See McKeachie, *Handbook of Research on Teaching*.

4. Glenn, "To Know and Be Known," abstract, iii.

relationships must be an intentional priority in any Christian educational endeavor. As Parker J. Palmer writes,

> ... life in community is also a continual testing and refining of the fruits of love in my life. Here, in relation to others, I can live out (or discover I am lacking) the peace and joy, the humility and servanthood by which spiritual growth is measured. The community is a discipline of mutual encouragement and mutual testing, keeping me both hopeful and honest about the love that seeks me, the love I seek to be.[5]

Engaging in meaningful community relationships will naturally lead to personal growth and development. Consciously determining to cultivate deeper community relationships in the context of education, however, will result in even greater rewards in the spiritual formation of the individual. A large body of research shows that efforts at community-building in online courses lead to successful learning outcomes.[6]

## 2. IMPLEMENT TWO MODELS OF RELATIONAL WAYS OF BEING

The model of the body of Christ stands as a powerful and applicable paradigm of community relations in education that is Christian.[7] Being a member of the body of Christ requires attitudes of openness, encouragement, and connection. When members of the body of Christ apply these together in the journey toward a deeper knowledge of God, a Christlike environment for Christian learning will be formed.[8] John Coe explains the importance of living the principles of God in the context of education that is Christian: "We can talk of the importance of love, faith, and spiritual formation all we wish, but until we intentionalize the process, make it part of the training and not merely something we talk about, then 'the medium

---

5. Palmer, *To Know as We Are Known*, 18. Woodson, "*Cura Personalis*," 111.

6. Granger and Benke, "Supporting Learners at a Distance," 127–37; Gunawardena, *Social Presence Theory*; Kazmer, "Coping in a Distance Environment"; McLellan, "Online Education as Interactive Experience," 36–42; Meye, *Online Education as Interactive Experience*; Ortiz-Rodriguez et al., "College Students' Perceptions," 98–105; Rovai and Baker et al., "Sense of Community"; Shea et al., "Teaching Presence and Student Sense," 175–90; Wegerif, "Social Dimension," 34–49; Wiesenberg and Hutton, "Teaching a Graduate Program."

7. Woodson, "*Cura Personalis*," 110.

8. Meye, "Imitation of Christ," 210.

is the message'—it is just talk."⁹ By modeling the pursuit of relationships with others as members of the body of Christ, educators are intentionally including a powerful force of formation in the educational process.

Another model of relationship applicable in Christian education is that of discipleship. In fact, the very Greek word used for "disciple" in the New Testament is *mathetes*, which described a teacher-student relationship. Education is therefore an inherent aspect of discipleship. However, discipleship to Christ goes beyond a mere teacher-student relationship, for it entails a complete and unbreakable dedication to Jesus (Matt 10:24, 37; Luke 14:26; John 11:16). Jesus' model of discipleship was less about gaining information and more about the formation that occurs while in a deep relationship with him.¹⁰ Gangel and Benson point out that Christ's method of teaching was revolutionary in its historical context. The usual approach of the rabbis in Jesus' era was to require rote responses of memorization. Jesus himself, however, often taught through conversational dialogue and storytelling. He allowed questions and asked questions in return. "For him, every event and conversation was an important learning situation."¹¹ Gangel and Benson contend that Jesus' method of teaching was fundamentally relational. This is true not only in its methodology, but also in a spiritual dimension as well. That is, a relationship with the Anointed One, the Savior, the Lord, is the center of Christianity. Discipleship to Jesus is a relationship that leads to ontological change. Jesus not only transforms his students (i.e., believers) through direct instruction, but also through relational connection.¹²

## 3. DIRECTLY EMPHASIZE INTERPERSONAL ONENESS

A key to proper education that is Christian is to emphasize interpersonal oneness. This first requires that the teacher view the student in a holistic manner.¹³ One of the reasons why onto-relational education must be enacted in the Christian context is that each person is a holistic being whose formation and education cannot happen only in the brain. An interpersonal approach to education treats students as multidimensional

---

9. Coe, "Intentional Spiritual Formation," 95, 85–110.
10. Schroeder, *Faculty as Mentors*, 29.
11. Gangel and Benson, *Christian Education*, 70–71.
12. Gangel and Benson, *Christian Education*, 70–71.
13. Woodson, "*Cura Personalis*," 32–33.

persons, and such multidimensional persons will not learn in sufficient depth if engaged without a view of their emotional and spiritual being, in addition to their mental, cognitive abilities. It is tautological that any approach to educating holistic persons must be holistic. The cognitive (mental), affective (emotional), and spiritual aspects of the student must all be of equal priority to the teacher. Further, since each person is a complex being—and therefore not reducible to a learning template or simplistic model—the teacher-student relationship must be a personal connection in which the student's particular personality and needs are taken into consideration in the teaching process.

The earliest American colleges were Christian institutions founded in the seventeenth and eighteenth centuries, including Harvard, William and Mary, Yale, Princeton, and Columbia. Boyer writes that "the early American college did not doubt its responsibility to educate the whole person—body, mind, and spirit; head, heart, and hands."[14] Such institutions, however, evolved toward a more secular focus, and in the process the holistic view fell out of favor. In its place stood a near exclusive emphasis on the cognitive capacities of humanity.[15] The holistic view of the human being must be reintroduced to education that is Christian, and it must be addressed in relational modes of teaching. This holistic view also includes the student's relationship with God. Claerbaut writes, "Whenever the Christian college places faith apart from learning rather than making it the context in which that learning occurs, it creates a Christian/secular dichotomy . . . It separates the Author of truth from the very truth it examines. That is neither Christian nor ultimately educational."[16]

The key to effective education that is Christian begins with the teachers themselves. Teachers include those in an educational institutional setting, as well as in the church setting, and include those who teach any age group. To approach teaching interpersonally, Christian teachers must create a space of interaction, acceptance, self-analysis, and hospitality.[17] These situational qualities are relational in nature, and they will not necessarily occur naturally in any learning setting without the intentional choice of the teacher. In this way, any sort of interpersonal approach to education begins with the person of the teacher.

---

14. Boyer, *College*, 177.
15. Strange, "Measuring Up," 122, 26. Noll, *Christian College*, 31.
16. Claerbaut, *Faith and Learning*, 74.
17. Palmer, *To Know as We Are Known*, 108.

A relational approach will dig deep into the learners' perspective and understanding. Kanitz asserts that "teachers should not assume that ... students, just because they are Christians, are less influenced by their culture than their non-Christian peers, that they are actively resisting the culture, or that they are able to take the principles of a Christian worldview and automatically harmonize them with their preexisting worldviews."[18] A faith that is never examined or challenged may suffer from being underdeveloped, or even faulty in its formation. Interpersonal teaching will help learners explore their beliefs honestly with the intent to develop them in concert with a cognitive understanding of Christianity.

One important aspect of interpersonal oneness that must be addressed in the classroom is its uncomfortability. Genuine interpersonal interaction cannot help but include dissonance—both for the two parties in the relationship as well as in the student's internal self-dissonance. This is nowhere truer than in a formal educational setting, in which addressing new ideas is a requirement. New ideas often lead to internal conflict, as the student wrestles incorporating new information with his preexisting knowledge. Lamoureux explains, "This kind of intentional and critical reflectivity is at the core of transformative learning as it creates the possibility for identifying and correcting distortions in feelings, perceptions, attitudes, knowledge, and behavior."[19] The teacher must therefore understand the creative nature of conflict in this setting and be present for the student(s) in an attitude of honesty, love, acceptance, and patience, even in the face of uncomfortable dissonance. As Palmer writes, "good teachers know that discomfort and pain are often signs that truth is struggling to be born among us."[20] Conflict is normal, natural, neutral, and necessary. In fact, conflict is a formative tool in the hands of a relational educator.

Parker Palmer suggests that the learning environment is of utmost importance. An effective environment is largely dependent upon the attitude and approach of the teacher. Palmer writes, "to study with a teacher who not only speaks but listens, who not only gives answers but asks questions and welcomes our insights, who provides information and theories that do not close doors but open new ones, who encourages students to help each other learn—to study with such a teacher is to know

---

18. Kanitz, "Improving Christian Worldview Pedagogy," 105.
19. Lamoureux, "Integrated Approach to Theological Education," 145.
20. Palmer, *To Know as We Are Known*, 73.

the power of a learning space."[21] Glenn recognizes this need in education that is Christian, and recommends what he terms the "Recursive Model of Conflict Management" (RMCM) as a relational approach to education. He writes:

> The RMCM model is relationally based in the reciprocity of personal interaction through active listening and dialoguing rather than monologuing. The principal factor for creating a paradigm of peace/flourishing is the spiritual being and emotional presence of its facilitators and participants. It is *relationship*, not competency, and *presence*, not technique that has the most profound effect on facilitating change, forming trust, and satisfying interests.[22]

Learning objectives and lesson plans for any level of Christian education would greatly benefit from an intentional prioritization of relationship between student and teacher, as well as student and God.

One way this kind of approach is implemented is through careful attention to how class discussions function. Discussion pursued with the intent to teach/learn is labeled "discourse" in educational circles. Anderson delineates the significance of discourse in the online learning environment:

> Discourse not only facilitates the creation of the community of inquiry, but also is the means by which learners develop their own thought processes, through the necessity of articulating them to others. Discourse also helps students uncover misconceptions in their own thinking, or disagreements with the teacher or other students. Such conflict provides opportunity for exposure to cognitive dissonance that, from a Piagetian perspective, is critical to intellectual growth. In fulfillment of this component of teaching presence, the teacher regularly reads and responds to student contributions and concerns, constantly searching for ways to support understanding in the individual student and the development of the learning community as a whole.[23]

Garrison and Anderson suggest a number of practical actions for educators to take in order to foster positive discourse, such as: acknowledging students at the beginning of a discussion, encouraging and supporting students in the process of directing the discussion, being authentic and allowing the students to see the teacher's personality, giving positive

21. Palmer, *To Know as We Are Known*, 18.
22. Glenn, "To Know and Be Known."
23. T. Anderson, "Teaching in an Online Learning Context," 280.

feedback to contributions when merited, assuming a conversational tone, and encouraging those who are not participating to chime in.[24]

## CONCLUSION

Accordingly, we can prioritize the spiritual, affective, and cognitive facets of the educational process by emphasizing relational approaches to holistic education. Concerted efforts to teach relationally, model a relational way of being, and directly emphasize interpersonal oneness are foundational. Education that does not develop the whole person is incomplete. The emphasis in education that is Christian should be on facilitating interaction with foundational knowledge, skills, and interpersonal experiences toward the student's growing relationship with God, his family, and the world surrounding us.

Benjamin Bloom's taxonomy (a set of three hierarchical models used to classify educational learning objectives into levels of complexity and specificity) consisted of three domains (head/cognitive, heart/affective,[25] and hand/psychomotor). The affective domain, however, is often underemphasized in Christian education at both the local church and higher educational levels. Three interpersonal and biblical strategies (dissonance, forming community, and modeling Christlikeness) are cited by Woodson as promoting affective learning in higher education that is Christian. She concluded "that although these strategies are mentioned widely in the literature, there is no research that describes their actual use in Christian online courserooms to date."[26] Her study was "designed to fill that gap by assessing the intentionality and . . . practices of Christian undergraduate online faculty members regarding their usage . . . as they relate to affective learning."[27]

Relationship that is Christian is love-based interpersonal oneness, shared life as caring compassion, or recursive and reciprocal community. Interpersonal life in community is, as Parker Palmer puts it, "a continual testing and refining of the fruits of love in my life."[28] Living from, not for,

---

24. Garrison and Anderson, *E-Learning*, 85.
25. See under "Active Domain" in Ford, *Design for Teaching and Training*.
26. Woodson, "*Cura Personalis*," 127.
27. Woodson, "*Cura Personalis*," 127.
28. Palmer, *To Know as We Are Known*, 70–71.

love (interpersonal being) is the Christian's highest calling. Releasing that love opens up the truth of being.

## REFLECTION

1. Why do students that are Christian tend to default to topical and non-relational answers to questions posed in exams or papers they write? Why is it normal for teachers and students to remain impersonal in the educational context?
2. Do you agree with the research finding that it is *relationship*, not competency, and *presence*, not technique, that has the most profound effect on facilitating change, forming trust, and satisfying interests? What experiences have you had that inform your position?

## Trinitarian Relationship

# PART II

## Why Is It Important to Define Reality?

"This is my command: Love one another the way I loved you. This is the very best way to love. Put your life on the line for your friends. You are my friends when you do the things, I command you. I'm no longer calling you servants because servants don't understand what their master is thinking and planning. No, *I've named you friends because I've let you in on everything I've heard from the Father.*"

—John 15:12–15 (emphasis added)

Philip said to him, "Lord, show us the Father, and *it is enough for us*."

—John 14:9 (ESV)

"As Jesus only did what he saw what his Father was doing, so we turn our eyes to Jesus to see what he is doing and to follow his work, empowered by the Spirit to practically work out our loving and joyful obedience in our homes and neighborhoods."[1]

—Marty Folsom

Could Western Christians be criticized for "saying so much about what Christ said so little about, and so little about what he said so much about"?

—Pete Buttigieg[2]

---

1. Folsom, "Dialog with Ben Myers."
2. https://www.lifesitenews.com/opinion/pete-buttigieg-wrong-about-christianity-abortion-and-homosexuality/.

# 5

# Trinitarian Thinking

## INTRODUCTION

OF ALL THE WAYS we might conceive of God, the Trinity presents the most complete picture. By containing three distinct persons of the Godhead, it provides more detail regarding the ontological truth of God's being in both distinct persons as well as in relational oneness. For this reason, the Trinity must be an ongoing, central consideration in all theological formulations. The Trinity must not disappear from view in any discussion of Christianity. Again, T. F. Torrance contends that:

> It is not just that the doctrine of the Holy Trinity must be accorded primacy over all the other doctrines, but that properly understood it is the nerve and centre of them all [a first-order doctrine], configures them all and is so deeply integrated with them that when they are held apart from the doctrine of the Trinity, they are seriously defective in truth and become malformed.[1]

What does Christianity look like when the Trinity is afforded a central place in its worldview? And what would Trinitarian thinking look like in a practical way? We can appreciate the importance of Trinitarian thinking by examining two issues.

---

1. Torrance, *Christian Doctrine of God*, 6. In this magisterial work, he concurs that the Trinity is a first-order doctrine.

## THE NATURE OF REALITY

While we assert that Trinitarian thinking is a central aspect of Christianity, others do not agree. The German philosopher Immanuel Kant claimed, "Taken literally, absolutely nothing worthwhile for the practical life can be made out of the doctrine of the Trinity."[2] Sir Isaac Newton, John Locke, and John Milton were all strong anti-Trinitarians. Some scholars see it as a post-biblical development. Stephen Holmes asserts that "The doctrine of the Trinity is necessary and precisely useless, and that point must never be surrendered."[3] He uses metaphors of distance, such as the unspeakableness of God in worship, to render the Trinity functionally meaningless.

Further, José Miguez Bonino lamented that the Trinity "has remained a generic doctrine which does not profoundly inform the theology, and what is worse, the piety and the life of our churches."[4] Admittedly, that statement is twenty years old and might not do justice to the last two decades. Bonino was referring to Latin American Protestantism, and that may have been equally true of Anglo-American Protestantism in that time frame. L. T. Jeyachandran, an international speaker and Christian thinker, laments that the doctrine of the Trinity tends to be viewed as "an outright and unnecessary complication":

> It is a sad fact that the doctrine of the Trinity has been believed in but rarely preached on in our churches. Living these last few years in Singapore, sandwiched between the two Islamic countries of Malaysia and Indonesia, I have half-humorously, half-seriously commented to Christian leaders, "We all believe in the Trinity, but we pray to the Trinity that nobody would question us about the Trinity!" The doctrine is felt to be irrelevant if not an outright and unnecessary complication imposed on the simple belief in the One God.[5]

2. Horrell, "Self-Giving Triune God," 4.
3. Holmes, in Sexton, ed., *Two Views on the Doctrine of the Trinity*, 47.
4. Bonino, *Faces of Latin American Protestantism*, 113.
5. Jeyachandran, "Trinity as a Paradigm."

> L. T. Jeyachandran hails from Tamil Nadu in South India. He graduated from PSG College of Technology, affiliated with University of Madras (Chennai), and later received a Master of Technology degree in Structural Engineering from the prestigious Indian Institute of Technology (IIT) in Chennai. L. T. worked in several parts of India for 28 years as a Senior Civil Engineer with the Central (Federal) Government. The last position he held was that

Certainly, Christians should be careful not to neglect any aspect of the faith. While the doctrine of the Trinity may be difficult to explain, it is certainly not irrelevant, nor an unnecessary complication. Rather, it is a glorious, mysterious, and majestic understanding of God. Without it, Christianity loses the power of the relationship between Father and Son, as well as the personal nature of the divine indwelling of the Holy Spirit within believers.

Many, however, still feel what Kant expressed. For example, take the considerable impact of a paper written by Maurice Wiles in 1957 doubting the biblical basis of the doctrine. Professor Horrell recounts "an ordination council in a large evangelical church in São Paulo, Brazil, after a pastoral candidate had floundered completely in trying to answer questions concerning the Godhead, a veteran denominational leader proffered in the young man's defense that the doctrine of the Trinity did not really matter: 'Most Evangelicals believe in three Gods anyway.'"[6] For this pastor, however, "as for Kant, the concept of the Triune God was irrelevant. When Christian leadership assumes indifference toward Trinitarian theology, it is hardly surprising that many people in the church feel the same."[7]

Two tendencies produce an unbalanced ecclesiology: failure to (1) maintain equally the oneness and threeness of God, that is, to reconcile threeness with oneness through *perichoresis* (mutual indwelling);[8] and (2) stress equally the humanity and deity of Jesus Christ. The result? A

---

of Chief Engineer in charge of 13 states of India in the Eastern Zone while based in the city of Calcutta.

L. T. discovered the meaning of new life in Christ Jesus during his undergraduate college days. He has been involved in preaching the Gospel in conferences and is well known as a Bible expositor. He is a keen student of theology and comparative religions, and also interested in the study of Indian and foreign languages. He is knowledgeable in both Hebrew and Greek and is thus able to handle Scripture effectively in his ministry.

He took early retirement from the Government in November 1993 to join Ravi Zacharias International Ministries in India and functioned as Director of Ministries there till December 2000. In that capacity, he had been training leaders in seminars for Christians and conducting open forums for people from other faiths. He also served as a Bible teacher for RZIM and other conferences.

6. Jeyachandran, "Trinity as a Paradigm."

7. Jeyachandran, "Trinity as a Paradigm."

8. Boff, *Holy Trinity*, xvi, 2. Boff views God's oneness and union as derived from the communion of God's threeness, and then describes how "they weave among themselves a bond of love so intimate and strong that they are a single God" (31).

distorted understanding of what the church essentially is and its mission in the world. J. I. Packer laments:

> Too often we evangelicals related the truth of the Trinity to the lumber room of the mind, to be put on display only when deniers of it appear, rather than being made the frame and focus of all adoration. The church then comes to be thought of as an organization for spiritual life support rather than as an organism of perpetual praise; doxology is subordinated to ministry, rather than ministry embodying and expressing doxology, and church life is thought out and set forth in terms of furthering people's salvation rather than of worshiping and glorifying God.[9]

Packer eventually concludes that "The American church is a mile wide and an inch deep!" Although the Trinity may be an afterthought in Western theology, many Christian thinkers are now reaffirming the central importance of Trinitarian theology for our daily lives. Both Catholic and Protestant theologians have been influenced in part by Karl Barth, the father of Trinitarian theology. T. F. Torrance considers Barth "the most outstanding and consistently evangelical theologian that the world has seen in modern times."[10] As Horrell put it, "Stimulated in part by Karl Barth's *Church Dogmatics*, Catholic and Protestant theologians have produced in the last forty years a significant corpus on the subject."[11] One of the most significant theological developments in the last quarter of the twentieth century has been a renewed emphasis on the ancient doctrine of the Trinity and its implications for understanding the church. Note such works by "Karl Rahner, Eberhard Jüngel, Bernard Lonergan, Bertrand de Margerie, Jürgen Moltmann, Leonardo Boff, Colin E. Gunton, T. F. Torrance," James B. Torrance, Alan Torrance, C. Baxter Kruger, "Catherine LaCugna, and Millard Erickson."[12]

In evangelical theology, the Trinity is affirmed as basic doctrine but seldom related in any fundamental way to ecclesiology. There is

---

9. Packer, *Stunted Ecclesiology*, 125.

10. Torrance, *Karl Barth*, 289–308.

11. Horrell, "Self-Giving Triune God."

12. Horrell, "Self-Giving Triune God." See Karl Barth's *Church Dogmatics*. Also, primary works include Rahner, *Trinity*; Eberhard Jüngel, *Doctrine of the Trinity*; Lonergan, *Way to Nicea*; Margerie, *Christian Trinity in History*; Moltmann, *Trinity and the Kingdom of God*; Boff, *Trinity and Society*; Gunton, *Promise*; LaCugna, *God for Us*; Torrance, *Trinitarian Faith*; Torrance, *Trinitarian Perspectives*; Erickson, *God in Three Persons*. Recent overviews include Schwöbel, *Trinitarian Theology Today*; Thompson, *Modern Trinitarian Perspectives*; and Vanhoozer, *Trinity in a Pluralistic Age*.

some light in the darkness. At the Los Angeles Theology Conference in 2014, the theme was "Advancing Trinitarian Theology";[13] and the ETS conference in 2016 in San Antonio also revolved all around the doctrine of the Trinity.

## THE PRACTICAL IMPLICATIONS OF THE TRINITY

In recent decades, a number of theologians have been exploring the implications of the doctrine of the Trinity for the whole theological enterprise.[14] Some have begun to ask: What would a truly Trinitarian model of the church look like? A functional theological recovery of how the doctrine of the Trinity would profoundly affect our understanding of what the church is and how it is to function.[15] Howard A. Snyder, when teaching church renewal at Wheaton Graduate School at the Billy Graham Center, uses the term "recovery" because, as a number of writers have noted, a robust Trinitarian theology functioned in the church's third and fourth centuries, and therefore the expansion of the doctrine of the Trinity in contemporary Christianity is not really an original exploration.[16] Millard J. Erickson noted that nearly every theological movement has recently sought in some sense to reflect upon and to reapply the doctrine of Nicea, and this has produced a harvest of literature in biblical, historical, and contemporary Trinitarian studies. Many have concurred with Wolfhart Pannenberg's judgment that the Trinity has become the most important of subjects in current theological discussion.[17]

---

13. Ware and Starke, *One God in Three Persons*.

14. Note, for example, Moltmann, *Trinity and the Kingdom*.

15. Note the discussion in Snyder and Runyon, *Decoding the Church*, ch. 3, "Church, Trinity, and Mission."

16. Snyder, "Fresh Streams," 15. See the excellent summary in Newbigin, *Open Secret*, 19–29 ("Mission of Triune God"). Using a Trinitarian model, Newbigin describes mission as "Proclaiming the Kingdom of the Father: Mission as Faith in Action," "Sharing the Life of the Son: Mission as Love in Action," and "Bearing the Witness of the Spirit: Mission as Hope in Action" (30–65).

17. Horrell, "Where Is Theology Going?," 122. See Whapham, "Pannenberg on Divine Personhood": "In the final analysis we can see, then, that much more is at stake in Pannenberg's definition of the term 'person' as it applies the Trinity than just a theoretical debate about the relative appropriateness or inappropriateness of a word. Instead, what is really at work here is a way of reflecting on who God is, who we are as human persons, and how God relates to the world. The result is not fundamentally an argument for holding onto a tired, old, worn-out word that has been over-burdened

A significant theological consensus seems to be emerging that our basic understanding of the church must derive not from culture or tradition but from the very nature of God as revealed in Scripture. Therefore, a Trinitarian ecclesiology must be "grounded in creation (what God the Trinity made and intended in creating the world), in redemptive history (which God the Trinity accomplished and is accomplishing through Jesus Christ by the Spirit), and in eschatology (the kingdom and economy of God finally consummated in Christ through the Spirit)."[18]

As in any faith, one's understanding of God should significantly define one's worldview. Accordingly, it is Horrell's belief that "the doctrine of the Three-in-One provides a macro-structure of reality that makes sense of life, one that gives a remarkable basis for our perception of ourselves as persons, for our relationships in marriage, family, the local church and community and, in point, the role of the local church in mission."[19] In this way, the doctrine of the Trinity is imminently applicable in our lives. The connectivity of the Trinity, their inter-identification, and their eternal love for each other are the bases for our own relationships within the body of Christ. And since Christlikeness is a central goal of the Christian faith, we must see Jesus' relationship with the Father and the Holy Spirit as models for our relationships with God and with one another.

The Trinity means fundamentally that "God is in himself a permanent conversation, a communion of love, an identity of purpose and unity of action: Father Son, and Holy Spirit," writes Bonino. The Trinity "is not an enigma to be solved, but rather the model on which all human relations, including the church, should be structured."[20] What would our relationships look like if we modeled them on the Trinity? They would be immediately more open, honest, intimate, and loving. Bonino continues that a Trinitarian relationship is "... neither the all-embracing authority of one over others, nor an undifferentiated mass uniformity, nor the

---

and out matched since the second century. It is the effort to revitalize the meaning of that word in light of our experience of the divine and to rediscover the centrality and practicality of the doctrine of the Trinity."

18. Gunton, *Promise*, 82.

19. Horrell, "Self-Giving Triune God."

20. Bonino, *Faces of Latin American Protestantism*, 115 (emphasis original). Bonino suggests a truly Trinitarian theology that offers "a structure of theological thought that can save us from [theological] reductionisms" and is "particularly significant... with reference to ecclesiology, the doctrine of sanctification, and eschatology" (117). However, he does not focus on the implications of Trinitarian thought for ecclesiology, rather for Christology.

self-sufficiency of the 'self-made man.'" Instead, Trinitarian relationships are based upon "The perichoresis of love [which] is our beginning and our destiny—as persons, as church, as society."[21]

The relationships between believers shape the nature of the church. While Christ is the head of the church, we are each members of his body, and therefore the way we choose to relate to one another defines the way the church acts and functions as a whole. Trinitarian interpersonal relationships must be the goal of a healthy church. In John 5:19–27 and 16:13–14, we see that the relationships between the Trinity are self-emptying and self-giving. The Father gives his authority and power to Jesus. Yet Jesus gives it all back by refusing to do anything apart from the Father. Further, the Holy Spirit speaks on behalf of Jesus, and gives glory to Jesus in the process. The model here is that of interdependence, unequivocal trust, mutual indwelling, and loving unity. This must be the model followed in Christian doctrine, as well as in the structure and function of the Christian church.

Again, Gunton asserts that "the manifest inadequacy of the theology of the church derives from the fact that it has never seriously and consistently been rooted in a conception of the being of God as triune."[22] Given the fact of the Trinity, Gunton argues that the body of Christ is essentially a community, a *koinonia*, that is a Trinitarian echo. Its calling is "to be a temporal echo of the eternal community that God is," to be the image of the Trinity in community. In other words, the members of the church must mirror the relationships of the Trinity. Further, "the being of the church should echo the dynamic of the relations between the three persons who together constitute the deity." Again, this requires "an ecclesiology of Perichoresis" in which "there is no permanent structure of subordination," but rather "overlapping patterns of relationships, so that the same person will be sometimes 'subordinate' and sometimes 'superordinate' according to the gifts and graces being exercised."[23] The church, then, as an actual, visible community, must function as the image

---

21. Bonino, *Faces of Latin American Protestantism*, 115–17.

22. Horrell, "Self-Giving Triune God." See Gunton, *Promise*, 56. Gunton does a fine job of tracing historically how the major problems of the church's self-understanding today derive from these theological distortions. See especially ch. 3, "Augustine, the Trinity and the Theological Crisis of the West" and ch. 4, "The Community: The Trinity and the Being of the Church." Gunton maintains that "the question of the being of the church is one of the most neglected topics of theology" (56).

23. Gunton, *Promise*, 78, 80.

of the sacred, divine relationships of the Trinity. The eternal perichoresis of Father, Son, and Holy Spirit should "provide the basis for the personal dynamics of the community."[24] It is only in this context that the true nature of the church will be seen. And it is only in this context that proper preaching, teaching, counseling, and discipline may occur, for it will then "echo the community of Father, Son and Spirit."[25]

## CONCLUSION

Therefore, we can appreciate the necessary influence that Trinitarian thinking must have on Christian theology and its application. Affording the doctrine of the Trinity a central place in the formulation of Christianity encourages a holistic approach to the faith that derives its view of life and Christianity from the very nature of God. If God is the basis of reality, then his way of being must be understood, accepted, and engaged in order to properly understand reality.[26]

God, in his existence as the Trinity, demonstrates a relational and holistic way of being. We must therefore interpret, evaluate, and understand Scripture and doctrine in a relational and holistic way. Further, we must judge our choices based upon their relational impact—toward God and toward others. In the Trinitarian context, the believer's onto-relationship with Christ is definitive regarding the believer's identity, for it is the open door to the relationship with the Father, with the Holy Spirit, and with other believers in the body of Christ. Holiness might therefore be redefined as being predicated upon being in right relationship with God and others.[27]

Trinitarian thinking is a robust and lively recognition of the nature of God in the practical pursuit of the Christin faith. It affects doctrine, personal identity, our view of human life, and the shape of the church. It is not an overstatement to say that any attempt to live a Christian life without due attention to the Trinity will result in an incomplete and eccentric religious pursuit.

---

24. Gunton, *Promise*, 78, 80.
25. Gunton, *Promise*, 82.
26. Jeyachandran, "Trinity as a Paradigm."
27. Jeyachandran, "Trinity as a Paradigm."

## REFLECTION

1. Do you find it difficult to simultaneously conceive of the oneness and threeness of the Trinity? In what ways does this tension help or hinder your conception of God?
2. In what ways do the relationships between the members of the Trinity inform or inspire your approach to personal relationships?
3. How do you view the connection between the nature of the Trinity and a holistic approach to life? What role do you give holistic thinking in the Christian life?

# 6

# Interpersonal Oneness

### INTRODUCTION

How is Trinitarian thinking applied? Primarily in relationships. While the previous chapter covered Trinitarian thinking, this chapter focuses on the relational results of such thinking, which is interpersonal oneness.

What is interpersonal oneness and why is it important? We can begin to understand the idea of interpersonal oneness by examining its characteristics in distinct theological contexts. This chapter will first investigate how interpersonal oneness is founded on a relationship with the Father. Second, it will review how interpersonal oneness allows us to understand Jesus, and to interpret the Bible in the way that Jesus would. Third, it will examine the close connection between the reconciliation found in Christ and the nature of the Trinity.

### INTERPERSONAL ONENESS IS FATHER-LED

Interpersonal oneness is first and foremost defined by the relationship between the Father and the Son. To be more specific, it is Father-led. Said Jesus, "I call you friends because I've let you in on everything I've heard from the Father" (John 15:12–15). "What I say, therefore, I say as the Father has told me" (John 12:50b). "I have made your very being known to them—who you are and what you do—And continue to make it known, so that your love for me might be in them exactly as I am in them" (John 17:25-26). "The Father entrusts all things to the Son: his authority, his power over life and judgment. But the Son will not do anything by himself; he will only do what he sees the Father doing. The Spirit will not speak of himself nor seek his own glory. He will bring glory to Jesus by taking what belongs to Jesus and showing them to us" (John 5:19-27; see also John 16:13-14). He sends his zeal for the Father's glory into our hearts. Jesus said that "the [interest] and purpose of my life is Father" (John 14:28). His relationship with the Father was his grounding wonder.

The Son attributed every action to his Father. When he began his ministry, he said, "Didn't you know that I had to be here, dealing with the things of my Father?" (Luke 2:49). When he ended it, he cried, "Father, I place my life in your hands!" (Luke 23:46). In the middle he indicated he could do no miracles of compassion unless the Father did them through him, that he could do no less than speak his Father's thoughts and Words. "The words that I speak to you aren't mere words. I don't just make them up on my own. The Father who resides in me crafts each word into a divine act" (John 14:10). Jesus was interdependent with his Father in obedient Sonship, out of which came his Spirit formation. "[T]ruly our fellowship is with the Father and with his Son Jesus Christ" (truth of being, 1 John 1:3). "I am in my Father, and you are in me, and I am in you" (John 14:20). Jesus is passionate about wanting his Father known. "He cannot bear for us to live without knowing his Father, without knowing his heart, his lavish embrace, his endless love—and the sheer freedom that works within us as we see his Father's face."[1] The Son's gospel is the character and nature of his Abba. As James B. Torrance summarizes:

> We allow the Spirit, in interpreting Christ to us, to evacuate the word of all biological, male, patriarchal, sexist content, to fill it with divine content, that we may more truly pray, 'Abba, Father.' . . . the name [Father] is not merely an arbitrary signifier, like Susan or Fred! It has semantic content, as has the name of Jesus. It is the name through which God discloses himself personally to us to draw us into intimate communion with himself in worship and prayer, not just to convey information about himself.[2]

---

1. Kruger, *Across All Worlds*, 166.
2. Torrance, *Worship*, 123-75.

Exegesis, for Jesus, began with what he heard from his Father! Being Father-led is Jesus' hermeneutical principle. It is amazing that one could read the Gospels and then preach or teach a Fatherless Jesus in fatherless America.[3] Could Western Christians be criticized for "saying so much about what Christ said so little about, and so little about what he said so much about?"[4] Most theological textbooks do not even have a chapter on Abba Father, which, according to Joachim Jeremias—the distinguished New Testament professor and scholar of Near Eastern studies at the University of Göttingen, Germany, and one of the most innovative and productive New Testament scholars of the twentieth century—is the central revelation of the New Testament![5] As he observed:

> No less than one hundred and seventy times do we encounter in the Gospels the word Father for God in the mouth of Jesus. Moreover, not only do the four Gospels attest that Jesus used this address, but they report unanimously that he did so in all his prayers. [21 times—16 times if parallels are counted only once]. There is only one prayer of Jesus in which 'my Father' is lacking. That is the cry from the cross: 'My God, my God, why hast thou forsaken me?' (Mark 15:34 par. Matt 27:46), quoting Ps 22:1.[6]

Jesus placed so much emphasis on God as Father that it is rather un-Christlike to diminish that relationship with God. If we intend to live as Jesus did, then our relationship with God must be defined by his characterization as Heavenly Father. Jeremias adds: "Abba . . . is a word which conveys revelation. It represents the centre of Jesus' awareness of his mission (*Sendungsbewusstsein*)."[7] "Abba" is Jesus' signature word for God. What would Christianity look like if its believers adopted the concept of Abba as their own? As Jeremias concludes:

---

3. David Blankenhorn, founder of the Institute for American Values, concluded that "the fact that 40 percent of America's children do not live with their biological fathers is the leading cause of crime, adolescent pregnancy, child sexual abuse, and domestic violence against women. Fathers are seen as superfluous in today's society." Quoted at https://www.kirkusreviews.com/book-reviews/david-blankenhorn/fatherless-america/.

4. Pete Buttigieg, quoted at https://www.lifesitenews.com/opinion/pete-buttigieg-wrong-about-christianity-abortion-and-homosexuality/.

5. Jeremias, *Central Message*. See also Jeremias, *Jesus and the Message*.

6. Jeremias, *Jesus and the Message*.

7. Jeremias, *Jesus and the Message*.

> But if it is true—and the testimony of the sources is quite unequivocal—that Abba as an address to God is ..."the very voice," (thought for thought), an authentic and original utterance of Jesus, and that this Abba implies the claim of a unique revelation and a unique authority ... We are confronted with something new and unheard of which breaks through the limits of Judaism. Here we see who the historical Jesus was, the man who had the power to address God as Abba and *who included the sinners and the publicans in the kingdom by authorizing them to repeat this one word, 'Abba, dear Father'*.[8]

If the vast majority of the biblical text were lost, reduced merely to Jesus' teaching of "Abba dear Father," would sinners who repeated them as an act of worship be included in the kingdom? Jesus' work invites every person to enter into the Father-child relationship with God. The term *Abba* certainly captures the central revelation of the New Testament covenant in Christ.

In examining this Father-Son relationship, one can start with the understanding that Jesus' use of Abba Father conveys his self-emptying love of God. Jesus' choice to humble himself in his incarnation all in service to the will of the Father exemplifies the nature of their relationship. God's love is red. It bleeds for others. Parker J. Palmer observes that Jesus' incarnation extends to those who live in him. This, in turn, creates a community based on this shared relationship with Christ (John 17:23).[9] Parker writes:

> In Christian understanding truth is neither an object 'out there' nor a proposition about such objects. Instead, truth is personal, and all truth is known in personal relationships. Jesus is a paradigm, a model of this personal truth. In him, truth, once understood as abstract, principled, propositional, suddenly takes

---

8. Jeremias, *Jesus and the Message*. J. B. Torrance cautions against anthropomorphizing the notion of the word "Father": "For us the word 'father' is a human class concept, which we predicate of creaturely male parents. How then can a word which is a human class concept be used to denote God who is not a member of that class? ... If the human word 'father' is to be used of God, there must be a shift in meaning to denote God the Creator, who is the only true Father, after whom all earthly fatherhood is named (Eph. 3:15). In the order of being, God's fatherhood is prior to ours, as the creator is prior to the creature ... We can only [compare and contrast God's fatherhood with ours theologically] by the content put into that word by Jesus Christ, as we reflect upon the life of Jesus, the words of Jesus, the sufferings of Jesus" (J. Torrance, *Worship, Community*, 123–25).

9. Palmer, *To Know as We Are Known*, 48–49.

on a human face and a human frame. In Jesus, the disembodied 'word' takes flesh and walks among us. Jesus calls us to truth, but not in the form of creeds or theologies, or worldviews. His call to truth is a call to community—with him, with each other, with creation and its Creator. If what we know is an abstract, impersonal, apart from us, it cannot be truth, for truth involves a vulnerable, faithful, and risk-filled interpenetration of the knower and the known.[10]

Jesus calls us to the truth of Abba.

The nature of God defines the nature of the reality he created. God is a Trinity, revealed to us in the person of Christ. Jesus Christ related to God as Father. From this perspective, the reality of humanity is Christ's reality: Father-led interpersonal oneness. In this reality, all knowledge and action are accomplished through the mediums of love, connection, and relationship. This truth is demonstrated in the examples of Christ's disciples. For Jesus, the disciples' friendship with him was based upon their inclusion into his personal relationship with the Father: "I've named you friends because I've let you in on everything I've heard from the Father" (John 15: 15).

The Western church tends to be largely unaware of *Abba* as Jesus' signature word for his Father and the central revelation of the New Testament. However, the degree to which we are not Father-led is the degree to which we are not Christlike. Jesus' personal view of his *gut-wrenched* God—a definition from the Greek word for compassion, *splagchnizomai*, used in the parable of the prodigal son in Luke 15:20—is the outline of our lives.

## INTERPERSONAL ONENESS IS A CHRISTOLOGICAL HERMENEUTIC

Jesus and his teachings cannot be understood except through the lens of interpersonal oneness. In particular, the interpersonal oneness of the Trinity must inform our understanding of Jesus, for Jesus' life and ministry were an outgrowth of his interpersonal oneness with the Father and the Holy Spirit. Graham Buxton views "the various dimensions of the Christological event as interconnected aspects of one multifaceted jewel, from the incarnation through to the *parousia* (the return of Christ), in which all three members of the Trinity are intimately and necessarily

---

10. Palmer, *To Know as We Are Known*, 48–49.

involved."[11] In this way, the incarnated Christ is, in himself, a reflection of the interpersonal oneness of the Trinity. As Andrew Thrasher emphasizes, "In the gospel of John we clearly see in Jesus' own understanding of himself in his relation to the Father in a way that reveals who he is *relationally* in and towards the Father . . ." How? ". . . by revealing himself through a humble relationality, or rather a self-disclosing revelation of who he is *in relation* to the Father."[12] In other words, Jesus defined himself through relational terminology that focused on his identification with the Father. This divine, spiritual identification was a hallmark of his interpersonal oneness with the Father.

Daniel L. Migliore, Professor of Systematic Theology at Princeton Theological Seminary, asserts that "The logic of trinitarian theology moves from the differentiated love of Father, Son, and Holy Spirit in the economy of salvation (the economic Trinity) to the ultimate ground of this threefold love in the depths of the divine being (Immanent Trinity)."[13] And further, the Trinity is necessary in understanding Jesus' incarnation. Migliore explains:

> The trinitarian communion of love is thus both ground and prototype of the union of true God and true humanity in Jesus Christ.[14] In the incarnation, God and humanity are fully free and fully united in love.[15] Each is totally free for and unconditionally faithful to the other. God elects Jesus as God's "chosen," God's "beloved" (Matt 12:18); in turn, Jesus is entirely devoted to God and freely subordinates his will to God's (Luke 22:42). In perfect mutual love, divinity and humanity are distinct yet united in Jesus Christ. In him the perfect love of God and a perfect human response to that love are united . . . The relationship of God to Jesus and of Jesus to God has its basis and fullest analogy in the eternal exchange of love in the life of the triune God.[16]

---

11. Buxton, *Dancing in the Dark*, 20.

12. Thrasher, "Substantial Persons in Trinitarian Relationality," 3.

13. Migliore, *Faith Seeking Understanding*, 151.

14. Migliore, *Faith Seeking Understanding*, 62. Migliore refers readers to Barth, *Church Dogmatics*, vol. 1, part 1, 384–748. According to Kasper, "In the last resort, the mediation of God and man in Jesus Christ can only be understood in the light of Trinitarian theology" (Kasper, *Jesus the Christ*, 249).

15. "The prime purpose of the incarnation, in the love of God, is to lift us up into the life of communion, of participation in the very triune life of the Trinity." Torrance, *Worship*, 32.

16. Migliore, *Faith Seeking Understanding*, 151.

For Christoph Schwöbel, a world-renowned systematic theologian, this is a paradigm shift:

> This also explains why Jesus' addressing God as Father and the church's invocation of Jesus as the Son could become the paradigm for the use of all other Christological models, since the Father-Son relationship exemplifies the mutuality and reciprocity of God's self-identification in Jesus and the identification of Jesus through his relation to God.[17]

Having graduated from several seminaries in the US and listened to many messages over many years, I cannot remember hearing a lecture or message on the relational distinction between a servanthood and friendship approach to Christianity. The relationship between interpersonal oneness and friendship never surfaced. However, we must recognize that the relational approach to Christianity is deeply supported by the perichoretic mutuality and reciprocity of self-identification in Jesus' relationship with the Father. Jesus says we are his friends if we are defined by the Father's words, spoken through Christ. God is friendship. Again, "I'm no longer calling you servants *because servants don't understand what their master is thinking and planning*. No, I've named you friends because I've let you in on everything I've heard from the Father" (John 15:14–15, emphasis added). Jesus and the Father are one (John 10:30). The members of the Trinity are unified. If Jesus calls us friends, then certainly each member of the Trinity would do so as well.[18] God loved the world before he sent his Son and while it was yet in sin (John 3:16).

We might see this aspect of Jesus as a *hermeneutical* consideration that allows us to properly interpret the personhood of Jesus. Hermeneutics is the study of the principles of interpretation. Seminary courses on hermeneutics focus on the means and methodology of properly interpreting the biblical text. In other words, how do we understand the meaning

---

17. Schwöbel, "Christology and Trinitarian Thought," 124.

18. Kinkade, *More to the Story*, 1–72. "The form of the word *call* in the beginning of this verse in the original Greek is present indicative active tense, which indicates that Jesus is no longer calling (that is, *continuously calling*) them servants. However, the second use of the word is in the perfect tense, which means the action was performed in the past with continuing consequences. The action is summarized and presented in its entirety. An English analogy is, 'He loosed the arrow.' The perfect tense is considered by many to be a third type of aspect (perfect or stative) that focuses on a state that arises from a previous action. This is complicated Greek grammar, but here is how it breaks down: Jesus is saying that, at some time in the past, he called us friends even though he was also calling us servants (Greek-slaves). He was a friend to the slave."

of the Scriptures? To say that "interpersonal oneness is a christological hermeneutic" has a double meaning. First, it means that interpersonal oneness is an ontological hermeneutical approach (*onto-hermeneutical*) that allows us to understand (or interpret) Jesus. We cannot understand Jesus' person, acts, or words without this foundation. Second, interpersonal oneness as a christological hermeneutic means that viewing the Scriptures through the lens of interpersonal oneness is the way Jesus himself would understand the Bible. Interpersonal oneness is christological because it is reflective of Jesus' way of being. In this way, we recognize that interpersonal oneness is applicable both to the personhood of Jesus and to the proper interpretation of the Bible.

My seminary courses on hermeneutics taught the grammatical historical approach because it was seen as being more scientific or logical in its methodology. This approach focused on the historical, cultural, literary, and linguistic contexts of the text. However, this approach tends to produce interpretive results that are linear, one-dimensional, atomistic (text-collation), rationalistic,[19] and propositional.[20] It is generally not reflective of a holistic approach. As Mark H. Glenn exclaimed, "The presupposition that the triune God can only be revealed by the parsing of Words through man-made rules of grammar and apart from not only cultural/historical context, but relationship is, in my opinion, absurd."[21]

19. Sanders, "Trinity Talk, Again," 271. "At times, contemporary evangelicalism has uncritically assumed a rationalistic biblical hermeneutic." He writes, "God the Trinity is revealed through word and deed in the Bible, even though not in propositional form."

20. Sanders, "Trinity Talk, Again." See Yarnell, *God the Trinity*. See Sanders, *Triune God*, 104.

21. Glenn, email to author, March 29, 2018: "I was surprised and intrigued to read that semiotics is mentioned in the dictionary definition of hermeneutics. It makes complete sense since so much of communication and thus decoding of that communication is non-verbal. John was a master semiotician with his continual reference to signs and the structure of his gospel in re Jewish feast/festivals. The presuppositions and preunderstandings of the message and the way/walk are so prevalent in the Enlightenment influenced the view of logos as something static instead of someone who reveals new and interesting facets of himself and therefore the triune God. If I need a proof-text: Philip said to him, 'Lord, show us the Father, and it is enough for us.' Jesus said to him, 'Have I been with you so long, and you still do not know me, Philip? Whoever has seen me has seen the Father. How can you say, "Show us the Father"?' (John 14:8–79 ESV); 'And he is the radiance of his glory and the *exact representation of his nature* and upholds all things by the word of His power. When he had made purification of sins, he sat down at the right hand of the Majesty on high' (Heb 1:3 NASB); 'He is the image of the invisible God, the firstborn of all creation' (Col 1:15 NASB); 'The spirit of this world

Malcom B. Yarnell III, Southwestern Seminary's retired Professor of Old Testament and Hebrew, suggests a valid caution: "Scripture is not a human document to be subjected to modern methods of historical-critical analysis; it is divine revelation which paints for us various portraits of God and his interactions with the world."[22] While the grammatical historical approach has its uses, is it up to the challenge of properly evaluating and understanding the onto-relational nature of the Trinity, and of Jesus himself?

Fred Sanders, Associate Professor of Theology, Torrey Honors Institute, Biola University, concludes, "In the field of Biblical studies, the overall trend of sober historical-grammatical labors has been toward the gradual removal of the trinitarian implications of passage after passage."[23] Moreover, he claims that "Many of our accounts of the foundational figures and decisions have become clichés and oversimplifications operating at considerable distance from any exposure to primary texts."[24]

Scripture gives rise to our understanding of the Trinity, but our understanding of the Trinity must also function in our interpretation of the Bible. The doctrine of the Trinity, Sanders argues, "arises from the totality of Scripture rather than from a congeries of scattered texts."[25] The unity

---

has blinded the minds of those who do not believe and prevents the light *of the glorious Gospel of Christ, the image of God*, from shining on them. For it is *Christ Jesus the Lord whom we preach*, not ourselves' (2 Cor 4:4 J. B. Phillips)."

> He (God) was manifested physically
> and proved righteous spiritually,
> seen by angels
> and proclaimed among the nations,
> trusted throughout the world
> and raised up in glory to heaven. (1 Tim 3:16 CJB)

22. Yarnell, *God the Trinity*.

23. Sanders, "Trinitarian Theology's Exegetical Basis," 79. See also Sanders, *Triune God*, 104. As reviewer Brent Rempel puts it: "Sanders specifies the relationship between God's triune self-disclosure and Holy Scripture." He "identifies three aspects of Trinitarian doctrine in New Testament. The Scriptures present (1) raw data in speaking of the Father, Son, and Spirit. The data occurs alongside (2) 'patterned reflection' which puts (3) 'pressure' on the interpreter to develop distinctions among the persons while maintaining unity." Rempel, Review of *The Triune God* by Fred Sanders. See also Sanders, "Trinitarian Theology's Exegetical Basis," 79.

24. Sanders, "Trinity Talk, Again," 271.

25. Sanders, *Triune God*, 104. See Sanders, "Trinitarian Theology's Exegetical Basis," 78–90: "The service that systematic theology can provide in the present state of disorder is not to do the exegesis itself, nor to dictate in advance what the exegetes are

of the Old and New Testament exhibits a unified narrative that reveals the 'agency of the triune God.'[26] As Yarnell states, "interpreters must read Scripture holistically and canonically" because "the canonical unity of the biblical text . . . serves as a presupposition of Trinitarian theology." [27] So, the nature and form of this doctrine should be explored throughout the divine drama of Scripture.

For example, a holistic approach in a course on hermeneutics might begin with Jesus' basic principle of interpretation rooted in the relationship with the Father. What difference would it make if the first session in a hermeneutics course was Father-led and featured interpreted Scripture based on what Jesus himself heard from his Father? How much deeper would reading of the Scriptures be if we interacted with them with the help of Jesus' insight from the Father? The Bible must be understood in the context of what the Father entrusted to his Son, what Jesus sees the Father doing, and what the Spirit shares with us, rather than a tendency toward one-dimensional, generalized responses. We must ask what approach to the interpretation of these texts would yield insight into the Father's values—that is, what was important for him to entrust to his Son, and to us? How might that motivate novices learning the art of interpretation?

---

required to find. The lines of authority in the shared, interdisciplinary task of Christian theology do not run in that direction, nor with such directness. But the theologian can draw attention to the larger structures within which the exegetical laborers can do their skilled work."

26. Sanders, *Triune God*, 105.

27. Yarnell, *God the Trinity*. Reviewer Brent Rempel puts it: "Yarnell addresses the weaknesses of a scientific or purely historical-grammatical interpretive method. Such an approach represses the Trinitarian pattern woven throughout the many literary genres of the Bible. Yarnell contends that deficient hermeneutical approaches result in similarly deficient accounts of Trinitarian theology. At times, contemporary evangelicalism has uncritically assumed a rationalistic biblical hermeneutic. In light of this trend, Yarnell revisions theological method in conversation with patristic and pre-critical exegetical models. This approach is decidedly a *via media* between modernism and postmodernism, between 'scientific measurement' and 'artistic inspiration' (27). Many contemporary theologians hesitate to speak of a doctrine of the Trinity located in the Bible, preferring rather to understand the doctrine as a faithful development of the early church. Offering an alternative to this trend, Yarnell argues that verbal revelation must remain the *sine qua non* of Trinitarian theology. He writes, 'God the Trinity is revealed through word and deed in the Bible, even though not in propositional form' (18). In setting a precedent for a theological appropriation of Scripture, the author aims to provide a biblical foundation of the doctrine of the Trinity. The extensive use of theological interpretation represents an important contribution of the work." Rempel, review of *God the Trinity* by Malcolm Yarnell.

## Part II: Why Is It Important to Define Reality?

Allowing truth to be defined by the Father's voice is the hermeneutic of interpersonal oneness. Can one say that the Western church is a friend of Jesus if it ignores this christological approach? Without this paradigm, we may only be servants who do not know the master's agenda. Accordingly, the American church's culturally normed servant leadership paradigm often makes goals of precisely the opposite of interpersonal oneness—such as performative self-generation, self-actualization, self-achievement, and self-fulfillment. Rather, recursively hearing the Father's voice, heart, and commitments inspires sonship, the kind that does not need a second thought because it flows so naturally and christologically. This is genuine Christian servanthood through recursive relationship, and it is a natural byproduct of prioritizing the Fathers voice, just as Jesus did![28] Ultimately, friendship and service are inextricable because it is not

---

28. Glenn gives a thoughtful analysis of the distinction between servant and friend that is contextual and clarifying (Mark H. Glenn, Napkin scribbles on Wess Pinkham's "Thoughts on Relational Christianity," July 3, 2017): "In the pericope of John 15, a new commandment is given in verse 12: 'love one another as I have loved you.' This commandment brings with it the preceding verse 11 of the joy of Jesus being in us and that joy would be full. The statement of a new relationship of friendship in verse 15 is preceded with a caveat: 'You are my friends if you do what I command you.' What is the command? Love one another. Thus, one-anothering love precedes the paradigm-shifting move from servant (*doulos* a bond-slave without any ownership rights of their own) to friends (*philos*) which according to the TDNT connotes a relationship becoming one's confidant and a relationship of mutual choosing. This volitional acting upon the call to one-anothering in love connects to both joy and friendship. Just as man was invited to participate in God's plan in Creation by naming, working/keeping, being fruitful/multiplying, and taking dominion; in the New Creation (John's theme), we are called friends—*philos*, confidants and participants in God's New Creation, with all the authority to accomplish the dominion set out in the expanding Kingdom of God/New Creation. To know and be known (1 Cor. 13:12) is only possible because of the Incarnation of Jesus as we come to know Jesus as the perfect representation of Abba, and we are called to be his friends without losing the title of servant. Perhaps this is because of the kenotic service of Christ in the Incarnation and procession toward laying down his life for his friends. Thus, friendship and service become inextricable as we accept by volition the invitation into a transformational relationship of being God's confidant and being in on the joy of his plan. This redemptive plan involves both *philos* & *doulos* in the movement toward redemption bringing ultimate joy (Heb 12:2) and fellowship with and in the triune God himself. Yes, "The plan of redemption that brought joy to Jesus, 'The joy set before him,' that motivated him to endure the cross, was us" [this insight on Heb 12:2 by Rebecca Bauer, email, May 20, 2019. The joy before him was us!]

TDNT, in regard to *doulos* or the plural *duloi*: "It is a recognition of the freedom which can come only with commitment to Christ, so that there is no contradiction when John speaks of the freedom which the Son brings (John 8:34), or when he has Jesus say that he calls his disciples, not *douloi*, but friends, for these are friends who do what he commands them. (John 15:14–15)." In John, "The link with joy comes out

an either/or choice. The servanthood modeled by Jesus was a byproduct of his love-based relationship with God.

An insightful aphorism is attributed to humorist, essayist, and novelist Mark Twain: "The two most important days in your life are the day you were born, and the day you find out why." In John 14:28, Jesus said through his Spirit (the bond of love between the Father and the Son): "the goal and purpose of my life is Father." Jesus' life purpose was Abba-centered. If we claim to be Christian, our own purpose in life must not contradict this! In Western Christianity it is far too easy to rely on the will of God as nation, geography, career, hobbies, and conduct. In this approach, the *what* (God's will as country, career, or conduct) tends to upstage the *who*. We need a value check! Why would one expect a godly life-purpose from a contractual, transactional, individualized, and non-relational quest that amounts to self-generation, self-actualization, self-achievement, and self-fulfillment?

## INTERPERSONAL ONENESS IS THE RECONCILIATION OF JESUS

Not only is interpersonal oneness necessary in accurately viewing Christ, but it is also a perfect representation of the reconciliation accomplished by Jesus' sacrifice. The interpersonal acceptance and love seen between the members of the Trinity has been extended to believers. God's interpersonal oneness is the motivating ontological fact behind his desire for closeness with humanity. As Daniel L. Migliore writes:

> If God is expressed to us in three distinct personal ways, then there is a basis of this structure of divine love in God's own immanent, eternal being. God's own life cannot contradict what God is in relation to the world. In God's own life there is an activity of mutual self-giving, community of sharing, a 'society

---

here and with table fellowship in 12:1. Lazarus is 'our friend' in John 11:1. The disciples are friends of Jesus by his free choice (15:13). He remains the Lord, but commands are commands of love (vv. 14) which he himself fulfils (v. 10)." In regard to *philos*, "Jesus breaks down the wall of an exclusiveness of fellowship and love. In Luke 14:12 friendship and table fellowship are correlative (15:6, 9, 29). Hospitality expresses the relation between friendship and table fellowship, as in Luke 11:5 where *philos* has almost the sense of 'good neighbor' in vv. 5, 8 and of 'guest' in v. 6. The friend as neighbor and host must be available for a friend . . . Joy stands closely related to friendship (Luke 15:6, 9, 29). Yet friends must be ready too, for service, concern and self-sacrifice (11:5). Friends may expect help from *one another* even when it is inconvenient" (emphasis added).

of love' (Augustine) that is the basis of God's history of love for the world narrated in Scripture.[29]

God cannot contradict himself, and therefore the interpersonal oneness at the heart of his being reveals itself in the Father's sending of his only begotten (John 3:17) and the Son's willingness to endure pain and shame in order to bring humanity back into oneness with the Father.

Further, a deep understanding of the mechanics of salvation also help us to define the nature of God. As Christoph Schwöbel captures it, "if the reconciliation of God with creation is truly unconditional, dependent on nothing but God's being of love, then the relationship between the Father and Son which constitutes Christ as the agent of salvation cannot be a temporal and transitory accident of God's being, but has to be seen as eternally rooted in God's being."[30] In this view, salvation arises from the nature of God. It was not done on a whim. Each personal experience of salvation is a magnificent insight into the personality of God. Particularly with Jesus, salvation is not just something he did, but rather someone he is. The Father's love and desire for intimacy with his creation form the essence of our salvation. Migliore explains that it is from this standpoint that Trinitarian theology is established and confirmed. He writes that

> ... proper trinitarian theology does not first speculatively posit a Trinity in eternity and afterward search for evidence of the Trinity in revelation and Christian experience. Rather, it begins concretely from the history of revelation and salvation attested by Scripture and experienced by Christians from the beginning of the church. Only on that basis do faith and theology declare that trinitarian communion belongs to God's own eternal being, as well as to God's relation to the world.[31]

Salvation and the personal reception of salvation are therefore integrally connected with God's Trinitarian nature. The interpersonal oneness found in the relationships of love and self-emptying between Father, Son, and Spirit cannot be separated from Christ's salvific work.

Yet salvation alone does not properly describe God's desire for reconciliation. In fact, reconciliation is the open door to a deep and intimate relationship with God. It is a relationship of interpersonal oneness that God has offered to every single one of us. And it is an invitation to partake

---

29. Migliore, *Faith Seeking Understanding*, 151.
30. Schwöbel, "Christology and Trinitarian Thought," 124.
31. Migliore, *Faith Seeking Understanding*, 151.

in the interpersonal oneness of the Trinity. This onto-relationship is one of delight and mutual giving. As Horrell describes:

> ... in the New Testament we see the Father delighting in and glorifying the Son, giving all things to the beloved One. Yet the Son appears delighting in and glorifying the Father. After conquering all things and reigning over his kingdom, the Son lays all things at the feet of the Father. And we find that the Holy Spirit delights in glorifying not himself but the Son and again in revealing the glory of the Father.[32]

The kind of relationships enjoyed between Father, Son, and Spirit are now available to us! This is the good news! Salvation is not limited to the forgiveness of sin. Rather, salvation paves the way for a much deeper and more personal relationship with the members of the Trinity, and with one another. As Royce G. Gruenler explains:

> In Jesus' disclosure of the divine Family the theme that runs repeatedly through his discourses is the generosity of the social God. The manner of Jesus' speech indicates his conviction that the persons of the divine Community inwardly enjoy one another's love, hospitality, generosity, and interpersonal communion, so much so that they are one God, and being one God, express such love to one another.[33]

Believers take on the nature of the Trinitarian relationship. This is interpersonal oneness expressed in the divine family. We receive the enabling to engage in this kind of relating due to the miraculous work of Christ. However, we are also able to reflect such interpersonal oneness as image-bearers of God.

## CONCLUSION

This chapter put forth three distinct ways in which interpersonal oneness functions in integral ways with the Christian faith. Interpersonal oneness reflects the incarnate Christ's relationship with the Father. It is also the lens by which we may properly interpret Jesus and the Bible. Finally, salvation is, in itself, a reflection of the Trinity's interpersonal oneness, particularly as it is offered to humanity in Christ's reconciliatory work.

---

32. Horrell, "Self-Giving Triune God."
33. Gruenler, *Trinity in the Gospel of John*, 121, 89–140.

In the power of his Spirit, the Son affirmed to his Abba Father: "I have made your very being known to them—who you are and what you do—and continue to make it known, so that your love for me might be in them exactly as I am in them" (John 17:25–26). Exactly! The interpersonal oneness between Father and Son was the motivation and the empowering of Jesus' salvific work. And not only that, it is now available to us through the sacrifice of Christ.

## REFLECTION

1. Do you agree that the interpersonal oneness of the Trinity aids in our efforts to define our reality? Why or why not?

2. What examples come to mind regarding how our understanding of Jesus, the Father, and the Scriptures may be distorted when attention to the doctrine of the Trinity declines?

3. What personal experiences have you had regarding the interpersonal oneness offered in Christ's salvation?

# 7

# A Relational View of Christ's Covenant

## INTRODUCTION

WE ARE NOT WHAT we think we are; rather, we are what we think! So, how do we think about God? Everyone has preexisting ideas about God. These ideas were formed by our upbringing and our experiences. Whether we would like to admit it or not, such ideas inform our theology.

One of the major categories of theology affected by our experience is our understanding of the nature of the God-human relationship. In Christianity, there are essentially two main ways in which we might approach God: contractual or covenantal (onto-relational). By examining these two opposing views, we will find that most of us have a preexisting contractual view of the God-human relationship. However, the approach supported by Scripture is the covenantal one. This chapter examines aspects of a relational vs. a contractual view of God, and unsurprisingly concludes that we must replace our contractual approach with a covenantal approach.

## COVENANT

What is a covenant? Keathley answers:

> A Covenant is an agreement between two parties. Sometimes the agreement required actions be performed by both parties. Such

as, if you do this, I'll do that. Sometimes the agreement or covenant was a unilateral covenant. Party number one promised to do something, and nothing was required of the other party. The covenants we are going to study are all unilateral or promisory covenants. God made promises that he would do something, and there was nothing required by the humans involved.[1]

One of the earliest major developments in theology was the view of God as being in a covenantal, not a contractual relationship. At Mt. Sinai, God made a covenant with those he had rescued from slavery in Egypt, declaring that he would be their God and they would be his people (Exodus 19–24). For the first time, God had a nation, a people, who belonged to him, and he established his relationship with them through a promise. Brennan Manning writes, "Yahweh is first perceived by the Jewish community as a personal, relating Being. Their concept of God was vastly superior to that of the pagans whose gods were quite human, fickle, capricious, erotic, as unpredictable as the forces with which they were identified—wind, storm, fertility, the nation, and so forth."[2]

The covenant at the root of the Judeo-Christian tradition is God's covenant with Abraham. It is instructive to start our discussion of the Abrahamic covenant in Galatians 3 before reading about it directly in Genesis 15. In Galatians 3:16, Paul specifies that the covenant promise to Abraham was to his seed, *in the singular*, which is Christ. Further, in verse 29, Paul explains that those who belong to Christ are Abraham's seed and "heirs according to the promise." For this reason, the promises of God to Abraham apply to us. If the promise to Abraham's seed is a particular promise to Christ as that seed, then Jesus' prayer that all his disciples be included in his relationship with the Father in John 17 includes us in that covenant. Our relationship with Jesus is the fulfillment of that covenant. Abiding in Christ means we are present-day recipients of the Abrahamic covenant.[3]

---

1. Keathley, "Relationship of the Church to Israel," https://bible.org/article/relationship-church-israel.

2. Manning, recording of conference at Alderwood Vineyard, October 1989, Tape 1.

3. Norquist, *"Heartbeat of God."* Adapted from a recording of a lesson given for Wednesday evening service at Christian Faith Center, May 4, 1994. Dr. Norquist developed the covenant theme beginning from Galatians 3:29 and tracing it to its origin in Genesis 15.

## A Relational View of Christ's Covenant

In Genesis 15, God promises that Abraham's descendants will be as numerous as the stars. Abraham's response was one of faith, and God credited that belief to Abraham as righteousness. God also promises the land, and Abraham asks what proof he could have that this would come to pass. In response, God commands Abraham to gather a cow, a goat, and a ram, and to cut them in half, with the two parts on either side of a path wide enough for Abraham to walk. This was a dramatic and visceral moment for Abraham. The work involved in cutting the animals, as well as the resultant gory mess, would have been unforgettable for him.

I hunted as a boy. The first bird I killed with a double-barreled shotgun was the whooping crane. At 5:30 on one cold, Northern Canadian morning, I remember coming out of a stuke of sheaves of barley in which I was hiding. I aimed, giving the crane the right lead, fired, and watched it fall to the ground. It made a lonely call as it landed. The noise from the voice box, the smell, the feel of its fading warmth all made an indelible impression upon me. It is a picture that helps to identify with Abraham's contractual/cultural ceremony.

In Abraham's time period, kings or oriental potentates (e.g., in Suzerain treaties) would make a bilateral (*suntheke*) contract in a similar way, by making a path between animals cut in two. The greater potentate would recite terms to the lessor as they stood on either end of the circle eight path, walk through it, and then declare that if the contract were broken, then the fate of those divided animals would be the fate of the parties to that contract. Certainly, God was using this brand of cultural ceremony to impress upon Abraham that the promises of a new position (the patriarch of multitudes) and land were genuine.

But Abraham's story of the making of this covenant is not over, for after cutting and arranging the animals, Abraham must wait for God to show up. And as he is waiting, birds of prey arrive, attracted by the easy feast laid out before them. Abraham has to continually scare them off to protect the scene of the covenant. The sun sets, and Abraham falls asleep in a state of fear.

Sometime later, a flame passes between the animals, and that moment solidified the covenant (Gen 15:17–18).[4] Theologians refer to this as a theophany—a preincarnate appearance of the Trinitarian God himself. Literally, the passage states that it was "a smoking firepot with a blazing torch" that moved down the path, symbolizing the Trinity passing

---

4. Hayford, *Spirit-Filled Bible*, 27.

through the pieces.[5] God (as Father, Son, and Holy Spirit) "cut" the covenant with himself while Abram snoozed![6] It was a one-sided, one-party, unilateral event. As Keathley puts it:

> That this is an unconditional covenant is also important because, since God is faithful, he will fulfill his promises to Abraham. He will use Abraham's seed to bless mankind. Any particular generation of Israelites could enjoy these promises if they were obedient to God. But ultimately God would fulfill these promises by raising up a generation that would be obedient. He would do this regardless of what Abraham or any of his descendants do.[7]

Contrary to the covenantal ceremonies of the time, which required two parties of a contract to walk through the sacrifices in a circle eight pattern, only God moved down this sacrificial aisle. Only the smoking oven and blazing torch passed between the pieces. In this theophany, God sees Abram snoozing on the ground, and, in a sense, cuts a deal with himself. This action would signify to Abraham that God would be the only one suffering the consequences if the covenant failed! In other

---

5. Glenn, email to author, September 24, 2019: "The Triune God made a covenant within the perichoretic union and therefore it is not unilateral. The Covenant was made by the Trinity (Rev 13:8). The Father sent (John 3:16) carried out by the Son (Heb 12:2) and the Son was empowered by the Spirit (Acts 10:38)."

Thrasher, "Substantial Persons in Trinitarian Relationality," 3, supports a tripartite understanding: "Linked to the biblical context and the development of Trinitarian theology in the early church what we find is a tripartite understanding of a relational God who works in creation to bring it back to its original intention via his self-revelation in the person and work of Jesus Christ and in the reconciliation and work of the Holy Spirit in humanity and creation."

Schwöbel, "Christology and Trinitarian Thought," 126–27: "Because the Son and the Spirit are not external to God's being, the Son and the Spirit can be seen as active in all divine works from creation to the consummation of the Kingdom. The eschatological ultimacy of the temporal identification of the Father, Son and the Spirit requires a recognition of their ontological ultimacy for the being of God."

6. In the Hebrew, a covenant is "cut" rather than "made." Certainly, the cutting of the animals here is a mirroring of this language.

7. Keathley, "Relationship of the Church to Israel," 3:

> ... the provisions of the Abrahamic Covenant are three: a land; a seed and blessing (personal, national, and universal). Here we have the beginning of the nation of Israel because Abraham is the Father of the Jews, the father of Israel. And we begin to see that the seed of Abraham, the nation of Israel, is going to be the vehicle of God's blessing on all mankind. It is important to understand this connection. They are not separate unrelated promises.
>
> The covenant is reaffirmed to Abraham in Gen 15:1–21, 17:4–21, 22:15–18; to Isaac in Gen 26:3–5, 24; and to Jacob in Gen 28:13–15; 35:9–12.

words, only God was responsible for the keeping of the covenant. And, since that covenant was broken many times by Abraham's descendants, God in Christ did, indeed, suffer the same fate as those Abrahamic sacrifices when he was made the sacrifice on Calvary. God knew that humanity would violate the covenant. Therefore, he ensured the covenant met its terms and consequences due to our failure to keep it.

The depth of this covenantal picture should not be missed. The Abrahamic covenant began the Judeo-Christian relationship to God with a paradigm shift. The Chaldean agreement was contractual or bilateral (*suntheke*, i.e., between two parties). However, God communicated his promise to Abraham in a unilateral manner. Abraham cut the animals and arranged them, following the command of God, and most likely he was anticipating the agreement to follow the common cultural contract of his time. The fulfillment of the covenant, however, is unilateral (*diatheke*), being wholly dependent upon God's strength, willingness, and ability. This, thankfully, runs contrary to the natural human instinct to attain self-perfection, for the covenant was sworn only upon the person of God, not any other person—even Abraham. By doing it in this way, God deconstructed Abraham's culturally based contractualism. Given that Abraham was a Chaldean, and Chaldean contracts were formalized at such a blood ceremony, it was likely that Abraham was thinking bilateral contract and not unilateral covenant. God cut the covenant with Abraham but made himself the only responsible party to see it enforced! Bruce Norquist writes that this picture is essentially God speaking to the sleeping Abraham: "If you mess up Abraham (and God could name each of us by name), may this happen to Me."[8] There is literally no room for failure in this covenant, because it is not dependent upon humans in any way. A unilateral covenant like this means that God will uphold his part of the bargain no matter what the other party does.[9] It should be noted, however, that some rabbinic scholars would disagree with this reading, as they maintain that there is not enough evidence in Genesis 15 to confidently assert that Abraham was asleep during the cutting of the covenant.[10] Regardless, it does seem in Genesis 15 that there are no

---

8. Norquist, "Heartbeat of God." Adapted from a recording of a lesson given for Wednesday evening service at Christian Faith Center, May 4, 1994. Dr. Norquist developed the covenant theme beginning from Galatians 3:29 and tracing it to its origin in Genesis 15.

9. Richards, *Let Day Begin*, 122.

10. Edery, email to author, April 15, 2017. Professor Edery believes that "most Jews

requirements put on Abraham. The covenant was an example of God's gracious selection and promise. In that sense one could argue that the covenant, though between parties, was dependent on the greater party, that is, God, who placed no requirements on the other.

We too enjoy the privilege and blessing of being the other party. The truth is that God's promises are not dependent upon us. This is cause for rejoicing! This should prompt us to worship God in his infinite patience and grace. The completion of this gifted covenant is found in Christ, who suffered the consequences of our breaking of the covenant. Just as with Abraham, our response is to believe and receive.[11] That is our agreement to the covenant, which God has executed.

Hebrews addresses this unilateral responsibility in this way: "When God made his promise to Abraham, since there was no one greater for him to swear by, he swore by himself . . . Because God wanted to make the unchanging nature of his purpose very clear to the heirs of what was promised, he confirmed it with an oath" (Heb 6:13, 17 NIV). The promise is clear, confirmed with an oath, unchangeable and sure. The purpose, passion, and potential of God began to take shape in the promise to Abraham. "The Abrahamic covenant is the OT model for the New Covenant in Jesus Christ."[12] The unconditional nature of God's promise towards us in Christ is the gist of the covenant—that in him all of the promises of God are found to be "yes" and in him "amen." "Unconditional" means there is no fine print in the agreement. Our behavior or performance is not a final issue, but rather God in Christ's performance through us. There may be conditions for growth, as we have the capability to make choices that, with the Spirit's power, render us response-able. God picks up both ends of the covenant—promise and penalty—for both its terms and any consequences for our failure to deliver the required response. Indeed, salvation is a covenantal gift of relationship. All we can do is receive it in a response of faith, gratitude, and love—or reject it. When we receive it, Christ lives his life and Spirit through us. We get to cooperate, so he can perform in and through us what Abba desires.

Scripture, after it was ratified in Christ's death and resurrection, affirms the unbreakable character of the promise. In Genesis 17:7, God

---

will tell you it is NOT clear from the scriptures if Abraham was awake or asleep. Is it a vision or a dream? That would be a risky move to conclude definitely that he was asleep, while rabbis and sages cannot agree on this issue. The scripture is not clear."

11. Hayford, *Spirit-Filled Bible*, 27.
12. Hayford, *Spirit-Filled Bible*, 27.

says the promise is "everlasting." It was confirmed to David and amplified to Jeremiah (Jer 31:35–38). God has a plan, a direction for history, a way to bless the world through a unique channel—a chosen race fathered by Abraham. In him we have a mirror of ourselves and a message from God. Abraham turned from any hope in his own goodness. We find in God's message about Christ (Abraham's seed) our way to the fulfillment of faith. God cannot break the promise, for an unconditional promissory covenant had been made. He bound himself and himself alone "to make the unchanging nature of his purpose very clear" (Heb 6:17 NIV).

It is important that we do not make the blood covenant in Christ into a contract. The cross was the fulfillment, a unilateral act that assumed the consequences of the sin of the human race. God closed the loop! Too many preachers on the blood covenant see its irrevocable and indelible nature, yet for some reason fail to see a closed loop. That is, their perspective is still contractual, as an if-then of mutual obligation. Yet God picked up both ends, the obligation (to be *present, provide, and protect*)[13] and the *penalty* (consequences for any failure), thus making the covenant a unilateral closed loop.

Why do so many Christians view this unilateral covenant (*diatheke*) as a bilateral (*suntheke*) contract? James B. Torrance's contrast of the bilateral covenant with a unilateral covenant relationship is helpful in clarifying the nature of God's covenant with us in Christ:

> Clearly in a bilateral covenant (*suntheke*) there can be no covenant without a response. So, in marriage a man cannot make a covenant for his beloved. He has to wait until she says yes to his proposal before they can enter mutually into a two-way covenant. Such a covenant is open ended and contingent upon the mutual response of both parties. This is not the nature of the New Covenant in Christ.[14]
>
> A unilateral covenant (*diatheke*) is quite different. God has made a Covenant for us in Christ—the New Covenant 'in my

---

13. In a Chaldean contract or Suzerain treaty there were at least three terms of a celebrated agreement. The greater king or potentate would promise the lesser: (1) *Presence*: Personal relationships are a sacred priority. Binding together in support out of love and devotion was highly valued. (2) *Provision*: Meeting needs was also an important value. Should you ever have a need and I have the goods, then what I have is yours and what you have is mine. (3) *Protection*: If anyone ever comes against you or your family, that person may automatically consider that he is going to have to deal with me and my family. See "Suzerain Treaties," https://www.fivesolas.com/suzerain.htm.

14. J. Torrance, "Covenant or Contract?," 4.

blood'. But it still demands a response . . . So, the New Covenant made by God for us in Christ demands the joyful, grateful, loving, 'Amen' of the whole man—which worship is.[15]

Or, as Buxton puts it:

> Our worship is not measured by how successful we are in "crossing the line" to God, for God has already crossed the line to us. We simply cannot come to God in perfect self-offering as Christ has done, for he alone is our righteousness, our holiness, and our redemption. All we can ever do is utter our "Amen" to Christ's perfect "Yes." This is our worship, gathered up in Christ and sanctified by his grace.[16]

Grace is a unilateral free gift. Our response is warranted, but not demanded. The covenantal relationship with God in Christ is not made up of obligation, but rather the gift-giving nature of perfect love.

As we pointed out, bilateral contracts were common in Abraham's lifetime as they are in ours. If the default state of mind is to see a relationship with God as contractual, we will miss the personal impact of God's unilateral promise. It is possible that the religious instinct resists the concept of the unilateral covenant because it wishes to gain glory and having nothing to do with the accomplishment of God's will does not lead to glory? A legalistic approach to Christianity maintains that there are a large number of requirements for maintaining a relationship with God in Christ. The unilateral covenant, however, is a powerful testament to God's grace. Legalism dies in the face of sheer gifted grace—God himself.

## CONTRACT

While the covenant we have in Christ is relational in nature, it is certainly possible (and fairly common!) to view it in a contractual way. A contract is about the terms and benefits of the agreement. A contract is based on living up to expectations and fulfilling requirements. God's covenant in Christ is intertwined with his love, grace, and everlasting commitment. However, to view it as a contract reduces it to an arrangement of if-then mutual obligation. Approaching God's covenant as a contract is to view it legalistically, rather than relationally.

---

15. J. Torrance, "Covenant or Contract?," 4.
16. Graham Buxton, *Dancing in the Dark*, 200.

We can trace how the contractual view came to ascendancy in the Western church by examining how the Federal theologians in the seventeenth century perverted John Calvin's understanding of covenant.[17] They recognized that the idea of covenant was a central one in both the Old and New Testaments. Yet, their theology categorized different types of covenants. By distinguishing a *covenant of works* from a *covenant of grace*, Federal Calvinists made God's grace conditional on man's obedience, thereby turning covenant into contract. In Galatians 3:17–22, Paul explains that the covenants of the Old Testament are fulfilled in Christ and are therefore assured in their fulfillment according to God's promise, not according to the observance of the law. If God were to give conditional covenants that rely on human faithfulness and works, such covenants would likely never by fulfilled due to human failings. James B. Torrance distinguishes between the obligations of love and the conditions of love in this regard.[18] There may be expectations on God's part for humanity, but this is different than considering God's love as dependent upon certain actions and behavior. It is doubtful that Calvin would have taught the distinction between a covenant of works and a covenant of grace. As James B. Torrance has it:

> For Calvin, all God's dealings with men are those of grace, both in Creation and Redemption. They flow from the loving heart of the Father. The two poles of his thought are grace and glory—from grace to glory. There has been only one eternal covenant of *grace* promised in the [Hebrew Bible] and fulfilled in Christ. 'Old' and 'New' do not mean two covenants but two forms of the one eternal covenant—the central theme of Book Two of the *Institutes*.[19]

So, novices upstaged the first-class mind of John Calvin. But they did not have their theological heads screwed on straight. The result? Costly grace was turned into conditional grace. Moreover, it was done to Martin Luther too! Bonhoeffer observed, "Lutheranism can sometimes turn free grace into cheap grace. Puritan Calvinism can sometimes turn costly grace into conditional grace."[20] Bad Calvinism or Lutheranism can

---

17. J. Torrance, "Covenant or Contract?," 5. "The sin of late Judaism—and it is the sin of the human heart in all ages—was to try to *turn God's covenant of grace into a contract*, with serious consequences for worship."

18. J. Torrance, "Covenant or Contract?," 5.

19. J. Torrance, "Covenant or Contract?," 62.

20. J. Torrance, "Covenant or Contract?," 5.

rabbit-trail the church for centuries by collapsing Christianity into legalistic contractualism or transactionalism. This view, in turn, becomes culturally reinforced in capitalistic societies.

In response to a contractually centered view of Christianity, Douglas A. Campbell and James B. Torrance contend for a theology of grace. However, a strong emphasis on grace stirred up considerable opposition throughout church history, due to contractual views of Christian theology.[21]

Covenant versus contract is an old debate. However, we think it should be renewed in Western theology in order to combat the prevailing cultural pressures toward transactionalism. An onto-relational covenant paradigm is a countercultural message. The merits of a covenantal approach to salvation need to be reexamined, rehearsed, and reinforced.[22]

In the unilateral covenantal view of salvation, humanity simply responds to God's freedom and love by receiving a gift in Christ and the gospel. As Campbell, following James B Torrance, puts it:

> A covenantal relationship for James Torrance is a relationship grounded in love for the other and hence one that is unconditional, permanent, and irrevocable. Because the basis for the relationship is precisely this ground, of love, the covenantal actor reaches out to the other and establishes the relationship independently of any action by that party. It is therefore an unconditional and gracious act, and the relationship with the other is a gifted one.[23]

Salvation is a gift to be received, not a deal to be made. To view salvation as dependent upon works is to diminish God's sovereign grace. Certainly, believers must respond to God's salvation, but salvation is not a conditional covenant which requires the fulfillment of certain obligations on the part of humanity. Are we saved by our act of believing? As Martin Davis clarifies T. F. Torrance's view:

> ... it is *Christ's own act* of believing that saves us. In other words, contra evangelicalism, it is not faith "in" Christ that saves us;

---

21. Campbell, "Covenant or Contract in Paul," 207.
22. Campbell, "Covenant or Contract in Paul."
23. Campbell, "Covenant or Contract in Paul," 198. "Torrance does not himself use language of 'the other' since its widespread use has largely postdated him, but it is useful for explicating some aspects of his thinking." Walter Kaiser, my professor of the Hebrew Bible, characterized it as the doctrine of promise in one of his classes at Trinity Evangelical Divinity School, Fall 1973.

rather, it is the faith "of" Christ that saves us.[24] For Torrance, we cannot talk seriously about "justifying faith" as a *condition* of our salvation, for we rely "wholly upon the vicarious faith of Christ and not upon ourselves even in the act of faith." It is only as we rely on the vicarious faith of Christ that we are truly free to believe without the "ulterior motive of using faith to secure our salvation" (p. cix). This last point is important, for if faith is exercised solely to avoid punishment, or even "hell," then personal faith is not an outwardly turned assent to the Father's love, as revealed in Jesus, but merely an inwardly turned attempt at self-preservation. For Torrance, faith must rest on "thanksgiving" for all that Christ has done for us, both from the side of God and from the side of man.[25]

Or as James B. Torrance applies it:

> It seems to me that in our pastoral situation our first task is not to throw people back on themselves with exhortations and instructions as to what to do and how to do it, but to direct people to the gospel of grace—to Jesus Christ, that they might look to him to lead them, open their hearts in faith and in prayer, and draw them by the Spirit into his eternal life of communion with the Father.[26]

Actions associated with salvation, such as faith and repentance, are the human responses to God's free salvation in Christ. If salvation is a contract, however, the contract stipulates that such things as faith and repentance are requisites to deserving, receiving, and maintaining salvation. Regardless of whether these requirements are said to be stringent or

---

24. "Knowing that a man is not justified by the works of the law, but by the faith *of* Jesus Christ, even we have believed in Jesus Christ, that we might be justified by the faith *of* Christ, and not by the works of the law: for by the works of the law shall no flesh be justified" (Gal 2:16 KJV). *Pistis Christou* is the genitive debate: subjective (faith *of* Christ—his love for me saves) or objective (my faith *in* Christ—my love, the subject's love for God saves). So, *Pistis Christou* can be interpreted as *Christ's faithfulness or my faith in Christ that saves. Toward or from?* Calvin and Barth emphasized Christ's faithfulness on our behalf. The continual role of the prophets in the Old Testament was to call people back to know the faithfulness of God and to live out of the faithfulness of God—that is our faith. Faith is not just a feeling or a commitment that one has; it is a way of being in relationship. Is our theology all about what we do? Or what God does? A big question. See Douglas A. Campbell, "Romans 1:17—A Crux Interpretum for the Pistis Christou Debate," 265-285. See Bryce Null, "Tracking the Pistis Christou Debate," 1-25.

25. Davis, "T. F. Torrance"; Torrance, *School of Faith*, cix.

26. J. Torrance, *Worship, Community*, 45.

lenient, if there are any requirements at all, this view demotes salvation from being a pure gift to being a transaction with a justice theme.

Accordingly, in a transactional paradigm, salvation is not primarily an endeavor of love, but a system of requirements. If you keep the law, God will love you. When the obligations of salvation are emphasized over and above his loving sacrifice on our behalf, salvation ceases to be a gift of grace and becomes a product of works. Salvation is then reduced to a moral point of contact which rescues the guilty only if the terms and conditions have been met. In this view, salvation is conditional, and only those who continue to meet the conditions of salvation are saved. God then becomes characterized by justice, judgment, and punishment rather than fundamental love. Christ's role in a conditional brand of salvation is actually a sacrilegious view of the Son of God, for it places human will and capabilities as a higher function than the person of Christ. This has a profound effect on the church's view of Christ, the believer's relationship with Jesus, and the approach to the teaching of the fundamentals of Christianity.

If salvation is based primarily on works and may be gained or lost based on human action, then the church must of necessity focus on those actions over and above Christ himself. Salvation is a gracious, unconditional, unilateral, and gifted relationship to be received in an act of worship, not a deal to be made. One can receive that gift or reject it and perish. It is important to note, though, that our human action of accepting Christ as our Savior does not save us in and of itself. "Christ's own act of believing"[27] saves us. When we believe in and receive the gift of salvation, or accept Christ as our Savior, the Holy Spirit makes us re-sponse-able—that is, able to respond—to receive it and we are rebirthed. Jesus accomplishes it, but we accept it. If we contrarily see salvation as a deal to be made, preaching and teaching then becomes focused on the obligations and requirements of salvation. This is what we currently see in many corners of Christianity. The relationship with God in Christ, by the Holy Spirit, has taken a backseat to works. The gospel is thereby transformed from an expression of love into a proclamation of sin, in order to motivate the individual toward the necessary performance to satisfy the penalty and sanctions for such sin. But Galatians 2:16a says, ". . . Knowing that a man is not justified by the works of the law, but by the faith of Jesus Christ . . ." (KJV). The conviction of guilt then becomes the

---

27. Torrance, *School of Faith*, cix.

chief aim of preaching, with the good news of Christ's grace and sacrifice relegated to a theological afterthought. As Campbell writes, "Even observably righteous behavior when it is motivated in extrinsic terms tends to be deeply sinful."[28] At the end of the day, contractualism reverses the order of grace and collapses into an anthropocentric survival system. As James B. Torrance warns:

> But if we take our eyes off Christ, like those to whom the epistle to the Hebrews was written, we fall back on ourselves with a false "self-confidence in the flesh" that we can keep the ordinances of worship (*dikaiomata latreias*, Heb 9:1) by our own religion, that we can offer worthy worship to God and meet his holy requirements. That is the road to apostasy, to sectarian divisions, to legalism, to weariness, where religion becomes a "yoke grievous to be borne." Then people will drift away from the church, we shall lose our young people who will want to cast off the "yoke," and our members will lose the motivation of grace to give time and service and money to the church.[29]

Unfortunately, such a pattern of law then gospel, emphasizes our short-fall and the requirements for resolution, and continues after salvation. We are left with "an overly guilt-ridden, obsessive, and anxious theology."[30]

The church must therefore return to the onto-relational understanding of covenant if it is to properly avoid the pitfalls of contractualism and transactionalism in its approach to Christ and his salvation. Christianity should not be seen primarily as a game of sin, with the Bible as a rulebook for winning. Rather, in a covenant paradigm, God's promises are motivated by the desire for intimate relationship, and his love is unconditional in Christ. Again, as Robert Schuller concludes in his book *Self-Esteem: The New Reformation*, "The classical error of historical Christianity is that we have never started with the value of the person. Rather, we have started from the 'unworthiness of the sinner,' and that starting point has set the stage for the glorification of human shame in Christian theology."[31] This reversal results from a failure to correctly understand the way in which God enacted his covenant of promise with Abraham.

---

28. Campbell, "Covenant or Contract in Paul," 201.
29. J. Torrance. *Worship, Community*, 119.
30. Campbell, "Covenant or Contract in Paul," 209.
31. Schuller, *Self Esteem*, 162.

## CONCLUSION

When viewing the stark contrast between a relational covenant and a transactional, if-then contract, we should be motivated to adopt an onto-relational view of God's covenant in the Christian context. As Geordie W. Ziegler[32] and Bruce Norquist[33] agree, grace should not be seen as a thing or as a commodity, but as a Person—specifically, Jesus Christ himself. Jesus' grace is found in his life, sacrifice, and resurrection, which allows God to live his life in and through us via participatory communion. Grace is not separate from God, and therefore Christ is the gift of grace in our lives, the promises of God expressed in relationship—the promises that extend all the way back to Abraham.

We are heirs according to the promise of a dynamic and holistic relationship. To see things whole is dynamic, for the grace or healing that God gives us is not something other than himself. Grace is not spiritual penicillin. It is not something he gives. He gives who he is. It is strong friendship (the Abrahamic covenant was also called the Covenant of Strong Friendship), Sonship, or quite simply, relationship. God is the friendship that he is and the grace that he gives! Or, as Thomas F. Torrance put it, "Grace is to be understood as the impartation not just of something from God but of God himself. In Jesus Christ and in the Holy Spirit God freely gives to us in such a way that the Gift and the Giver are one and the same in the wholeness and indivisibility of his grace..."[34] "God is the content of what God is towards us in God's love and grace."[35] Real covenant love, mutual self-giving, and perichoretic unity are what the gospel is all about.

---

32. Ziegler, "Is it Time," 4. As Ziegler puts it: "The critical point is this: grace is not a 'thing' separate from Jesus himself. Grace is a person—and this person lived, died, and rose again that we might participate in the life of the God who is for us, to the end that we might live a holy life *with* God, not merely *for* God. The goal and means of the Christian life are participatory communion."

33. Norquist, "Heartbeat of God." "We think God has given us His grace, a commodity. 'Here's some grace.' *Grace is not something other than God himself! The grace of God is gift of God himself in the person of Jesus Christ.* The same for healing, for faith or for all of the essential attributes of God. These promises are the gift of himself, not something other than himself in his Son, Jesus. Likewise, the promise is God himself in the Son. So, the promise of God to Abraham will bring forth this seed, in whom all nations of the earth will be blessed. How? In Christ."

34. Torrance, *Reality and Evangelical Theology*, 14, 15.

35. J. Torrance, "Covenant or Contract?," 80.

## REFLECTION

1. Why is it important to distinguish between the idea of a covenant and a contract?
2. Why do the merits of a covenantal approach to salvation need to be reexamined?
3. Why is the Abrahamic covenant at the root of the Judeo-Christian tradition?

# 8

# Incarnational Paradigms for Transforming the Church

## INTRODUCTION

WHILE IN A SERVICE at a conference in Iowa, I looked across the aisle at a father whose son suffers from cerebral palsy. Symptoms often include poor coordination, stiff or weak muscles, and tremors. There may be problems with sensation, vision, hearing, swallowing, and speaking. An offering was being received in the service, so the father wrote two checks and placed one in the uncoordinated hand of his son, and then, arm in arm, took him to the front to deposit their gifts in a basket.

Returning into their seats, the son twisted to look up at a man standing behind their pew and wiggled his fingers in a gesture of "Hi" with a guttural groan. If he could have smiled, he would have. The man smiled down at him. Then father and son stood to sing arm in arm. The look on the father's face in worship was heartbreaking in its earnestness and love: a smile with head and hand tilted upward in interpersonal oneness! I was stunned by such a deep example of the Father's love manifest in relationship. Here was this book's message found in the here and now: Father-led interpersonal oneness as reality!

What struck me, humbled me, was the father's way of being with his son—gentle, loving, or kenotic (self-emptying or self-offering) otherness.

This story captures a paradigm of Christianity. Love has no rejections, only redirections! Love is red; it bleeds for others! The Bible is God's personal love letter to us. I felt the spirit of the apostle Paul, of being willing to lay down my life for another. We all die, but how many of us live unconditionally in the here and now? The paradigm is a loving intimacy of pure and relentless acceptance shown in acts of selfless giving.

A paradigm is more than a worldview. It is a mental map of concepts, values, perceptions, and practices. For a community, their paradigm is a vision of reality. It is the basis on which a community reshapes and reorganizes its life. An individual may have a worldview, but a community has a paradigm.[1] A paradigm is often based on a vision—perhaps a vision of an ideal life, or a vision of a particular interest. And when change is necessary, a vision is a necessary motivator. In order to inspire congregations to become relational communities through love-based paradigms, a Trinitarian vision of reality is necessary. Vision in much of today's church is thing-ified. It tends to be made up of events and activities. In the Christian context, however, a vision should involve more than natural-level goals.

Walking out the true vision of the church requires being Spirit-formed. Jack W. Hayford likens those who are Spirit-filled to being like a typical hot-air balloon. Everyone looks about the same and is empowered to float and do what balloons do. However, being *Spirit-formed* is different. It is like the Macy's Thanksgiving Day Parade balloons. They too are filled so that they do what balloons do. But they are also *formed* into a recognizable likeness, such as Charlie Brown, Snoopy, Garfield, or any of the hundreds of Disney characters. So, as Spirit-formed believers, we are not only to be filled, but also formed so that people see Jesus when they look at us. Being filled helps us to do our balloon thing, but it is primarily focused on us as believers. Being formed means allowing ourselves to be Jesus so that others are attracted to him. It is directed outward rather than inward—incarnationally! *Becoming Spirit-filled may enable us, but being Spirit-formed enables him through us.*[2]

Spirit-filling is individual, whereas Spirit formation is corporate/communal. Becoming Spirit-filled enables us. Spiritual formation is a byproduct of Christ's love, which surpasses knowledge and fills us with the fullness of God ("to know the love of Christ which passes knowledge;

---

1. See Kuhn, *Scientific Revolutions*, for an extensive discussion on paradigms and paradigm shifts.

2. Hayford, Autumn Leadership Conference.

that you may be filled with all the fullness of God . . .";  Eph 3:19 TNKJV). Christ's love (as shared caring or compassion) is the engine of spiritual formation! When it becomes about a community being enabled through him, we have a new vision, a paradigm shift.

This illustration helps to explain the difference between just wanting the Holy Spirit to fill us, so we are more "spiritual" or "mature," and wanting to be Holy Spirit–formed incarnationally. This distinction must be made in today's church, because just wanting the Holy Spirit to fill individuals can easily become a self-centered focus. The church should not be defined by an individual man or woman of the hour with the power! If many are inclined to see Spirit-filling as Christ enabling me, then we are missing the distinctive element of Christian spiritual formation: Christ himself.

If we see Spirit formation as Christ being enabled to love through us in a Trinitarian-like community, then we may see a breakthrough paradigm shift in the church. At stake here is the inner logic of being the body of Christ, his community, consisting of persons both filled and formed, with Jesus as the head. Incarnational thinking and way of being is what Christianity is all about.

The prevenient vision of Christianity has to do with Spirit-formed persons as a way of incarnational being in community. This communal Spirit formation allows Christ to partner with us—to be yoked with him, so to speak (Matt 11:30). This relational partnering leads to his transforming purposes. So, the larger question that this chapter leads into is: "What is the basis for Spirit formation that leads to cultural transformation?" Church leaders need to make the paradigm shift from spirit-filled community to Spirit-formed community. Only a filled *and* formed spiritual community can transform culture! But the motivation and outcome will be misdirected if one does not have the right paradigm or map in one's Christian head.

Paul's message and methodology were driven by his motivation that he would go down for Spirit-formed people, whom he referred to as his joy and crown (1 Thess 2:20). Paul had a passion that made his message penetrate other people's hearts because he was not preaching from his mind but his heart! He used the word picture of a mother nursing her child to convey his motivation in ministry: "but we cared for you the way a mother cares for her children. We loved you dearly. Not content to just pass on the Message, we wanted to give you our hearts. And we did" (1 Thess 2:7). "We were gentle among you as a mother feeding and caring for her children" (TLB). "So, being affectionately desirous of you, we were ready to share with you not only the gospel of God but also our own selves, because you had become very dear to us" (1 Thess 2:8 ESV). How many ministers have we met in our lives that felt like this about their people? "With each of you we were like as a father with his child" (1 Thess 2:12). Paul not only had the message of his Lord; he had the heart of his Lord. In effect, Paul said, "I was not only ready to give you the Gospel. I was ready to go down for you!"

Limitless love is recursive (hearing another's voice, heart, and commitment) and reciprocal *kenōsis* (reciprocal communion views personhood as emerging from interpersonal and dynamic oneness). It is kenotic, gracious self-giving, and not individualistic! Love is only love when it is shared. Love does not function when limited to a single individual. Love, by nature, is perichoretic. Love exists in community rather than in individuals. As Pastor Len Vander Zee put it:

> . . . let's start here: At the center of all reality, at the heart of the universe, there exists an eternal divine community of perfect love. The Bible calls this community the Father, the Son, and the Holy Spirit. There's a certain logic to trinitarian belief. The Bible says that God is love, but the only way God can be love is for God to be a community of divine persons. Love does not exist in a monad. God is that eternal community of love.[3]

In this way, God is love only as Trinity. Richard St. Victor (d.1173) chose the preposition "between," rather than "in," when discussing love.[4] Victor writes:

> Love cannot be love if there is not a beloved. That love must be mutual is required by the fact that supreme happiness cannot exist without the mutuality of love . . . a further analysis of the nature of true charity reveals that three persons, not two, are necessary. For charity to be excellent, as well as perfect, it must desire that the love it experiences be a love shared with another . . . Thus, charity is not only mutual love between two; it is fully shared love among three.[5]

---

3. Zee, "Holy Trinity."

4. Zinn, *Richard of St. Victor*, 47–48. Zinn also observes with insight that this view of love is most nearly paralleled, in our own century, in the writings of the Oxford "Inkling" Charles Williams.

5. Richard St. Victor was a twelfth-century spiritual writer. Although Richard was best known and most influential as a writer on Christian spirituality, he was also the author of several works of theology, the most original of which was his *De Trinitate*. Baron, *Hugue et Richard de Saint-Victor*, 49. Richard argued that God is in fact a

Victor's insight here is that the Trinity perfectly captures the divine attributes of love and charity. In *De Trinitate*, he said that true love always necessitates another who can receive that love.[6] Love requires two entities, for it exists between, not in. And genuine love will always extend to share and include, which necessitates the participation of a third entity. The Trinity, therefore, demonstrates the paradigm of love and charity that must be present and expressed in the Christian community.

Spirit formation, like personhood itself, occurs in community, not individualistically. The word "saint" does not appear in the New Testament in the singular. It is always plural. The New Testament is about him in "we," as self-emptying otherness or community. Spirit formation will involve discipling as a mutual communal-formation process. The implication is that our Spirit-formation strategies must be communal. Being spirit-formed enables him through his body. Loving others is loving Christ and loving Christ is loving others. Paul said it succinctly: "For everything we know about God's Word is summed up in a single sentence: Love others as you love yourself . . . Stoop down and reach out to those who are oppressed. Share their burdens, and so complete Christ's law" (Gal 5:14; 6:2).

Why should church leaders move toward this shift? The most significant paradigm for Spirit-formed friendship is the divine pathos—the manifestation of the Father's care and concern. God's people should serve as extensions of the care and concern that God has (or is), because we have embraced the Father in the Son. One hug from God, and the rest is details. And once hugged, we can hug. Godly compassion means being moved to action. It is giving people in need a cup of water, binding wounds, and providing food and shelter.

When we follow Jesus as a friend, we enter into moments of conflict as opportunities for ministry. We become involved for the purpose of healing or helping the hurt or brokenhearted. Real ministry means becoming involved in the lives of people. Love is a verb. God acts in unconditional love, but never reacts. Again, love has no rejections, only redirections!

---

*Trinity* and not a *Binity* of persons. Why must God be a Trinity of persons? Richard argues from *his notion of perfect love*. "Though he stresses the equality and symmetry of the persons, the geometry of Richard's doctrine of the Trinity is not that of a triangle but rather that of a straight line: a line, moreover, to whose structure the *filioque* is integral!"

6. Ribaillier, *Richard de Saint-Victor*, I.20.

The church's curriculum is people. God so loved the *kosmos*, not just the church (John 3:16). The Creator Father brought the universe into being through a motivation for communion. The Trinity itself, in its dynamic of love, forms the basis of relationship between beings with their Creator.[7] Relational exchange—of love, not mere knowledge—is at the heart of our coexistence with God as Trinity, as one personal way of being to another. Jesus acted out of divine pathos. As Eugene Peterson renders John 1:18, "This one-of-a-kind God Expression, who exists at the very heart of the Father, has made him plain as day" (John 1:18). Jesus came from the Father's heart to be his heart in us.

To move the church toward this relational way of being, we must identify and utilize transformational paradigms. The right paradigm, taught and pursued in a congregational community, will establish a holistic map leading to incarnational thinking and living. Three such paradigms are explored here.

## THE ABBA PARADIGM

The church must be the foremost example of Jesus' relational dynamic in the earth. God desires a formed community that reflects his character.[8] As Horrell points out, the teachings of the New Testament address the believer's relationships with others more often than the believer's relationship with God.[9] A church without deep friendships and interdependent relationships is failing in its calling to reflect the character of Christ. The Trinity does not function by rules, but from love. The church must do the same if it is to reflect the genuine nature of God.

The Western church tends to focus on conduct (behavior modification), rather than first principles of motivation (why we do what we do). Accordingly, it operates from a weak *why* structure, and lacks a sense of purpose and vision. Jesus gave us his core value and life cause when he said in John 14:28, "the goal and purpose of my life is Father." Being Father-led was Jesus' way of being. The extent to which Abba is not our core value is the extent to which we are not Christlike. If the Father was the goal and purpose of Jesus' life, should it not be the goal and purpose of the life that is Christian? Often, however, the will of God is merely

---

7. Gunton, *Father, Son and Holy Spirit*, 24.
8. Fee, *Paul*, 66.
9. Horrell, "Self-Giving Triune God."

understood as a calling to a country, conduct, or character. The astounding idea that Abba—as person and relationship—is the central revelation of the New Testament is largely unknown, ignored, or downplayed in the Western church. The results of this lack is nearly catastrophic for the heart of Christianity in the West.

When Jesus uses his signature word *Abba* to describe the heart of the Father, a sense of awe should ripple through our hearts. *Abba* (אַבָּא) is a tender Aramaic child's word, meaning "Precious Father." It is the symbol of a close, personal, intimate, caring and profound being in relationship, a life-long partnership experience. Jesus was Abba-centered. To be Abba-centered is to be Christlike. Paul echoes this view when he discusses the Spirit of adoption, which cries out of the deepest recesses of a true believer, "Abba Father" (Rom 8:15). To be Abba-centered is an expression of Spirit formation. Again, the degree to which we are not Abba-centered is the degree to which we are not Christlike.

C. Baxter Kruger, President of Perichoresis Ministries in Jackson, Mississippi, gives an illustration of this relational stance.[10] As he waited at the airport for his brother, he noticed another man about his age standing there, looking up at the monitor and then out the window, then back. This man was waiting for somebody too. When Baxter looked out of the windows, he could see the jetways to the planes. He was watching this man, of all the people there, for some reason. He saw a little bit of blond hair bouncing in the jetway—a boy. He thought that little boy must be the one for whom the man was waiting. All of a sudden, the little boy saw his dad, and everything went in slow motion for Baxter. The dad took three or four steps. The son ran. It was an event. An embrace of sheer delight! Sheer welcome home–ness! A sense of awe rippled through the airport. As Baxter sat there and watched, God spoke to him as clearly as he had ever heard: "That's the resurrection! That's my son coming from the very pit of hell with all haste to meet me." And that Child embraced his Abba, and the good news is that he had the world in his heart. That is the Abba connectivity, and that is the gospel![11]

Appropriate here are Brennan Manning's best and eloquent inputs on the Father theme in the Hebrew Bible and the Father-Son paradigm in the New Testament.[12] Manning expounds upon the premise of Joachim

---

10. Kruger, "Real Christian Life."

11. Kruger, "Real Christian Life."

12. I had the pleasure of meeting my charismatic hero, Richard Francis Xavier Manning, known as Brennan Manning (April 27, 1934–April 12, 2013), an American

Jeremias—distinguished New Testament professor and scholar of Near Eastern studies at the University of Göttingen, Germany—that Abba is the central revelation of the New Testament. Brennan Manning eloquently states:

> listening to the Rabbi's [Jesus'] heartbeat is immediately a Trinitarian experience. The moment you press your ear against his heart, you instantly hear Abba's footsteps in the distance. I do not know how this happens. It just does. It is a simple movement from intellectual cognition to experiential awareness that Jesus and the Father are one in the Holy Spirit, the bond of infinite tenderness between them. Without reflection or premeditation, the cry, "Abba, I belong to You," rises spontaneously from the heart. The awareness of being sons and daughters in the Son dawns deep in our souls, and Jesus' unique passion for the Father catches fire within us. In the Abba beggars' speech. As our hearts beat in rhythm with the Rabbi's heart, we come to experience a graciousness, a kindness, a compassionate experience we prodigals, no matter how bedraggled, beat-up, or burnt out, are overcome by a Paternal fondness of such depth and tenderness that surpasses our understanding. That is the enigma of the gospel: How can the Transcendent Other be so incredibly near, so unreservedly loving.[13] We have only one explanation—the Teacher says that is the way he is.[14]
>
> Wise men and women have long held that happiness lies in being yourself without inhibitions. Let the Great Rabbi hold you silently against his heart. In learning who he is, you will find out who you are: Abba's child in Christ our Lord.[15]

Abba was a Jesus landscape. His relationship with his Father was reality. The nature of the unilateral covenant (the faithfulness of the Father) is best illustrated through the Abba paradigm. The central revelation of the New Testament is that Jesus and the Father exist only *in* each other. What is true in eternity is true in the incarnation—the Word of God is with God and the Word is God. The Abba paradigm illustrates the truth that we realize our individuality, identity, and destiny in and through the Sonship of Jesus, in connection with the Fatherhood of God, and only

---

author, laicized Catholic priest, and world-renowned public speaker.

13. Gray, *Jesus*, 69.
14. Manning, *Abba's Child*, 168.
15. Manning, *Abba's Child*, 171.

then in and through each other (John 17:21). Thus, communion or community with the Father, through the Son, and by the Holy Spirit is the basis of spirituality—being in relationship that is Spirit-formed. The Abba paradigm is the central revelation of the New Testament ("new covenant" or *kainē diathēkē*) view of God and a satisfying explanation and fulfillment of the Hebrew Bible view of God as יהוה, his sacred Name.[16]

## THE PARACLETE PARADIGM

Both Jesus and Paul provide models of a way of being stemming from participation in Abba's life. This way of being is a serving partnership with God and with community. The example set by Jesus became a sign and a wonder to a wounded world. His kenotic heart of a friend and servant reached out first to connect personally, then to help and comfort, and finally to function together. This way of being is encapsulated in the Greek term *paraclete*. This word is used to describe the Holy Spirit, and it means "one who comes alongside and comforts."

A powerful image of this idea is the expression of care seen in whales. They travel in pods and offer help and support to one another. With empowering presence, they carry their wounded babies on their backs or support them through miles of ocean with a supportive fin. This is exactly what the Holy Spirit does for us. And further, the Holy Spirit's empowering presence is ascribed to us. Paul says, "For you did not receive the spirit of slavery to fall back into fear, but you have received the Spirit of adoption as sons, by whom we cry, 'Abba! Father!' The Spirit himself bears witness with our spirit that we are children of God" (Rom 8:15–16 ESV). But dig deeper.

> Paul is not saying that the Holy Spirit bears witness to my spirit that I am a child of God, but rather that the Holy Spirit witnesses, *with* my spirit, that I am a child of God. In other words, at the same time that I am praying and calling God my father from within my Spirit, the Holy Spirit is doing the same thing from within me so that there are two who call God Father every

---

16. The true pronunciation of these four Hebrew letters has possibly been lost, but *Yahweh* is an English-styled version of them. It is important to note that some in the Orthodox Jewish community view *Yahweh* as a distortion of God's real name. Regardless, the writings of the Hebrew Bible (both Old and New Testament) confirm יהוה and Abba as teaching a covenantal way of being. These twin concepts capture an ontological definition of Christianity and represent the controlling theme of the Bible.

time I pray, the Holy Spirit and my spirit. It's a dual evidence of my sonship. When I call God Father, the Holy Spirit is witnessing right alongside me. He's saying yes . . . Father. He's yours. He belongs to you.[17]

In fact, the whole Trinity "paracletes," defends, or comforts us. As Thomas F. Torrance put it, "God is a fullness of personal Being within himself, just as he is full of Love within himself."[18] Abba paracleted Jesus. Jesus paracleted his disciples. If we understand how this relational approach to each other shapes lives in profound direction, we will mostly likely change how we approach church leadership and parenting.[19]

In 2 Corinthians 1:3–7, Paul uses the word *paraclete* as a noun and a verb, meaning "comfort," ten times. By repeating it, Paul is emphasizing in a compelling and vivid way that the whole Godhead can stand beside a person to encourage when one is undergoing severe testing. As Philip E. Hughes says in his commentary on 2 Corinthians:

> This work of encouragement is indeed a work of the blessed Trinity: as Paraclete, the Father comforts and consoles us; as Paraclete, the Holy Spirit strengthens and guides us (John 14:16, 26: 15:26; 16:7—Greek); and as Paraclete, Jesus Christ the righteous is our Advocate with the Father and our helper in the hour of temptation (I John 2:1; Heb 2:18—Greek). The present tense of the verb shows that this God of ours comforts us consistently and unfailingly, not spasmodically and intermittently; and he does so in all our affliction, not just in certain kinds of affliction. If one person knew the experimental proof of this great assurance it was the Apostle Paul, who later in this same epistle justly speaks of himself in comparison with others as "in labors more abundantly, in prisons more abundantly, in stripes above measure, in deaths oft" (2 Cor 11:23). And the comfort God gives enables the Christian not only to endure, but even to rejoice "in weaknesses, in injuries, in necessities, in persecutions,

---

17. Jeremiah, "Ministry of The Holy Spirit." Sermon given on the television program *Turning Point*, July 31, 2021.

18. Torrance, *Christian Doctrine of* God, 133.

19. See Marty Folsom's discussion on "Paracletic Life and Ministry" in *Face to Face*, 3:352–60. This was fairly groundbreaking work that brought together the Trinity and paracletic ministry. The only other reference to paracletic ministry is in Ray Anderson's work *Shape of Practical Theology*, 189. Marty started using the phrase in 1992, so Ray Anderson and Marty Folsom are pioneers worth mentioning.

in distresses, for Christ's sake" (2 Cor 12:10), so dynamic and vitalizing is its effect.[20]

Rather than being anthropocentric—that is, being all about humanity in a self-absorbed manner—we must become God-centered, paracleted by the Trinity. We must live without separation from the Godhead. Only then we can discover who we are. Growth comes from knowing God's love and expressing it, not being self-focused. This is why the kenotic paraclete paradigm is so necessary.

We must begin with who the Trinity is, for in the "jewel of theology" is the outline of life itself. We access the reality of the Trinity through Christ. That is, we can begin to comprehend the Trinity through Christ, or Christ through the Trinity. The *perichoresis*, or "mutual indwelling," is expressed in the concept of paracleting. God's own revealing of himself to humanity can be seen as an act of paracleting. In 1 Corinthians 2:2–16, Paul discusses how God makes himself known. He does not do it through human wisdom; he does it through his Spirit. The Spirit knows the depths of God and delivers his understanding to humanity. God also reveals himself in Jesus Christ. Christ knows the Father and the Holy Spirit in the most intimate of ways, and he paracletes us into the Trinity's relation of oneness (Matt 11:27; Luke 10:21–22).

We can only know God as he reveals himself to us. He has decided to do so through the heart of the Son, the communion of the Spirit, and the body of Christ. Knowing the depths of God occurs when we have communion with the Holy Spirit. Grace enables us to share those depths. Thus, we can mutually indwell the Son, the incarnate Word. And we can know the Father and be known by him.

## THE RELATIONAL ONENESS PARADIGM

Jesus spoke of the relationship between Father and Son as a mutual indwelling when he said, "No one knows the Son the way the Father does, nor the Father the way the Son does. But I'm not keeping it to myself; I'm ready to go over it line by line with anyone willing to listen" (Matt 11:27; see also Luke 10:21–22). The Father is everything the Son is, but he is

---

20. Hughes, *Commentary on 2 Corinthians*, 11. "The title Paraclete is not as such used of the Father in the New Testament, but its application to the Father is fully justified by Paul's terminology here, for . . . 'the Comforter,' the One who constantly comforts"—a timeless present participle (n. 12).

not the Son. The Son is everything the Father is, but he is not the Father. The Spirit is everything the Father is, but he is the Spirit of the Father. They indwell and interpenetrate each other in dynamic oneness—the real Trinity we can know. The relational oneness of mutual indwelling is a necessary paradigm for Christianity. The life of Christianity is found in participation and partnership with a person. Look at 1 John 1:1–3:

> That which was from the beginning, which we have heard, which we have seen with our eyes, which we have looked upon, and our hands have handled, concerning the Word of life. The life was manifested, and we have seen, and bear witness, and declare to you that eternal life which was with the Father and was manifested to us—that which we have seen and heard we declare to you, that you also may have fellowship with us; and truly our fellowship is with the Father and with His Son Jesus Christ.

"Participation" and "partnership" are the key words there. John's words must ever resonate in our being: "truly our fellowship is with the Father and with his Son Jesus Christ" (1:3). If the Christian reality is participation or partnership with the person(s) of the Trinity, then it is not enough to participate in a God-idea (a truth statement), or to partner with a thing. Consider the relationship with a spouse. One relates to a spouse as a person, rather than relating to the good idea of marriage. One fellowships with a spouse as a being, rather than fellowships with a thing, such as a marriage license.

It is far too easy to have an idea of God without relating directly to God. This is not what God wants from his believers. Persons meet needs, while ideas or things cannot. Relational interconnection is a network center of reality and is replicated through interpersonal relationships of love. True Christian revival will come when we get interconnected, interrelated, and interdependent with the Father, through the Son, by the Holy Spirit, and then with other persons. The Trinity plays in the field of the interpersonal.

A transactional or contractual approach to relationships is in opposition to this paradigm of relational oneness. Unfortunately, the bulk of the Western approach to relationships is based on contracts. Friendships, business relations, and even marriages can be seen as contractual realities. It is a "What can you do for me?" situation. Contracts are based in control, not trust. A transactional relationship allows each party to remain self-centered, and it focuses on the products (things) of the relationship, rather than the people in the relationship.

An unfortunate example of how the transactional approach might detrimentally affect Christian practices is seen in salvation and Communion. Salvation is not a transaction in which humans proclaim Christ's status as Savior in return for his perfect forgiveness. Salvation arises out of a relationship with Jesus Christ. It may be the starting point of a relationship, but salvation is not meant to be merely a "sign on the dotted line" experience. It is not the entry ramp to a freeway; it is the freeway! It is meant to usher us into a deep relationship with the Father through the person of Christ and by the person of Holy Spirit.

Similarly, Communion in American churches tends to be a Greco-Roman transaction or event, not a Judeo-Christian interrelational experience. Communion is meant to be an intimate moment with Jesus Christ. It is the partaking of his being in a deep, connective sacrament. It is not a business deal in which Jesus requires us to eat bread and drink wine in order to be forgiven. If Communion lapses into an empty ritual, this most transformational Christian act has become merely a business deal with Jesus: we do what he wants, and we get what we want. If the elements of Christianity are approached transactionally, rather than relationally, the very purpose of the Father in sending Christ is lost or ignored. We speak here of God's motivation of love in sending his only begotten Son (John 3:16).

True communion requires entering what T. F. Torrance called the "closed circle of knowing." This closed circle is the mutual intimacy of the Trinity, which can only be known when invited to see it from the inside. As Torrance states regarding Matthew 11:27:

> we learn that there is a closed circle of knowing between the Father and the Son and the Son and the Father. The Father and the Son are inherently and reciprocally related with one another in God in such an exclusive way that there is no knowledge of the Son except that of the Father, and no knowledge of the Father except that of the Son. And so, there is no way for us to know the Son except through the Father, and no way for us to know the Father except through the Son, unless a way is freely opened up by the Son for us to share in the communion of knowing within God himself. That is precisely what may happen through the revealing activity of Jesus Christ the incarnate Son and Word of God, for in him God has anchored within our own existence the mutual knowing which the Father and the Son have of one another, so that it is in union with him and through him that we

human beings may share in the knowledge which the Father and the Son have with one another.[21]

Christ and the Father have invited us into this closed circle of knowing by sending to us the Holy Spirit. In 1 Corinthians 2:9–12, we find that our reception of the Spirit shares with us the depths of God. The Spirit is God and knows God, and, positioned within us, the Spirit is able to bring us into an intimate communion with the Trinity. Torrance writes, "The Holy Spirit is the Spirit of the Father and the Son, who in being given to us enables us beyond any capacity of our own to participate in God's knowing of himself through himself, and thus really to know the one God in the inner relations of his divine being, as Father, Son and Holy Spirit."[22] The Holy Spirit is one with both Son and Father. Their relationships are both coinherent and reciprocal. Therefore, the Spirit interned within us enables access to the closed circle of knowing. One way this is expressed is in the language of adoption used by Paul in Romans 8:15. The Holy Spirit is the Spirit of adoption, who causes us to be counted as God's sons and daughters. The oneness we share with Christ is to such a powerful degree that we find ourselves in a similar Father-child relationship. The Holy Spirit amplifies the atoning and reconciliatory work of Christ in our life.

The "closed circle of knowing" is not a legal relationship but a dynamic one. After being away from home for some time, would you rather embrace a marriage license or a person? The marriage license may contain proof of a relationship, but it is not the relationship itself. Perhaps the license does not make mistakes, and it does not hurt you, but it is only a lifeless statement of legal truth. The real truth of the marriage (truth of being) is lived out by the couple. It is found while being in the relationship. This speaks to the paradigm of relationship. Participating in the relationship is the life of the marriage, just as participating in the relationship with the Trinity is the life of Christianity.

## CONCLUSION

Paradigms for transforming the church are needed to give us holistic maps that lead to incarnational thinking and living. The three incarnational paradigms examined here are focused on the larger question:

---

21. Torrance, *Mediation*, 116.
22. Torrance, *Mediation*, 116–17.

"What is the basis for Spirit formation that leads to cultural transformation?" Church leaders need to make the paradigm shift from getting a Spirit-filled community to being Spirit-formed. Only filled *and* formed spiritual community can transform culture! But the motivation and outcome will be misdirected if one does not have the right paradigm. The church needs an incarnational, recursive, or kenotic map. Interpersonal oneness leads to his transforming purposes. However, the church must institute new ways of being that encourage interpersonal oneness, through the paradigms of Abba, paraclete, and relational oneness.

## REFLECTION

1. How do you respond to J. Scott Horrell's assessment that "the largest percentage of imperatives in the New Testament do not address the believer's relationship directly to God, nor his relationship to the world, but his relationship to others in the local church"?[23] Why is this a significant insight?

2. How would you describe the process of Spirit formation that would lead to cultural transformation?

3. Of the three paradigms discussed in this chapter, which one resonates the most with you, and why?

---

23. Horrell, "Self-Giving Triune God." See Houston, "Community and Nature of God," chapel lecture no. 2526 (recording), Regent College, Vancouver, British Columbia (cited in Horrell). See also Gunton, *Promise*, 81–85; O'Donnell, "Trinity as Divine Community," 5–34; and Plantinga, "Perfect Family," 24–27.

# 9

# The Defining Relationship of Christianity

## INTRODUCTION

> Picture a rabbi sitting at the head of a Bar Mitzvah table, with his kippah or yarmulke, thick black beard, black suit, white shirt, tie. His wife and children are eating dinner with him. Midway through the meal the rabbi's four-year-old son, bored with the adult conversation, gets up and wanders fifteen feet away from the table. Then he loses his bearings. Not knowing where he is, in minor panic, he turns around, spots his father at the head of the table, and goes running as fast as his little legs would carry him. Two feet from the table, he flings himself on his father's lap and shouts, "Abba, Abba."[1]

IN THE PREVIOUS CHAPTER, we reviewed three Scriptural paradigms that, if implemented, could transform the Christian church. These paradigms are all central to the proper understanding and functioning of the church, but none more so than the Abba paradigm, which will be explored in depth in this chapter.

---

1. Manning, recording of conference at Alderwood Vineyard, October 1989, Tape 1.

The Abba paradigm comprises more than simply a view of God as Father. The Abba paradigm is the central revelation of the New Testament (or new covenant) view of God as revealed in Jesus Christ. Further, it is a satisfying explanation and fulfillment of the Hebrew Bible's view of God's sacred name (יהוה). The true pronunciation of these four Hebrew letters has possibly been lost, but *Yahweh* is an English styled version of them. It is important to note that some in the Orthodox Jewish community view *Yahweh* as a distortion of God's real name. Regardless, the writings of the Hebrew Bible (both Old and New Testament) confirm יהוה and Abba as teaching a covenantal way of being. These twin concepts capture an ontological definition of Christianity and represent the controlling theme of the Bible.

The basis for true Spirit formation, participation, and partnership that transforms culture is sonship. This concept is captured in the Father-Son paradigm and communicated in the term *Abba*. T. F. Torrance explicates a framework for spiritual formation as "trinitarian participation," which corrects "spiritual formation programs that are christologically stunted."[2] "Spiritual formation must be theologically grounded in *trinitarian* christology, in contrast to approaches that are more human-centered and more virtue-oriented or imitation-driven."[3]

We can begin to discover that Abba is the defining relationship of Christianity by asking three questions:

---

2. Ziegler, "Is It Time?," 76. "Thomas F. Torrance (1913–2007), who sadly is not as well known or read in the United States as he deserves to be, offers a deep theological vision permeated through and through by its grounding in trinitarian theology as one of mutual love between the Father, the Son, and the Holy Spirit. Torrance is widely considered to be the greatest British theologian of the twentieth century, and by more than a few as the most significant English-speaking theologian of the second half of the twentieth century. Regardless of rankings, the fact that Torrance was able to publish more than 600 works during a career spanning six decades undeniably establishes him as a scholar's scholar and a theologian's theologian. The significance of Torrance's intellectual contribution is demonstrated by the steady appearance of scholarly analysis of his thought over the last three decades of the twentieth century. Reflection and application upon Torrance's theological works have only increased since his death in 2007. Torrance's theological vision carries significant implications for the who, why, and how of Spiritual formation."

3. Ziegler, "Is It Time"

## 1. WHAT IS THE NEW TESTAMENT VIEW OF GOD?

When the disciples request that Jesus teach them their own special prayer, Jesus' response begins with *Abba* (Matt 6:9). The Lord's Prayer is the quintessential Christian prayer, and it establishes the major elements of the Christian life. The disciples, and we today, are meant to address God as "Father." Christ extended his intimate relationship with the Father to include the disciples, and all those who pray in the name of Jesus. The four-letter word *Abba* is one of the central, primary revelations of Jesus Christ in the New Testament. It opens up the possibility of "undreamed-of, unheard-of intimacy" with Father God in prayer.[4] Joachim Jeremias, the great Lutheran theologian, notes that Abba "is the presence of the kingdom even here, even now. It is a fulfillment, granted in advance, of the promise."[5]

Actually, the word "Father" applied to God is found only fourteen times in the Old Testament, possibly because we do not have the revelation of the Son until the New Testament. There we discover that Jesus began nearly every prayer with *Abba* (except one)—twenty-one in all, or sixteen if the parallels are counted together. *Abba* is consistently the first prayer word of Jesus. In addition, Jesus refers to God as "Father" 170 times in the Gospels. There is no doubt that "Father" was Jesus' designation for God. This is particularly true in the Gospel of John, wherein "Father" becomes almost a synonym for God.[6]

Jesus' special use of the Aramaic word *Abba* can be appreciated when one notes that not only in the Hebrew Bible, but in Palestinian Judaism in the time before Jesus, there was a great reluctance to speak of God as "Father." Joachim Jeremias concluded, "To date, nobody has produced one single instance in Palestinian Judaism where God is addressed as 'my Father' by an individual person."[7] Matthew deliberately uses "Father" forty-four times in his gospel to make the point that things have changed. To address God as *Abba* was very unusual in Judaism, since *Abba* was the language of family intimacy.[8] As James D. G. Dunn,

---

4. Manning, recording of conference at Alderwood Vineyard, October 1989, Tape 1.

5. Jeremias, *Parables of Jesus*, 190.

6. Jeremias, *Central Message*, 23.

7. Jeremias, *Central Message*, 16.

8. Dunn, *Jesus and the Spirit*, 22. The word *abba* (אַבָּא), a common form of *av* (אָב), meaning a parent, "father" in English, is adopted from the Syrian Aramaic as is,

the Lightfoot Professor of Divinity at the University of Durham, England, comments on the significance of Jesus' word for God:

> The significance of this address to God is clear. The OT has made us familiar with the Hebrew concept of fatherhood as implying a relationship of care and authority on the one side and of love and obedience on the other (Deut 1.31; 8.5; 14.1; Isa 1.2; Jer 3.19; Mal 1.6). 'Father' for the Hebrew denoted 'absolute authority and tenderness'. Significantly, both of these aspects find clear expression in the Gethsemane prayer. This, together with his more negative attitude to traditional Jewish worship, strongly suggests that Jesus' calling on God as 'Father' was the language of experience rather than a formal address. It was his experience of God which found expression in the *Abba-prayer*. It was because he found God in the experience of a love and authority which constrained him as from beyond that he addressed God as 'Father'.[9]

Given his contention that we do not have a single example of God being addressed as *Abba* in Judaism and that Jesus addressed God this way in his prayers, Jeremias concludes that Jesus' Abba prayer expressed an unusual sense of intimacy and becomes a *"fact of fundamental importance"*[10] for his self-understanding, for Christian theology, and for the historical Jesus. Although some would argue that Jesus' use of *Abba* was not unprecedented, as there are some examples of a Jew saying "my Father" to God,[11] we can say that *Abba* was Jesus' signature word for God

---

according to the Academy of the Hebrew Language (https://hebrew-academy.org.il/):

In Aramaic the ending ah אָ originally signifies a definite article "The", the word then would be Av אָב father, with the ending אַבָּא meaning 'the father'. For example, מַלְכָּא (Mal-kah) would be הַמֶּלֶךְ (Ha-Melekh) meaning 'The King.' עָלְמָא (al-mah) would be הָעוֹלָם (Ha-Olam) meaning 'The World.' This ending became inseparable part of the word and is used even in names that are not characterized with definite article.

The terms אַבָּא father and אימא mother and סבא (sa-bah) grandfather, and סבתא (sab-tah) grandmother, were adopted as is, including the ah אָ ending and used for parents but without adding in writing or in spoken Hebrew the definite article. Nevertheless, אֵם וְאָב (Em and Av) 'mother and father' are still used as well.

9. Dunn, *Jesus and the Spirit*, 22. Cf. Ceroke, "Is Mark 2:10 a Saying of Jesus?," 369–90.

10. Bultmann, *History of the Synoptic Tradition*, 158.

11. Dunn, *Jesus and the Spirit*, 26.

and his regular way of approaching him, and this appears to have been unusual in his day.[12]

Interestingly, the one time when Jesus does not use the familial *Abba* when addressing God was in his agony on the cross. In that moment, he did not feel the closeness with God that he normally felt, and thus addressed him as "God." As James D. G. Dunn has it:

> It is significant that the only occasion we know of where Jesus did not use Abba in prayer to God was in his cry of dereliction on the cross (Mark 15:34)—in his awful experience of *abandonment* by God he could not cry 'Abba'. It is difficult therefore to escape the conclusion that Jesus said 'Abba' to God for precisely the same reason that (most of) his contemporaries refrained from its use in prayer—viz., because it expressed his attitude to God as Father, his experience of God as one of unusual intimacy.[13]

The early Christians' experience of sonship—a term that encompasses both genders—was understood as an echo of Jesus' own experience. Romans 8:5 and Galatians 4:6 clearly imply that it is precisely the Spirit of the Son who cries "Abba." Dunn concludes that "This reinforces the testimony of the gospel traditions that the Abba-prayer was the distinctive characteristic of Jesus' own prayer."[14] Jesus did not want his Father-Son relationship to be unique to him. While this relationship with the Father is available with the same intimacy on display with Jesus, it is still dependent upon Jesus himself. Jesus is the door to the Father and is the only one who knows the Father. He chooses, however, to include us in this beautiful intimacy.[15]

---

12. Dunn, *Jesus and the Spirit*, 23.

13. Dunn, *Jesus and the Spirit*, 23.

14. Dunn, *Jesus and the Spirit*, 22.

15. Dunn, *Jesus and the Spirit*, 26. See Mcray. "Abba." Mcray agrees that Jeremias' studies on *abba* are significant for Jesus' self-understanding, for Christian theology, and for the historical Jesus. Yet he suggests that caution needs to be exercised in accepting his conclusions because he feels that Jeremias argues from silence and has not proved that *abba* necessarily always lies behind the Greek for "father," and that he assumes that the Synoptics are antecedent to the Fourth Gospel.

However, Dunn nicely balances the matter: "This conclusion, however, does have to be qualified at two points. First, it is not in fact true that we have no examples of a Jew saying, 'my Father' to God. I am thinking here particularly of Ecclus. (Ben Sira) 23.1, 4: that the Greek πάτερ is like the πάτερ of Jesus' prayers (except Mark 14.36) and denotes a sense of intimate trust, is strongly suggested by Ecclus. (Ben Sira) 51.10. We cannot therefore maintain that Jesus' use of *abba* was *unprecedented*. Of course, 'Abba' was not simply an occasional usage by Jesus, rather, so far as we can tell, his *regular* way

## Part II: Why Is It Important to Define Reality?

We must ask, though: Can the tenderness in the Aramaic word *Abba* be heard in the spirit of a Westerner? Are there barriers in our culture and in our worldview that prohibit us from finding this experience of God as Father that is so desired for us by Jesus himself? Perhaps we can sympathize that Jesus' contemporaries were offended by Jesus' Son-Father relationship with God.[16] If so, we should strive to overcome this hurdle and accept Jesus' invitation.

It is interesting to note that the intimacy of Abba finds stark contrast to the unuttered personal name of God (*YHWH*). His sacred name was never pronounced in Judaism in a reverential desire to never take it in vain.[17] However, doing so caused a religious emotional distance between

---

of speaking to God in prayer. All we can say then is that when we compare the literature available to us, Jesus' regular approach to God as 'Abba' appears to be *unusual* for his day."

Second, Hans Conzelmann, in *Jesus*, points out that *abba* need not have had a connotation of familiarity:

> This is quite true. Jeremias does note that *abba* was used in the pre-Christian period as a respectful address to old men. But this usage is clearly an extension of the family usage. The more regular and typical use of *abba* at the time of Jesus was within the family and did express family intimacy. Obviously, it was precisely because of this note of intimacy that *abba* was so little used by Jesus' contemporaries in addressing God. More important, this is the note which is present in the uses of *abba* in the NT (Mark 14-36; Rom 8:15; Gal 4:6), as in Matt 11:25; Luke 23:46. In all these cases 'Abba/Father' expresses more than respect viz., childlike confidence and obedience. It is significant that the only occasion we know of where Jesus did not use abba in prayer to God was in his cry of dereliction on the cross (Mark 15-34) in his awful experience of abandonment by God he could not cry 'Abba'. It is difficult therefore to escape the conclusion that Jesus said 'Abba' to God for precisely the same reason that (most of) his contemporaries refrained from its use in prayer viz., because it expressed his attitude to God as Father, his experience of God as one of unusual intimacy.
>
> It would appear then that Jeremias has pressed his argument too far. But nevertheless, much of value remains from his researches. In particular, we are not being over bold if we conclude that Jesus' use of *abba* enables us to see into the heart of his relationship with God as he understood it. The divine reality he experienced in those moments of naked aloneness was God as Father. This experience was so vital and creative that it had to find expression in an address to God which would have sounded shockingly familiar to the great majority of his contemporaries. We may presume that this language alone could express the unusual intimacy he found in prayer the intimacy, trust and obedience of a child with his father.

16. Manning, recording of conference at Alderwood Vineyard, October 1989, Tape 1.

17. Payne, *Theology of the Older Testament*, 147. My professor asserts: "Next, when the medieval Jewish scholars, the Masoretes, began to write in vowels to accompany the consonantal Old Testament text, they added to the original consonants of Yahweh

## The Defining Relationship of Christianity

the human and God. Jesus eliminated that emotional distance by calling him "Father" and encouraging believers in Christ to do the same. As Brennan Manning writes:

> Until Jesus' revolutionary approach to God as Father, God was most often understood to be transcendent, ineffable, unapproachable. To Plato and Aristotle, he was the impersonal first cause, or the unmoved mover. For the prophets of Israel, God was mighty, overpowering, holy. They knew him as a covenant relationship, the One who is faithful and personal. However, in spite of all their visions and encounters with God, none of them knew God as Father. To a Jewish mind, it would have been irreverent and, accordingly, unthinkable to talk to God in tender terms like, "Our Father."
>
> What Jesus Christ is teaching his people is that we may dare to address God—the God under whose presence Moses had to remove his shoes because he was standing on holy ground; the God from whose fingertips this universe fell; the God beside whose beauty the Grand Canyon is only a shadow; the God beside whose power the nuclear bomb is nothing—we may dare to address this infinite, transcendent, almighty God in baby talk, with the same intimacy, familiarity and reverence as a sixteen-old-month baby sitting on his father's lap calling, "*da, da,* daddy."[18]

The particular address of *Abba* as a terminology is less important than what it signifies. It signifies not only a fundamental change in the human relationship with God, but also the availability of an intimate relationship with the God formerly known from afar. All of the best qualities we could imagine of the pinnacle of fatherhood or motherhood would pale in comparison to the person of God the Father. In his love, patience, kindness, goodness, understanding, compassion, and commitment, the Heavenly Father is unparalleled to the point wherein he is impossible to describe in human language.

Paul picks up the Abba theme in his concept of the Holy Spirit as the Spirit of adoption in Romans 8:15. It is the Holy Spirit who allows us to cry out to God by addressing him as *Abba*. All who have received Christ have received the Holy Spirit (Eph 1:13). In this way, the Father-child

---

the Masoretic vowel points of Adhonai, and the actual written result became the impossible Y-H-W-H."

18. Manning, recording of conference at Alderwood Vineyard, October 1989, Tape 1.

relationship is available to any who have received Christ's salvation. God's person as Father is a fundamental part of the gospel, and we must recognize it as such. The average Christian should feel the closeness and encompassing love of the Heavenly Father as a matter of course. Our prayer life, our expressions of worship, and our acts of service should all reflect this fundamental truth of the relationship inaugurated and made available by Jesus Christ himself.[19]

If Christians see God as the supreme divine being, they would not be wrong, of course. In Christ, however, that view is rather incomplete. If we do not know God as Father, there is a missing element in our Christian life. But more than that, it also reflects that our true knowledge of Jesus is lacking. Jesus himself wants to include us in this intimate relationship. If we are stuck in a paradigm that sees God as personal, but only in a contractual way, then we are not relating to the God of Jesus, to God as Father. Personally, and communally, Christians must attempt to get past this roadblock of an incomplete view of the Christian God. As Jesus said:

> All things have been transmitted to me by my Father.
> And as only a father knows his son
> so also, only a son knows his father
> and he to whom the son wants to reveal it.
> (Matt 11:27; Luke 10:22).

Jesus wishes to reveal the Father to us. We must be willing, however, to learn a new way of relating to him. Jesus' distinctive way of addressing God implies a unique sense of sonship: "the sense that God cared for him as an individual with a fatherly care, the sense that he had a filial duty to God which no personal wishes could set aside (Mark 14:36)..."[20] But this relationship is not just a unique artifact of Jesus' person as the Son of God. Jesus wants us to take on his signature word for God, to live it out as children to our Heavenly Abba, and in doing so we find ourselves as members of God's divine family, seeing each other as brothers and sisters living together in Abba's care. And then, from that place of sonship and daughterhood, we serve our neighbors, extending the same relationship we have found with the Father to others.

---

19. Manning, recording of conference at Alderwood Vineyard, October 1989, Tape 1.

20. Dunn, *Jesus and the Spirit*, 26.

## 2. WHAT IS THE MISSION OF THE ABBA RELATIONSHIP?

*Abba* does not just represent an intimate relationship with God the Father. *Abba* is also a word with the ring of destiny in it, the sense of distinctive mission and purpose, foreshadowed in messianic expectation:

> He shall cry to me, "Thou art my Father,
> my God, and the Rock of my salvation."
> And I will make him the first-born,
> the highest of the kings of the earth. (Ps 2:7)

The connection made here between Jesus as Son and Jesus as King is dramatic. The Abba relationship was not only a sweet, intimate relationship, but is also directly associated with Jesus' status as King of kings. Jesus' ultimate fulfilment of his authority in the earth cannot be divorced from his role as Son. His Sonship was not a dignity to be claimed, but a responsibility to be fulfilled.[21] Out of his sense of Sonship came the confidence to fulfill his mission. In Matthew 11:27, we find that Jesus was conscious of being a distinctive "recipient and mediator of knowledge of God."[22] As Dunn has it:

> In the same way and for the same reason, 'Abba' became the expression of the complete surrender of Jesus as son to the Father's will (Mark 14:36). In other words, Jesus' consciousness of sonship was probably a fundamental element in his self-consciousness out of which his other basic convictions about himself and his mission arose. To put it another way, this experience of intimacy in prayer gave Jesus his deep insight into both the character and the will of God. These insights probably lie at the heart of his unique claim to authority.[23]

Out of his sense of Sonship, Jesus counted on his Abba to be there for him for every needed compassionate word, deed, and miracle. Jesus lived from Abba's covenantal faithfulness and took on his mission to include us in sonship. Out of Sonship came his sense of compassion, as an expression of the Father's lovingkindness (*hesed*).

The primary basis for mission springs from knowing God in an intimate way, as Abba. Just as Christ was motivated by love to include all

---

21. Fuller, *Mission and Achievement of Jesus*, 84.
22. Joachim Jeremias, *Prayers of Jesus*, 51.
23. Dunn, *Jesus and the Spirit*, 39.

of humanity in the Father-Son relationship, so too must we be reflections of that motivation and mission in our own participation in the Abba relationship. As James D. G. Dunn writes of Jesus' relationship with the Father, "out of this intimacy sprang the compulsion to bring others into the same living relationship [Spirit formation] with God as Father (Luke 11:2; 'your Father'; Luke 22:29; Matt 11:27)."[24] This relationship imbues Christian experience and Spirit formation with its dynamism. Our partnership with God is about bringing others into sonship with Abba Father where profound intimacy, loving approval, interdependence, and response-enablement (rather than performance-oriented responsibility) truly lives. Such bonding, attachment, and basic trust is the bedrock and glue of healthy person formation.

However, when invitations for the gift of salvation are extended throughout much of today's church, the emphasis is more on getting a deal rather than receiving a gift—a release from the guilt of failure or escaping future punishment, and less (if at all) on entering into dynamic sonship with a waiting Father who loves, lifts, listens, leads, and never leaves! When the *what* comes before the *Who*, the order of grace tends to be inverted and Spirit formation eclipsed. Our guilt can get in love's way or our being there for others.

So, think and live a balanced life from the grace-gifted future in Abba Father (the *Who*), like a Mount Rainier in your vehicle's windshield, and the rearview mirror (the *what*) as your past. Our biblical ethos is that "out of every greatest problem can appear the greatest promise. Out of every obstacle we can find the greatest opportunity."[25] We can triumph over tragedy. This is our new birth certificate.[26] Trey Gowdy, hosting "Sunday Night in America," asks, "What is the right balance between the pain, the past, the present, and the promise of tomorrow?"[27] Senator Tim Scott answers:

> "I wish that we would spend more time in that big windshield that we are driving than we do in the little rearview mirror. The past is something that teaches us but some place that we don't dwell. Too often we are dwelling in the past, not for its lessons but almost reliving it as if 1855 and 1955 are somehow embedded in 2021. I think the ratio for the past, the present

---

24. Dunn, *Jesus and the Spirit*, 41.

25. Sen. Tim Scott, R-SC, on unity and the state of America, on *Fox News*, June 6, 2021.

26. Sen. Tim Scott, R-SC, on *Fox News*, June 6, 2021.

27. Trey Gowdy, "Sunday Night in America," on *Fox News*, June 6, 2021.

## The Defining Relationship of Christianity

would be the big windshield representing the present. The little rearview mirror represents the past. It should teach us, but we shouldn't dwell there. We can't wallow in it. There are some very important lessons, painful lessons. Lots of people bear the scars of that pain but the burden of living there is too high of a price to pay. And the more time you spend in the past, the less time you spend in the future.[28]

In our mirroring of Christ's missional foundation—that is, the Abba relationship—we must also recognize that it is a Trinitarian endeavor. Jesus' ministry functioned out of his understanding of himself as God's Son and as anointed by the Spirit.[29] In other words, Jesus' missional attitude springs from Trinitarian waters: the Father-Son relationship, and the empowering of the Holy Spirit. While the Abba relationship stands at the center of Christ's ministerial acts (John 5:19[30]), it cannot be divided from its Trinitarian ecosystem. We must live out Jesus' Trinitarian approach to mission—to share his Father's remarkable compassionate love.

Evangelism should be relationship oriented, rooted in the Trinity, and expressed in a Father-child dynamic. Jesus experienced sonship in a direct and distinctive way, out of an intimacy expressed in Abba. Jesus, the One for the many, represents the many. There is, therefore, a collective sonship available to God's people.[31]

Paul's writings reveal that the first Christians were aware that the two primary relationships of Christianity—to God the Father and Jesus as Lord—were enabled by the Holy Spirit (Rom 8:15; 1 Cor 12:3). Early Christians understood the Trinitarian relations at the foundation of their faith. Thus, the anchor points for the doctrine of the Trinity are that it is grounded "in the experience of Spirit, Spirit as Spirit of sonship, Spirit as Spirit of the Son."[32] The Holy Spirit makes us conscious of the Trinitarian relationships, and enables these relationships in a spiritual manner. Indeed, Sonship births Jesus' self-emptying compassion for the world. Now partnership has its clear agenda. Likeness has its context. For to be

---

28. Sen. Tim Scott, R-SC, on unity and the state of America, on *Fox News*, June 6, 2021.

29. Dunn, *Jesus and the Spirit*, 67.

30. Dunn, *Jesus and the Spirit*, 67: "the Son can do nothing by himself; he can do only what he sees his Father doing, because whatever the Father does the Son also does."

31. Dunn, *Jesus and the Spirit*, 39.

32. Dunn, *Jesus and the Spirit*, 326.

like God is to be compassionate. That is who God is. That is who Christ is in us. That is his mission through us, compassion that births a sense of true sonship.

## 3. HOW DO WE LIVE IN THE ABBA RELATIONSHIP?

Obviously, my dad was not God. And neither was yours. My dad was there for me, but he was also not there for me. I knew he was not perfect, but he still had the ability to hurt me or let me down, simply because he was a human being. But even if our fathers drop the ball, we end up in Abba's arms anyway (Ps 27:10)! When you end up in the Father's arms, you can forgive anyone—even a dad who could not give what he did not have. I learned I could not continue to over-expect from my dad given his life experience. Near the end of his life, I wanted to hug him and close the loop, but he died near the Canadian Rockies on me one twenty-seven-degree-below-zero day in March.

As young children, it is easy to see our fathers as perfect. They are the strongest, the smartest, and the best. But as we grow older, we recognize their imperfections. That experience of disillusionment can be hurtful enough on its own. But as Mike Hayes writes, "We tend to put Dad on a pedestal and look at him as a source. But he isn't God! If he hurt you, if you came down the stairs and you spun around in the living room in your new dress, and you desperately needed him to look from behind the paper and affirm you and he didn't, forgive him."[33] It is inevitable that your father let you down, disappointed you, or hurt you. We cannot avoid those experiences in life. We must be willing, however, to do two things: forgive our fathers, and refuse to allow their failings to influence how we see the Heavenly Father.

Forgiveness of our earthly fathers is the first step toward finding the deep relationship with Abba. If we cannot move past our prior hurts in the father-child relationship on a human level, how can we possibly find a healthy Father-child relationship on the divine level? Through forgiveness and the restoration of trust, we can find the willingness and openness we need to experience the relationship with Abba.

Relatedly, in wanting to trust and love people again, we must reconnect with the parts of us that have gone into hiding due to injury. When we are mocked about something personal, we tend to put that thing into

---

33. Hayes, "We Cry Abba."

hiding to avoid being mocked again. If we go out on a limb and express a love for a hobby or a desire to pursue certain projects, and our passion is either diminished or ignored, our response is to disassociate with that passion, even when it is a fundamental part of who we are.

It can be a painful process to come out of hiding, to uncover the personal things we have buried, or to address our denial. Developing safe and healthy relationships is ever so important in repairing injury. Many times, these issues stem from our relationship with our fathers. Perhaps he misspoke, or perhaps he did not realize that what you were expressing was so important to you. Or perhaps he was jaded and obstinate and lashed out of his own hurt. Either way, the effects can be lasting. But they must be addressed, or they will end up prohibiting or tainting our relationship with the Heavenly Father. As Mike Hayes explains it, we cannot accept sonship or daughtership from God if we have an unforgiving heart. We cannot accept the Father's blessings when we are opposed to our own father.[34] For this reason, the healing of our hearts in our relationships with our earthly fathers is of utmost importance in creating a deep relationship with Abba.[35]

An important point that helps us in this process is to recognize that Jesus specifically bundled our pain of abandonment with his on the cross. He knows what it feels like to be abandoned by the One he trusted the most. While on the cross, he cried out "My God, my God, why have you forsaken me?" (Matt 27:46) That moment was not just an expression of his doubts or his volatile emotion. He truly felt it. This is a moment that has the potential to free us from our own sense of abandonment. If you feel your dad was not there for you when you needed him, Jesus' own experience of abandonment on the cross can remove it from you. He knows the feeling, and he moved past it. Jesus can carry your hurt, so you do not have to.[36] Believe in Jesus' cleansing of this for you and choose forgiveness and healing.

Once we have received our healing and restoration, and have established our own Abba relationship, then we can turn around and help others into their own healing and restoration. As John Calvin writes, "No one gives himself freely and willingly to God's service unless, having tasted his

---

34. Hayes, "We Cry Abba."
35. Hayes, "We Cry Abba."
36. Hayes, "We Cry Abba."

fatherly love, he is drawn to love and worship him in return."[37] As those in the church, we are meant to carry one another into the arms of Abba. By finding our own intimate relationship with the Father, as Jesus had, we can then do as Jesus did and bring others into sonship and daughtership.

The restoration of the father-child relationship in all our lives goes beyond the benefits of emotional healing. The healing and connection between fathers and children is prophetically connected to the end times. In Malachi 4:5-6, it is prophesied that the ministry of Elijah would return to restore the hearts of the fathers to the children and the hearts of the children to the fathers. *The Message* Bible translates it this way: "But also look ahead: I'm sending Elijah the prophet to clear the way for the Big Day of God—the decisive Judgment Day! He will convince parents to look after their children and children to look up to their parents. If they refuse, I'll come and put the land under a curse." The restoration of earthly relationships between parents and children is important to God, precisely because it has such a profound effect on our relationship with him.

## CONCLUSION

This chapter explored three questions about a Christian Abba paradigm. First, what is the New Testament view of God? Second, what is the mission of the Abba relationship? Third, how do we live in the Abba relationship?

Jesus' use of *Abba* embodied an intimate Father-Son relationship, and it represented a major shift in the Judeo-Christian relationship with God. Jesus is the model of all Christian behavior, and therefore his view of God should be adopted by all believers. The New Testament view of God does not replace or abandon God's status as creator and king, but rather emphasizes Jesus' work to initiate a new personal, intimate, and familial connection with God.

The relationship embodied by the Abba paradigm is missional. Just as Jesus' earthly ministry was driven by the vision and leading of his Father, so too should Christian mission today be similarly motivated. Christlike evangelism should reflect the attitude of Jesus and be relationship oriented, rooted in the Trinity, and expressed in a Father-child dynamic. Accordingly, Abba is the defining relationship of Christianity.

However, in order to properly experience God as Father, all believers must be sure to sort out their view of their earthly fathers. Our

---

37. Calvin, *Institutes* 1.5.3.

experience as children will deeply influence our conception of a fathering relationship. If we are not careful, we could easily project the problems (e.g., detachment issues resulting in emotional distance) of our earthly fathers onto God. For this reason, believers must accept forgiveness and the healing work of Christ in order to enter into a pure Father-child relationship with God.

## REFLECTION

1. Do you agree that the Abba paradigm is the central revelation of the New Testament (new covenant or *kainē diathēkē*) view of God and fulfillment of the Hebrew Bible view of God as יהוה? If not, why not?

2. How would an Abba-centered approach to Christian formation contrast with the American gospel of self-actualization, self-achievement, and self-fulfillment?

3. How would an implemented Father-child paradigm transform the culture of your church? How would it transform the culture of your community at large?

4. How do we help those who have experienced abandonment by a father and project their attachment issues onto Father God?

## Trinitarian Relationship

# PART III

## How Do We Experience Reality?

Do nothing out of selfish ambition or vain conceit, but in humility consider others better than yourselves. Each of you should look not only to your own interests, but also to the interests of others.

—Phil 2:4

How is interpersonal oneness released in us? How does the Holy Spirit, who makes us conscious of a Trinitarian relationship, love through us?

We need to develop and practice a practical theology of interest satisfaction as applied relational leadership.

# 10

# Releasing Interpersonal Oneness through Interest Satisfaction

## INTRODUCTION

ONCE WE HAVE A biblical worldview, we can be motivated to develop and practice a practical theology centered on self-giving relationship, rooted in Trinitarian connection. We will find that interpersonal oneness is exercised in mutual interest satisfaction. Caring about satisfying the interests of the people around you is an other-centered attitude that cultivates the ways and means by which the Father loves through us. Interest satisfaction is how the Spirit makes us conscious of the Trinitarian relationship as both theological truth and model of behavior.[1] We can be motivated to release interpersonal oneness through interest satisfaction by considering several aspects of paradigm and practice.

## THE PARABLE OF THE ORANGE

A mother walked into her kitchen to find her daughters screaming at each other and tugging back and forth on an orange. Both daughters said

---

1. The author's interest-satisfaction approach, as applied relational theology, is extensively developed in two unpublished texts: Pinkham, "Truth and Truthfulness," and Pinkham, "Pastor as a Change Agent" (2002).

they wanted the orange, and it was unfair that the other was not giving it up. Mom, applying a Solomon solution without the wisdom, sliced the baby in half with a butcher knife and exclaimed, "There, the problem is solved!" She left the kitchen, ready for some peace and quiet. It never came. The two girls continued to argue, but now over two halves of an orange. The mother's solution did not work because she did not truly understand the problem.

Had the mother listened for the interests or needs of her girls and asked one important question—"Why do you want the orange?"—she could have solved the problem. It turns out that one daughter wanted the skin to make an orange-flavored icing for her cake, while the other wanted the fruit to eat. They had two different interests that were not mutually exclusive! One daughter wanted the pulp, the other the peel. Mom framed the problem in terms of a simplistic problem: there's only one orange, so who gets it? And even though the problem required more understanding, it was easier to solve than the mother's simplistic version.

The point? The cardinal principle of relational conflict management is that we need to allow the interests to drive the discussion of issues or positions to avoid getting into strife. As the former Secretary of State Henry Kissinger once said, "America has no permanent friends or enemies, only interests."

When lecturing in Hong Kong, I gave an orange to each student in a conflict-management seminar. I asked them what it was. They looked at me like my cheese had slid off my cracker. I asked, "An orange? A gift? A paradigm? A map? A parable? Or all of the above?" Then I told them the parable of the orange.

So, in this chapter, we are handing you a proverbial orange. Please treasure it and place it in your proverbial display case for your proverbial friends and family to see. We must all have an orange that reminds us of Philippians 2:4: "Do not merely look out for your own personal interests, but also for the interests of others" (NASB).

## A PRACTICAL THEOLOGY OF INTEREST SATISFACTION

Once we recognize the fundamental importance of relationships in Christianity, it naturally leads us to the realization that we need to develop and practice a theology of interest satisfaction. How do we love like the Father? How do we become God's love, as Christ was? We do so through a Christ-based theology of interest satisfaction. Interest satisfaction is one of the most practical ways to act in a Christlike, self-emptying manner. It is a primary expression of interpersonal oneness, and it is a way by which the Spirit makes us conscious of Trinitarian relationship and loves through us. Interest satisfaction is therefore a model of Father-led interpersonal oneness.

Before providing the biblical basis for interest satisfaction, we should clarify what we mean by it. Consider the parable of the orange, which sets the table for us because it illustrates the basic idea of how to listen for the interests of others.[2]

The parable of the orange emphasizes the difference between strife and conflict. Strife is purely negative, while conflict is not. Conflict is normal, natural, necessary, and neutral. It can energize, sharpen, and mature us. Strife, however, is destructive aggression that emerges from discord, misunderstanding, and the refusal to listen for interests and needs. When we listen for the interests of others, we are validating *who*-ness, because we are focusing on the person. On the other hand, attempting to solve the issues at hand validates *what*-ness by focusing on the problem. Asking "Who is to blame?" or "What caused this?" is a defensive and accusatory perspective. It is reactionary, rather than reformative and relational. Strife therefore emphasizes problems over people.

What-ness encapsulates the view that reality is made up of things, ideas, and rules that we must navigate properly in order to be valued, accepted, and loved. What-ness leads to a static and fragmented spirituality. It is a view of God that does not address the *who* of God. This becomes a paradigm in which right living is all about right doing and right thinking, without prioritizing love and relationship. What-ness alone, therefore, defaces the image of God, and turns the loving, personal Jesus into a concept. We need listeners in the church who are orange peelers not orange splitters!

Relational Christianity is about listening for and responding to the interests of others—starting with Father God! It is about being led by the Holy Spirit and the attitude of listening for God's interests. Asking Jesus,

---

2. Fisher et al., *Getting to Yes*, loc. 1246–47. Adapted. "Yet all too often negotiators end up like the proverbial children who quarreled over an orange. After they finally agreed to divide the orange in half, the first child took one half, ate the fruit, and threw away the peel, while the other threw away the fruit and used the peel from the second half in baking a cake."

"What would you do in this situation?" leads to responding to God's interests. Doing the right thing starts with a relationship to the One who dictates what is right! Listening for the godly interests is therefore a practical way to walk out Jesus' prayer that God's will be done (Matt 6:10).

Listening for the interests of others is also a practical way in which to walk out the second greatest commandment: to love others as we do ourselves (Mark 12:31). We are called to become orange peelers, and not orange slicers. Orange peeling is interest satisfaction, which leads to genuine Christian community. By learning to listen and place the interests of others above our own, we give the Holy Spirit more room to work in our relationships. Common sense is not so common. It seeks common ground. Common interests create common ground. Loving others in this way helps solve problems in such a way that relationships are enhanced, rather than diminished.

This way of life is characterized by love expressed in *kenōsis* (see Phil 2:5). *Kenōsis* is the action of emptying ourselves for the benefit of another. It is a selfless attitude that subordinates our desires to the needs of another. When practicing *kenōsis* in relationships, it leads to free self-limitation and free self-expenditure.[3] According to W. H. Vanstone, an English parish priest, "Christ's self-emptying (*kenōsis*) in his incarnation, far from impairing the fullness of his revelation of God, contains the very heart and substance of that revelation, which is of a kenotic God who is ever self-giving in authentic love."[4] Christ's self-emptying is precisely what allowed the perfect union of humanity and divinity in his being. In Jesus Christ, God and humanity are united in mutual and gracious self-giving love.[5]

It must be emphasized again that the act of *kenōsis* as described above does not entail a negation or diminution of God's nature, as some kenotic Christologies mistakenly taught.[6] It is the very nature of God to be self-giving, other-affirming, and community-creating. The Trinity is defined

---

3. For a more comprehensive examination of the historical development of the concept of *kenōsis*, see Martin, *Hymn of Christ*.

4. Vanstone, *Love's Endeavour, Love's Expense*, 22, 39–54.

5. See Richard, *Kenotic Christology*. See Zachariades, "Διπλην Επαγγελιαν": his thesis is that "Athanasius advocates a 'double account of the Savior' approach to explaining the Person of Jesus Christ, which may be utilized to offer an alternative Christology to those encountered in Kenotic proposals."

6. Gunton, *Act and Being*. Gunton critiques the use of negative (apophatic) theology in the construction of the attributes of God.

*Releasing Interpersonal Oneness through Interest Satisfaction*

by relationship. Life in mutuality does not diminish but defines the reality of God. In the eternal life of God there is interaction and exchange between Father and Son in the uniting love of the Spirit. The unity of the triune God is a union of kenotic, reciprocal, and self-giving love. God's essential way of being is to go outward-bound in kenotic otherness, to be self-giving and self-offering, to bond within us, and to show up as shared love in our lives. Thus, "all knowledge and action are for the purpose of friendship."[7] Again, as Jesus said, "I've named you friends because I've let you in on everything I've heard from the Father" (John 15:15).

Graham Buxton, following Irenaeus, suggests it is far more helpful to accentuate the positive and interpret the incarnation as a positive filling (*plerōsis*) of personhood, rather than a negative emptying *(kenōsis)* of the Godhead. "So, we might follow Iraneus's suggestion that Christ filled the manhood with and much of the Godhead as he was able to bear, in the same way that a skilled carpenter, working with the grain and capacities of the wood in his hands, exploits them to the full as a craftsman in woodcarving."[8] In this way, we must recognize that any act of self-emptying, when done in relation to God, will lead to filling. In other words, the emptying is done for a purpose, which is to be filled by God. This is also true in relationships in which *kenōsis* is the guiding principle for both parties, for if all in Christ's community maintain kenotic attitudes, then we can be sure that our own interests and needs will be addressed.

## INTEREST SATISFACTION IN CHURCH LEADERSHIP

Nowhere is the concept of interest satisfaction more applicable than in the church setting. Church leadership should be concerned with community formation, not with the mere management of things. Dietrich Bonhoeffer (1945), a German pastor, theologian, spy, anti-Nazi dissident, and key founding member of the Confessing Church, viewed community formation as a descending gift from God.[9] Thus, the key question: What must be in the soil of congregational life so that genuine Christian community may descend from above? Our answer? Relational interest

---

7. Folsom, *Face to Face*, 3:382.

8. Buxton, *Dancing in the Dark*, 22.

9. Bonhoeffer viewed community as God's gift of himself in Christ to us, not the result of a Xeroxed twelve-step program. Bonhoeffer, *Life Together*, 21.

satisfaction! We must look to the model of Christ as King, who administrates relationally by the leading of the Holy Spirit and the Word of God.

Christlikeness in leadership will therefore be founded upon interpersonal oneness and expressed in interest satisfaction. Wise leadership is one of those essential roles—along with prophetic preaching and priestly pastoral roles—that helps shape the witness of Christ's people to God's work among them. These church roles embody and express the caring love of Jesus' lordship. When we talk about wise leadership, we are referring in a contemporary way to the ministry of Christ the King as caring for his people. Any sort of authority or leadership in the Christian context must reflect Christ's person and must rely on Christ's lordship.

One of the New Testament Greek words behind the idea of administration is *kubernesis*, which carries the metaphorical meaning of "steering the ship away from rocks and reefs."[10] Even Hans Küng, an excommunicated Catholic theologian, put his finger on this need in the church today:

> Particularly in the storm, particularly in the towering difficulties and a hopeless situation, the tossing and rolling ship—it is a question of human beings—needs us to *remain in* all truthfulness, *to share in steering it.* Believing and trusting, to try *in the ship* to secure what has worked loose, to stop up leaks, to bring the ship back to the right course laid down by its Lord, to make it seaworthy again. Should not this be possible?[11]

How do leaders of today's church steer her correctly? Through a practical theology of interest satisfaction or wise rule, an ontological administration of the kingly office of Christ. Through a pastoral view that emphasizes interpersonal oneness in all aspects of the church.[12]

Governance is an activity that is practical, concrete, and a profound expression of theological reflection. Protestantism has overemphasized the

---

10. The Greek word *kubernesis* means "helmsman" or "governor." "All of its uses in Scripture refer to leadership and administration in some form of secular enterprise, except where Paul impregnates the word with spiritual meaning and church context in 1 Corinthians 12:28. (Other uses appear in Proverbs 1:5; 11:24; 24:6 of the Septuagint and Acts 27:11 and Revelation 18:17 in the New Testament.) It is a clear carry-over of the idea of organizational and superintending leadership. The administrator is the [one] who is qualified to direct the ship. Kittel puts it well when he refers to the Christian who is 'a [helmsperson] to his congregation, i.e., a true director of its order and therewith of its life'" (Kittel and Fredrich, eds., *Theological Dictionary of the New Testament*, 3:1036). Gangel, "Gift of Administration," 20.

11. Küng, *Truthfulness*, 60, emphasis added.

12. Cartledge, *Practical Theology*.

prophetic-preaching and priestly-pastoral (worship, prayer, and counseling) roles, neglecting the kingly office of Christ.[13] However, leadership in the relational domain of the church is neglected at the peril of Christ's perfect love. We should intentionally pursue Christ's wise rule in our churches and make it an integral aspect of the ministry of pastors, lay leaders, and church members. Wise rule is about preserving the headship of Christ in his church and seeing his person and nature in the church community.

While the Western church generally appears to operate in a contractual manner, a biblical mindset rejects that in favor of Spirit-enabled participatory interest satisfaction. What has been traditionally called "church administration" or "strategic servanthood leadership administration" (its theory and practice) tends to be a secular/human creation that is built on Western cultural, contractual, and transactional pragmatism that results in "mechanistic individualism"—self-generation, self-actualization, self-fulfillment, and self-perfection. Such a focus on self-approval is naturally antithetical to the growth of community, which is built on relationships.[14] Individuals may be the basic building blocks of community, but individuals with a self-focus will never coalesce into genuine community.

---

13. When we view the total ministry of Christ as a higher doctrine, we can see why interest satisfaction is a balancing factor and a practical way to be community and do wise rule. We can appreciate one of Calvin's major distinctions. He described the office (function) that was assigned Christ in his ministry as having three parts: *prophetic*, *priestly*, and *kingly* (Calvin, *Inst.* 2.15.1–6, oS 111, 471–81). Calvin maintained that these *three* activities were necessary for our knowledge of God's work in Christ and for receiving the benefits of this work: the prophetic office (prophesying, preaching), the priestly office (worship, intercession, counseling, etc.), and the kingly office (wise rule, administration, governance). We must emphasize that the *prophetic* (preaching) *priestly* (counseling, prayer, worship), and *kingly* (wise rule) offices were all essential in the witness, sharing, and expression of God's work in Christ and in caring for God's people.

We have tended to split the office of Christ, putting the emphasis on the prophetic and priestly activities and so devaluing the kingly office. Is the King dead? Is his headship protected and preserved in the Western church? Thus, there is a need to resurrect a major understanding of Christ's ministry in order to emphasize that practical theology with regard to administration or wise rule is a profound theological activity. Wise rule is about preserving the headship of Christ in his church—the kingly office—through the spiritual gift of *kubernesis*, metaphorically depicted as "steering the ship away from rocks and reefs."

14. As Zizioulas elaborates: "as each person becomes a member of the church, they bear the 'image of God' and take on His way of being, which is the 'way of *relationship* with the world, with other people and with God, an event of *communion*, and that is why it cannot be realized as the achievement of an *individual*, but only as an *ecclesial* fact." For a critical look at how closely Zizioulas links his anthropology with ecclesiology, see A. Torrance, *Persons in Communion*, 295–96.

We should not dismiss individual personhood, which is a prerequisite to interpersonal oneness, but we should not overemphasize it either.

There is certainly a tension between the importance of interest satisfaction—which seems to prioritize individual needs—and our warning against self-focus. We must remember, however, that the medium of interest satisfaction is relationship. Individuals do not focus on their own interest satisfaction. Rather, each person recognizes that others are made in God's image, that they are worthy of time and attention, and that God has called us to encourage, support, and care for one another. Interest satisfaction is therefore an inversion of the Western approach to self-focus in that each person sees the needs of others as being at least as important as their own. In the Christian context, interest satisfaction focuses on the other.

Interest satisfaction is motivating and personal. When someone experiences the attention and blessing of their interests being satisfied by brothers and sisters in Christ, that person will feel personally engaged, and will more likely make changes and participate in solutions on both an individual and communal level. Addressing interests can provide a growth focus in a personal manner. When people's priorities are addressed, it can give a real reason for behaviors to realign with core values. Addressing personal interests is an effective way to achieve structural change. Why? It unifies a church community toward personal interests and outcomes, which translates into communal interests and outcomes. As believers engage each other on a personal level, they will naturally define the problems to be addressed together as a community. In worship, Communion, preaching, counseling, and fellowship, church leaders should focus on community-based interest satisfaction. The church should not primarily be about getting things done, but about getting the relationships done in the love of God! By focusing on relationships, the conflict does not become the focus, and neither does the goal. However, the people become unified in addressing conflict and satisfying interests.

Further, church leaders should revisit their own hopes and commitments. Are your commitments aligned with your vision and your hope? Often, organizational needs may take precedence over spiritual needs, sometimes in invisible ways. When this occurs—and it occurs often—the church must engage in a process of revitalization. And this revitalization cannot occur unless the leader(s) are willing to address their own personal spiritual interests in an honest fashion.

Systems that prioritize anything other than God's people should be subordinated to systems that prioritize community. A relational focus can do this. Making interest satisfaction a priority can do this. Interdependent interest satisfaction pursued in the context of core values will realign congregational behaviors and create cultural transformation.

The usual single-variable approach to changing the culture of a church organization (e.g., targeting one avenue of change such as leadership styles, structure, information patterns, technology, climate, etc.) will not work. A culture is like a spider's web, held in place by numerous self-reinforcing strands that connect in complex relationships. For this reason, focusing on relationships is the simple answer to a complex problem. A kenotic-interest-satisfaction approach takes on the whole system through the unifying power of Christlike relationships.

## THE KENOTIC INTEREST SATISFACTION MODEL

The approach to church leadership we suggest could be described as the kenotic-interest-satisfaction model. This model involves exercising Christlikeness through self-emptying and the elevation of other people's needs. This approach is ontological, futuristic, and practical.

Kenotic interest satisfaction is an *ontological* approach, for it is both a way of being, and a perspective that respects and interacts with other people's being. As a way of being, it is not merely characterized by strategy, requirements, or even action, but rather is a lifestyle of the heart. Genuine kenotic relationships cannot be faked. Further, the ontological view of others in relationship recognizes and responds to their personhood. In other words, church members are not reduced to projects to accomplish or problems to solve, but are rather those who carry the image of God. People are ontologically valuable because they are our fellow brothers and sisters in Christ and are therefore deserving of love and attention. The Father is committed to supplying every need, and therefore concentrating on identifying interests and needs is a godly way of being. When we choose to react instead of listen, we choose to blame instead of applying the grace of God, and then we pay the price in the loss of intimacy, health, vitality, well-being, happiness, satisfaction, freedom, self-expression, passion, and creativity. If we want vitality in ourselves and our communities, we cannot lead by dominating or avoiding, by justifying ourselves and invalidating others. For this reason, church leadership and church community must be ontologically focused.

Framing life from our interest commitments is also a *futuristic* approach. One could say that it is prophetic, because it frames the future through relational activity today. The interconnected relationships of community are like a net, and a net cannot be pushed, only pulled. It must be guided by forward thinking. It must be guided by questions such as: what is the Father-led future the community wants to cocreate? And: what are the Father-led interests of the community that should be explored and answered together? The kenotic-interest-satisfaction model is also futuristic in that it does not rely on the past in guiding the future. Focusing on the past is a reactive and obligatory lens that is sure to ruin relationships. In Christ, everyone is a new creature (2 Cor 5:17). We should live in faith and hope in him, creating the future from his transcendent presence, protection, provision, power, peace, plan, and purpose. The truth is that what we cannot let live will not let us live. What we will not let be will not let us be. What we run from we will run into. Christianity is at its heart a religion of forgiveness. The church must reflect this core value. By letting go of the past and focusing on the promise of God's future together, we avoid destructive reactions and exercise proactive reframing.

Framing life from our interest commitments is also a *practical* approach with a benefit basket. It can result in *spiritual satisfaction* that facilitates Spirit formation. It can provide *procedural satisfaction* that gives order to the negotiation process prior to, during, and after a conflict-management process. It can bring about *substantive satisfaction* when the actual substance or content of a settlement agreement is framed from the love-based future we want to coinvent. Finally, it can give *psychological satisfaction* where people feel confident that agreements will not unravel once their issues have been resolved.

## An Example of This Model in Action

In the interests of what God was doing in our congregation when I was pastor of Forest Glen Church in Chicago, I asked my board members to take three sheets of paper, with no names, and answer three questions: (1) What do you see to be the strengths of our church? (2) What are the barriers that keep us from using our strengths to the fullest extent? and (3)

What specific steps can we take to overcome these barriers? Note the flow: positive, negative, positive. Then I asked them to circulate and read each page. On a whiteboard, we listed the strengths on the first page, weeding out duplicates, and praised the Lord for what he was doing among us. Then we listed the weaknesses, eliminating duplicates. Next, we recorded any suggested next steps minus duplicates. I closed in prayer thanking the Lord for our insights. I typed everyone's responses without corrections (I wanted members to see that I had not doctored their data) and their listed summaries. At the next meeting I distributed and reviewed the findings and asked them how we might complete the next steps. It took three months to do so. In that time frame we experienced a positive history of working together and the trust level came up. Our open, non-defensive, and authentic way of being with each other resulted in interpersonal oneness and community. In applying a biblical philosophy of management in a ministry situation, I had followed Myron Rush's suggestions: "Create a trust relationship between you and your group; give decision-making power to all individuals within the group; turn failures and mistakes into positive learning experiences for the group; constantly give proper recognition to the group and its individuals for accomplishment."[15]

Then I asked the board if we could have the choir ("Battle Stars Ecclesiastical") take the same three-pronged questionnaire. They balked. They did not want to open up "a can of worms." I indicated that I wanted to live on the knife-edge of time and suggested they might choose a board member to assist me in leading the process and that we would bring all responses back to the board. I wanted board members to compare their answers to the three questions with those of the choir to motivate their authorization for going to our entire congregation to sense the Lord's direction or vision for the next five years. They approved.

How does a pastor act as a change agent in the revitalization of an established congregation vs. starting a new one? The Forest Glen congregation experienced the four phases of the work process of revitalization that led to a more truthful church community (Diagnosing, Strategizing, Implementing, and Assessing):

---

15. Buxton, *Dancing in the Dark*, 24.

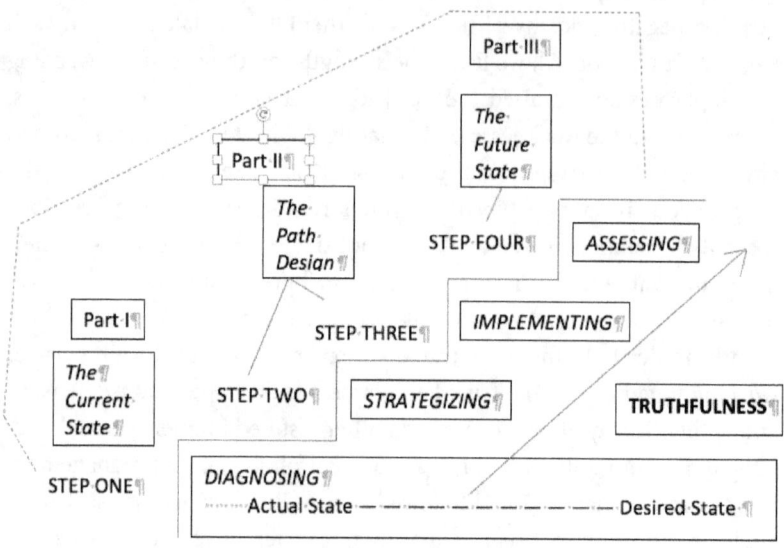

Figure 5: Steps toward Truthfulness

These are the phases of interest-satisfaction actions that I took with the congregation. The Forest Glen congregation experienced their pulling power and made systemic changes in their organizational culture.

The first actions by my intervention with the board (obtaining authorization and gathering their data and that of the choir) were illustrated earlier. These data sets were bumped together, causing conflict. When the board saw the disparity of interests between them, they began to own (buy into) the value of gathering personal perspective data from the congregation as a whole. During the entire process they saw how the old wineskins could not hold new wine. Thus, they had to align new structures to satisfy their interests, thereby becoming a truthful church.

The first revitalizing cycle took more than five years to complete. Revitalization was achieved as hopes and theological commitments were expressed, interpreted, and acted out concretely in this congregation's life.[16] These were formed by exploring the congregants' personal inter-

---

16. The process of interest gathering, the disparities within the church, and the author's interest-satisfaction approach as applied relational theology, is extensively developed in two prepublished texts: Pinkham, "Truth and Truthfulness" (2001), and Pinkham, "The Pastor as a Change Agent" (2002).

ests. Along the way, I provided timely and relevant biblical support for these theological commitments, mindful of Ray Anderson's caution:

> The leader is the servant of the mission of the people of God. This mission must be perceived as the "vision" that informs the goals and strategy of the people. The vision does not come through predicting what will come to pass in the future by reading past performance and extending present goals, but through reading the signs of the future in the present.[17]

Revitalization occurs through Father-led interest satisfaction distinguished by kenotic leadership, actions, and results.

Revitalization through an empirical interest-satisfaction or interpersonal-oneness process, diagrammed below, can be used as a guide at a weekend retreat or over a one-year term. But there is no Christian equivalent to instant coffee. Our children do not grow up overnight. It takes room and time for growth to occur. But love happens when shared. We are defined in community or family by substantiating limitless love, the currency of transformation.[18]

---

17. Anderson, *Soul of Ministry*, 474–76.

18. A pastor could support this revitalization effort by preaching/teaching on the Father-Heart Ministries (https://www.fatherheart.net/) themes: "We believe in experiencing Father's love and becoming his love. We value the closeness of His comfort & the joy of his approval. We celebrate the glorious freedom of the Sons of God." Such a message has implications for supporting the reorganization of a congregation's life.

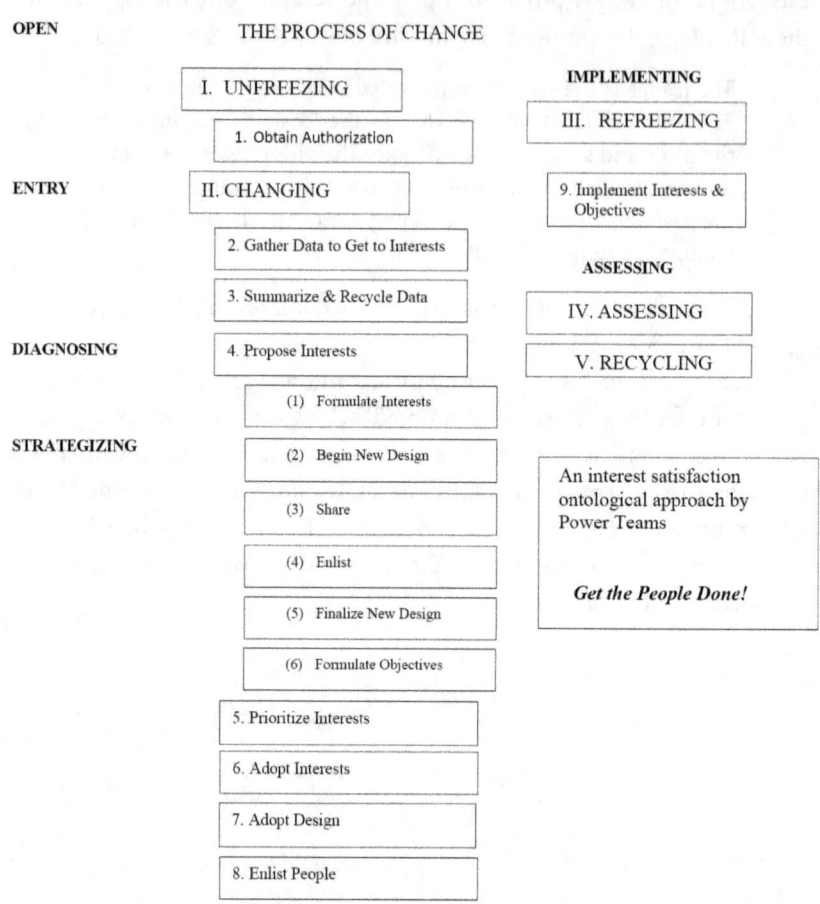

Figure 6: The Process of Change

## CONCLUSION

We can be motivated to release interpersonal oneness through interest satisfaction by developing and practicing a practical theology of interest satisfaction. Such a revitalization effort is possible, plausible, and probable in a church culture that prioritizes relationship. When we ascribe to a higher doctrine of Christ's Father-led ministry, we assume a way of being that is compassionate and other-centered. This is the practical theology of wise rule at its cutting edge.

## REFLECTION

1. Think about some recent or memorable conflicts you have experienced and review them through the lens of the parable of the orange. Are you able to see how you could have managed the conflict more successfully by becoming more aware of the other party's interests?
2. What practical steps might you take to discover and address the interests of others? Relatedly, are you able to articulate your own interests (values, needs, desires), and would you be willing to communicate these interests with others?
3. Why is sin essentially the loss and lack of community?
4. Think about situations in which you are a leader (whether in church, home, work contexts), and consider the idea that Christlikeness in leadership must be founded upon interpersonal oneness and expressed in interest satisfaction. What concrete steps can you take to implement the kenotic-interest-satisfaction model as a leader?
5. Revitalization of church and culture is possible, plausible, and probable if we accept the paradigm shift to a higher doctrine of Christ's Father-led, relational ministry. Do you agree? Why or why not?

# 11

# Living in Interpersonal Oneness

**INTRODUCTION**

How does one live from interpersonal oneness? This chapter explores the practical elements involved in exercising interpersonal oneness, beginning with the foundational importance of listening. Our God idea in this chapter revolves around these questions: (1) Why must we be good listeners? (2) Why is it imperative that we listen for the interests of others? (3) How do we listen actively and recursively? In other words, how do we listen to the voice, heart, and commitments of others?

**REALIZE THE IMPORTANCE OF LISTENING**

One of the ways to live in interpersonal oneness is to listen with the intent to prioritize our family's and friends' interests. We can express God's love by satisfying the interests of others. Some needs may be substantive content interests, such as money, time, goods, and resources. Other needs may be psychological interests, such as needs regarding emotions, how one is treated, and conditions for an ongoing relationship. Other interests may be procedural in nature, such as how one speaks or relates in the process of a relationship. Some interests may be about perspective, such as sharing and clarifying viewpoints, as well as proposed solutions to conflicts.[1] In all these cases, we cannot assume that we immediately understand or know anyone's desires or needs unless we listen. Without listening, our relationships will fail.

Our family doctor is a good listener. We had to find a new doctor a few years ago for various reasons, and we were given a list of potential physicians. One doctor's ad said, "My ability to be a good listener allows me to be a more compassionate physician." That sold me more than anything else! One of the greatest strengths in a physician is the ability to accurately discern and identify health problems. A key tool in that endeavor is listening to the patient.

Kevin, age five, was a good listener. His mother was preparing pancakes for him and his brother Ryan, age three. The boys began to argue over who would get the first pancake. Their mother saw the opportunity for a moral lesson. "If Jesus were sitting here, he would say, 'Let my brother have the first pancake. I can wait.'" Kevin turned to his younger brother and said, "Ryan, you be Jesus!" Kevin certainly knew how to apply lessons to his advantage!

In a study of the abilities managers considered to be most critical for their success, they rated listening as the primary competency to be developed. In another study, executives that were earning more than $250,000 a year were asked to cite the primary factors in achieving success.[2] Here is their list in order of importance:

1. Communication Skills
2. Intelligence
3. Integrity
4. Experience
5. Positive Attitude

It is important to note that these are all elements of emotional or relational intelligence, rather than technical or informational expertise. And the most important elements among these skills of success is communication, which begins with listening.

The key to goal achievement is communication. "We spend 70% of our time communicating with others. Of this communications time,

---

1. Pinkham, "Creative Conflict Management," 273.
2. Steel, "Primary Factors in Achieving Success."

we spend 16% Reading, 9% Writing, 30% Talking, [and] 45% listening."[3] We easily overemphasize the utility of words, but they amount to about 7 percent of communicated meaning in our interpersonal interactions and are often overridden by facial and vocal cues (body language pitch, volume, rate, quality, articulation, etc.). As Yaffe notes, "words are profoundly inadequate as a sole means of communication and the written digital platforms are converting back to what is common and that is that non-verbal signals are as important as words."[4]

Listening skills are critical for success in relationships of any kind. They occupy a large percentage of our communication behavior, yet no communication training toward developing active listening skills is given in our years of schooling! No training like this is given in seminary either. So, when it comes to communicating feelings and attitudes, the key component of listening is severely underdeveloped in the West.

## UNDERSTAND THE BIBLICAL VIEW OF LISTENING

Three good rules for communication are given in James 1:19: "You know this, my beloved brothers and sisters. Now everyone must be quick to hear, slow to speak, and slow to anger." First, be "quick to hear." This rule is about engaging in active listening. Being "quick" to do something means to do it readily. It should be the first thing we do in a conversation! The priority in any interaction should not be to talk, but rather to listen.

The second biblical competency is to be "slow to speak." This is an obvious corollary to the first rule. Listening should be prioritized, and speaking should be subordinate. This attitude gives proper attention to the other person in the conversation. Listening more and better enhances the prospect that what one says will be qualitative and congruent. Romans 12:10 teaches that we should "prefer one another," and this paradigm of conversation in James 1:19 gives a practical run down of what that means in conversation. Being slow to speak also means to choose your words carefully. Do not say something without thinking about it and asking the Holy Spirit to lead the conversation. Peter R. Garber offers four listening tips for preferring one another:

    3. Garber, *50 Communications Activities*, 9.
    4. Yaffe, "7% Rule." When dealing with feelings and attitudes, Albert Mehrabian's (currently Professor Emeritus of Psychology, UCLA) research suggested three elements of communication: 7 percent of meaning in words, 38 percent in tone of voice, and 55 percent in body language (the so-called 7%-38%-55% Rule).

1. Concentrate on what the speaker is saying, both with his or her words as well as with voice inflections, rate of speech, body language, etc. There are many things that can influence these communications and paying attention to as many as you possibly can help keep you focused.

2. Try not to think about how you are going to respond to the other person while he or she is speaking to you. This will cause you to lose your concentration on what the other person is saying.

3. Interact nonverbally with the other person with small gestures or verbal affirmations, such as nodding your head or saying very brief comments such as "I see" or other words that would not interrupt the other person. This tells the other person that you are fully engaged in listening and also keeps you involved in the process.

4. Do not interrupt or finish the other person's sentences. This takes your concentration completely away from what the other person is saying and focuses your attention on your own words.[5]

Third, James adds that we should be "slow to anger." This is an interesting addition to the first two rules because it almost seems out of place at first. A good conflict manager, however, will always encourage participants to be "slow to anger." Why? Because angry words wound people deeply. Angry words wreck friendships and family relationships. Angry words are out of line with the character of God. James does not say that we should avoid anger, but rather be slow to anger. It is okay to be angry. We should never deny our true emotions. But slowing down the process of anger allows genuine communication without inordinate reactions.

Also, Paul mandates that we listen actively: "let each of you esteem and look upon and be concerned for not merely his own interests, but also each for the interests of others" (Phil 2:4, Amplified). As humans with a sin nature, it is all too easy to be self-centered, even in selfless relationships! Perhaps we demonstrate selflessness when it comes to working hard to support our family or doing the necessary chores around the house. But do we also demonstrate selflessness by maintaining genuine interest in our spouse and children and parents and friends? Are we concerned for their well-being to the point that we have uncomfortable conversations, or that we listen to them when they talk about their hobbies

---

5. Garber, *50 Communications Activities*, 24.

that we do not care about? Be swift to hear about the passions of your sons and daughters.

This is all deeply related to the idea of *kenōsis*, which describes Christ's self-emptying. *Kenōsis* is about one's capacity to love selflessly. These admonitions in James 1, Romans 12, and Philippians 2 describe the kenotic attitude we must have as followers of Christ in relationship to others. Jesus came under his church and exalted her to the heavens to satisfy the Father's interests and to bless us, and he died that others might live. These were ultimate kenotic acts that should inspire and guide us. In the face of Jesus' *kenōsis*, can we respond in simplicity by being swift to hear and slow to speak? Can we prefer one another? Can we place others' interests above our own? These are Christlike, kenotic acts in miniature, but they mean all the world to the Father.

How do I teach best? I string stories (metaphors) themed together. Why? Stories are a way to discover truth. Sharing a story can be cathartic. Allowing one to laugh at shared frustration is healing—illustrating how understandable it is to get angry and snap. Stories connect with universal struggles because they connect emotionally and cognitively. Story has the ability to move the heart and open up the mind to truth. By the way, if Jesus were here, he would tell stories.

## FIND A PATHWAY FOR INTEREST AND NEED

Below, I will tell several stories that illustrate how one listens for the interests of others. So, these stories are about how I listened for interests and experienced interpersonal oneness in my best teaching moments, and hopefully they will help us to listen from the Father's heart. I am not saying that I am always a good listener; I am just saying, here are a few interpersonal times when I listened well.

The first story makes the point that we need to find a pathway for people who are hurting. My stepson was having a conflict with his three-and-a-half-year-old daughter. Mom had gone to the hospital for minor surgery. Laura Grace was clutching her dad, crying, "I want my mom!" She yelled out her need several times.

Dad replied each time, "Laura, Mom is coming home in two days."

Mom was Laura's closest friend. There was no one to play with. There was no one to be there for her. Laura's world had been turned upside down. If you were Laura's dad, how would you handle the conflict?

They say there are two methods of parenting. The first is to direct a child from the outside. This method can fail to consider the child's emotions or level of security. This is commonly called "extrinsic" or "outside-in" motivation or behavior modification. Laura's dad could have stood her in the corner for a time-out, attempting to shut down her emotions.

My stepson went beyond the first method. He heard what Laura needed, and he was going to respond in a way that filled that need. He said, "Laura, guess what? I am going to set the timer on the microwave and when the bell rings I will tell you a secret."

Laura stopped crying when she heard the bell ring! Dad said, "Laura, would you like to put on your coat? We will get in the car and go see Mom at the hospital."

It stopped every tear in Laura's soft blue eyes. Amazing how kids turn on a dime! Her golden curls bounced. Her face no longer looked like a suitcase that had gone a million miles. She smiled largely. They were off to see Mom!

After Laura arrived at the hospital and got her hug from Mom, she asked, "Mom, when are you coming home?"

Mom replied, "Sweetie, I'm coming home in two days!"

Laura asked, "Why?"

Mom replied, "Well, Mom has an owie and the doctor has to put medicine and new Band-Aids on it today and tomorrow."

Laura responded, "Can I see your owie?" When she glanced at the stitches, her face winced with an expression of pain, "But Mom, you have got staples in your tummy!"

To which Mom said, "Yes, and the doctor will take them out when he feels my owie is better. Would you like to pray for Jesus to make Mom's owie better?"

Laura said, "Sure." She loves to pray. They prayed.

When it was time to go, Mom said to Laura, "Guess what. When you get home, and have your bath, I am going to call you on the phone, tell you a story, and sing to you just like always. Would that be cool?" Laura went home with a hug on the inside and faith that a phone call would tuck her in for the night.

Dad did not treat Laura as an object or a bug annoying him. Even though he was preoccupied about his wife, he took the time to listen for his daughter's interests and needs. He treated her as a real little person with a real big need. Dad did not make Laura measure up; he found a pathway for her to treasure up! Dad and Mom worked with their little girl to meet her need and were successful because they mirrored Laura's need. They did not say, "Grow up, Laura; you are a big girl!" They didn't tell her it was wrong to feel what she was feeling, nor did they just give her a scripture to quiet her. He did not sentence her to a corner for a time-out or administer the board of education on her gluteus maximus. Even though Laura could not say, "I felt like Daddy really heard me," she knew Dad understood her world. He was a real servant-parent.

Dad and Mom, we are happy to say, spent a lot of time with Laura. They listened to her, played with her, and affirmed her. They told her stories that made her say, like Tinker Bell to Peter Pan, "If you want to find me, look for the 'second star to the right, and straight on till morning!'"

There are many little "Lauras" around us who are emotionally stuck. We keep handing them a formula in the attempt to isolate them in their pain, causing them to feel distant without any source for comfort. But those hugged the most are changed the most! What is needed is a process giving the "Lauras" of the world the ability to work through their thoughts and feelings. They need to know they are valued as people.

This creates a safe environment for them to get in touch with their being, their person, and their gifts. It gives them a safety net to explore and develop their emotional maturity. Then the "Lauras" grow into productive healthy adults who creatively make a difference in their world.

When folks are emotionally stuck, they become hug-hunters, dependent upon others, always searching for expressions of acceptance that rarely come. They try to find security in measuring up to performance formulas because their strength and security is all contractual and transactional. Emotionally stuck people become shaped or defined from the outside. They are conformed, not transformed.

I love this scripture: "This resurrection life you received from God is not a timid, grave-tending life. It's adventurously expectant, greeting God with a childlike 'What's next, Papa?' God's Spirit touches our spirits and confirms who we really are. We know who he is, and we know who we are: Father and children" (Rom 8:15–16). This captures how we must relate to our children and to one another in an emotionally healthy manner.

## EXPAND THE POWER BASE FOR THOSE WITH INNER CONFLICT

The following story makes the point that we need to expand the relational power of people who are hurting. Do you know how to expand another's person's relational power by being a good listener?

It happened at 8:45 a.m. in room 321 of The King's Tower in a class on conflict management. I finished lecturing on the first and second of the eight dynamic steps in managing conflict creatively: expand the power base (one's ability to trust and accept) and develop a relational base.

The way to expand someone's relation power is to foster the growth of their trust. I had pointed out to the class that trust formation is necessary. Without trust we cannot accept, and if we cannot accept, we cannot listen. When the trust level is high, communication flows. When it is low, there is distortion.

As relationships are dynamic, not static, trust and acceptance levels fluctuate. Relationships do get out of focus! When this occurs, two concepts are helpful. First, we remember that acceptance begets acceptance, and estrangement begets estrangement. Second, trust is also catching, so we should choose to give the benefit of the doubt.

I then asked the class, "Do you understand how relationships are built?" They all replied, "Yes."

I countered, "No, you do not . . ."

Then it happened. Frank raised his hand, saying, "Prof, Sheryl seems to be struggling. Can we pray for her?"

I ignored his request at first. I am not against praying for people, but I had been teaching long enough to know that it is important not to let a lecture get hijacked unless absolutely necessary.

But I soon realized that the finest illustration of how to build a relationship was right in front of us. I asked myself the question "What is missing here?" and it opened a way to one of the best miracle moments of my long teaching career.

It was actually not in the interest of Sheryl or the class to be prayed for in that moment. So, I created a story for the entire class to live in and from which to learn.

I asked, "Sheryl, where are you at now?" The tears came. The class was emotionally stuck. We had arrived in white-knuckle city, full of awkward emotional traffic!

She blurted out, "I am a failure as a mom, and I always wanted to be the best mom I could." A conversation with her son that morning had ended badly. He was up for an award at school and had missed practice. He feared he would not play well today and then be a huge disappointment to his coach, class, and parents.

Sheryl had responded, "Your dad and I really believe in you. We know you can win. You have our genes, and we were both star athletes in college." Now, the rest of us are rolling our eyes because we are beginning to get it. Are you getting it?

She was not getting through. He went off to school troubled, stuck, and locked up. She went to her class feeling like she had not gotten her son free and had done a "bad" as a mom.

I asked her to come and take a seat next to me. Facing her, I asked if I could tell her a story and to think about why I was doing so.

Fellow class members were raptly listening, wondering where this was going. Do not worry, we will get back to Sheryl in a moment.

## BUILD RELATIONSHIPS IN REVERSE

The story I told Sheryl is the third story of this chapter, and it is about the need to build relationships in reverse. We do not validate and then ventilate; we ventilate, then validate. In other words, we cannot get through to someone with our love and acceptance if they are still clouded in negative emotion. This is because negative emotion—such as self-hatred, frustration, anger, confusion, or depression—must be ventilated and removed or it will taint every attempt at communication. However, if the negative emotion is addressed, processed, and left behind, the words of validation can then be accepted. Let us illustrate this point.

We were in Chattanooga. I went to a girl's Little League soccer game. Mattie, a ten-year-old girl, had invited me to join the family in watching her play. During the second half, Mattie was appointed goalie. Within minutes the other team scored two goals.

I looked at her dad and said, "You are in trouble!"

To which he replied, "It's not my problem."

"She looks so defeated," I said. "How can you communicate that she is loved, and that just playing the game should be the joy part, even if she loses the game for her team?"

To which he replied, "I can't rescue her."

Before the game ended, she let three more goals in the net. Mattie was in tears. Her mom hugged her, trying to put the emphasis on how many goals she had prevented. Mattie was not listening or feeling any hugs. The coach came over to comfort her in the same way, complimenting her on her saves and good moves. He told her not to worry about the game loss. Mattie's aunt chimed in and took her off to the store to smother her with candy. Mom, coach, and aunt put bandages on the problem. Dad stood silently by observing that Mattie was not listening to them. Mattie was still wiping the tears away as she headed off the field.

When Mattie came home thirty minutes later, her father took her aside to talk with her. Later, I asked him how he had handled the situation. He said, "I did not do what she expected. In fact, I avoided talking about the game at first. I started with, 'Mattie, mom told me you were struggling with your homework last night and did not want to ask for my help because Wess was here.'"

"Yes," she replied, "He is important."

Replied Dad: "God comes first, then Mom, then you and your sisters. Then Wess, because I consider him a part of my family. But I want you to know that you can talk to me any time—when Wess is here, when I am at work, anytime. Because you are very important to me."

She said, "Okay."

Continued Dad, "I can tell you have been having a bad week. You lost your favorite watch. You went to the fridge and you forgot why. Yesterday you came in last in the mile race at school, and today you had a bad game."

Mattie broke into tears, agreeing she had a very bad week indeed. Dad let her know he had bad weeks too. He told her how special she was simply because she was his daughter. He then asked how she thought he could help. She came up with several suggestions.

First, he validated her perspective. Mattie was right to be upset! He acknowledged the validity of her feelings. Only then did he help her find solutions for her problem. Dad wanted to show her that she was ever so important to him—unconditional acceptance regardless of performance. But in order to get there, he had to begin with where she was at.

## VENTILATE, THEN VALIDATE

I then asked Sheryl why I told her this story.

She replied, "I was not ventilating my son then validating him. I was validating before ventilating him. I see that I was not giving him room to fail. I could have asked him, 'How do you think your dad or I would feel if you did not get the award having missed practice? How would the coach treat you? You know we care about you?' Or I could have said, 'Son, we love you if you get the award, and we love you if you do not.' That's a win-win deal. By saying 'You can do it; we believe in you,' I was not letting him vent his feelings. I was increasing the pressure creating a no-win situation for him, failing the coach, himself, and us."

She took a breath. "He needed to be free to win or lose. That freedom probably would make the difference in being able to succeed."

Now the class was ready for the point that in-depth listening and constructive sending are essential ingredients in managing conflict creatively.

When she got it, the class got it! What did they get?

As our power base goes down, our peripheral vision is lowered. If we have a negative self-image, or are insecure and threatened in each situation, we will be unable to think about creative ways of getting ourselves out of conflict.

Rather than help people see their problem, we must help them get some psychic ground on which to stand in relationship to the conflict. That is, we must act out of a positive power base first.

How do we do that?

Relationships are built in reverse. Ventilate, then validate. Address and discuss where someone is at in real time before attempting to lead them somewhere else.

My finest teaching moment came because I did not pray for Sheryl first. I ventilated her, listening for her interests, then stood with her on a breakthrough for her son. Then I knew how to pray for her and her son. Had I prayed for her like Frank had asked, I would have missed a miracle ministry moment. And I knew she would now go back home and get her son free. So, we must first be swift to hear, and listen closely for the interests!

## NUKE IT

My fourth story is about nuking it. Here I do not mean to invoke microwaves, but rather powers of great destruction. Nuking a situation can actually cause great listening. The idea of nuking here is a way to ventilate—to cause enough disruption to a normal, guarded conversation that the conflict is more easily addressed. In some ways, nuking a situation escalates it to the point where the truth boils to the surface.

Julie flew over five hundred sorties as a navigator off an aircraft carrier in the A-6 Intruder—an attack plane that was in service between 1963 and 1997—which sucks the cloudy night through its turbines and spits it out backside in a twirling vapor.

Julie was in my class. I was lecturing. My theme at that moment was that leadership that facilitates Spirit formation deals with equipping members with inner qualities that function successfully in an educational/ministry setting. Leaders must have a way of being that reflects truthfulness translated into action.

I was discussing the inner quality of authenticity when Julie hijacked the class by raising her hand and bursting into tears.

It was white-knuckle city! The entire class looked frozen and wide-eyed, like deers in headlights.

I had observed Julie walking through the stacks in the library adjacent to the lab before class began and she had seemed upset or depressed.

What would you have done were you the professor? I left the podium and took an empty seat in front of her desk, swiveled and asked her to unpack what she was experiencing. She shared that she could not handle any more. I knew it was not about my chosen teaching method for the day—death by PowerPoint with appropriate movie clips, songs, and lecture points.

She vented for a while and then apologized for interrupting the class. She asked me to forgive her. Nuking it, I said, "No!" I paused. It was so unexpected. It did not follow the usual script of our polite conversations. This reset the entire conversation and caused everyone to look for a way back to equilibrium, and this expectancy is exactly what we need sometimes to find a solution to our conflicts.

I responded by thanking Julie for hijacking the class. She looked surprised, her eyes getting larger. I said, "Thank you for giving us the gift of authenticity!"

Everyone relaxed and the class opened up. I had disrupted the conversation and then set it on a better course. I had gone against the grain of the polite scripts we often use with one another. I had resisted the temptation of rote relating. The nuclear option brings a sense of the irrational and unsafe. Irrationality can be a great gift to a peacemaker. When we feel irrational and unsafe, we will fight for rationality and safety. I look for those moments when things go nuclear or I cause critical pauses. Why? Because it allows for ventilation. And after one ventilates, one will move toward safety and rationality. People cannot stand irrationality for very long! At that point, movement toward safety and problem-solving is on fast-forward.

## LISTEN RESPONSIVELY AND GENEROUSLY

John Edward Hasse, a music historian, pianist, speaker, and award-winning author and record producer, gives some good advice about listening closely. He explains that there is no precise script for jazz music. Instead of following sheet music, the players must listen to one another and respond. When jazz players are in sync with each other, it is not because they have all followed an exact plan. It is because their ears are attuned to each other with the intent to respond and work together. Hasse writes:

> How does a jazz master listen? He or she listens keenly, listens for direction, listens responsively, and listens with generosity. What do I mean by "listens with generosity?"
>
> I mean that Duke Ellington wasn't listening for the shortcomings of his players, for the inevitable mistakes. No, he was listening for the beauty in Johnny Hodges' sax playing, for the brilliance in Cootie Williams' trumpet solos, for the ingenuity of Ray Nance's violin solos. And by listening for their greatness, maestro Ellington was inspiring his players to fulfill his lofty expectations of them.
>
> As in jazz, there's often no word-for-word script in businesses, hospitals, and other organizations. If you have no exact script, you have to listen closely.[6]

As in jazz, we have to listen to each other in order to be in sync. And not only that, but we must listen with generosity, to look past the problems to get to the music of the person. So, we listen for cues and ask, "Where do we go from here?"

We could pass by any moment of growth and transformation by not listening to people and being sensitive to the movements of a relationship. We could ignore conflict and fail to give the Holy Spirit the room to guide our conversations. Authentic personhood is lived out in our honest interactions. Leaders and teachers must be willing to play jazz with

---

6. Zhou, "What to Listen to."

their congregants and with their students. The interpersonal domain is the primary place of learning, and the interpersonal domain does not follow a script.

Had I asked Sharon to meet with Julie out in the lounge area adjacent to the lab to share and pray, and then moved on, the educational train would have left the station with no one aboard. My left-behind learners would have been pondering how insensitive I was by making the lecture more important than a person. A short verse in the Bible says it all. The crowd was pressing. An interrupted cry for help was heard. The disciples tried to shut him down. "And Jesus stopped . . ." (Matt 20:32). Jesus ignored the demands of the crowd to help one person. Will we, too, escape the demands of polite society or cultural obligations in order to love like Jesus loved?

All it takes to start a transformative conversation is one question that moves beyond the scripted interactions we follow every day. That day when Julie opened up, there were five guys leaning against the back wall of the computer lab in tears. At one point, I asked if it was time for lunch. They said, "No. We want to process!" When men want to process and not go to lunch, you have genuine transformation on your hands!

I am under no illusions that my students would remember all the details presented in class, but I am sure that they will always prize the interactions that were out of the ordinary. If we play it safe and only follow the scripts we are given, we will never see the honesty and humility that leads to a Christlike response of love and acceptance. Authenticity in relationships means we must listen for the interests (the heart, voice, and commitments) of others and respond. Without this, our community is merely following a script with no room for growth. Perhaps this is what is missing in your relationship with your kids, your husband, wife, or friends. Relate differently. Allow the conversations to follow the rules of jazz.

## CONCLUSION

This chapter examined some practical actions by which to engage in interpersonal oneness and suggested that the primary way to do so is through listening. In the entire spectrum of human communication, listening accounts for 45 percent of it. As James admonishes us, we should be quick to hear and slow to speak (Jas 1:19). Without actively listening, we will never truly connect with someone. A relationship must be a recursive flow of informational and emotional exchange, and a lack of listening halts any level of interchange. Listening is an act of *kenōsis*, for it prioritizes others over and above self.

Once we begin listening, we have two options. The first is to react by script. A script is a fixed way of non-being. It is a self-soothing defense system that amounts to running a scam on others. Reacting by script does not represent Christian responsiveness.

The other option is creatively engaging and responding. When someone is in need, we can choose to provide what is missing. We can listen for someone's needs and interests and respond organically. This is a way of being that does not avoid conflict, but instead sees it as the crucible for prophetic possibility. Stand in interpersonal oneness of "I AM." Listen and live from the foundation of oneness. Function in self-emptying love and be Christlike. This is done by validating others' personhood by showing them that what they think and feel matters. By listening and responding to interests, we empower others to address their problems as they are.

## REFLECTION

1. How do we listen actively and recursively?
2. How can you listen for the interests of others? In other words, what practical things can you do to hear the voice, heart, values, concerns, and commitments of others?
3. Why must we be good listeners?

# 12

# The Study of Being

## INTRODUCTION

ONENESS WITH THE FATHER in Christ by the Holy Spirit is a state of being. In other words, we are loved, valued, and affirmed through an intimate connection with them, not as a result of what we do or fail to do. This concept must be examined closely in order to be understood, because humans are much better at understanding doing than being. We could describe what is at play here as "ontological dynamics." As Emma Pavey writes, relational exchange, or love, "is at the heart of our co-existence with God, as one personal being to another."[1] Oneness with the Father in Christ and by the Holy Spirit (the participation in their life of love) is a state of being, rather than a doing-in-order-to-be dynamic in which believers attempt to perform the right set of actions in order to be loved, valued, and affirmed. This distinction can be appreciated by examining ontological dynamics.

## A STORY OF REVIVAL

This foundational issue of ontology as relational oneness is illustrated in this story.

---

1. Pavey, "Examining Theological Approaches," 6.

My wife was watching a revival on TV that occurred in Florida several years ago. She asked me to join her in prayer that this revival would be transported to LA.

I replied, "No."

She wondered out loud how a professor at The King's University could say "no" to such a prayer request. Maybe she thought that she would have to tell Chancellor Jack Hayford on me, if only to have integrity with God!

I asked her, "Are all the treasures of heaven in Christ?"

She answered "yes" and said that was from Ephesians. "Blessed be the Father of our Lord Jesus Christ, who has blessed us with all the treasures in heaven in Christ Jesus" (Eph 1:3, 4, 5).

I asked her, "Is the whole Godhead in Jesus?"

"I think that verse is in Colossians," she replied.

I quoted it for her: "For *in him* dwelleth all the *fullness* of the Godhead bodily.[2] And ye are *complete* in him, which is the head of all principality and power" (Col 2:9–11 KJV, emphasis added). I asked her, "Is revival a return to the life of God? Is Jesus the way, the truth, and the life of God?"

She replied, "Yes."

I responded, "So we both agree that Christ's prayer for oneness in John 17 should be answered?"

> Holy Father, guard them as they pursue this life
> That you conferred as a gift through me,
> So, they can be one heart and mind
> As we are one heart and mind. (John 17:11–12)

All together, these scriptures tell us that we have all the treasures of heaven in us, that we are positionally complete in Jesus, and that we are one with the whole Godhead. So, we will never be more anointed because the three are our anointing. We will never be more awesome because they are so awesome in us.

Christianity is not about a changed life; it is about an *exchanged* life! This means that we have abandoned the old person upon receiving Christ. The exchange has already occurred. We do not measure up; we treasure up! This means that we are not meant to work so hard at becoming better

---

2. Torrance, *Christian Doctrine of God*, 133. He clarifies, "we cannot have communion with all three, for they are who they are precisely as one indivisible Being, three inseparable Persons/three inseparable Persons, one indivisible Being."

in our own estimation, but rather to continually allow Christ to live his love-based life through us and value our treasure in heaven.

In other words, I concluded to my wife, "We do not need a 'revival' because we could not be more revived!"

Do not get the wrong idea. I do not have a completely negative view of revivals. I know that God does mighty things in revivals. People do return to the Lord ("Return to him, and he will return to you"; Zech 1:3). But my question here is about what motivates them to do so—doing in order to be loved? And further, how long does this motivation last in a lifetime relationship with the heavenly Father?

My point here is that Christians should not always be looking for the next revival—the next big spiritual thing—because the Scriptures clearly teach us that our revival has been accomplished upon receiving Christ. Revival is a return to life in God. That is, Life with a capital L—genuine Life! True revival is not a momentary meeting, but a relationship that we already have. If we seek revival as though we do not have it, we have missed the message of Christ! The Christian life is not characterized by a "name and claim" or "grab and get" approach. This is because we have already positionally received everything pertaining to life and godliness (2 Pet 1:3). However, a relationship must be maintained on a daily basis.

My final thought for my wife was this: "I will pray with you that revival is released in this city in and from us. But I will not pray for something I already have or am! I will release him."

The foundational issue illustrated in this story is that of *ontology*. Ontology is the study of being. To discuss one's ontological state, one is describing who one *is*. To discuss God's ontology is to discuss the nature of his being. For "to-be is to-be-in-communion" argues Catherine Mowry LaCugna. "A relational ontology focuses on personhood, relationship, and communion as the modality of *all* existence."[3] Again, love or relational exchange "is at the heart of our coexistence with God, as one personal being to another."[4]

Therefore, stating that the Christian life is not a changed life, but rather an exchanged life, is to say that the fundamental nature of a person's being has been traded in death for life, old for new. Christians should accept their new ontological state in Christ. Many Christians, however, are trying to get into a room they are already in!

---

3. LaCugna, *God for Us*, 250, emphasis original.
4. Pavey, "Examining Theological Approaches," 6.

For this reason, the very concept of a revival is not sufficiently ontological because it is so transitory. All historical revivals have come and gone. None yet have remained. True spiritual revival is living in the life of God! It is a relationship with the Trinity, by the Holy Spirit. True revival is to be a daily reality for the Christian whose being is now defined by Jesus and his life. It is not a thing—like a meeting—but a Person. True revival is ontological, and it happens in the supernatural salvific power of Christ.

Yet so many are chasing an ill-defined destination of perfection, a quest for self-approval, as though it is something to be attained rather than something to be owned in the present as an ontological reality. Working hard to obtain something (or Someone) you already have is an act of insanity.

The bottom line here is that oneness with the Father in Christ and by the Holy Spirit—the participation in their life—is a state of being. Is it true, however, that Christianity is fundamentally ontological (a way of being) in nature?

## THE ONTOLOGICAL TRUTH OF CHRISTIANITY

Ontology is the philosophical study of being, and dovetails with the study of reality and existence. This specific philosophical term is important because our state of being is an integral concern of God. For example, the categories *saved* and *unsaved* are ontological states.

The conflict between doing and being is often unaddressed in the church. In fact, most branches of Christianity tend to emphasize doing over being. We should not see these two as enemies, however. Rather, doing occurs from being. Being must come first, or the doing will be inauthentic, inconsistent, and unsustainable. Stated in theological terms, we will only do the right things (orthopraxy) when we have our beings oriented in Christ (ortho-ontology).

We do because we are, not in order to be. In other words, attempting to form our ontological state by doing the right things will not be effective unless we understand that ontology comes first. Those who try to work their way into being good end up being religious shells of self, without genuine personhood, for their ontological state is based on what they do, rather than who they are one with, that is, Jesus. Our actions must arise out of the lived truth that Christ's character is expressed in and through us. This is the ontological basis of Christianity.

Only the Father is good (Mark 10:18). But he shares his goodness with us. That is an ontological dynamic.

Of course, the questions must arise: How does one do this? How can a believer accept Christ's character in a real way? There are two steps involved. First, we receive. Second, we release.

## 1. Receiving Christ

One of the foundational scriptural principles behind the act of receiving Christ in an ontological manner is found in Paul's use of the term "in Christ" (or, alternately, "with Christ"). This term encapsulates the idea that the believer's being is connected to Christ's eternal being. The relationship of the believer to Christ—that is, being "in Christ"—explains the way in which the believer's being is affected by Christ. It is a relational understanding of an ontological truth. The believer's ontology is affected by this specific relationship with Christ and being "in Christ" is an ontological state that can be accepted by any believer.

Kierspel,[5] following Rehfeld, states that the term "in Christ" is "the hub of Paul's theological wheelhouse."[6] Since the concept of being "in Christ" was central to Paul, the foremost author of the New Testament, then perhaps we should pay closer attention to its significance.

Rehfeld makes an important distinction between viewing being as *substance* or seeing being as *an expression of relationship*. If ontology is based on substance, then internal qualities are naturally occurring and fixed. In other words, our interior state is a defined thing, and therefore concretized. In this paradigm, relationships merely influence being. On the other hand, if ontology is an outgrowth of relationship, then being and personhood are enhanced through relationships with others. Further, in this second paradigm, being is externally defined, and therefore there is no genuine ontological life without relationships.[7] In this view, our chosen relationships are the basis of our ontology. These relationships may be to people, concepts, media, or even physical belongings.

---

5. Kierspel, review of *Relationale Ontologie bei Paulus* by Emmanuel L. Rehfeld.

6. Kierspel, personal correspondence, September 23, 2017. Rehfeld, *Relationale Ontologie bei Paulus*. See also Wissenschaftliche Untersuchungen zum Neuen Testament 2.

7. Kierspel, personal correspondence, September 23, 2017.

The Pauline concept of "in Christ" follows this second paradigm in that it is fundamentally onto-relational. Therefore, to accept that we may live in Christ (or Christ lives in us) is to accept the good news of an exchanged life. Personal identity is based on relationship, and isolation results in the loss of personhood.[8] The believer's being—that is, our being—can and should be defined by the being of Christ. In this view, identity is not formed without relationships. Individualism is a dead end in the search for meaningful personhood.

Rehfeld, claims Professor Kierspel, argues that relational ontology is an organizing principle of Pauline thought about a "supremely dynamic relationship."[9] Kierspel writes,

> Rehfeld employs the Trinitarian term *perichoresis*, the mutual indwelling and interpenetration of Father, Son, and Holy Spirit, to describe the relational unity between Christ and the believer. That unity is experienced in the "heart" of the believer, which is in Paul's understanding not a substance of any kind but the "affective and intentional [center] of the human being" (321); it is the Holy Spirit who enables life "in Christ" as well as Christ's life "in me" (321–23, e.g., Rom 5:5).[10]

Receiving Christ is therefore the act of enjoining the relational oneness of the Trinity. The idea of "mutual indwelling" describes an ontological relationship. It is mutual in that there is a back-and-forth relationship. It is ontological because it involves indwelling—that is, finding a place in each other's internality. If Christ indwells me, then my ontology is defined by him. It is important to recognize that this ontological relationship is not just a possibility but is also the Father's desired outcome (John 14:23).

How does one engage this ontological potential? The act of reception is done in the heart (Eph 3:17; 2 Cor 3:3; Heb 8), which is not a static substance, but rather the center of the human being's faculties of affect (emotion) and intention (will). Further, this act is aided by the Holy Spirit (John 15:26; Rom 5:5, 8:9; 1 Cor 6:11; 2 Cor 3:3), who facilitates the ontological reception of Christ. This, therefore, answers the *how* question. We receive Christ in an ontological manner by allowing him to live in our hearts, by the help of the Holy Spirit.

---

8. Kierspel, personal correspondence, September 23, 2017.
9. Rehfeld, *Relationale Ontologie bei Paulus*, 413–24.
10. Kierspel, personal correspondence, September 23, 2017.

However, the concept of relationship is appropriate in another sense here, for a relationship must be maintained. A relationship is not made up of a one-time affirmation of love. No, a relationship must be maintained on a daily basis. For this reason, the acceptance of Christ in the heart cannot be relegated to a one-time salvific encounter but must be a maintained state of being by continually taking a stance of mutual indwelling in our hearts. In the words of C. S. Lewis, "Each day we are becoming a creature of splendid glory . . ."[11]

## 2. Releasing Christ

However, the reception of Christ is not the end point. God intends that we not only receive him, but also release him. Ontology not only determines who or what one is, but also determines the products of personhood. In other words, being in Christ will naturally lead to Christlike behavior. And God intends for us to express and release into the world what we become in Christ. First Pet 4:20–11 describes the act of releasing:

> Be generous with the different things God gave you, passing them around so all get in on it: if words, let it be God's words; if help, let it be God's hearty help. That way, God's bright presence will be evident in everything through Jesus, and he'll get all the credit as the One mighty in everything—endures to the end of time. Oh, yes!

What we have received in Christ as an ontological rootedness should naturally lead to the giving out from that Christlike state of being. We give out both words and help. We release his blessings within us through our speech and our acts. And in so doing, we release his bright presence. Oh, yes! We must be generous in releasing out what God has given us.

This choice to release reflects the nature of the Trinity. As Horrell points out, the self-sacrificing love that was taught and modeled by Christ is not just meant to be a measuring stick for goodness. Rather, it is a reflection of the *imago dei*—that is, the image of God in humanity. Horrell writes,

> part of our human constitution is that we *must* give of ourselves in order to fulfill the way we are designed. One rightly supposes that members of the Godhead *freely* give of themselves and are not under obligation by design. However, the human being

---

11. Lewis, *Mere Christianity*, n.p.

seems to be by very ontology under a kind of *free obligation* to give of himself to others. It may be that he can *only* enter more fully into the divine image, into full personhood, by giving himself away. By placing others first—God and then fellow man—he is completed as a human being and made truly "Christ-like" and "God-like" as a person.[12]

The picture that comes into focus here is that of the believer's ontology, transformed through relationship, leading to a self-denying release of the product of that exchanged being. The giving here is not of external things, but rather an act of giving from the self. This is why it is a "release." The Trinity models this self-giving relational ontology, and the three have not only invited us to participate in this ontological relationship of release but have also made a way for us in Christ to do so in a very real way.

We are called to receive and release his presence in divine actualization. No one can live out Christianity in independence, or out of self-determination. The only way is relational. If Christ lives his life for, in, and through us, then his presence is released for, in, and through us. God in Christ will reign in, through, and over his creation when we proleptically and prophetically receive and release him. We simply release who God is in us. "Let the Lion out of the cage, and he will defend himself," said St. Jerome and Charles Spurgeon. Or, As Ray Anderson put it, "our ministry is not what *we* do but is determined and set forth by God's own ministry of revelation and reconciliation in the world, beginning with Israel and culminating in Jesus Christ and the church."[13]

The twin concepts of receiving and releasing further reveal the faults with the being-vs.-doing mindset. The only way for a believer to act properly is to do so out of a state of relational ontology, which occurs in the reception of Christ. Godly doing will always, and only, emerge from godly being.

## THE I-AM ONTOLOGY

Moses led from God's bright presence (1 Pet 4:11). The point of departure for his leadership was I-AM. It did not, however, start out that way!

When God first called him, Moses experienced an internal conflict, carrying his nobody-ness too far. God spoke to him at eighty years of

---

12. Horrell, "Self-Giving Triune God."
13. Anderson, "Theology of Ministry," 7.

age, announcing that his youthful dream of a vision to deliver his people would be fulfilled. Moses balked, seeing several reasons why he could not be one with his future.

"What if they do not believe me?"

"Lord, I have never been eloquent."

"Lord, please send someone else."

God was okay with Moses' fear and sense of inadequacy. God was not okay, however, with Moses' last reaction. He got angry at Moses for not being available and willing. One lesson here: God's ability often gets trumped by our personal unavailability! But with God, there are no rejections, only redirections.

God's response to Moses's unwillingness and unavailability was ontological in nature and centered on himself. "God said to Moses, 'I-AM-WHO-I-AM.' Tell the People of Israel, 'I-AM sent me to you.'" God continued with Moses: "This is what you're to say to the Israelites: 'God, the God of your fathers, the God of Abraham, the God of Isaac, and the God of Jacob sent me to you.' This has always been my name, and this is how I always will be known" (Exod 3:14–15).

This name is as ontological as one can represent in the form of language. "I am" is the first-person singular present form of "to be." "To be" is the most common, functional, and foundational verb. This has several ontological ramifications for us. Firstly, it states that God is. He exists. Secondly, as the Creator, God is the source of all being. He is literally I-AM, as in he is being itself. Thirdly, God wants us to relate to him in the present—not as "I WAS" or "I WILL BE" but "I AM." Fourthly, and most importantly in the context of this chapter, because this Name is in the first person, when one says it aloud, one is at least tangentially associated with that being. To even say this Name is to include oneself in the being of God.

This is further shown in Jesus' use of "I am" in the Gospel of John. Jesus expresses his participation in the Father's identity as I-AM throughout this Gospel. Jesus' "I am" sayings reveal his character and mission, and directly tie into the I-AM name of God.[14] Why? Because Jesus loved, lived, and led from the divine Name. Jesus' person is formed and revealed by an ontological connection to I-AM. These are the "I am" sayings of Jesus:

---

14. Elwell and Comfort, *Tyndale Bible Dictionary*, 623.

"I am the Bread of Life. The person who aligns with me hungers no more and thirsts no more, ever." (John 6:35; cf. John 6:48, 51)

"I am the world's Light. No one who follows me stumbles around in the darkness. I provide plenty of light to live in." (John 8:12)

"I am the Gate. Anyone who goes through me will be cared for—will freely go in and out, and find pasture." (John 10:9; cf. John 10:7)

"I am the Good Shepherd. The Good Shepherd puts the sheep before himself, sacrifices himself if necessary." (John 10:14)

"I am, right now, Resurrection and Life. The one who believes in me, even though he or she dies, will live. And everyone who lives believing in me does not ultimately die at all." (John 11:25)

"I am the Road, also the Truth, also the Life. No one gets to the Father apart from me." (John 14:6)

"I am the Vine, you are the branches. When you're joined with me and I with you, the relation intimate and organic, the harvest is sure to be abundant. Separated, you can't produce a thing." (John 15:5; cf. John 15:1).

Many believe that Jesus used this same formula of "I am" from the Hebrew Bible to relate his deity. The "I am" statements in John's Gospel help the reader identify Jesus as divine, as God. Importantly, many of these statements are made in connection with miracles performed by Jesus. After stating that he is the light, Jesus heals a blind man, thus bringing literal light to his life. When Jesus says he is the resurrection and the life, it is in the context of raising Lazarus from the dead. Jesus says he is "the bread of life" immediately following his miraculous feeding of the five thousand.[15]

The "I am" sayings highlight the significance of Jesus miracles, which were not just acts of power or mercy. The miracles were products of Jesus' ontology. He did not just perform these miracles in a formulaic way. Rather, the miracles were a natural outgrowth of his being. He is not just capable of resurrection. He is resurrection. He is not just capable of miraculously multiplying food but is the life behind the bread. All of these miracles, at their root, are due to Jesus' identification with I AM. And Jesus modeled the participation, intimacy, and oneness that he had with the Father, both in his "I am" sayings and the miraculous signs that

---

15. Elwell and Comfort, *Tyndale Bible Dictionary*.

proved his words to be true. Jesus led from God's bright presence. His point of departure, his "come from," was I AM. Further, Jesus was ontologically I AM. These sayings explain his being and his relationship with the Father.

Further, these "I am" sayings also speak to us concerning Jesus' relationship with us. After every "I am" statement, Jesus explains its significance to humanity. For example, in John 6:36 Jesus states that he is "the bread of life," then proceeds to explain that those who come to him will not hunger. Kierspel writes, "Jesus only exists by giving himself to others. The [Hebrew Bible] precedents reveal that Jesus is saying, being, and doing here only that which he had learned from his Father."[16] Here we see the interrelational ontology of Jesus, who lived in I AM, and invites us to participate in his being through intimate communion.

How do we apply this discussion of ontology? We must recognize Christ as I AM, and that we are in Christ. The focus of the Christian life should be our being in Christ. This is meant in two ways. First, our being—that is, who we are—is found in Christ. He determines our identity. A relationship with Jesus defines our person ontologically. Second, he lives within us and we live in Christ—that is, we are always being in him. It is important in all of this to recognize that God is not trying to get something into us. Rather, he is trying to get someone out of us! The Father wants Christ to exude from every believer.

Christ Jesus has blessed us with heaven's treasures to share. And the greatest treasures are the relationships with God, Christ, and the Holy Spirit. The awareness of the whole Godhead, the Trinitarian relationship, is presented and represented by the Holy Spirit within us and is the outline of our new life. In turn, we are also in Christ, and may share in his ontological oneness with the Father. We too can be in the I AM, and may say, "I am in the I AM." We were made in the image of God, and Christ brings that image back into perfect focus in the I AM. It is an ontological reality that we must understand, accept, and live. Just as Christ's point of departure was the I AM, so too must it be ours. In other words, this ontological reality must be where we come from in all other matters.

The ever-present problem, however, is the conflict between being and doing. The ontological understanding of I AM must guide us toward Father-led interpersonal oneness. We do not do in order to prove what we are. Instead, we must partake of the very nature of God, and then

---

16. Kierspel, personal correspondence, September 23, 2017.

correct doing will naturally arise. If this choice is not made, the Christian will attempt to do right things in order to deserve love. Attempting to act without a proper ontology in place is like attempting to drive without first getting into the car. Doing can never come from non-being. And being only comes in Christlike relationship with the Father. The innate drive to do the right thing in order to be pleasing to God is tantamount to working hard in order to gain something that one already has. Our destiny in God is not a destination, but a grand relationship. Unfortunately, for the church in the West, an individualized and self-actualized, contractual, and transactional cultural value ends up being the default pattern. Paul writes of this in Colossians 2:10–11: "When you come to him, that fullness comes together for you, too. His power extends over everything. Entering into this fullness is not something you figure out or achieve. It's not a matter of being circumcised or keeping a long list of laws. No, you're already *in*—insiders . . ."

Believers are in the throne room (Eph 2:6; Heb 4:16). We do not need to try to work our way in. Jesus allows us to be as he is: in oneness with the Father. This is an ontological state that is not earned. And while it is available to each Christian, most do not take advantage of this gift of Christian existence.

## THE NATURE OF THE CHURCH AS DERIVED FROM THE NATURE OF GOD

We pointed out earlier that a significant theological consensus seems to be emerging that our basic understanding of the church must derive not from culture or tradition but from the very nature of God as revealed in Scripture.

Gunton maintained that "the question of the being of the church is one of the most neglected topics of theology."[17] Particularly, the Trinitarian understanding of God's person and nature must define the nature of the church. Gunton continues elsewhere, "The being of the church should echo the dynamic of the relations between the three persons who together constitute the deity."[18] This view is simultaneously relational and

---

17. Gunton, *Promise*, 56. See esp. ch. 3, "Augustine, The Trinity and the Theological Crisis of the West" and ch. 4, "The Community: The Trinity and the Being of the Church." Gunton maintains that "the question of the being of the church is one of the most neglected topics of theology."

18. Gunton, *Promise*, 78, 80.

ontological. The church must be an actual, visible community that reflects the community of the Father, Son, and Spirit. Again, such a Trinitarian ecclesiology will necessarily be "grounded in creation (what God the Trinity made and intended in creating the world), in redemptive history (which God the Trinity accomplished and is accomplishing through Jesus Christ by the Spirit), and in eschatology (the kingdom and economy of God finally consummated in Christ through the Spirit)."[19] All of these individual concepts—creation, redemption, and eschatology—are ontological aspects of Christian life. They come together to form a unified whole in an ecclesiology which prioritizes being and relationship.

Here, we are primarily concerned with how the concept of ontology should be reflected in the church. The apostle John discusses the internalized ontology of Christ as resulting in the love of neighbor: "No one has seen God, ever. But if we love one another, God dwells deeply within us, and his love becomes complete in us—perfect love! This is how we know we're living steadily and deeply in him, and he in us: He's given us life from his life, from his very own Spirit" (1 John 4:12–13). Loving one another is an expression of Christ in us. This is a distinctive marker of Christian community. As Cherry M. Chan puts it, "God's reality is at first not accessible but becomes accessible with a relational mode of knowing God. The role of the Spirit here is significant as God's life-giving presence for his creation and makes the creation capable to respond to the presence of God in this mutual indwelling."[20] Our reception of the Holy Spirit is a relationally ontological act that allows God's very presence to indwell us. This, in turn, causes us to recognize Christ's similar internalization within us. The Trinitarian love in which all believers are immersed causes proper interrelations in the church.[21] The being of each believer, now in Christ, establishes an interpersonal connection of love and mutual recognition of one another as persons in God's image. As J. Scott Horrell writes:

> Summarily, then, the key to human ontology is the *imago dei* within a trinitarian framework: (1) in man's personal nature which, although fallen, reflects the personal aspects of the divine nature; (2) in his capacity for divine indwelling, paralleling the intra-trinitarian *perichoresis*; and (3) in his design for

---

19. Gunton, *Promise*, 82.

20. Chan, "Living Love." See Schwöbel, "God Is Love," 310. See also, Kruse, *Letters of John*, 152–55.

21. Grenz, *Named God and the Question of Being*, 339–40.

fulfillment through self-giving, mirroring the disposition of the Godhead itself.[22]

The church must first and foremost express this Trinitarian dynamic. If it does not, the church will continue to languish in irrelevance and its influence in the lives of humanity will continue to decline.

## CONCLUSION

Interpersonal oneness with the Father in Christ and by the Holy Spirit (the participation in their life of love) is a state of being, not a doing-in-order-to-be (loved, valued, affirmed), and can be appreciated by examining ontological dynamics. Each person is made in a way that allows for the indwelling of God in three persons. "Threeness is the way God actually is in his essential being."[23] God himself promises such indwelling throughout the Scriptures. When this indwelling occurs as a way of being, it is expressed in relationships with others. Christianity must reflect these ontological dynamics of the Trinity.

## REFLECTION

1. Do you agree that a relational ontology insists that a person is not just influenced by relationships but primarily exists in and through them? Why or why not?
2. Do you agree that the gifts of the Spirit are ontological—God's way of kenotically gifting himself through us? If so, what are the implications?
3. Do you agree that spiritual formation is a byproduct of Christ's kenotic love? If so, how would that develop dynamic communion?

---

22. Horrell, "Self-Giving Triune God."
23. Grenz, *Theology for the Community of God*, 66.

# 13

# Signs of Interpersonal Oneness

## INTRODUCTION

While looking through our lunch menus at the Paris Cafe in Van Nuys, California, one of my brightest students announced that he was very upset, to the point that he was disappointed in the university. He explained, "Nine months ago, they approved my request to satisfy the pre-language requirement by taking it at Regent University in Virginia. Today I was told my credits would not transfer and I needed to retake Greek I here. This is so unfair!" That set off the other two students into airing their grievances, and soon we were having lunch in Complaint City, rather than Van Nuys.

I could have asked the first domino question, "What is missing for you here?"

His answer would have been "fairness" or "justice."

"Then how can we envision that happening?" I could have asked. "Maybe we could get you an appointment with the dean, so you can explain what happened. He might reverse the decision. Especially if you pointed out that the agreement had already been made, the requirement was fulfilled, and students were bound by the catalog under which they entered. Even if you do not get what you want, by talking with the dean, you would have approached the situation in a way that the Lord could honor."

With this suggestion, I could have created a new context, a new opening, a new possibility—by encouraging him to stand in the answer, rather than in the problem.

A complaint is a scripted way of being that makes others wrong so we can be right. It is a fixed reaction to conflict that justifies oneself and invalidates others. Complaining is a reaction that quickly turns into a way of non-being unless it is addressed and reframed. If one's perspective of complaint is not reframed through an interpersonal solution, it becomes a self-soothing survival system that often results in the loss of love, intimacy, vitality, well-being, happiness, satisfaction, self-expression, passion, and creativity. This is because complaining produces distance, rather than closeness. Complaining pushes others away and focuses on divisive problems instead of connective solutions. Rather than living as a free-will agent, the paradigm of complaint becomes a fixed, scripted way of being that embraces futility.[1]

The student with the "justice" issue was living in complaint. What he could not let be would not let him be. He may have been right that the decision was unfair, but his reaction to that offense amounted to making others wrong so he could be right, thus giving up his own agency of creativity and passion. In that frame of mind, so all-consuming as to be a reactive way of being, it would not readily occur to him that he was missing the core value of justice—and that making choices to restore justice in an interpersonal manner would be the solution. We cannot always control our reactions, but we can control our responses.

He not only needed to live out his answer himself, but also needed to connect with someone else in order to come to a conclusion through oneness. This is the Christian solution: finding answers in God together. Choosing actions that align with divine interest is a prophetic approach. The Word of God must lead our lives. For this reason, living out the principles of God through reframing is an ontological declaration of the prophetic Word. In this way, we change outcomes through the Word of God. Personal, relational solutions are therefore reflective of the Christian view of reality.

---

1. Cf. McNamara, Carter. "Basic Guidelines to Reframing — to Seeing Things Differently," 02/02/2012. https://managementhelp.org/blogs/personal-and-professional-coaching/2012/02/02/basic-guidelines-to-reframing-to-seeing-things-differently/.

As the German philosopher Friedrich Nietzsche said, "If you know the why, you can live any how."[2] In a state of complaint, the way of being is focused on conduct (the *how*), rather than the underlying divine principles (the *why*). For this reason, his reactionary state would define his present, and worse, his future, unless he took intentional steps to change it through a process of reframing.

In this story above, choosing to get an appointment with the dean to review the matter would constitute a declaration of the prophetic Word in which the student refused bitterness, disconnection, and impersonality, and instead chose to walk out the divine interests of forgiveness, oneness, and whole personhood. This is a Christian relational approach to finding a prophetically creative solution. This student would then be living from a reframe rather than a reaction. He would, in effect, be coinventing and costanding in a Word-driven future. This is an active, creative approach, rather than coming from a reactionary way of being in which he is passively stuck in the consequences of a past event. His past-based defense mechanism would settle for a low level of moral judgment or cause, but it would not be Word-driven. Instead, the personal and prophetic approach mirrors the I AM ontology, being creative and transformational. This is interpersonal oneness in action, on the ground, in Christian relationships.

If we are to live this kind of life with one another, It is important to look at indicators of interpersonal oneness. This chapter does just that. What are the markers of a way of being? What are the measures of spiritual formation and/or personal transformation? Before attempting to answer these questions, however, we should examine the story above in a bit more depth in order to identify why looking at personal and interpersonal indicators are important in the Christian context. An objective assessment of the church and its members along these lines will help us to know whether we are living out our relationship with Christ in a genuine manner. As Gene Getz points out:

> Paul exhorted the Corinthians to "*prove*" themselves (2 Cor 13:5): to put themselves to the test, examine themselves, scrutinize themselves. To the Galatians he wrote, "Let every man prove his own work" (Gal 6:4); and he admonished the Thessalonians to "prove all things" (1 Thess 5:21). Paul also practiced this concept in his own ministry. He sent Timothy back to Thessalonica to evaluate the state of the church to see how they were (1 Thess

---

2. Nietzsche, *Twilight of the Idols*.

3:5). He was constantly anxious to get reports from various sources, as to what was happening in all the churches, regarding their problems, their needs, their concerns, and their progress.[3]

This becomes even more important in the recognition that most objective measurements of success are not adequate measures of interpersonal oneness. It could be objectively proven, for example, that the complaining student had learned new knowledge, skills, and abilities in a course on Matthew's Gospel. This could easily be measured through an exam on the Beatitudes in Matthew 5. However, even though such knowledge is measurable in an objective manner, the student's way of thinking and being with them has not been measured. Knowledge does not always lead to transformation. The mental understanding of God's Word does not always lead to commensurate behavior. So, the student may have proved he had learned something, but his way of being and thinking may still have been passive scripted reactions rather than proactive, Word-based choices. In this scenario, the student may have had great knowledge, but still lacked in personhood and Trinitarian interpersonality. Head knowledge is of great importance, but it can never be a substitute for functioning from relational being. Those who do not shift from reactionary non-being to a reframing agency will be stuck in a legalistic view of God's Word. If we are to take interpersonal oneness as the true criterium for Christian success, then we must dig deeper into how we may identify it. We can identify interpersonal oneness in several ways.

## 1. THROUGH INTERPERSONAL ONENESS INDICATORS

Indicators of interpersonal oneness are found in the list of twenty "one another" statements found in the New Testament. These are descriptions of interpersonal oneness by the authors of the epistles—particularly Paul, James, and Peter. If we want to know how to detect interpersonal oneness, these statements give a clear run-down of how the New Testament authors viewed Christian relationships.[4] The New Testament does not give us a mere dictionary definition of love (e.g., acceptance, affirmation, or caring). Rather, it gives an operational or behavioral definition—a view of love that is visibly expressed through action.[5]

---

3. Getz, *Sharpening the Focus*, 259.

4. See Rehfeld, *Relationale Ontologie bei Paulus*. See also *Wissenschaftliche Untersuchungen zum Neuen Testament 2*.

5. Richards, "Meaningful Interaction." Notes given at a Step 2 seminar in Chicago,

## Signs of Interpersonal Oneness

The twenty kenotic "one anothers" each have a relational context and a Jesus focus.[6] Interpersonal oneness will be a significant part of our congregation's life when these "one another" statements are followed. Twenty interpersonal indicators of Spirit formation are about "one-anothering" as a way of being with others in Christ's community. Meaningful interaction in the body of Christ can be measured through these twenty kenotic "one anothers." We can tell that meaningful interaction is a significant part of our congregations' life when we find these paraphrased twenty aspects of interpersonal oneness put into action.

Rom 14:1: Bear one another's burdens.

Rom 12:10: Love each other with brotherly affection and take delight in honoring one another.

Rom 12:16: Work happily together. Don't try to act big. Don't try to get into the good important people but enjoy the company of ordinary folks. And don't think you know it all.

Rom 12:18: Don't quarrel with anyone. Be at peace with everyone, just as much as possible.

Rom 14:13: Don't criticize each other anymore. Try instead to live in such a way that you never make your brother stumble by letting him see you doing something he thinks is wrong.

Rom 15:5: May God who gives patience, steadiness and encouragement to help you to live in complete harmony with each other—each with the attribute of Christ toward the other.

Rom 15:7: So warmly welcome each other into the church, just as Christ has warmly welcomed you; then God will be glorified.

1 Cor 11:33: So, dear brothers, when you gather for the Lord's supper—the communion service—wait for each other.

1 Cor 12:25: This makes for happiness among the parts, so that the parts have the same care for each other that they do for themselves.

Gal 5:13: For, dear brothers, you have been given freedom; not freedom to do wrong, but freedom to love and serve each other.

Gal 5:26: Then we will not need to look for honors, or arid popularity, which lead to jealousy and hard feelings.

---

Illinois, January 1975.

6. Richards and Hoeldtke, *Theology of Church Leadership*, 219.

Gal 6:2: Share each other's troubles and problems, and so obey our Lord's command.

Gal 4:2: Be humble and gentle. Be patient with each other, making allowances for each other's faith because of love.

Heb 4:32: Instead, be kind to each other, tenderhearted, forgiving one another, just as God has forgiven you because you belong to Christ.

Col 3:9: Don't tell lies to each other, it was your old life with all its wickedness that did that sort of thing, now it is dead and gone.

Col 3:13: Be gentle and ready to forgive; never hold grudges. Remember, the Lord forgave you, so you must forgive others.

Heb 10:24: Provoke (stimulate, encourage) one another. In response to all he has done for us, let us outdo each other in being helpful and kind to each other and in doing good.

Jas 4:11: Don't criticize and speak evil about each other, dear brothers. If you do this you will be fighting against God's law of loving one another, declaring it is wrong. But your job is not to decide whether this law is right or wrong, but to obey it.

Jas 5:16: Admit your faults to one another and pray for one another so that you may be healed.

1 Pet 4:9: Cheerfully share your homes with those who need a meal or a place to stay for the night.

1 Pet 5:5: Be submissive to one another.

What emerges here is a clear and concrete picture of Christian relationships in the church. These "one-anotherings" are practical, enactable, and down to earth. Further, they reflect the Trinitarian approach to relationships, grounded in love, *kenōsis*, and reciprocal communion.

The importance of these "one another" statements is illustrated best by their application in the incorporation of new church members. These twenty guidelines for Christian relationships should permeate the experiences of new congregants in any church. Robert C. Worley, my professor and Dean of Doctoral Studies at McCormick Theological Seminary in Chicago, gives us a context for "one-anothering": "The time of incorporation of new persons is probably most important. During this period, the climate or character of an organization needs to be lifted up so that entering persons can see it, understand it, and make the critical decision about the meaning of membership in the organization."[7] When a new member enters the environment of the church, what kinds of reception will they receive? What kind of witness will they observe? How do congregants relate to newcomers? These questions emphasize the pivotal importance of enacting these "one another" actions, for they not only reflect God's will, but they provide a concrete, experiential witness of the transformative power of Christ. The incorporation process of new members into a congregation is a telling example of the need for a paradigm shift into interpersonal oneness in the church.[8]

As a young pastor in an identity crisis, fresh out of seminary, however, I attempted to build commitment in new members' classes by doing the opposite—lecturing on the history of our congregation, the history of our denomination, contemporary theology, and how the local church operates. It was information without formation. I had unwittingly tried to begin a heart journey from the head. The longest distance any of us will travel, however, is eighteen inches, the distance between our hearts and heads. By beginning my new members classes in this way, I was not setting a foundation of relationship, but a foundation of concepts and ideas.

Gene Getz takes the more practical approach of making the life of the congregation available to new members—and was able to clarify the biblical and theological base as he did so. He introduced new members to the twenty "one another" statements.[9] The new members then experienced who the church was, first and foremost. It was a relational beginning to a relational journey. When the class was over, the new members went into the congregation and engaged in "one-anothering." Pastor Getz found that he had a revival on his hands through his new members class!

The paradigms that direct these two differing approaches have to do with the distinction between orthodoxy and orthopraxy. Orthodoxy is about thinking the right thing. This is certainly something we should all aspire to! We may have proper orthodoxy, however, without doing anything about it. Orthopraxy, however, is about correct action. We do not need to know all the theological intricacies of Christian doctrine prior to "one-anothering" each other. Further, it seems likely that orthodoxy will be discovered more readily in an environment of interpersonal oneness with Jesus Christ. In this way, it seems the relational oneness in the church should take precedence over doctrinal efforts. My original approach to

---

7. Worley, *Change in the Church*, 121.
8. Worley, *Change in the Church*, 122.
9. Getz, *Building Up One Another*.

new congregants was non-interpersonal and information driven. Getz's approach was about releasing interpersonal oneness, a way of formation, based on who God is. Each approach produced a different result. One merely propositionalized people. The other interpersonalized them.

## 2. THROUGH CONVERSATION

Further, being can be altered through interpersonal oneness expressed in conversation, which is one of the primary human expressions of personal exchange. Just as the Trinity's ontology (way of being) is interwoven together ("the life of God is a life of self-giving and other receiving love"[10]), so too should the persons in the church be interwoven. This is accomplished practically through the sharing from ontology. This is practically accomplished in a number of ways, but certainly honest conversation (speaking the truth in love) is an expression that cannot be ignored.

Listening for interests and sharing spiritual truth are creative conversational acts of *prolepsis*. Prolepsis is a theological viewpoint centered on hope, relating to future promises as presently available. As Peters explains, "Like hearing the first Christmas carol in late October, our ears perk up at the prospect: Christmas is coming! That first Christmas carol does not merely point us to a future Christmas on December 25; it actually participates in the very Christmas ambiance mood, and celebration."[11] A proleptic approach therefore expresses faith for the future in the present tense. Doing so is a prophetic stance. Goss writes, "By learning to uncover the concealed aspects of your current conversations and learning to engage in different types of new conversation, you can alter the way you are being, which, in turn, alters what's possible."[12] This can be

---

10. Moltmann, 137.
11. Peters, *God—The World's Future*.
12. Goss, *Last Word on Power*, 19. Goss summarizes:

> The idea of changing your actions (and the events in the world around you) through conversation feels alien for many people, partly because it is so abstract, and partly because it contradicts the conventional psychological view of a person's personality. From a psychological perspective, actions stem from deeply seated motives in a person's subconscious. You have to probe deeply into a person's past to see what's really going on behind his or her actions. Psychologically, no one can really alter those deep motives except, perhaps, through years of arduous analysis. From an ontological perspective, by contrast, everything is apparent in the conversation being held at that moment. This gives everyone a starting place for making dramatic alterations and the tools for doing so. By learning to uncover the concealed aspects of

## Signs of Interpersonal Oneness

a creative approach in conversations—reaching into God's rich Word, rehearsing the Scriptures, and edifying one another through encouragement and love. After all, Jesus states (in the context of church discipline), "When two of you get together on anything at all on earth and make a prayer of it, my Father in heaven goes into action. And when two or three of you are together because of me, you can be sure that I'll be there" (Matt 18:19–20). This is a proleptic view of Christian conversation in a prophetic vein, for it emerges from the ontology of each believer.

## 3. THROUGH AVOIDING THE PITFALLS OF ATTEMPTING TO MEASURE

Here is a surprising question: is Father-led oneness measurable? First, we should ask whether we should even try to do so. As Paul writes in 2 Corinthians 10:12, "For we dare not to make a *geder* [classification] for ourselves or to compare ourselves with some of the ones commending themselves, but when they measure themselves by the standard of one another or compare themselves with one another, they do not show *seichel* [spiritual perception]."[13] Comparing and measuring are easily done without spiritual perception. In other words, measurements we make will often not be reflective of God's truth. Perhaps measuring relationship is antithetical to what a relationship really is. Perhaps

---

your current conversations and learning to engage in different types of new conversation, you can alter the way you are being, which, in turn, alters what's possible. When you create a new context, you create a new realm of possibility, one that did not previously exist.

See also Geoff Broughton. "Authentic dialogue: Towards a Practical Theology of Conversation," Academia May 23, 2022. https://www. Academia.edu/10253559/Authentic_dialogue_Towards_ _Practical_Theology_of_Conversation. See "Theology of the Trinity and Conversation," perichoretic space for "self-giving and other receiving," 72-73.

13. "*Sechel* is both a Hebrew and a Yiddish word, the Hebrew meanings having been absorbed into Yiddish. Pronounced *sekhel* in Modern/Israeli Hebrew and *seykhel* in Yiddish, it can mean intelligence, smarts, brains, reason, common sense, cleverness or even wisdom. *Sechel* is defined in the authoritative *Eben Shoshan Hebrew Dictionary* as 'the spiritual ability to think, to weigh, the strength to judge and to come to a resolution.' Michael Swirsky, an Israel-based educator and translator of Hebrew texts, distinguishes *sechel* from *chochma*, and other Hebrew words for wisdom, as 'a trait, like IQ or good sense' that one is endowed with. '*Chochma, binah* and *da'at,*' Swirsky explains, 'are skills, talents or traits that could take a lifetime to acquire.'" Johnson, "Jewish Word / Sechel," https://momentmag.com/jewish-word-sechel.

interpersonal oneness is something that simply is—it is on or off and does not require measurement.

Perhaps attempting to measure our maturity is simply not a mature thing to do. The primary issue with the attempt to measure anything ontological is that doing so usually arises from the attempt to self-actualize, self-fulfill, or self-perfect. These attitudes are driven from the need for self-approval and resist the relational oneness of Christ, which is self-emptying (kenotic). It is the attempt to do in order to be. Genuine doing, however, comes from authentic being. It is a grave mistake to try to measure our performance for Christ, primarily because it is a mistake to try to perform *for* Christ at all.

For this reason, even if we could measure our interpersonal oneness with Jesus, we should be careful to even want to do so. It is easy for one to misunderstand the lifestyle that is Christian. A misguided Christian may take a performance-oriented culturally shaped approach to life, attempting to earn God's love. Too many Christians think they must work to earn God's love. This wrong way of thinking supposes that if we do not perform the correct actions at all times, then God's love is removed from us. This perspective is destructive. For example, the apostle Paul portrays a counter meaning in our Baptism in Christ:

> Going under the water was a burial of your old life; coming up out of it was a resurrection, God raising you from the dead as he did Christ. When you were stuck in your old sin-dead life, you were incapable of responding to God. God brought you alive—right along with Christ! Think of it! All sins forgiven, the slate wiped clean, that old arrest warrant canceled and nailed to Christ's cross. He stripped all the spiritual tyrants in the universe of their sham authority at the Cross and marched them naked through the streets. (Col 2:12–15)

When Christ died for our sins, he died for our future sins. Eternal forgiveness for all our sins—past, present, and future—is available to those who receive it. In Christ, we are forgiven and free! As Paul says in Romans 8:1–2 (ESV), "There is therefore now no condemnation for those who are in Christ Jesus. For the law of the Spirit of life has set you free in Christ Jesus from the law of sin and death." There are no tears of regret in heaven (Rev 21:3–5)![14] It cost God an entire dimension of time—that

---

14. "I heard a voice thunder from the Throne: 'Look! Look! God has moved into the neighborhood, making his home with men and women! They're his people, he's their God. He'll wipe every tear from their eyes. Death is gone for good—tears gone,

is, our past, present, and future sins—to bear the weight of world sin and make eternal forgiveness available through Christ's death and destitution. Our unconfessed false guilt, however, can get in the way of our being there for others! As the philosopher Soren Kierkegaard put it, "The most painful state of being is remembering the future, particularly one you'll never have" or "Life must be understood backwards; but . . . it must be lived forward."[15] And the reassuring words from the apostle Paul also show that we can never lose his love in life's journey:

> So, what do you think? With God on our side like this, how can we lose? If God didn't hesitate to put everything on the line for us, embracing our condition and exposing himself to the worst by sending his own Son, is there anything else he wouldn't gladly and freely do for us? And who would dare tangle with God by messing with one of God's chosen? Who would dare even to point a finger? The One who died for us—who was raised to life for us!—is in the presence of God at this very moment sticking up for us. Do you think anyone is going to be able to drive a wedge between us and Christ's love for us? There is no way! Not trouble, not hard times, not hatred, not hunger, not homelessness, not bullying threats, not backstabbing, not even the worst sins listed in Scripture. (Rom 8:31–35)

A performance orientation approaches Christian ontology from the wrong direction. Doing anything in order to be accepted, loved, or valued is essentially non-being. In this sense, insecurity is the enemy of divine ontology! Rather, our actions should naturally come out of who we are or who he is within us.

Further, it is absurd to think that we need to measure something that was given to us as a gift. After all, we are "being filled with the fruits of righteousness which *are* by Jesus Christ, to the glory and praise of God" (Phil 1:11 NKJV). Again, as Ray Anderson explains, "ministry is not what we do, but is determined and set forth by God's own ministry of revelation and reconciliation in the world, beginning with Israel and culminating in Jesus Christ and the church."[16] In this way, any measurement is an attempt to quantify God's activity in our lives! This kind of

---

crying gone, pain gone—all the first order of things gone.' The Enthroned continued, 'Look! I'm making everything new. Write it all down—each word dependable and accurate'" (Rev 21:3–5).

15. https://www.goodreads.com/author/quotes/6172.S_ren_Kierkegaard.

16. Anderson, "Theology of Ministry," 7.

desire runs contrary to divine oneness and love. In a sense, measuring his performance in and through us is not our role. As Paul writes, "May you abound in and be filled with the fruits of righteousness (of right standing with God and right doing) *which come through Jesus Christ* (the Anointed One), to the honor and praise of God (that his glory may be both manifested and recognized)" (Phil 1:11 AMPC, emphasis added). And when God inspects or judges us, what will really make heaven sing is our complete willingness to see Christ move in and through us, not our measured performance for him. Our attempts to do things perfectly for God is what the prophet Isaiah calls "filthy rags" righteousness (Isa 64:6). Again, "Even observably righteous behavior when it is motivated in extrinsic terms tends to be deeply sinful."[17] We should remember Paul's exhortation: "[Not in your own strength] for it is God who is all the while effectually at work in you [energizing and creating in you the power and desire] both to will and to work for his good pleasure and satisfaction and delight" (Phil 2:13 AMPC). As Moises Silva quotes John Murray:

> God's working in us is not suspended because we work, nor our working suspended because God works. Neither is the relation strictly one of cooperation as if God did his part and we did ours so that the conjunction or coordination of both produced the required result. God works, and we also work. But the relation is that *because God works, we work. All working out of salvation on our part is the effect of God's working in us* . . . We have here not only the explanation of all acceptable activity on our part, but we also have the incentive to our willing and working . . . *The more persistently active we are in working, the more persuaded we may be that all the energizing grace and power is of God.*[18]

Do we think the Christian life is about our progress, or about Christ's proficiency through us? Let us personally affirm Christ's proficiency without hesitation!

The way out of this being-vs.-doing dilemma is to view the things we do in our relationships with God and community as expressions of his divine being in us. In other words, such measurable attitudes and actions, as the gifts of the Spirit, the fruit of the Spirit, and one-anothering, are the outworkings of the Holy Spirit expressing Trinitarian relationship through us. Further, that kenotic relational overflow can be recognized and valued in ourselves and in others. If our genuine motivation comes

---

17. Campbell, "Covenant or Contract in Paul," 201.
18. Silva, *Philippians*, 123, emphasis added.

from a place of Father-led interpersonal oneness, then it releases gifts of the Spirit, the fruit of the Spirit, and the acts of one-anothering as ontological expressions of the Father in us. These are the ways in which the Father expresses his being. Thus, we get to reflect his likeness, his character, his treasure, in interpersonal oneness—with him and with one another. In this way, we stand in his Life-release as our proleptic point of departure, for our interest, hope, and way of being one is defined by who he is within us.

Our acceptance with God is based not on what we do for God, but what Christ has already done for us. So, in Christ God makes us his children, and then he asks us to obey in a totally different process. It is not a contractual or transactional (if-then) process. This difference is captured by the distinction between being responsible and being response able. If we think we are responsible to merit God's love, we clearly do not know Jesus and his sacrifice. However, if we realize that our greatest strength in our relationship with God is to respond to his preexisting love and acceptance, then we are living a life that is truly Christian.

A covenantal Father calls us, through his Son, to participate in his own loveliness—the place of peace, protection, and provision. As Paul summed it all up in Galatians 5:6, "For in Christ, neither our most conscientious religion nor disregard of religion amounts to anything. What matters is something far more interior: faith expressed in love." The only thing that matters is a faith that expresses itself in response-able love in a life of spiritual, joyful, thankful, obedient response-ability (the hyphen means it is not our responsibility). We cannot live the life that is Christian. Christ must live his life in and through us. We cooperate with the Holy Spirit, who reproduces Christ's life within us, with a response-ability that is given by God. We are empowered by the Spirit to live a joyful, thankful, obedient Christian life. Romans 8:10 says that the Holy Spirit who lives in us is the spirit of life who brings us his life. The Holy Spirit's empowering presence is ascribed to us. Paul says, "For you did not receive the spirit of slavery to fall back into fear, but you have received the Spirit of adoption as sons, by whom we cry, 'Abba! Father!' The Spirit himself bears witness with our spirit that we are children of God" (Rom 8:16 ESV). Dr. David Jeremiah suggests that we dig deeper.

> Paul is not saying that the Holy Spirit bears witness to my spirit that I am a child of God, but rather that the Holy Spirit witnesses, *with* my spirit, that I am a child of God. In other words, at the same time that I am praying and calling God my Father

from within my Spirit, the Holy Spirit is doing the same thing from within me so that there are two who call God Father every time I pray, the Holy Spirit and my spirit. It's a dual evidence of my sonship. When I call God Father, the Holy Spirit is witnessing right alongside me. He's saying yes . . . Father. He's yours. He belongs to you.[19]

So, the Holy Spirit comes along side bringing his life, to empower and enable us to respond, to accept the gift of the glory of his love. It is not about our self-help, self-generation, self-actualization, or self-fulfillment. It is about Christ being enabled in us. Again, becoming Spirit-filled enables us. Being Spirit-formed enables him through us and is released through us.[20] We treasure up, not measure up.

While we should be careful with attempting to measure a way of being such as interpersonal oneness, what we can measure is the quality of our openness. After all, our openness to God and to others seems to be a quintessential aspect of relational success. Our degree of openness is usually visible in moments of honesty, need, and conflict. How do we respond to someone's honesty toward us? How do we respond when we see someone's need? How do we respond when a conflict arises? Do we remain close in the relationship, or pull away? Do we choose to prioritize love, acceptance, and forgiveness, even when it is uncomfortable or even painful?

When anyone reveals their need or interest, it creates the potential for an open exchange of love in the oneness of Christ. Our openness is expanded when we ask, "What is missing?" Then we turn that answer into a commitment/interest to stand in God's love together. In this way, we reframe the issue in Christlikeness, addressing it together in hope and faith. All of this requires a high degree of openness! As Winston Churchill put it, "A pessimist sees the difficulty in every opportunity; an optimist sees the opportunity in every difficulty."[21] Our openness is enacted when we are willing to enter into the realm of the uncomfortable and the difficult in order to express Christlikeness.

If we can discover what interest, care point, or miracle is lacking, it creates a divine opening where we may stand proleptically and prophetically in the relational answer of "I AM." We are then one with the only

---

19. Jeremiah, "Ministry of the Holy Spirit."

20. Hayford, Autumn Leadership Conference, The Church on the Way, November 2000.

21. https://www.goodnewsnetwork.org/a-pessimist-sees-the-difficulty-in-every-opportunity-an-optimist-sees-the-opportunity-in-every-difficulty-winston-churchill/.

true answer, which is God himself as Father, Son, and Holy Spirit. In this way, we are being with the problem in and through him. This is the ontological stance that allows for transformation. This breaks out of the performance orientation because it is completely reliant on the relationship with God—living loved, not struggling to be loved. The doing then comes from being. This is the interpersonal life. "But for right now, until that completeness, we have three things to do to lead us toward that consummation: *Trust steadily in God, hope unswervingly, love extravagantly.* And the best of the three is love" (1 Cor 13:13, emphasis added).

So, our openness can be measured, or at least perceived. It is a clear marker of interpersonal oneness. Other aspects of a stand that creates an opening would be a proleptic perspective and a prophetic faith. A proleptic perspective expresses faith for the future in the present tense. Prophetic faith looks for possibilities in God, rather than obstacles. Our proleptic and prophetic expressions can be measured, as well.

An example of a stand that creates a proleptic and prophetic opening happened when I was reacting or complaining about the irritating noise from daily fire-and-rescue vehicles that came down "The Strand" in front of our condo on Coronado Island. I resented the noise and wondered why they had to have their sirens on past midnight. However, I decided to invert my negative reaction into a reframing, instead of complaining. I asked myself, "What is missing here?" I started praying for God's healing presence for every person involved. Doing so was prophetic in that I saw a possibility for God's hand to affect change in the situation. It was also proleptic in that I took time in the present to call for God's perfect will in the future.

When we proleptically and prophetically release his Trinitarian love in Father-led interpersonal oneness in the laboratory of real life, we enable good things by bringing God into any situation through our oneness with him. In other words, our oneness with God brings him wherever we go! As the psalmist puts it, "Your beauty and love chase after me every day of my life. I'm back home in the house of God for the rest of my life" (Ps 23:7). We will always be with him if we accept the oneness he has offered us (Eph 3:17, 5:31–32; 1 Cor 1:30; 2 Cor 13:5). And even if we are absent from a situation, we can pray ourselves into it! Our partnership with Christ in intercession (Rom 8:34) is a proleptic and prophetic relationship. However, it requires our openness to see and stand in the needs and interests of others. In this discussion on measuring interpersonal oneness, we have therefore identified its most visible aspects: a stand that creates an openness marked by a proleptic view and a prophetic attitude.

## CONCLUSION

The fullness of God cannot be measured, only expressed through his Son's Trinitarian love in us through expressions of interpersonal oneness. We cannot measure spiritual growth. Leave that to God. It is a byproduct of Christ's kenotic love which surpasses knowledge and fills us with the fullness of God ("to know the love of Christ which passes knowledge; that you may be filled with all the fullness of God"; Eph 3:19 NKJV). So, the fullness of God cannot be measured, only expressed through his Son's Trinitarian love in us. That love is the engine of spiritual formation!

So, treasure up in response-ability. Do not measure up with a false sense of responsibility! The future is now! Receive and release divine treasure proleptically and prophetically! Stand in his awesome presence! Release interpersonal oneness! Lead from the divine Name, I AM! Live from a remarkable vision of God (the Trinitarian relationship within you)! Live loved! Be who you are in Christ—the greatest source, course, and force in our watching world (1 Cor 13:13). For we are defined by who he is within us—the unrelenting, unlimited, and immeasurable love of God! We are defined by the glory of his love (Col 1:27).

## REFLECTION

1. Which one of the twenty "one another" statements resonated with you the most, and why? How would your community be affected if that admonition were followed to the utmost?

2. Why do we tend to merely propositionalize people, rather than interpersonalize them? What behavior could you change about yourself to pursue interpersonalization—such as listening, reframing, engaging in difficult conversations, and other ways of personal connection?

3. Do you agree that creative speech acts can alter being through interpersonal oneness conversations? Can conversations be prophetic and proleptic? If not, why not?

4. Are you able to measure your own openness? What markers would you look for in order to recognize when and where you are truly open (or not) to engage with people's needs and interests?

# 14

# The Heart of Christianity

IN CONCLUSION, WE HAVE claimed that Father-led interpersonal oneness is the heart of Christianity. It is a remarkable vision of God. It is a reflection of the Father's heart. It is a root paradigm about the glory of his love. It should motivate the church to release kenotic interpersonal oneness, the image of God. Consequently, a summary of our positions on the heart of Christianity will bring closure.

## 1. RECAPITULATED

Accordingly,

### 1.1 What Is Reality?

Reality is a macro structure of relationship, a Father-led interpersonal oneness that is limitless love, presence, kenotic otherness, or self-giving, self-offering, or interest satisfaction.

### 1.2 Why Is It Important to Flow from Reality?

The person of the Spirit reveals and glorifies the eternal love shared between the Father and Son within the triune God—God is love only as

Trinity,[1] and given that reality is Father-led interpersonal relationships, then all knowledge and action are "for the purpose of friendship." And Jesus' friends are defined by his Father: "I've named you friends because I've let you in on everything I've heard from the Father" (John 15:15).

How do we explore God? Through God's glasses—the person of Jesus Christ, who is revealed in Scripture. Jesus is our source for knowing the Father.

God's glasses are his Son. Again, Jesus was Father-led. Again, the degree to which we are not Father-led is the degree to which we are not Christlike. Jesus' personal view of God is the outline of our lives. Paul said, however, that "There are a lot of people around who can't wait to tell you what you've done wrong, but there aren't many fathers willing to take the time and effort to help you grow up" (1 Cor 4:15). *But do we have many Jesus-defined, Father-led fathers around?*

As Jesus is the One who expresses the very relating life of Father, Son, and Holy Spirit, we too must *release their relating life*. This is to be on mission with a message! Release the Spirit, who makes us conscious of a Trinitarian relationship that kenotically loves through us. Do not seek what you already have to be self-fulfilled and self-actualized; share who he is because the Trinitarian relationship is divinely actualized in you as relating life—your heart, voice, and commitment! As C. S. Lewis said about "Gift-love," "What draws people to be friends is that they see the same truth. They share it."[2]

## 1.3 How Is Reality as Father-led Interpersonal Oneness Experienced and Expressed?

Be God's gift-love through the art and act of interest satisfaction.

So, what is the measure of Father-led interpersonal oneness, this Trinitarian grace as *a gifted way of divine Being*? How is this spiritual DNA released within us? Is it through kenotic otherness, self-giving, or shared love, expressed in Christlike interest satisfaction? Does that release the byproduct of attachment, bonding, or dynamic communion?

To search for it is non-being—humanistic doing in order to be (loved, accepted, or valued). Again, the search for significance or acceptance is non-being. It is to not allow *the gift of the Trinitarian relationship*

---

1. Grenz, *Theology for the Community of God*, 374.
2. Lewis, *Four Loves*.

*through the ministry of the Holy Spirit* (interpersonal community or oneness), our "come from," to be present inside every grace day because it *is the outline of our lives*!

Reality is discovered through satisfying these interests, argues Andrew D. Thrasher:

1. a reevaluation of human personhood as the *imago dei* dependent upon a triune God through

2. a perichoretic relationality of otherness and love that

3. defines God via a Trinitarian communion of three persons as ontologically constituted as persons in relation by and subsisting in love wherein

4. human personhood may be understood via the *imago dei* conformed to the *Imago Christi*

5. oriented to the church via a communion ontology that finds its completion as created existence through the biblical narrative as grounded in

6. a theological ontology of love that defines both divine and human personhood through the contexts of otherness and communion

7. to show a theological alternative to postmodern ontology ["the demise of the centered, rational self of modernity, the postmodern self that seeks unity in diversity finds an alternative answer within a Trinitarian ontology of communion that affirms the difference of the other as other in a creational reorientation of the human person as created for communion."][3]

## 2. REINFORCED

### 1.1 Integratively

As one renewed church organization, having embraced and been redefined by Trinitarian theology, concluded:

> The doctrine of the Trinity has enriched our understanding of many other doctrines, and we will continue to learn more about it as we grow in grace and knowledge. It makes sense that God's nature is reflected in everything that God does, and that means

---

3. Thrasher, "Communion Ontology and Personhood," 5, 20.

it affects all other doctrines, because our doctrines are based on what God is doing in the people he has created.

We see God's *love* throughout the story, from before creation and in the cross of Christ, and on into eternity in the future. We see the Father, Son and Spirit in creation, in salvation, and in eternity. God wants to live with us, and us to live with him, in love, forever and ever. In his love and grace, he has *given* this to us—and in our love for him, we enjoy learning about it. But we know that this is only the beginning of our understanding.

In I Cor 13:12, the apostle Paul says that now, "we see only a reflection as in a mirror; then we shall see face to face. Now I know in part; then I shall know fully, even as I am fully known." We have knowledge, but our knowledge is partial, and we look forward to learning more. We rejoice that God knows us fully, and we can be confident that he will continue to draw us toward himself, so that on some future day, we will see him face to face and know him fully, sharing in his life and love forever and ever."[4]

Or, as Professor Marty Folsom posted his response to theologian Ben Myers, on avoiding heresy with the Trinity:

Ah yes, the practical. Some theologians are concerned that a primary focus in Trinitarian thinking is to lead the uneducated into using the Trinity to merely meet human needs and desires. We might shape the Trinity into the answer for our vision of happiness and fulfillment. We would miss the mystery and holiness of God who is wholly other than us. If making God to fit us is the only option for thinking practically about the Trinity, then, yes, we can abandon the quest.

However, if by "practice" we mean that understanding the Trinity allows us to discover the Father and cry out "Abba," knowing that we are a child sharing the Abba cry of Jesus by the Spirit, then that is a practical outcome that responds to the intent of the Bible. Theory and practice are held together in unity as a life of worship that acts like we really are impacted and respond to the living God. Active response is a practical outcome. We are not loved for responding, but our response is the fruit of the reality of our relation.

We ought not to want any impractical doctrine of the Trinity. If we better understand the Trinity, then we are better positioned to share in the life, mission, and ministry of the Triune

---

4. Morrison, "Theology," https://www.gci.org/articles/an-introduction-to-trinitarian-theology/.

God to us and through us. We are instructed to love as they love, to be one as they are one, and to be sent as Jesus was sent (see the Gospel of John). This orientation in theological thinking that affirms our coming to know how the Triune God acts is a proper formatting for how we are to practically live in this world. We are not separated, merely following an example; no, we are participating practically in the acts of God. As Jesus only did what he saw what his Father was doing, so we, too, turn our eyes to Jesus to see what he is doing and to follow his work, empowered by the Spirit to practically work out our loving and joyful obedience in our homes and neighborhoods.

Idealized Christianity is what we need to avoid. To merely be able to think great thoughts and articulate concise doctrine is not enough. If those ideas do not take practical form in the life of community as the outworking of the work of the Triune God, we are most to be pitied. "Love one another as I have loved you" is a call to practical application of the Incarnation of God in Christ. His love is not solitary; it is shared from his Father. It is poured on the first community and beyond as the Spirit facilitates the ongoing life of gathering, worship, witness, and service.

If we do not discuss the practical implications of the Trinity, we will default to naturalistic thinking for how we define success; we will think of God in pure terms, but we will act out of what works practically as defined by the culture in which we live. With self-interest, the priority of the thinking self, and the urge to have power over our circumstances, we will be cast back on Western ideals of the primacy of the individual. Our practices reflect the soil in which we are nourished.

All people live a practical life. If our practices are shaped by discovering the Triune God, we enter a life of faith that is not a blind leap in the dark. We will begin to act in response to the God who acts in ways that are not disconnected or merely good ideas. We will be practicing life as an act of worship that will practically change everything as our values are formed in the renewal of our minds in Christ.

If we smile and move along when people are interested in discovering the Trinity, we will be abandoning those who are loved by that Trinity. Whether we teach, admonish, reprove or encourage, we could always be those who see that deep-down people want to meet and know the living God—this is what is behind their quest. *We need to do better theology, theology that is connected to life, and deeply connected to the living, Triune God.*[5]

---

5. Folsom, "Dialog with Ben Myers," emphasis added.

And "we need to do better theology" that is life-connected to each other. As Horrell concludes with a practical note on biblical ecumenicity:

> The same mutual caring is not limited to believers in the local church or single denomination. Sensitivity to the unity and diversity of the Body of Christ should extend our care to other Christian churches as well—seen not as religious competition or as "errant brethren" but as fellow congregations in the universal Church of our Lord. The triune nature of the Godhead reminds one of the values and beauty of traditional, cultural and ethnic diversity manifest in sometimes radically diverse styles of worship and service. Often local churches and denominations have failed to appreciate the pluralism of God's people, a people nevertheless united by "one Spirit . . . one Lord, one faith, one baptism, one God and Father of all" (Eph 4:4–5).[6]

## 1.2 Metaphorically

Finally, two sea-going stories become metaphors that highlight this book's plea for a paradigm shift to an ontological way of being with life from kenotic life.

I am the older professor, eighty-one on Saturday, February 12. First, I identify with and live to grade the wise words of one of my bright students.

> Hemingway's work, "The Old Man and the Sea", reminds me of many things. It speaks honestly about a life wrought with victory mingled with defeat and pain. Life is a mixture of experiences and it can be lived in denial of its honest brutality or it can be faced full on. At first it can be faced with vigor and romanticized idealism with pride mixed into it all. However, an honest person over time becomes wearied and humbled looking to find meaning where it seems to be wearing thin. As the saying goes, "Death comes to us all." The coward pretends it won't come while those that look for courage face it. There are moments, as we brave the waters of life that seem to come and lift us into *the transcendence of eternal purpose*. Such moments like these are not fabricated by our hands, but rather seem to find us. The old man in Hemingway's book is past the days of ability and seems to be no longer effective at the craft he has spent a lifetime learning.

---

6. Horrell, "Self-Giving Triune God."

> He hooks up on the biggest catch of his life. A marlin pulls him out to sea. Moments like these are rare. It would seem that the right thing to do is cut the fish loose and move away from the situation. In his youth, maybe he would have been able to bring this fish in and receive the adulation and admiration of his fellow fishermen. Maybe the old man doesn't need to prove anything to anyone. Maybe he needs to know something for himself. The beauty of this moment isn't without pain or struggle. The man is wounded in his hands in the process. The greatest catch of his life then ends with the fish being ripped to shreds with only the skeleton attached to the boat. Only he was able to see the moment in its full scope. Others would be able to behold the bones and appreciate this magnificent fish, *but the old man was the only one that saw it.* (emphasis added)

He knew something more, however, than how to catch:

> The works of Christ is the emanating light that shines from him. Yet the light shines forth from the glory of his beauty and splendor. I don't want to know the actors that pretend to know how to brave the waters selling their advice of kingdoms they have built in their own strength. I want to know the old man that caught a kingdom at his weakest with no strength of his own. This generation, old and young, feels their weakness. We are tired of pretending to be strong while the world is at turmoil around us. We are ready for the old man's wisdom from the sea.[7]

So, this is how we exemplify transcendence. Like *The Old Man and the Sea*, we turn "loss into gain, defeat into triumph, and even death into life."[8]

Second, as captain of my yacht, Perichoresis, I identify with and live from my own revelation that hopefully are wise words about being with life from Life: "Behind every breakdown, there can be a breakthrough, and then a breakout."

---

7. Lee, "Reflection."
8. Lee, "Reflection."

**Figure 7: Perichoresis**

My 46.5-foot yacht, Perichoresis, arrived in Cherry Cove, Catalina Island, off the coast of Southern California, at 11:30 p.m., in pitch black. We were happy to be out of 21-knot winds and honest 6-foot swells. Now it is 8:30, Friday morning, July 4. I have just woken up. The harbor master's assistant is hailing me, "Good morning, Perichoresis. You must now leave your buoy as it is owned by a power-boater from Long Beach for the third through the fifth." I reply, "But we are registered until Saturday morning!" I wanted to report him! I waved my receipt!

I complained that it was a dishonest practice to take your money for two nights and not inform you that most of the moorings for July 3 and 4 were already registered, giving no alternative. So, I gave in and returned home, saddened that our island vacation had been cut short, with no barbecue, no fireworks for the Fourth of July. But what happened next is a divine surprise that happens to very few in whale world . . . For behind a *breakdown* is a *breakthrough* and then a *breakout*!

Finally, there was good news for the blue whales (*Balaenoptera musculus*) of the Pacific Ocean, a return to a historic migration pattern makes whale-sense. Recent studies reported the first documented migration that summer of the blue whale from the waters of Alaska and southern British Columbia since the end of commercial whaling in 1965.

We released from our buoy at Cherry Cove on Catalina Island and were halfway home to Marina Del Rey in Los Angeles. A 100-foot-long, over-200-ton blue whale swam 3 feet from my stern quarter, portside. I could reach out and touch his back! Charles Koekemoer, my first mate, grabbed a camera and started shooting rapid-fire shots, catching it surfacing a hundred feet beyond us. He continued to snap pictures as Big Blue circled around us at 5 knots (the speed of a feeding blue whale) in a soft-ball-diamond area, scaring its food into a ball and then attacking it to consume a good portion of daily krill.

In the movie *Caddyshack 2*, Chevy Chase says to Danny as he is about to tee off, "Be the ball!" But we are in the center of the diamond pattern and this whale is circling his lunch . . . We think we are the ball! Research on blue whale behavior, however, suggests we were not in danger from the biggest animal that has ever lived.

The implications are stunning! Dwarfed by the vast expanse of the open ocean is the biggest animal that has ever lived on our planet. Blue whales can measure over 100 feet in length. Adult weights typically range from "a maximum recorded weight of 173 tons" (190 short tons)[9] and probably reaching over 181 tons (200 short tons),[10] 300,000 pounds, the equivalent of 30 African elephants. It is the longest of any animal. It is far larger than the biggest dinosaur, and almost twice as heavy. Its tongue weighs as much as an elephant. Its vast ribcage houses its lungs, carrying 2,000 liters of air, 500 times the capacity of human lungs. Its powerful 20-foot jaws take in 16,000 gallons of water in one gigantic gulp. Blue whales can hear each other up to 1,000 miles away. They use their sounds to communicate and to navigate the ocean with echolocation. Their heartbeats can be heard from 19 miles away. Their hearts are the largest of any animal, the size of a VW Beetle car, weighing up to 600 pounds, "which beats 5 or 6 times a minute and pumps 10 tons of blood through a million miles of blood vessels."[11] And some of its blood vessels are so wide that one could swim down them. Their tails alone are the width of a small aircraft's wings. Thank God they do not flip their tails when feeding! Streamlining close to perfection enables them to cruise at 20 knots. They

9. https://en.wikipedia.org/wiki/Blue_whale.

10. COSEWIC, *Assessment and Update Status Report*.

11 "Inside the Blue Whale," *The Life of Mammals*, BBC, July 28, 2009. https://www.bbc.co.uk/programmes/p004t035.

are some of the fastest creatures in the sea. They can cover up to 283.2 miles per day. Although they are the world's largest animals, they feed on the smallest—krill, a crustacean a few centimeters long. Adult blue whales can eat up to 40 million krill in a day. Their migration routes are a mystery. Despite their enormous size, we know very little about them. Where do they breed? We do not know. *They can teach, learn, cooperate, scheme, and grieve.* They dramatically remind us of how much we have to learn about the ocean and the creatures that live there.[12]

We did not know then that federal regulations mandate that people stay 100 yards from a swimming whale. We could not be whale-wise because this one surfaced in our space. We were not complaining, because we would not be spending a year in federal prison and paying a $10,000 fine. Obviously, we were not showing our snapshots. Hopefully, the statute of limitations has run out!

Ten minutes went by. Suddenly, maybe 300 spinning dolphins appeared, some diving in threes beneath our yacht, others swimming ahead of our bow to our delight. It was dinner time, and they were chasing the same broods of krill, meaning small-fry fish in the aquatic food chain.

What are the chances of seeing a big blue whale, the largest creature on earth, coming across our stern quarter 3 feet from us, and about 300 dolphins spinning by ten minutes later on a July 4? Does this ever happen to a sailor on a Friday afternoon in Southern California waters? According to a sailing magazine picked up later that day, there were only three recorded sightings that first migration summer. But they need to rewrite history! There were four, and, by the way, the summer before I saw a blue whale (and have a snapshot), 200 feet off my starboard side. There were five.

Did God, however, send a 300,000-pound, 30-African-elephant-sized animal to get my attention and impress on my spirit on a bad-hair day, "I love you sailor?" Now, I am not a break-dancing charismatic! But like *The Old Man and the Sea*, that was like a miracle boat-pulling moment by "a magnificently splendored fish in which one doesn't need to prove anything to anyone but needs to know something for himself." That is, "there are moments, as we brave the waters of life that seem to come and lift us into *the transcendence of eternal purpose*. Such moments like these are not fabricated by our hands, but rather seem to find us."[13] Only,

---

12. https://en.wikipedia.org/wiki/Blue_whale.
13. Lee, "Reflection."

*this* old man did not find a marlin. The biggest creature on earth traveled many ocean miles and found me on a Friday, the Fourth of July, 3 feet away. So, that was a benchmark day for me! A sailor's biggest and best Fourth of July gift is a blue whale 3 feet off your stern quarter, followed by 300 spinning dolphins 10 minutes later—some scooting beyond our bow, others diving beneath our hull! When I get discouraged, like the Hebrews of old who remembered a grace-gifted day of plan, purpose, peace, power, provision, protection, and presence, I too treasure how God uniquely singled me out for love-gifted transcendence. The astronomical odds are in favor of my miracle moment. I did the math!

*The Old Man and the Sea* is only a story about seeing and catching a glorious boat-pulling fish. Again, that was a story about a paradigm shift in which the old man does not need to prove anything to anyone but needs to know something for himself. But *this* old man actually saw, and could have touched, not a marlin, but a mighty whale at his weakest moment with no strength of his own. The beauty of my moment is not without pain or struggle. I was angry at being unfairly put out of my favorite mooring, which overlooks a beautiful and rugged pastoral scene. I was wounded. I was reacting, making the harbor master's assistant so wrong so I could be so right (how dare he ruin our Fourth of July), thereby losing creativity and empowerment. *He was wrong, but my way of being with him was wrong. I was not looking for or being from an anticipated moment of "the transcendence of eternal purpose."* I was not living from a remarkable vision of God until he sent Big Blue and love-gifted me with a whale of a day!

*The point?* We can do a reaction to life's losses, defeats, and death, or we can be with life's interruptions from a reframe that creates a new opening as one stands in an answer to what is often missing, the satisfaction of a love-gifted transcendent interest that turns "loss into gain, defeat into triumph, and even death into life," or a breakdown that becomes a breakthrough, and then a breakout.

That is how Abraham got into Hebrews 11, the Bible's hall of fame! He stood in proleptic and prophetic position—God called him to be a father of all nations before he was a father. So, the question:

> So how do we fit what we know of Abraham, our first father in the faith, into this new way of looking at things? If Abraham, by what he *did* for God, got God to approve him, he could certainly have taken credit for it. But the story we're given is a God-story, not an Abraham-story. What we read in Scripture is, "Abraham

entered into what God was doing for him, and that was the turning point. He trusted God to set him right instead of trying to be right on his own." (Rom 4:1–3)

Now we can practice life as an act of worship! Is that impressive and unique? To get out in front of a blind spot (a *skitoma*) by accessing a breakthrough by being with what life throws at us from a new "come from"—a transcendent interest of eternal purpose satisfied through love-gifted kenotic interpersonal oneness inspired by a remarkable vision of God. So, this is how we live into transcendence, are defined, and get named in the eternal hall of fame!

Given these sea-going metaphors, how about a turning point? Why not experience a paradigm shift, and get into the eternal hall of fame, believing that loss can be turned into *gain*, defeat into *triumph*, and even death into *life*? That behind every *breakdown* there can be a *breakthrough*, and then a *breakout*?

## CONCLUSION

Therefore, a summary of our positions on the heart of Christianity brings closure. Trinity, as limitless kenotic Love, is "the frame and focus of all adoration."[14] The loss of human connection can be restored and life need not be without "meaning, value, and purpose."[15]

Hopefully, the case for kenotic interpersonal oneness as "a human rational construct" was "developed under the constraints of revelation and inspiration and was a process of thinking theologically under the impact of the economy of creation and redemption."[16]

The late Charles Krauthammer, who suffered much and yet lived as he intended, said it well: "Playwright Tom Stoppard once said the reason he writes is because every once in a while, you put a few words together in the right order and you are able to give the world a nudge."[17] Krauthammer responded: "And sometimes I'm able to do that."

---

14. Packer, *Stunted Ecclesiology*, 125. James Innell Packer (born in Gloucester, England) is a British-born Canadian Christian theologian in the Calvinistic Anglican tradition.

15. Craig, "Absurdity of Life without God."

16. Manastireanu, "Perichoresis," 63. See Gunton, *One, the Three and the Many*, 164.

17. The actual quote is: "Words are sacred. They deserve respect. If you get the right ones, in the right order, you can nudge the world a little."

Hopefully, although the writers of this book do not have the massive intellect, enigmatic world knowledge, and wordsmithing skill of a Charles Krauthammer, the readers of this inspired word will give the world a new nudge!

## REFLECTION

1. What is reality?
2. Why is it important to flow from reality?
3. How is Reality as kenotic Father-led interpersonal oneness experienced and expressed?
4. Do you agree with the ontological principle of looking for or being from an anticipated moment of "the transcendence of eternal purpose"? If so, what is the basis for such an approach to life?

# Resources[1]

ONLINE FORUMS AND COMMUNITY websites, research journals and reputable research sites, and physical publications and physical events are used by the Relational Theology community.

One will not, however, find the term "Relational Theology" used. But anything that affirms the work of T. F. Torrance, Karl Barth, Ray S. Anderson, Colin Gunton, Alan Torrance, C. Baxter Kruger, etc. will be in the mode of thinking that undergirds relational theology. Marty Folsom has a lot more engagement with family systems, attachment theory, addiction theory, etc. than most theological thinkers.

1. Websites or conversations:
    a. academia.edu
    b. T. F. Torrance Fellowship
    c. Karl Barth for Dummies
    d. John Macmurray Fellowship
    e. Evangelical Calvinists—Bobby Grow
    f. Trinity in You (Perichoresis Australia)
    g. Grace Communion International
    h. Perichoresis—C. Baxter Kruger
    i. Open Table Conference—Portland, OR

1. Folsom, "Resources," email to author, December 3, 2018.

2. Journals:
   a. *Scottish Journal of Theology*
   b. *International Systematic Theology Journal*
   c. *Cultural Encounters*
3. Events:
   a. At the AAR
      i. Karl Barth Society
      ii. T. F. Torrance Fellowship
   b. Karl Barth Conference—Princeton
   c. Inhabit Conference—The Seattle School of Theology and Psychology

Marty Folsom is establishing the field of Relational Theology (the most common term used is Trinitarian-Incarnational Theology). There are theology conferences that call themselves "Trinitarian," but they are classical in orientation (Augustine, Aquinas) and tend to be philosophical more than relational.

# About the Authors

## WESLEY M. PINKHAM (WESS)

Dr. Wess holds a Bachelor of Arts in Biblical Literature and Philosophy from Seattle Pacific University, a Master of Arts in Educational Ministries from Wheaton College, a Master of Education in Adult Education and Higher Educational Administration from the University of British Columbia, a Master of Divinity and Master of Theology in Church Administration and Homiletics from Trinity Evangelical Divinity School, and a Doctor of Ministry in Church Change Agentry and Conflict Management from McCormick Theological Seminary. He did postgraduate work in Higher Adult Education for the EdD degree at Northern Illinois University (one year) and for the EdD in Adult Education and Higher Educational Administration at the University of British Columbia (three years). Shiloh University conferred the Doctor of Literature Degree (DLitt) in June 2019.

Wess brings new meaning and power to the term "master communicator." His relational and transparent teaching and writing style assists students and readers in discovering life-changing truths. Wess brings a dynamic, holistic approach to relational theology. He is a leader and educator with six earned degrees, plus the DLitt *honoris causa*.

Wess served for twelve years as a senior pastor, a youth minister, and a minister of Christian education. He was an administrator and associate professor at Wheaton College graduate school for six years and served for seven years as Academic Dean, Senior Vice President and professor at Dominion College, an undergraduate liberal arts school. He served for fifteen years at The King's University, Los Angeles, as an accreditation specialist in the capacities of Dean of Assessment, Dean of Institutional Effectiveness, and Dean of Doctoral Studies. Wess served as Vice President for Academics and Dean of Doctoral Studies at Shiloh University for four years. He served there as a trustee. Prior to retirement, he served for one year as Vice President for Academics at The New International University in Bellevue, Washington.

## JEREMIAH GRUENBERG

JEREMIAH HOLDS A BROAD range of interests, from theology to music to writing. He is passionate about leading individuals to discover new levels of creativity and life satisfaction in God. He has served as a pastor and as teacher in Christian higher education.

His research interests center on spiritual formation and practical theology, but he is particularly engaged with the transformative impact of authenticity in the Christian church. He currently works as a speaker, coach, and consultant on authenticity in the corporate, church, and family settings. He also hosts *The God Experiment* podcast.

Jeremiah holds a Bachelor of Arts in English from the University of California, Los Angeles, a Master of Divinity from Shiloh University, and a Doctor of Philosophy in Theology from South African Theological Seminary. His articles have been published in *God and Nature* and *The Journal of Spiritual Formation and Soul Care*.

# Bibliography

Ables, Travis E. *Incarnational Realism: Trinity and the Spirit in Augustine and Barth.* T & T Clark Studies in Systematic Theology 21. London: Bloomsbury, 2013.
Adams, Ken. "How Do You Measure Being?" May 11, 2017. https://impactdisciples.com/how-do-you-measure-being/.
Anderson, Bernhard W. *Understanding the Old Testament.* Englewood Cliffs, NJ: Prentice-Hall, 1966.
Anderson, Ray S. "A Theology of Ministry." In *Theological Foundations for Ministry*, edited by Ray S. Anderson, 7. Edinburgh: T. & T. Clark, 1979.
———. *The Shape of Practical Theology: Empowering Ministry with Theological Praxis.* Downers Grove, IL: InterVarsity, 2001.
———. *The Soul of Ministry: Forming Leaders for God's People.* Louisville: Westminster John Knox, 1997.
———. *Theological Foundations for Ministry.* Edinburgh: T. & T. Clark, 1979.
Anderson, T. "Teaching in an Online Learning Context." In *Theory and Practice of Online Learning*, edited by T. Anderson and F. Elloumi, 273–94. Edmonton, Alberta: Athabasca University Press, 2004.
Atkinson, William P. "The Trinity and Servant-Leadership." *Evangelical Review of Theology* 38.2 (2014) 30, 138–50.
Augsburger, David W. *Caring Enough to Confront: How to Understand and Express Your Deepest Feelings toward Others.* 3rd ed. Grand Rapids: Revell, 2009.
Awad, Najeeb G. "Between Subordination and Koinonia: Toward a New Reading of the Cappadocian Theology." *Modern Theology* 23.2 (2007) 181–204.
———. "Personhood and Particularity: John Zizioulas, Colin Gunton, and the Trinitarian Theology of Personhood." *Journal of Reformed Theology* 4 (2010) 2–22.
Ayres, Lewis. "Augustine, Christology, and God as Love: An Introduction to the Homilies on 1 John." In *Nothing Greater, Nothing Better: Theological Essays on the Love of God*, edited by Kevin J. Vanhoozer, 67–93. Grand Rapids: Eerdmans, 2001.

Badcock, Gary D. "The Concept of Love: Divine and Human." In *Nothing Greater, Nothing Better: Theological Essays on the Love of God*, edited by Kevin J. Vanhoozer, 30–46. Grand Rapids: Eerdmans, 2001.
Baron. R. *Hugue et Richard de Saint-Victor*. N.p.: Bloud & Gay, 1961.
Barth, Karl. *Church Dogmatics*. Edited by G. W. Bromiley and T. F. Torrance. 4 vols. Edinburgh: T. & T. Clark, 1936–1962.
———. *The Epistle to the Romans*. Translated by Edwyn C. Hoskyns. London: Oxford University Press, 1976.
———. *The Humanity of God*. Translated by J. N. Thomas and T. Wieser. Richmond, VA: John Knox, 1960.
Battle, Michael Jesse. "Reconciliation: The Ubuntu Theology of Desmond Tutu." Rev. ed. Cleveland: Pilgrim, 2009.
Beale, G. K., and Mitchell Kim. *God Dwells among Us: Expanding Eden to the Ends of the Earth*. Downers Grove, IL: InterVarsity, 2015.
Beether, Willis J. *The Prophets and the Promise*. Grand Rapids: Baker, 1963.
Belliotti, Raymond Angelo. *Roman Philosophy and the Good Life*. Lanham, MD: Lexington, 2009.
Bernard David K. *Essentials of Oneness Theology*. Hazelwood, MO: Word Aflame, 1985.
Bilaniuk, Petro B. T. "The Mystery of Theosis or Divinization." In *The Heritage of the Early Church: Essays in Honor of the Very Reverend Georges Vasilievich Florovsky*, edited by David Nieman and Margaret Schatkin, 337–59. Orientalia Christiana Analecta 195. Rome: Pontifical Oriental Institute, 1973.
Bird, Joseph E. "Give the World a Nudge." June 22, 1018. https://josephebird.com/2018/06/22/give-the-world-a-nudge/.
Blair, Leonardo. "Most Adult US Christians Don't Believe Holy Spirit Is Real: Study." *The Christian Post*, September 10, 2021. https://www.christianpost.com/news/most-us-christians-dont-believe-holy-spirit-is-real-study.html.
Boethius. *Theological Tractates. The Consolation of Philosophy*. Translated by H. F. Stewart, E. K. Rand, S. J. Tester. Loeb Classical Library 74. Cambridge, MA: Harvard University Press, 1973.
Boethius. *Liber De Persona et Duabus Naturis Contra Eutychen Et Nestorium*. Edited by H. F. Stewart. Cambridge, MA: Harvard University Press, 1918.
Boff, Leonardo. *Holy Trinity, Perfect Community*. Translated from the Portuguese by Phillip Berryman. Maryknoll, NY: Orbis, 2000.
———. *Trinity and Society*. Translated by Paul Burns. Wellwood, Kent: Burns & Oates, 1988.
Bonhoeffer, Dietrich. *Life Together*. Translated by John W. Doberstein. New York: Harper & Row, 1954.
Bonino, José Miguez. *Faces of Latin American Protestantism*. Translated by Eugene L. Stockwell. Grand Rapids: Eerdmans, 1997.
Borysov, Eduard. *Triadosis: Union with the Triune God*. Eugene, OR: Pickwick, 2019.
Boyer, E. L. *College: The Undergraduate Experience in America*. New York: Harper & Row, 1987.
Bradshaw, David, ed. *Philosophical Theology and the Christian Tradition: Russian and Western Perspectives*. Russian Philosophical Studies 5; Cultural Heritage and Contemporary Change, Series IV A, Eastern and Central Europe 44. Washington, DC: Council for Research in Values and Philosophy, 2012.
Broughton, Geoff. "Authentic dialogue: Towards a Practical Theology of Conversation," *Academia* May 23, 2022. https://www.academia.edu/10253559/ Authentic_dialogue_Towards_a_Practical_Theology_of_Conversation.

Brown, David. "Trinitarian Personhood and Individuality." In *Trinity, Incarnation and Atonement: Philosophical and Theological Essays*, edited by Ronald J. Feenstra and Cornelius Plantinga, ch. 2. Notre Dame: University of Notre Dame Press, 1990.

Brümmer, Vincent. *The Model of Love: A Study in Philosophical Theology*. Cambridge: Cambridge University Press, 1993.

Bruner, Frederick Dale. *The Holy Spirit, Shy Member of the Trinity*. Eugene, OR: Wipf & Stock, 2001.

Buber. Martin. *Between Man and Man*. Translated by Ronald Gregor Smith. London: Routledge and Kegan Paul, 1947.

Bultmann, Rudolph. *The History of the Synoptic Tradition*. Translated by John Marsh. Rev. ed. New York: Harper & Row, 1976.

Butner, Glenn, Jr. "For and Against De Régnon: Trinitarianism East and West." *International Journal of Systematic Theology* 17.4 (October 2015) 399–412. doi:10.1111/ijst.12117

Buxton, Graham. *Dancing in the Dark: The Privilege of Participating in the Ministry of Christ*. Milton Keynes, UK: Paternoster, 2001.

Buzzard, Anthony. "Does Everyone Believe in the Trinity?" http://www.mindspring.com/~anthonybuzzard/articles.htm.

Calvin, John. *Institutes of the Christian Religion*. Translated by Henry Beveridge. Peabody, MA: Hendrickson, 2007.

Campbell, Douglas A. "Covenant or Contract in the Interpretation of Paul." In *Trinity and Transformation: J. B. Torrance's Vision of Worship, Mission, and Society*, edited by Todd H. Speidell, 193–212. Eugene, OR: Wipf & Stock, 2016.

———. *Pauline Dogmatics: The Triumph of God's Love*. Grand Rapids: Eerdmans, 2019.

———. "Romans 1:17—A Crux Interpretum for the Pistis Christou Debate." *JBL* 113.2 (1994) 198, 207.

Canlis, Julie. *Calvin's Ladder: A Spiritual Theology of Ascent and Ascension*. Grand Rapids: Eerdmans, 2010.

Capes, David B., et al. *Rediscovering Paul: An Introduction to His World, Letters, and Theology*. 2nd ed. Downers Grove, IL: IVP Academic, 2017.

Caquelin, Ron. "Final Reflection Paper." Assignment for the course "Mentored Ministry" (MM 501), Shiloh University, August 2017.

Carl, Harold F. "Against Praxeas—How Far Did Tertullian Advance the Doctrine of the Trinity?" 2015. https://core.ac.uk/display/101168578. oai:CiteSeerX.psu:10.1.1.532.618

Carson, D. A. "Contrarian Reflections on Individualism." *Themelios* 35.3 (2011) 380.

Cartledge, Mark J. *Practical Theology: Charismatic and Empirical Perspectives*. Milton Keynes, UK: Paternoster, 2003.

Casanova, Amanda. "Less than 1/5 of Americans Believe Life's Purpose Is Knowing, Loving God, Survey Finds." *Christian Headlines* (blog), May 8, 2020. https://www.christianheadlines.com/blog/less-than-1-5-of-americans-believe-lifes-purpose-is-knowing-loving-god-survey-finds.html.

Chan, Cherry, Hiu Ki. "God in Classic Theism and Contemporary Thought." TMCT 510. Spring 2015. https://www.coursehero.com/file/43491158/Living-Love-An-Exploration-on-God-is-Lovpdf/.

Coe, J. "Intentional Spiritual Formation in the Classroom: Making Space for the Spirit in the University." *Christian Education Journal* 4.2 (2000) 95, 85–110.

Colyer, Elmer M., eds. "T. F. Torrance's Theology." In *The Promise of Trinitarian Theology: Theologians in Dialogue with T. F. Torrance*, 205–38. Lanham, MD: Rowman and Littlefield, 2001.

Conzelmann, Hans. *Jesus*. Minneapolis: Fortress, 1973.

Copeland, Kenneth. World Communion Service, audio recording, Fall 1984, Fort Worth, Texas.

COSEWIC (Committee on the Status of Endangered Wildlife in Canada). *Assessment and Update Status Report on the Blue Whale: Balaenoptera Musculus*. Ottawa, ON: COSEWIC, 2003. https://www.sararegistry.gc.ca/virtual_sara/files/cosewic/sr_blue_whale_e.pdf.

Craig, William Lane. *The Absurdity of Life Without God*. Biola University Christian Apologetics Program (January 1, 2005).

———. *The Kalām Cosmological Argument*. Eugene, OR: Wipf and Stock, 2000.

Davidson, Robert. *Genesis*. Cambridge: Cambridge University Press, 1979.

Davis, Martin M. "T. F. Torrance." *God for Us!* (blog), July 19, 2017. https://martinmdavis.blogspot.com/2017/07/tf-torrance-communion-of-spirit-pt-1.html.

Dean, Kendra Creasy. *Almost Christian: What the Faith of Our Teenagers Is Telling the American Church*. Oxford: Oxford University Press, 2010.

Deddo, Gary W. "The Holy Spirit in T. F. Torrance's Theology." In *The Promise of Trinitarian Theology: Theologians in Dialogue with T. F. Torrance*, edited by Elmer Colyer. Lanham, MD: Rowman and Littlefield, 2001.

Dickson, Ben. "Holistic Discipleship—How the Recapturing of the Trinity Can Address Underrepresentation within the Next Generations in the Western Church." February 2016. https://www.academia.edu/27320441/Holistic_Discipleship_How_the_recapturing_of_the_Trinity_can_address_underrepresentation_within_the_next_generations_in_the_Western_Church.

Dodds, Michael J. *The Unchanging God of Love: Thomas Aquinas and Contemporary Theology on Divine Immutability*. Washington, DC: Catholic University of America Press, 2008.

Dubin, Robert, and Thomas C. Taveggia. *The Teaching-Learning Paradox: A Comparative Analysis of College Teaching Methods Center for the Advanced Study of Educational Administration*. Eugene: University of Oregon, 1968.

Dunn, James D. G. *Jesus and the Spirit*. Grand Rapids: Eerdmans, 1997.

Durst, Rodrick. *Reordering the Trinity: Six Movements of God in the New Testament*. Grand Rapids: Kregel, 2015.

Eastman, Blake. "How Much of Communication Is Really Nonverbal? An Extensive Breakdown." August 2011. http://www.nonverbalgroup.com/2011/08/how-much-of-communication-is-really-nonverbal/.

Edwards, James R. *The Gospel According to Mark*. Pillar New Testament Commentary. Leicester: Apollos, 2002.

Eichrodt, Walther. *Theology of the Old Testament*. 2 vols. Philadelphia: Westminster, 1961.

Elmer, Duane. *Cross-Cultural Conflict: Building Relationships for Effective Ministry*. Downers Grove, IL: InterVarsity, 1993.

Elwell, Walter A., and Philip Wesley Comfort. *Tyndale Bible Dictionary*. Tyndale Reference Library. Wheaton, IL: Tyndale, 2001.

"Epistemology." https://en.wikipedia.org/wiki/Epistemology/.

Erickson, Millard J. *God in Three Persons: A Contemporary Interpretation of the Trinity*. Grand Rapids: Baker, 1995.

———. *Where Is Theology Going?: Issues and Perspectives on the Future of Theology*. Grand Rapids: Baker, 1994.

# Bibliography

Fayis, F. "Some Concepts of the Trinity from Different Angles." https://www.academia.edu/37742137/Some_concepts_of_the_trinity_from_different_angles.

Fee, Gordon D. "On Getting the Spirit Back into Spirituality." Lectured delivered at the Wheaton Theology Conference, 2009.

———. *Pauline Christology: An Exegetical-Theological Study*. Peabody, MA: Hendrickson, 2007.

Feenstra, Ronald J., and Cornelius Plantinga Jr., eds. *Trinity, Incarnation, and Atonement: Philosophical and Theological Essays*. Notre Dame: University of Notre Dame Press, 1989.

"15 Motivational Quotes for Patients." https://www.caringbridge.org/resources/motivational-quotes-for-patients/.

Fisher, Roger, et al. *Getting to Yes: Negotiating Agreement without Giving In*. Kindle ed. Originally published, New York: Penguin, 1922.

Fohrer, George. *Introduction to the Old Testament*. Nashville: Abingdon, 1965.

Folsom, Marty. "A Comparative Assessment of the Concept of Freedom in the Anthropologies of John Macmurray, John Zizioulas, and Karl Barth." PhD diss., University of Otago, Dunedin, New Zealand, 1995.

———. "A Dialog with Ben Meyers' 'Tweeting the Trinity' #10, #11, #12." https://www.academia.edu/34971758/A_DIALOG_WITH_BEN_MEYERS_TWEETING_THE_TRINITY_10_11_12.

———. *Face to Face*. 3 vols. Eugene, OR: Wipf & Stock, 2013–2016.

———. "Recursion: A Theological Axiom for Relationships." *Marriage and the Family, A Christian Journal* 7.2 (2004) 199–214.

———. "Relational Theology: A Primer." Edited and transcribed by Wesley M. Pinkham. Vol. 1. Prepublished lectures given at Dominion College, Seattle, WA, 1996.

Ford, Leroy. *Design for Teaching and Training: A Teacher's Guide for Interactive Learning and Instruction*. Eugene, OR: Wipf & Stock, 2002.

Frame, John. *The Doctrine of God: A Theology of Lordship*. P&R, 2002.

Freedman, R. David. "Woman, a Power Equal to a Man." *Biblical Archaeology Review* 9 (1983) 56–58.

Frey, Jörg, ed. *Wissenschaftliche Untersuchungen zum Neuen Testament 2*. Reihe 326. Tübingen: Mohr Siebeck, 2012.

Frymier, Jack R. *The Nature of Educational Method*. Columbus, OH: Merrill, 1965.

Fuller, R. H. *The Mission and Achievement of Jesus*. London: SCM, 1954.

Gabbatt, Adam. "Stephen Hawking Says Universe Not Created by God." *The Guardian*, September 1, 2010. https://www.theguardian.com/science/2010/sep/02/stephen-hawking-big-bang-creator.

Galen, Greg Gordan. "The Dynamic of the New Birth." Unpublished DMin paper, Shiloh University, Kalona, IO, 2021.

———. "Proclaiming God's Goodness across Cultures." Doctoral-level class discussion on the effects of the Enlightenment on mission in Western Culture. "Culture and Mission," Shiloh University, June 13, 2017.

———. Post in the course "The Pastor as a Change Agent" (DM766), Shiloh University, April 7, 2018.

———. Post in the course "The Pastor as a Change Agent" (DM766), Shiloh University, April 22, 2018.

Gangel, Kenneth O. "The Gift of Administration." *The Standard*, May 15, 1973.

———. "Has the Church Had It?" A baccalaureate message given to Trinity College and Trinity Evangelical Divinity School, Deerfield, IL, May 27, 1970.

Gangel, Kenneth O., and Warren S. Benson. *Christian Education: Its History and Philosophy*, Eugene, OR: Wipf & Stock, 2002.

Garber, Peter R. *50 Communications Activities, Icebreakers, and Exercises*. Amherst, MA: HRD, 2008. https://downloads.hrdpressonline.com/files/6820080609105844.pdf.

Garrison, D. R., and Terry Anderson. *E-Learning in the 21st Century: A Framework for Research and Practice*. London: Routledge/Falmer, 2003.

Gesenius, Wilhelm, et al. *Gesenius' Hebrew Grammar*. Edited by E. Kautzsch, translated by A. E. Cowley. Mineola, NY: Dover, 2006.

Getz, Gene A. *Building Up One Another*. N.p.: David C. Cook, 2002.

———. *Sharpening the Focus of the Church*. Eugene, OR: Wipf & Stock, 2012.

Gibson, C., ed. *Distance Learners in Higher Education: Institutional Responses for Quality Outcomes*. Madison WI: Atwood, 1998.

Giles, Kevin. "The Evangelical Theological Society and the Doctrine of the Trinity." *Evangelical Quarterly* 80.4 (2008) 323–38. https://biblicalstudies.org.uk/pdf/eq/2008-4_323.pdf.

Girdlestone, James P. "Our Potential Late-Modern 'God Problem.'" Lecture presented in the doctoral seminar "The American Crisis" (DM721), Shiloh University, 2017.

Glenn, Mark H. "Joy of the Trinity." November 2021. https://www.youtube.com/watch?v=omIEDFYZwLM.

———. Lecture notes for online session 12, "Eastern vs. Western," of the course "Proclaiming God's Goodness across Culture" (DM722), Shiloh University, Summer 2017.

———. "To Know and Be Known: A Recursive Model for Conflict Management." PhD diss., Trinity College and Seminary, 2016.

Godway, Eleanor M. "The Crisis of the Personal: Macmurray, Postmodernism, and the Challenge of Philosophy Today." *Appraisal* 8.1 (2010) 2.

Gordon, James R. "The Presence of the Triune God: Persons, Essence, and Equality." April 2021. https://www.academia.edu/35740324/The_Presence_of_the_Triune_God_Persons_Essence_and_Equality.

Goss, Tracy. *The Last Word on Power*. New York: Doubleday, 1996.

Granger, D., and M. Benke. "Supporting Learners at a Distance from Inquiry through Completion." In *Distance Learners in Higher Education: Institutional Responses for Quality Outcomes*, edited by C. C. Gibson, 127–37. Madison, WI: Atwood, 1998,

Gray, Donald. *Jesus: The Way to Freedom*. Winona, MN: St. Mary's, 1979.

Green, Bradley G. *Colin Gunton and the Failure of Augustine: The Theology of Colin Gunton in the Light of Augustine*. Cambridge: Clarke, 2012.

Green, J., and M. Turner, eds. *Jesus of Nazareth Lord and Christ: Essays on the Historical Jesus and New Testament Christology*. Grand Rapids: Eerdmans, 1994.

Greenleaf, Robert K., and Larry C. Spears. *Servant Leadership: A Journey into the Nature of Legitimate Power and Greatness*. Minneapolis: Paulist, 1983.

Greenman J., and G. Kalantzis, eds. *Life in the Spirit: Spiritual Formation in Theological Perspective*. Downers Grove, IL: InterVarsity Academic, 2010.

Grenz, Stanley J. *The Named God and the Question of Being*. Louisville: Westminster John Knox, 2005.

———. *Rediscovering the Triune God: The Trinity in Contemporary Theology*. Minneapolis: Fortress, 2004.

———. *The Social God and the Relational Self: A Trinitarian Theology of the Imago Dei.* 1st ed. Louisville, KY: Westminster John Knox, 2007.

———. *Theology for the Community of God.* Grand Rapids: Eerdmans, 1994.

Gruenler, Royce G. *The Trinity in the Gospel of John: A Thematic Commentary on the Fourth Gospel.* Reprint. Eugene, OR: Wipf & Stock, 2004.

Gunawardena, C. N. *Social Presence Theory and Implications for Building Online Communities.* Paper presented at the Third International Symposium on Telecommunications in Education, Albuquerque, NM, 1994.

Gunton, Colin E. *Act and Being: Towards a Theology of the Divine Attributes.* Grand Rapids: Eerdmans, 2003.

———. "Augustine, the Trinity and the Theological Crisis of the West." *Scottish Journal of Theology* 43.1 (1990) 56.

———. "Authority." In *The Oxford Companion to Christian Thought*, edited by Adrian Hastings et al., 55–56. Oxford: Oxford University Press, 2000.

———. *Christ and Creation.* Milton Keynes, UK: Paternoster, 1992.

———. *The Christian Faith: An Introduction to Christian Doctrine.* Oxford: Blackwell, 2002.

———. *Father, Son and Holy Spirit: Toward a Fully Trinitarian Theology.* London: T. & T. Clark, 2003.

———. *The One, the Three and the Many: God, Creation and the Culture of Modernity.* Cambridge: Cambridge University Press, 1993.

———. *The Promise of Trinitarian Theology.* 2nd ed. London: T. & T. Clark, 2003.

———. "Trinity, Ontology and Anthropology: Towards a Renewal of the Doctrine of the Imago Dei in Persons Divine and Human." In *Persons, Divine and Human*, edited by C. Schwoebel and C. Gunton. Edinburgh: T. & T. Clark, 1991.

———. *Yesterday and Today: A Study of Continuities in Christology.* Grand Rapids: Eerdmans, 1983.

Grudem, Wayne. *1 Peter.* Downers Grove, IL: InterVarsity, 1988.

Gryboski, Michael. "Disciples of Christ on Track to Lose Half of Its Membership in 10 Years." *The Christian Post*, August 25, 2019. https://www.christianpost.com/news/disciples-of-christ-on-track-to-lose-half-of-its-membership-in-10-years.html.

Haase, Albert. *Living the Lord's Prayer: The Way of the Disciple.* Downers Grove, IL: InterVarsity, 2009.

Habets, Myk. "The Essence of Evangelical Theology: Critical Introduction to Thomas F. Torrance." In *The Trinitarian Faith: The Evangelical Theology of the Ancient Catholic Church*, by Thomas F. Torrance, 2–13. Edinburgh: T. & T. Clark, 2000.

Hall, Shannon. "Wild Theory: 5-Dimensional Black Holes Could Break Laws of Physics." February 23, 2016. https://www.space.com/32008-five-dimensional-black-holes-theory.html/.

Hallman, Joseph M. "The Mistake of Thomas Aquinas and the Trinity of A. N. Whitehead." *Journal of Religion* 70 (1990) 36–47.

Hargrave, Gary. *Bring God's Kingdom to Earth: The Disciples' Prayer.* N.p.: Living Word, 2014.

Hart, Trevor. "How Do We Define the Nature of God's Love?" In *Nothing Greater, Nothing Better: Theological Essays on the Love of God*, edited by Kevin J. Vanhoozer, 1–29. Grand Rapids: Eerdmans, 2001.

Hastings, A., et al., eds. *The Oxford Companion to Christian Thought.* Oxford: Oxford University Press, 2000.

Hawking, Stephen, and Leonard Mlodinow. *The Grand Design.* New York: Bantam, 2012.

Hawkins, Michael R. "Net Mending: An Essential Element in Facilitating Perichoretic Community." DMin paper, The King's Seminary, 2008.

Haworth, Craig. Book reflection submitted to the doctoral studies seminar "The Pastor as Change Agent" (DM766), Shiloh University, February 2018.

———. "Transformation by Relationship: A Study in Conflict Management Style Formation." Paper submitted for the course "Creative Conflict Management" (DM721), Shiloh University, December 10, 2017.

Hawthorne, Gerald F. *Philippians*. Word Biblical Commentary 43. Dallas: Word, 1983.

———. *The Presence and the Power: The Significance of the Holy Spirit in the Life and Ministry of Jesus*. Eugene, OR: Wipf & Stock, 2003.

Hayford, Jack W. Lecture given at the Autumn Leadership Conference, The Church on the Way, November 2000.

———. *Prayer Is Invading the Impossible*. Gainesville, FL: Bridge-Logos, 2002.

———, ed. *Spirit-Filled Bible*. Nashville: Thomas Nelson, 1991.

Hayes, Mike. "We Cry Abba: The Father's Anointing." Sermon delivered at Covenant Church, Carrollton, Texas, January 1, 1995.

Hays, Richard B. *The Moral Vision of the New Testament*. New York: Harper Collins, 1996.

Hebblethwaite, Brian. "Perichoresis—Reflections on the Doctrine of the Trinity." *Theology* 80.676 (1977) 255–61.

Heidegger, Martin. *Being and Time*. Reprint. New York: Harper Perennial Modern Classics, 2008.

Highfield, Ron. *God, Freedom, and Human Dignity: Embracing a God-Centered Identity in a Me-Centered Culture*. Downers Grove, IL: InterVarsity, 2012.

Hemingway, Ernest. *The Old Man and the Sea*. New York: Scribner, 1995.

Hendricksen, William. *New Testament Commentary: Exposition of Galatians*. Grand Rapids: Baker, 1968.

Highfield, Ron. *God, Freedom, and Human Dignity: Embracing a God-Centered Identity in a Me-Centered Culture*. Downers Grove, IL: InterVarsity, 2012.

Hirsch, Emil G. "Son of Man." http://www.jewishencyclopedia.com/articles/13913-son-of-man.

"Homoousios." *Encyclopedia Britannica*, July 30, 2019. https://www.britannica.com/topic/homoousios.

Hooke, Robert. *Micrographia*. 1665. Republished in electronic format: Palo Alto, CA: Octavo, 1998

Hooker, Morna D. *The Gospel According to St. Mark*. Black's New Testament Commentaries. London: A. & C. Black, 1991.

Horrell, J. Scott. "The Self-Giving Triune God, the Imago Dei and the Nature of the Local Church: An Ontology of Mission." 2004. https://bible.org/article/self-giving-triune-god-iimago-deii-and-nature-local-church-ontology-mission.

Hughes, Philip E. *Commentary on the Second Epistle to the Corinthians*. Grand Rapids: Eerdmans, 1962.

Huizing, Russell L. "Leaders from Disciples: The Churches Contribution to Leadership Development." *English Review of Theology* 35.4 (2011) 333.

Hunter, James Davison. *To Change the World: The Irony, Tragedy & Possibility of Christianity in the Late Modern World*. Oxford: Oxford University Press, 2010.

"The Importance of Living in the Present Moment." Last updated November 15, 2018. https://exploringyourmind.com/importance-living-in-the-present-moment/.

Jeremiah, David. *Romans VIII: The Greatest Chapter in the Bible*. San Diego: Turning Point, n.d.

Jeremias, Joachim. *The Central Message of the New Testament*. Minneapolis: Fortress, 1981.

———. *Jesus and the Message of the New Testament*. Minneapolis: Fortress, 2002.

———. *New Testament Theology: The Proclamation of Jesus*. New York: Scribner, 1971.

———. *The Parables of Jesus*. Rev. ed. London: SCM, 1963.

———. *The Prayers of Jesus*. Translated by John Bowden, Christoph Burchard, and John Reumann. London: SCM, 1967.

Jeyachandran, L. T. "The Trinity as a Paradigm for Spiritual Transformation." In *Beyond Opinion: Living the Faith We Defend*, edited by Ravi Zacharias, 231–52. Nashville: Thomas Nelson, 2007.

Johnson, George E. "Jewish Word / Sechel." *Moment*, November–December 2013. http://www.momentmag.com/jewish-word-sechel/.

Jones, E. Stanley. *Abundant Living*. New York: Abingdon-Cokesbury, 1942.

Jones, Josh. "The Social Lives of Trees: Science Reveals How Trees Mysteriously Talk to Each Other, Work Together & Form Nurturing Families." October 26th, 2017. https://www.openculture.com/2017/10/the-social-lives-of-trees.html.

Jüngel, Eberhard. *The Doctrine of the Trinity: God's Being Is in Becoming*. Translated by H. Harris. 2nd ed. Edinburgh: Scottish Academic, 1976.

"J. Warner Wallace." https://en.wikipedia.org/wiki/J._Warner_Wallace/.

Kaiser, Walter C., Jr. "The Old Promise and the New Covenant." *Journal of the Evangelical Theological Society* 15.1 (Winter 1972) 12–23. http://thepromise.typepad.com/197201.pdf.

Kant, Immanuel. *Der Streit der Fakultäten*. PhB 252. Felix Meiner, 2005.

Kanitz, L. "Improving Christian Worldview Pedagogy: Going Beyond Mere Christianity." *Christian Higher Education* 4 (2005) 99–108.

Kärkkäinen, Veli-Matti. *The Trinity: Global Perspectives*. Louisville: Westminster John Knox, 2007.

———. *The Trinity and Religious Pluralism: The Doctrine of the Trinity in Christian Theology of Religions*. Aldershot: Ashgate, 2004.

Kazmer, M. M. "Coping in a Distance Environment: Sitcoms, Chocolate Cake, and Dinner with a Friend." *First Monday* 5.9 (2000). http://www.firstmonday.dk/issues/issue5_9/kazmer/index.html.

Kasper, Walter. *Jesus the Christ*. Translated by V. Green. New York: Paulist, 1961.

Keathley, Hampton, IV. "The Relationship of the Church to Israel." May 27, 2004. https://bible.org/article/relationship-church-israel.

Keil, C. F., and Franz Delitzsch. *The Pentateuch*. Edinburgh: T. & T. Clark, 1886.

Keller, Timothy. *The Reason for God: Belief in an Age of Skepticism*. New York, Riverhead, 2008.

Kierspel, Lars. Review of *Relationale Ontologie bei Paulus: Die ontischeWirksamkeit der Christusbezogenheit im Denken desHeidenapostels*, by Emmanuel L. Rehfeld. *RBL* 11 (2014). https://www.academia.edu/9104120/Bookreview_Rehfeld_Relationale_Ontologie_bei_Paulus_WUNT_2012_.

Kinkade, Mark. *More to the Story: Savoring Details in God's Word*. Bloomington, IN: Westbow, 2021.

Kinnaman, David. *You Lost Me: Why Young Christians Are Leaving Church ... and Rethinking Faith*. Grand Rapids: Baker, 2011.

Kittel, Gerhard, and Gerhard Fredrich, eds. *Theological Dictionary of the New Testament*. 10 vols. Grand Rapids: Eerdmans, 1979.

Koukoura, Dimitra. "The Nature of Luther's Preaching." July 29, 2017. https://pemptousia.com/2017/07/the-nature-of-luthers-preaching/.

Kruger, C. Baxter. *Across All Worlds: Jesus Inside Our Darkness*. Jackson, MS: 2007. Kindle ed.

———. "The Real Christian Life." Galatians lecture, Dominion College, May 31, 1995.

Kruse, Colin J. *The Letters of John*. 2nd ed. Grand Rapids: Eerdmans, 2020.

Kuhn, Harold. "Relationalism: Principle or Slogan?" *Christianity Today*, February 28, 1975.

Kuhn, Thomas. *The Structure of Scientific Revolutions*. Chicago: University of Chicago Press, 1962.

Küng, Hans. *Truthfulness: The Future of the Church*. New York: Sheed and Ward, 1968.

Kynes Bill. "Postmodernism: A Primer for Pastors." *The Ministerial Forum* 8.1 (1997) 47.

LaCugna, Catherine Mowery. *God for Us: The Trinity and Christian Life*. San Francisco: HarperCollins, 1991.

Lamoureux, P. "An Integrated Approach to Theological Education." *Theological Education* 36.1 (1999) 141–56. http://www.ats.edu/resources/tearch/1999fall.pdf.

Lange, John Peter. *Genesis, or the First Book of Moses*. Edinburgh: T. & T. Clark, 1868.

Larson, Bruce. *No Longer Strangers: An Introduction to Relational Theology*. Waco, TX: Word, 1971.

———. *The Relational Revolution: An Invitation to Discover an Exciting Future for Our Life Together*. Waco, TX: Word, 1976.

Leake, Mike. "Why Pastors Are Stepping Down—and What Congregations Can Do to Help." *Crosswalk*, July 2021. https://www.crosswalk.com/church/pastors-or-leadership/why-pastors-are-stepping-down.html.

LeBar, Lois E. *Education That Is Christian*. Colorado Springs, CO: David C. Cook, 1995.

Lee, Sung S. "Reflection of the 'Old Man and the Sea.'" Paper submitted for the course "The Old Man and the Sea" (GTHE661-62), The King's University, May 21, 2014.

Lett, Jonathan. "'God in Three Persons, Blessed Trinity!' Pneumatology and Participation in the Theology of John Calvin." https://letu.academia.edu/JonathanLett. In *Calvinus Pastor Ecclesiae: Papers of the Eleventh International Congress on Calvin Research*, 355–64. Reformed Historical Theology 39. Göttingen: Vandenhoeck & Ruprecht, 2016. https://www.academia.edu/11937288/_God_in_Three_Persons_Blessed_Trinity_Pneumatology_and_Participation_in_the_Theology_of_John_Calvin.

Levin, Faitel. "The Nature of G-d." https://www.chabad.org/therebbe/article_cdo/aid/294299/jewish/The-Nature-of-G-d.htm.

Levine, Amy-Jill. *The Misunderstood Jew: The Church and the Scandal of the Jewish Jesus*. Reprint. San Francisco: HarperOne, 2007.

Lewis, C. S. *The Abolition of Man*. New York: Macmillan, 1947.

———. *The Four Loves*. San Francisco: HarperCollins, 2017.

———. *Mere Christianity*. New York: Macmillan, 1952.

Liddell, Henry George, and Robert Scott. *A Greek-English Lexicon: With a Revised Supplement*. 9th rev. ed. Oxford: Oxford University Press, 1996.

Loder, James E. *The Transforming Moment*. 2nd ed. Colorado Springs, CO: Helmers & Howard, 1989.

Lonergan, Bernard. *The Way to Nicea: The Dialectical Development of Trinitarian Theology*. Translated by C. O'Donovan. Philadelphia: Westminster, 1976.

## Bibliography

Lossky, Vladimir. *In the Image and Likeness of God*. Edited by J. H. Erickson and T. E. Bird. Crestwood, NY: St. Vladimir's Seminary Press, 1974.

———. *The Mystical Theology of the Eastern Church*. Translated by the Fellowship of St. Alban and St. Sergius. London: Clarke, 1957.

Luther, Martin. *Lectures on Minor Prophets. Luther's Works*, vol. 18. Edited by Hilton C. Oswald. St. Louis: Concordia, 1978.

Lytvynenko, Viacheslav V. "The Doctrine of God and Deification in Athanasius of Alexandria: Relations and Qualities," Unpublished PhD diss., Charles University, Prague 2014.

Macmurray, John. *Freedom in the Modern World: Broadcast Talks on Modern Problems*. London: Faber, 1934.

Magee, John Gillespie, Jr. "High Flight." http://www.davidpbrown.co.uk/poetry/john-magee.html/.

Manastireanu, Danut. "Perichoresis and the Early Christian Doctrine of God." November 22, 2019. https://www.academia.edu/4794642/Perichoresis_and_the_Early_Christian_Doctrine_of_God.

Manning, Brennan. *Abba's Child: Cry of the Heart for Intimate Belonging*. Colorado Springs, CO: NavPress, 2002.

———. *The Ragamuffin Gospel*. Sisters, OR: Multnomah, 1990.

———. *The Signature of Jesus: On the Pages of Our Lives*. Portland, OR: Multnomah, 1992.

———. "What It Means to Be Cool in Christ Jesus." Sermon delivered at the Kingdom Works 1999 conference. Video recording posted by City Vision University. https://www.youtube.com/watch?v=QY7c6XPagmA.

Marenbon, John. "Anicius Manlius Severinus Boethius." *Stanford Encyclopedia of Philosophy*, Winter 2021 ed., edited by Edward N. Zalta. https://plato.stanford.edu/archives/win2021/entries/boethius/.

Margerie, Bertrand de. *The Christian Trinity in History*. Translated by E. J. Fortman. Still River, MA: St. Bede's, 1982.

Martin, Ralph P. *The Epistle of Paul to the Philippians: An Introduction and Commentary*. Grand Rapids: Eerdmans, 1998.

———. *A Hymn of Christ: Philippians 2:5–11 in Recent Interpretation and in the Setting of Early Christian Worship*. Downers Grove, IL: InterVarsity, 1997.

Martland, T. R. "A Study of Cappadocian and Augustinian Trinitarian Methodology." *Anglican Theological Review* 47.3 (1965) 252–63.

Maule, Will. "Well-Known Yale Professor Rejects Darwinism, Says Intelligent Design Is a 'Serious Theory.'" *Christian Headlines*, August 26, 2019. https://www.christianheadlines.com/contributors/will-maule/yale-professor-rejects-darwinism-says-intelligent-design-is-a-serious-theory.html.

May, Simon. *Love: A History*. New Haven, CT: Yale University Press, 2011.

"Maya Angelou Quotes." https://quotefancy.com/maya-angelou-quotes.

McFadyen, Alistair I. *The Call to Personhood: A Christian Theory of the Individual in Social Relationships*. Cambridge: Cambridge University Press, 1990.

McFarlane, "The Strange Tongue of a Long-Lost Christianity: The Spirit and the Trinity." *Vox Evangelica* 22 (1992) 63–70.

McGee, Quentin. *Prison Epistles: Ephesians, Philippians, Colossians, & Philemon*. Walnut Shade, MO: Faith and Action, 2017.

McGrath, Alister. *Christian Theology: An Introduction*. 2nd ed. Oxford: Blackwell, 1997.

McHugh, Phill, et al. "That's Where His Mercy Begins." https://songselect.ccli.com/Songs/1608620/thats-where-his-mercy-begins.

McIntyre, John. *On the Love of God.* London: Collins, 1962.
McKeachie, Wilbert J. *Handbook of Research on Teaching.* Edited by N. L. Gage. Chicago: McNally, 1963.
McLaughlin, J. F., and Judah David Eisenstein. "Names of God." In *The Jewish Encyclopedia*, originally published 1901–1906. http://jewishencyclopedia.com/articles/11305-names-of-god/.
McLellan, H. "Online Education as Interactive Experience: Some Guiding Models." *Educational Technology* 39.5 (1999) 36–42.
McNamara, Carter. "Basic Guidelines to Reframing — to Seeing Things Differently," 02/02/2012. https://managementhelp.org/blogs/personal-and-professional-coaching/2012/02/02/basic-guidelines-to-reframing-to-seeing-things-differently/
Mcray, John. "Abba." *Restoration Quarterly* 10.4 (1967) 222–24.
Melissaris, Athanasios G. "The Challenge of Patristic Ontology in the Theology of Metropolitan John (Zizioulas) of Pergamon." *Greek Orthodox Theological Review* 44 (1999) 473.
Meye, R. P. "The Imitation of Christ: Means and End of Spiritual Formation." In *The Christian Educator's Handbook on Spiritual Formation*, edited by K. O. Gangel and J. C. Wilhoit, 199–212. Grand Rapids: Baker, 1994.
Meyer, K. A. "The Web's Impact on Student Learning." *T.H.E. Journal* 30.10 (2003) 14, 16, 20, 22, 24.
Michaels, J. Ramsey. *The Gospel of John.* New International Commentary on the New Testament. Grand Rapids: Eerdmans, 2010.
Migliore, Daniel L. *Faith Seeking Understanding: An Introduction to Christian Theology.* Grand Rapids: Eerdmans, 1991.
Miller, Samuel. *The Dilemma of Modern Belief.* San Francisco: Harper & Row, 1963.
Minear, Paul S. "The Promise of Life in the Gospel of John." *Theology Today* 49.4 (1993) 485–99. https://doi.org/10.1177/004057369304900405.
Moltmann, Jürgen. *The Trinity and the Kingdom: The Doctrine of God.* Translated by Margaret Kohl. San Francisco: Harper & Row, 1981.
Montuori, Alfonso. "Transformative Leadership." Evolutionary Strategies, California Institute of Integral Studies, February 2017. https://www.academia.edu/34089742/TRANSFORMATIVE_LEADERSHIP.
Morrison, Michael. "Theology: An Introduction to Trinitarian Theology." https://www.gci.org/articles/an-introduction-to-trinitarian-theology/.
Mounce, Robert H. *Romans.* New American Commentary 27. Nashville: Broadman & Holman, 1995.
Murdock, Deroy. "Deroy Murdock: The Trump-Hating Media Are Demolishing Themselves." *Fox News*, January 26, 2019. https://www.foxnews.com/opinion/deroy-murdock-the-trump-hating-media-are-demolishing-themselves.
Murphy, Nancy. *Beyond Liberalism and Fundamentalism: How Modern and Postmodern Philosophy Set the Theological Agenda.* Harrisburg, PA: Trinity, 1996.
"Negative Theology." http://www.theopedia.com/negative-theology/.
Niebuhr, H. Richard. "Theological Unitarianisms." *Theology Today* 40.2 (July 1953) 150–57. https://doi.org/10.1177/004057368304000205.
Nietzsche, Friedrich. *Twilight of the Idols.* Translated by Richard Polt. Indianapolis: Hackett, 1997.
Newbigin, Lesslie. *The Open Secret: An Introduction to the Theology of Mission.* Rev. ed. Grand Rapids: Eerdmans, 1995.
———. *Proper Confidence: Faith, Doubt, and Certainty in Christian Discipleship.* Grand Rapids: Eerdmans, 1995.

———. *Trinitarian Doctrine for Today's Mission*. Eugene, OR: Wipf & Stock, 2006.

Newlands, George. *Theology of the Love of God*. Atlanta: John Knox, 1980.

Noll, Mark. *The Christian College: A History of Protestant Higher Education in America*. 2nd ed. Grand Rapids: Baker Academic, 2006.

Null, Bryce. "Tracking the Pistis Christou Debate." April 1, 2010. https://www.academia.edu/370699/Tracking_the_Pistis_Christou_Debate.

Nygren, Anders. *Agape and Eros*. Translated by A. G. Hebert et al. 2 vols. London: SPCK, 1932, 1938.

O'Carroll, Michael. "Circumincession." In *Trinitas: A Theological Encyclopedia of the Holy Trinity*, 68–69. Wilmington, DE: Glazier, 1987.

O'Donnell, John J. "The Trinity as Divine Community" *Gregorianum* 69.1 (1988) 5–34.

Oord, Thomas J., ed. *Relational Theology: A Contemporary Introduction*. Eugene, OR: Wipf & Stock, 2012.

Osborn, Eric. *Tertullian, First Theologian of the West*. Cambridge: Cambridge University Press, 2001.

Ortiz-Rodriguez, M., et al. "College Students' Perceptions of Quality in Distance Education: The Importance of Communication." *Quarterly Review of Distance Education* 6.2 (2005) 98–105.

Packer, J. I. *A Stunted Ecclesiology: The Theory and Practice of Evangelical Churches*. N.p.: Touchstone, 2002.

Palmer, Michael D. *Elements of a Christian Worldview*. Springfield, MO: Logion, 1998.

Palmer, Parker J. *To Know as We Are Known: A Spirituality of Education*. San Francisco: Harper Collins, 1983.

Palu, Ma'afu. "Does God Exist?" December 1, 2019. https://www.academia.edu/30652625/Does_God_Exist.

Pannenberg, Wolfhart. *An Introduction to Systematic Theology*. 2 vols. Grand Rapids: Eerdmans, 1991.

———. *Jesus: God and Man*. 2nd ed. Philadelphia: Westminster, 1977.

Parker, Nathaniel B. "A Biblical Understanding of the Trinity Through an Evaluation of the Eternal Generation and the Eternal Functional Subordination of the Son." University of Eldoret, January 2018. https://www.coursehero.com/file/80225606/A-Biblical-Understanding-of-the-Trinitypdf/.

Pattison, Stephen. *Pastoral Care and Liberation Theology*. London: Cambridge University Press, 1994.

Pava, Emma. "Examining Theological Approaches to the Personhood of God." September 16, 2019. https://www.academia.edu/8425276/Examining_theological_approaches_to_the_personhood_of_God.

Payne, J. Barton. *The Theology of the Older Testament*. Grand Rapids: Zondervan, 1962.

Pearcey, Nancy R. *Total Truth: Liberating Christianity from Its Cultural Captivity*. Wheaton, IL: Crossway, 2005.

Peters, Ted. *God as Trinity: Relationality and Temporality in Divine Life*. Philadelphia: Westminster John Knox, 1993.

———. *God—The World's Future: Systematic Theology for a New Era*. 3rd ed. Minneapolis: Augsburg Fortress, 2015.

Peterson, Derrick. "Gods, August and Otherwise: How Neo-Thomism Secretly Affected the 20th Century Trinitarian Renaissance." April 24, 2019. https://www.academia.edu/12407612/Gods_August_and_Otherwise_How_Neo_Thomism_Affected_the_20th_Century_Trinitarian_Renaissance.

Peterson, Eugene H. *The Message: The Bible in Contemporary Language*. Colorado Springs, CO: NavPress, 2005.

Pinkham, Wesley M. "Creative Conflict Management." Lecture materials, 2021.

———. "Identity Formation: The Journey Toward Person-Formation." Lecture materials, 1993.

———. "Listen for the Interests." Sermon delivered at Living Word Community Church, San Diego, June 25, 2017.

———. "The Pastor as a Change Agent." Lecture materials, 2002.

———. "Truth and Truthfulness: An Image for the Future of Today's Church." Lecture materials, 2001.

Pinnock, Clark H. *Flame of Love: A Theology of the Holy Spirit*. Downers Grove, IL: IVP Academic, 1996.

Polo-Wood, Chiqui. *The Abba Foundation: Knowing the Father through the Eyes of Jesus*. N.p.: Burkhart, 2018.

Powers, Kirsten. "Mayor Pete Buttigieg's Countercultural Approach to Christianity Is What America Needs Now." *USA Today*, April 3, 2019. https://www.usatoday.com/story/opinion/2019/04/03/mayor-pete-buttigieg-christian-right-2020-democratic-primary-trump-column/3342767002/.

Prestige, G. L. *God in Patristic Thought*. 2nd ed. London: SPCK, 1952.

"Prolepsis." https://www.merriam-webster.com/dictionary/prolepsis/.

Quinn, Philip L., and Charles Taliaferro, eds. *A Companion to Philosophy of Religion*. Oxford : Wiley-Blackwell, 1999.

Rad, Gerhard Von. *Genesis*. Philadelphia: Westminster, 1972.

———. *Old Testament Theology*. Vol. 1. New York: Harper & Row, 1962.

Rahner, Karl. *The Trinity*. Translated by Joseph Donceel. London: Burns and Oates, 1970.

Rayburn, Robert S. "Hearing Sermons." January 11, 1998. https://www.faithtacoma.org/uncategorized/1998-91-11.

Rehfeld, Emmanuel L. *Relationale Ontologie bei Paulus: Die ontische Wirksamkeit der Christusbezogenheit im Denken des Heidenapostels*. Tübingen: Mohr Siebeck, 2012.

Reid, Duncan. "Patristics and the Postmodern in the Theology of John Zizioulas." *Pacifica* 22.3 (2009) 308–16.

Rempel, Brent. Review of *God the Trinity: Biblical Portraits*, by Malcolm Yarnell. *Southwestern Journal of Theology*, 2018. https://www.academia.edu/38083402/Review_of_The_Triune_God_by_Fred_Sanders.

———. Review of *The Triune God*, by Fred Sanders. *Southwestern Journal of Theology*, 2018. https://www.academia.edu/38083402/Review_of_The_Triune_God_by_Fred_Sanders.

Review of *Fatherless America: Confronting Our Most Urgent Problem*. Kirkus Reviews, December 15, 1994. https://www.kirkusreviews.com/book-reviews/david-blankenhorn/fatherless-america/.

Ribaillier, J. *Richard de Saint-Victor, De Trinitate. Texte Critique*. Paris: n.p., 1958.

Rich, Tracey R. "The Name of G-d." *Judaism* 101. http://www.jewfaq.org/name.htm/.

———. "The Nature of God." *Judaism* 101. https://www.jewfaq.org/g-d.htm.

Richard, Lucien J. *A Kenotic Christology: In the Humanity of Jesus the Christ, the Compassion of Our God*. Lanham, MD: University Press of America, 1982.

Richards, Larry. *Let Day Begin*. Elgin, IL: David C. Cook, 1977.

Richards, Lawrence O., and Clyde Hoeldtke. *A Theology of Church Leadership*. Grand Rapids: Zondervan, 1980.

Ross, Hugh. *Beyond the Cosmos*. Colorado Springs, CO: NavPress, 1966.

———. *The Creator and the Cosmos: How the Greatest Scientific Discoveries of the Century Reveal God*. Colorado Springs, CO: NavPress, 1995.

Rovai, A. P., and J. D. Baker. "Sense of Community: A Comparison of Students Attending Christian and Secular Universities in Traditional and Distance Education Programs." *Christian Scholar's Review* 33.4 (2004) 471–89.
Rusch, William G. *The Trinitarian Controversy*. Philadelphia: Fortress, 1980.
Sahinidou, Ioanna. "On the Use of Perichoresis by Modern Theologians." September 19, 2019. https://www.academia.edu/36524177/%CE%9Fn_the_Use_of_Perichoresis_by_Modern_Theologians.
Sanders, Fred. "Trinitarian Theology's Exegetical Basis: A Dogmatic Survey." *Midwestern Journal of Theology* 8.2/9.1 (2010) 78–90.
———. "Trinity Talk, Again." *Dialog: A Journal of Theology* 44.3 (2005) 271.
———. *The Triune God*. Grand Rapids: Zondervan, 2016.
Schaeffer, Francis. "Christianity and the Humanities." Lectures recorded by the media department of Wheaton College, Wheaton, IL., 1967.
Schroeder, D. "Faculty as Mentors: Some Leading Thoughts for Reevaluating Our Role as Christian Educators." *Christian Education Journal* 13.2 (1993) 28–39.
Schuller, Robert Harold. *Self Esteem: The New Reformation*. Waco, TX: Word, 1982.
Schuller, Wayne. "Colin Gunton on the Trinity." Personal blog, November 9, 2005. http://schuller.id.au/2005/11/09/colin-gunton-on-the-trinity/.
Schumacher, Lydia. *Divine Illumination: The History and Future of Augustine's Theory of Knowledge*. Oxford: Wiley-Blackwell, 2011.
Schwöbel, Christoph. "Christology and Trinitarian Thought." In *Trinitarian Theology Today*, edited by Christoph Schwöbel, 113–46. Edinburgh: T. & T. Clark, 1995.
———. "God Is Love: The Model of Love and the Trinity." *Neue Zeitschrift für Systematische Theologie und Religionsphilosophie* 40 (1998) 310.
———, ed. *Trinitarian Theology Today: Essays on Divine Being and Act*. Edinburgh: T. & T. Clark, 1995.
Seamands, Stephen. *Ministry in the Image of God: The Trinitarian Shape of Christian Service*. Downers Grove, IL: InterVarsity, 2005.
Sellers, R. V. *The Council of Chalcedon: A Historical and Doctrinal Survey*. London: SPCK, 1953.
Sexton, Jason. *The Trinitarian Theology of Stanley J. Grenz*. New York: Bloomsbury, 2013.
Sexton, Jason, ed. *Two Views on the Doctrine of the Trinity*. Grand Rapids: Zondervan, 2014.
Shea, P., et al. "A Study of Teaching Presence and Student Sense of Learning Community in Fully Online and Web-Enhanced College Courses." *Internet and Higher Education* 9.3 (2006) 175–90.
Shivers, C. Christopher. "Trinitarian Communion as It Might Relate to Church Leadership: Reclaiming Personhood for Life in the Spirit." MA diss., London School of Theology, 2014.
Šijaković, Bogoljub, ed. *Ad Orientem: Essays from Serbian Theology Today*. Belgrade: Faculty of Orthodox Theology; Los Angeles: St. Sebastian Orthodox Press, 2019.
Silva, Moisés. *Philippians*. Baker Exegetical Commentary on the New Testament. 2nd ed. Grand Rapids: Baker Academic, 2005.
Smith, William. *A Dictionary of the Bible*. Revised and edited by MacDonald Peloubet. Grand Rapids: Zondervan, 1948.
Snyder, Howard A. *Decoding the Church: Mapping the DNA of Christ's Body*. Eugene, OR: Wipf & Stock, 2011.
Soulen, R Kendall. "YHWH the Triune God." *Modern Theology* 15.1 (1999) 25–54.

Speidell, Todd, ed. *Trinity and Transformation: J. B. Torrance's Vision of Worship, Mission, and Society*. Eugene, OR: Wipf & Stock, 2016.

Speiser, E. A. *Genesis*. Anchor Bible 1. New York: Doubleday, 1964.

Steel, Lyman K. "Primary Factors in Achieving Success." *US News & World Report*, May 26, 1980, 65–66.

Stoop, David. *Making Peace with Your Father*. Rev. ed. Grand Rapids: Revell, 2004.

Strange, C. "Measuring Up: Defining and Assessing Outcomes of Character in College." *New Directions for Institutional Research* 122 (2004) 25–36.

Studer, Basil. *Trinity and Incarnation: The Faith of the Early Church*. Translated by M. Westerhoff. Edited by A. Louth. Edinburgh: T. & T. Clark, 1993.

Suh, Edward Y. "The Inherent Goodness of God and Its Implications for Overcoming Believer's Relational Fears of Him: A Kenotic Trinitarian Paradigm of God's Emotionality." DMin paper, The King's University, 2010.

"Suzerain Treaties & The Covenant Documents the Bible." Notes from lectures of Dr. Meredith Kline, presented at Westminster Theological Seminary in Escondido, California, Westminster Theological Seminary in Philadelphia, Pennsylvania, and Gordon-Conwell Theological Seminary in Massachusetts. https://www.fivesolas.com/suzerain.htm.

Swindoll, Charles S. *Killing Giants, Pulling Thorns*. Portland, OR: Multnomah, 1981.

Tanner, Kathryn. *Jesus, Humanity and the Trinity: A Brief Systematic Theology*. Minneapolis: Fortress, 2001.

Tauber, Yanki. "What Is Sin?" https://www.chabad.org/library/article_cdo/aid/2830/jewish/What-Is-Sin.htm.

Taylor, Charles. *Sources of the Self: The Making of the Modern Identity*. Cambridge, MA: Harvard University Press, 1989.

Taylor, Daniel. *The Myth of Certainty: The Reflective Christian the Risk of Commitment*. Downers Grove, IL: InterVarsity, 1999.

Thielicke, Helmut. *The Waiting Father*. New York: Harper & Row, 1959.

Thompson, Craig. "What Marcel Proust Really Said about Seeing with New Eyes." *Clearing Customs* (blog), December 17, 2013. https://clearingcustoms.net/2013/12/17/what-marcel-proust-really-said-about-seeing-with-new-eyes/.

Thompson, John. *Modern Trinitarian Perspectives*. Oxford: Oxford University Press, 1994.

Thrasher, Andrew D. "Communion Ontology and Personhood: A Trinitarian Alternative to Postmodern Ontology." May 10, 2018. https://www.academia.edu/33564851/Communion_Ontology_and_Personhood_A_Trinitarian_Alternative_to_Postmodern_Ontology.

Thrasher, Andy. "Substantial Persons in Trinitarian Relationality: Trinitarian Theology, Imago Dei, and Personhood." July 18, 2020. https://www.academia.edu/31595395/Substantial_Persons_in_Trinitarian_Relationality.

Burgess, Paul. "Three Are the Perfection of Charity: The *De Trinitate* of Richard of St. Victor." http://www.paulburgess.org/richard.html#fn02.

Tinkham, Mathew L., Jr. "Hierarchy or Mutuality in the Trinity? A Case Study on the Relationship of the Son and the Holy Spirit in the New Testament." May 2, 2021. https://www.academia.edu/37762568/Hierarchy_or_Mutuality_in_the_Trinity_A_Case_Study_on_the_Relationship_of_the_Spirit_and_Son.

Toomey, Diane. "Exploring How and Why Trees 'Talk' to Each Other." *Yale Environment 360*, September 1, 2016. https://e360.yale.edu/features/exploring_how_and_why_trees_talk_to_each_other.

Torrance, Alan J. *Persons in Communion: Trinitarian Description and Human Participation*. Edinburgh: T. & T. Clark, 1996.

Torrance, James B. "Covenant or Contract? A Study of the Theological Background of Worship in Seventeenth-Century Scotland." *Scottish Journal of Theology* 23.1 (1970) 80.

———. "The Doctrine of the Trinity in our Contemporary Situation." Lecture delivered at Seattle Pacific University, Spring 1986.

———. *Worship, Community and the Triune God of Grace*. Downers Grove, IL: IVP Academic, 1997.

———. "Worship in the Reformed Church: The Purpose and Principles of Public Worship." Unpublished paper delivered to a graduate group at University of Aberdeen, Spring 1989.

Torrance, Thomas F. *The Christian Doctrine of God: One Being Three Persons*. Edinburgh: T. & T. Clark, 1996.

———. *Christian Theology & Scientific Culture*. Belfast: Christian Journals Limited, 1980.

———. *The Ground and Grammar of Theology: Consonance between Theology and Science*. Edinburgh: T. & T. Clark, 2005.

———. *Karl Barth: Biblical and Evangelical Theologian*. Edinburgh: T. & T. Clark, 1990.

———. *The Mediation of Christ*. Colorado Springs, CO: Helmers & Howard, 1992.

———. *Reality and Evangelical Theology*. Westminster, 1981.

———. *The School of Faith: The Catechisms of the Reformed Church*. London: Clarke, 1959.

———. *Theology in Reconciliation: Essays towards Evangelical and Catholic Unity in East and West*. London: Chapman, 1975.

———. *Trinitarian Faith: The Evangelical Theology of the Ancient Catholic Church*. 2nd ed. London: Bloomsbury Academic, 2016.

———. *Trinitarian Perspectives: Toward Doctrinal Agreement*. Edinburgh: T. & T. Clark, 1994.

Tow, Richard W. "Interest-Satisfaction Conflict Management: Measuring the Value of the Seminar for Increasing Christian Leaders Understanding of Effectively Managing Conflict." DMin paper, The King's College and Seminary, 2010.

Tozer, A. W. *The Knowledge of the Holy*. New York: Harper, 1961.

———. *The Pursuit of God*. Minneapolis: Bethany, 2013.

"Trinity." https://en.wikipedia.org/wiki/Trinity/.

Trueblood, Elton. *The Incendiary Fellowship*. New York: Harper & Row, 1967.

Tutu, Desmond. *No Future Without Forgiveness*. New York: Image, 2009.

Ury, William M. *Trinitarian Personhood: Investigating the Implications of a Relational Definition*. Eugene, OR: Wipf & Stock, 2002.

Vander Zee, Len. "The Holy Trinity." *The Banner*, February 2016. https://www.thebanner.org/features/2016/02/the-holy-trinity-the-community-of-love-at-the-heart-of-reality.

Vanhoozer, Kevin J., ed. *The Trinity in a Pluralistic Age: Theological Essays on Culture and Religion*. Grand Rapids: Eerdmans, 1997.

Vanstone, W. H. *Love's Endeavour, Love's Expense: The Response of Being to the Love of God*. Rev ed. London: Darton, Longman and Todd, 2007.

Varghese, Roby. "Stanley James Grenz's Communitarian Ecclesiology: An Explorative Analysis and Its Implications for the Indian Church." December 14, 2019. https://www.academia.edu/36847168/Stanley_James_Grenzs_Communitarian_Ecclesiology_An_Explorative_Analysis_and_Its_Implications_for_the_Indian_Church.

Velde, R. T. *The Doctrine of God in Reformed Orthodoxy, Karl Barth, and the Utrecht School*. Boston: Brill, 2013.

Volf, Miroslav. *After Our Likeness: The Church as the Image of the Trinity*. Grand Rapids: Eerdmans, 2021.

———. "The Nature of the Church." *Evangelical Review of Theology* 26.1 (2002) 69.

Volf, Miroslav, and Michael Welker, eds. *God's Life in Trinity*. Minneapolis: Fortress, 2006.

Waldinger, Robert. "What Makes a Good Life?" TED Talk, TEDxBeaconStreet, November 2015. https://www.ted.com/talks/robert_waldinger_what_makes_a_good_life_lessons_from_the_longest_study_on_happiness.

Wallace, J. Warner. "The Three Things I Wish Someone Had the Guts to Tell Me When I Graduated from College." *Fox News*, May 20, 2018. https://www.foxnews.com/opinion/2018/05/20/three-things-wish-someone-had-guts-to-tell-me-when-graduated-from-college.html.

Waltke, Bruce K., et al. *Theological Wordbook of the Old Testament*. Chicago: Moody, 1980.

Ware, Bruce, and John Starke, eds. *One God in Three Persons: Unity of Essence, Distinction of Persons, Implications for Life*. Wheaton, IL: Crossway, 2015.

Warrington, Keith. *Ephesians*. N.p.: Word & Spirit, 2015.

Wegerif, R. "The Social Dimension of Asynchronous Learning Networks." *Journal of Asynchronous Learning Networks* 2.1 (1998) 34–49.

Weng, Ng Kam. "T. F. Torrance on Perichoresis." *Krisis & Praxis* (blog), May 24, 2006. https://krisispraxis.com/archives/2006/05/t-f-torrance-on-perichoresis-mutual-indwelling-of-persons-within-the-trinity/.

Wessling, Jordan. "Colin Gunton, Divine Love, and Univocal Predication." *Journal of Reformed Theology* 7 (2013) 91–107.

Westermann, Claus. *Genesis 1–11*. London, SPCK, 1984.

"What Was the Great Schism?" https://web.archive.org/web/20210302054610/https://www.gotquestions.org/great-schism.html/.

Whapham, Ted. "Pannenberg on Divine Personhood." December 2, 2019. https://www.academia.edu/34807586/Pannenberg_on_Divine_Personhood.

Wiesenberg, F., and S. Hutton. "Teaching a Graduate Program Using Computer-Mediated Conferencing Software." *Journal of Distance Education* 11.1 (1996) 83–100.

Willard, Dallas. *The Divine Conspiracy: Rediscovering our Hidden Life in God*. San Francisco: HarperSanFrancisco, 1997.

———. *The Great Omission: Reclaiming Jesus's Essential Teachings of Discipleship*. New York: HarperOne, 2006.

———. *Renovation of the Heart: Putting on the Character of Christ*. Carol Stream, IL: Tyndale, 2014.

Wilson, Marvin R. *Our Father Abraham: Jewish Roots of the Christian Faith*. Grand Rapids: Eerdmans, 1989.

Wolterstorff, Nicholas. *The Contours of Justice in God and the Victim*. Grand Rapids: Eerdmans, 1999.

Wood, George, et al. *First and Second Corinthians: Student Manual*. Faith & Action Team. February 3, 2012.

Wood, Kerry V. "Participating in the Ministry of Christ: The Contribution of Trinitarian Theology to an Understanding of the Nature of Pastoral Leadership." DMin paper, The King's University, 2012.

Woodson, Sandra K. "*Cura Personalis* in Online Undergraduate Christian Higher Education." PhD diss., Capella University, 2010.

Worley, Robert C. *Change in the Church: A Source of Hope*. Philadelphia: Westminster, 1971.

Wozniak, Robert J., and Giulio Maspero, eds. *Rethinking Trinitarian Theology: Disputed Questions and Contemporary Issues in Trinitarian Theology*. London: T. & T. Clark, 2012.

Wright. N. T. *Simply Christian: Why Christianity Makes Sense*. San Francisco: HarperOne, 2006.

Yaffe, Philip. "The 7% Rule: Fact, Fiction, or Misunderstanding." *Ubiquity*, October 2011, 2–5. https://ubiquity.acm.org/article.cfm?id=2043156.

Yannaras, Christos. *Elements of Faith: Introduction to Orthodox Theology*. Edinburgh: T. & T. Clark, 1991.

———. *Truth and Unity of the Church*. Athens: n.p., 1977.

Yarnell, Malcom B., III. *God the Trinity: Biblical Portraits*. Nashville: B&H Academic, 2016.

Yates, Larry L. "The Divided God—Apostolic Theology and the Biblical Challenge to Contemporary Trinitarianism." December 23, 2019. https://www.academia.edu/21150767/THE_DIVIDED_GOD_Apostolic_Theology_and_the_Biblical_Challenge_to_Contemporary_Trinitarianism.

Yong, Amos. *Spirit-Word-Community: Theological Hermeneutics in Trinitarian Perspective*. Aldershot: Ashgate, 2002.

Zachariades, Doros. "Athanasius's Christology: A Methodology to Counter Kenotic Notions of the Incarnation." April 29, 2021. https://www.academia.edu/3704373/Double_Account_in_Athanasius.

———. "Διπλην Επαγγελιαν in Athanasius's Christology: A Methodology to Counter Kenotic Notions of the Incarnation." *American Theological Inquiry* 5.1 (January 2012) 55–77.

Zhou, Li. "What to Listen to and Watch for When Enjoying Jazz." *Smithsonian Magazine*, March 31, 2015. https://www.smithsonianmag.com/smithsonian-institution/what-to-listen-to-and-watch-for-when-enjoying-jazz-180954723/.

Ziegler, Geordie W. "Is It Time for a Reformation of Spiritual Formation? Recovering Ontology." *Journal of Spiritual Formation and Soul Care* 11.1 (2018) 4.

Zinn, Grover A. *Richard of St. Victor: The Twelve Patriarchs; the Mystical Ark; Book Three of the Trinity*. Classics of Western Spirituality. New York: Paulist, 1979.

Zscheile, Dwight J. "The Trinity, Leadership and Power." *Journal of Religious Leadership* 6.2 (2007) 54.

Zizioulas, John. *Being as Communion: Studies in Personhood and the Church*. Contemporary Greek Theologians 4. Crestwood, NY: St. Vladimir's Seminary Press, 1997.

———. *Communion and Otherness: Further Studies in Personhood and the Church*. Edinburgh: T. & T. Clark, 2007.

# Subject Index

abandonment
    pain of, 159
    perceived, 18
*Abba*, 7–8, 104–5, 149, 153, 228
    Western church and, 106
Abba paradigm, 137–40, 147–48
*Abba* relationship
    living in, 158–60
    mission of, 155–58
Abraham, 235–36
    God's covenant with, 118, 120n7
active listening, 182
Adam and Eve, xiv, 67
adult development study, xxvi
affective domain, 88
American colleges, 85
American dream, 59
Anderson, Ray, 73, 141n19, 177, 202, 219
Anderson, Terry, 87
Angelou, Maya, 19, 20
anger, 183
apothecary, xvii
Aramaic, 150n8
Aristotle, 153
Arius, 42
Athanasius of Alexandria, 39, 42
Atkinson, William P., 45

Augustine, 65
authenticity, 191, 193
authority, 56

Barth, Karl, xiii, xix, 31–32, 43, 47–48, 77n40, 96, 127n24
Basil of Caesarea, 39, 42
behavior modification, 185
being, 38
    alteration through interpersonal oneness, 216–17
    in Christ, 205
    of the church, 206
    connection to Christ, 199
    as expression of relationship, 199
    I-AM ontology, 202–6
    implementing relational ways, 83–84
    state of, 195
    vs. doing, 195, 198, 202, 205–6, 220
beliefs, worldview and, 26
believers, 206
believer's ontology, 202
Benson, Warren S., 84
Bible, 27. See also New Testament; *and Scripture index*
    hall of fame, 235–36
    Hebrew, 148

Bible (*cont.*)
   Hebrew mindset within, 37n7
   King James Version, 66
   as love letter, 133
   metaphors and imagery, 61
   as relational, xiv
biblical (Hebraic) worldview, 59
biblical ecumenicity, 230
biblical truth, 43
bilateral (*suntheke*) contract, 119
   vs. unilateral, 123
Bloom, Benjamin, 88
blue whales, 233–35
body of Christ, xiv, 27, 83, 99, 134
   unity and diversity, 230
Boethius, 63
Boff, Leonardo, 43
Bonhoeffer, Dietrich, xix, 125–26, 169
Bonino, José Miguez, 94, 98–99
Borysov, Eduard, 53n62
Boyer, E.L., 85
breakdown, breakthrough, or breakout, 231, 236
Brunner, Emil, xix
Bullinger, Heinrich, 76
Buttigeig, Pete, 91
Buxton, Graham, 106, 124, 169

*Caddyshack* (film), 233
Calkin, Ruth Harms, prayer, 13–14
Calvin, John, 76, 76n37, 125, 127n24, 159–60, 171n13
Campbell, Douglas A., 21, 126, 129
Cappadocians, 39
caring, 163
Carson, D.A., xxxi, 64
Chaldean agreement, 121, 123n13
Chan, Cherry M., 207
change, process of, 178f
character, Word as, 71
children
   relating to, 185–86
   trust, 70–71
Christ. See Jesus
Christian education, 80–81, 88
Christian ethics, replacing, xxvii

Christian lifestyle
   best way to live, 25
   consequences, 70
   faking, 218
Christian reality, and holism, 27–28
Christianity, 196
   conceptual scheme of, 25–26
   discipleship paradigms, 29
   essence of, xxix–xxxiv
   exchanged life in, 197
   externalized forms, xiv
   Greek view as works based, 60
   idealized, 229
   individualized forms, xiv
   interpersonal oneness and, 225
   legalistic approach, 124
   meaning of, xxv
   mental and relational approaches, 75–76
   mind and, 78
   obstacles to understanding spirituality, 52
   ontological truth of, 198–202
   relational, 76, 211
   search for unifying center, xxvi
   Trinity and, 93
   worldview, 26
*Christianity Today*, xii
Christlikeness in leadership, 169
Christological hermeneutic, 109
   interpersonal oneness as, 106–13
Christology, 44–46
church, 31, 53, 98, 227
   as community, 64, 207
   focus on conduct, 137
   history, xiv
   interpersonal oneness in action, 212–13
   loss of young adults, xxviii
   nature of God and, 206–8
   new members, 214–16
   objective assessment, 211
   operation, 171
   as organism or corporation, xxix
   relationships in, 51–54, 214
   revitalization process, 172
   servant leadership paradigm, 112
   Trinitarian theology and, 96

church leadership
    interest satisfaction in, 169–73
    nature of, 54
Churchill, Winston, 222
Claerbaut, David, 85
closed circle of knowing, 144–45
Coe, John, 83
collectivism, and individualism, 64
comfort, 141
commands of God, 70
communication, and goal achievement, 181–82
communion, 73
    consubstantial, 49
    dynamic, 47–51, 52
    perichoretic, 43
    personal dynamic, 54–57
    relational ontology focus, 197
    relationships of, 43
    of the Spirit, 44
community, 229
    church as, 64, 207
    formation, 169
    interconnected relationships, 174
    paradigm for, 133
    relational aspects and education, 82–83
    vs. individualism, xxvi
community relationships, spiritual power of, 32
community-based interest satisfaction, 172
compassion (*splagchnizomai*), 12, 106, 155
    Godly, 135
complaint, 209–11
concepts, Word as, 71
conduct, way of being and, 211
confidence, xiv
conflict, 167, 194
    between being and doing, 205–6
    expanding power base for those with, 187–88
    relational management, 166
congregations. See church
consequences, 71
consubstantial communion, 49

contractual view of God-human relationship, 117, 124–29
conversation, 216–17
Conzelmann, Hans, 152n15
covenant, 60, 63, 117–18, 221
    with Abraham, 118
    breaking of, 122
    fulfillment, 121, 123
    of works vs. grace, 125
covenantal view of God-human relationship, 117–24
Craig, William Lane, xxxii–xxxiii*n*16
creation, xxviii
Creator, xxix
cultural perspectives, 62
culture, 58
    relational, interpersonal, communal, 72–78

Davis, Martin, 126–27
Dean, Kenda Creasy, *Almost Christian*, xxvii
demythologization, xxvii
denominations, 230
Descartes, René, 63–64
destruction, 190
*diatheke* (unilateral contract), 118, 126, 139
    vs bilateral, 123–24
Dickens, Charles, 8
Dickson, Ben, 29, 31, 32
disciples, friendship with Jesus, 106
discipleship, 30, 84
    with downward focus, 31–32
    inward, 30–31
    outward, 32
    upward, 30
    web of, 32
discourse, 87
discovery, xviii
disillusionment, xxvi
divine pathos, 135
doing vs. being, 195, 198, 202, 205–6, 220
*doulos*, 112n28
downward discipleship, 31–32
dualism, 59–60

Dunn, James D.G., 149–50, 151, 155, 156
dynamic communion, 47–51, 52

Eastern Church, 52n58
ecclesiology, 28, 36n3, 56
    unbalanced, 95
Edery, David S., 3nn1
education
    Christian, 80–81, 88
    discipleship and, 84
    holistic approach, 85
    interpersonal oneness and, 84–88
    reality and, 81
*eis* (in; into), 31n40
*ekstasis*, 50
Elijah, 160
Ellington, Duke, 192
Elmer, Duane, 62
emotion, negative, 188
emotionally stuck, 186
Erickson, Millard J., 97
evangelicalism, 111n27
evangelism, relationship oriented, 157
extrinsic motivation, 185

faith, 86, 127
    of Abraham, 119
    for future, 216
    love and, 221
Father. See also God; Trinity, 28, 105n8
    expression of being, 220–21
    intimacy with, 149
    of Jesus, 63
    oneness with, 195
    vision in Luke, 16
fathers, relationships with, 158–60
Father-Son paradigm, 148
Father-Son relationship, 17, 108, 151, 156, 160
Federal theologians, 125
Fee, Gordon, 36, 52, 55
Folsom, Marty, 24, 28, 42, 58, 74, 78, 91, 228–29
forgiveness, 21, 158, 174, 218
Freedman, R. David, 66–67, 67n22
freedom to win or lose, 190

friendship, and interpersonal oneness, 108
fullness (*pleroma*), 18n15
futuristic approach to interest satisfaction, 174

Gangel, Kenneth O., 84
Garber, Peter R., 182
Garrison, D.R., 87
*geder* (classification), 217
Gethsemane prayer, 150
Getz, Gene, 211, 215
giving, 202
Glenn, Mark H., 82, 87, 109, 112n28
God. See also Trinity, 100
    commands of, 70
    desire for closeness with humanity, 113
    direct relationship, 143
    eternal life, 78
    finding answers in, 210
    fullness of, 224
    Greek view as controller, 59
    of Hebrew people, 60
    as I-AM, 203
    ideas about, 117
    *Imago Dei*, xix, 201, 207, 227
    as individual, xxx
    indwelling of, 208
    interpersonal nature, 35–57, 56
    Jesus' personal view of, 226
    knowing, 229
    love of, 14, 137, 218
    as Monad, 63
    nature of, xxx, xxxii
    nature of, and church's nature, 206–8
    New Testament view of, 149–54, 160
    personhood. of, 36–44
    promises, 129
    reality created by, 106
    relationality of, xii
    revelation, 64, 142
    revelation in Scripture, 98
    student relationship with, 85
    Western Christian view, xxix
Godhead, personal dynamic communion of, 35

## Subject Index

God-human relationship
    contract view of, 124–29
    covenantal view of, 117–24
    understanding of, 117
Godly compassion, 135
Goss, Tracy, 216
governance, 169
Gowdy, Trey, 156
grace, 10, 16, 17, 124, 126
    covenant of, 125
    Jesus as, 130
Graham, Billy, 19–20
great command, xiv
Greco-Roman tradition, 59
Greek cultural perspective, 62
Greenleaf, Robert, 54n64
Gruenler, Royce G., 115
guilt, 15
Gunton, Colin, xxxiii, 4, 36n6, 37, 39, 41, 42, 43n33, 47–48, 64, 99, 206

Hasse, John Edward, 192
Hayes, Mike, 158, 159
Hayford, Jack W., xvii, 133
heaven, treasures of, 205
Hebrew Bible, 148
Hebrew cultural perspective, 62
Hemingway, Ernest, *The Old Man and the Sea*, 230–31, 234
hermeneutics, 108
hierarchical system, 29
holiness, 100
holism
    and Christian reality, 27–28
    in Christian worldview, 27
    as educational approach, 85
    in hermeneutics, 111
    and human reality, 22–25
    and relationships, 26
    and theological thinking, 28–32
    in Trinity, 27, 32
holistic discipleship model, 29f
Holmes, Stephen, 94
Holy Spirit, 17, 19, 28, 30, 33, 128, 134, 140, 157, 205, 220, 221–22, 225
    and closed circle of knowing, 145
    communion of, 44
    and conversations, 192
    Jesus' dependence on, 46
    reception of, 207
    recognition of role, 52
    in relationships, 168
    releasing, 226
    role in church, 53
homoousion, 39
Hooke, Robert, *Micrographia*, 22
hope, 216, 223
Horrell, J. Scott, 3, 95, 96, 115, 137, 201, 207, 230
Hughes, Philip E., 141
Huizing, Russell L., 54n64
human being
    Christian view, xxx
    holistic view of, 85
    individualistic view of, 65
human connection, 236
human mind, 64
humanity, 45
    God's desire for closeness with, 113
    Jesus' relationship with, 205
    reality of, 22–25, 106
    reintegration within God's life, xi

"I am" sayings, 203–5
I-AM ontology, 202–6
identity, 77, 200
identity crisis, xxix
idolatry, 15
Ignatius of Antioch, 38
imagery in Bible, 61
*imago dei* (image of God), xix, 30, 201, 205, 207, 227
imitation of Christ, xxxi
"in Christ," 199–200
incarnation, 169
    kenotic theories of, 48
    Trinity and, 107
independence, 16
individual, God as, xxx
individualism, xi, 63, 200
    and collectivism, 64
    mechanistic, 62, 65, 74
    Trinity and, xxx
    vs. community, xxvi

individuality, 47
  responsiveness and, 73
indwelling of God, 208
informational exchange, 76
inner conflict
  expanding power base for those with, 187–88
  new ideas and, 86
insecurity, narcissism in, xii
interconnectedness, 16, 22
interdependence, 99
interest satisfaction
  in church leadership, 169–73
  community-based, 172
  kenotic model, 173–77
  relationships in, 172
  theology of, 166–69
interpersonal oneness, xxix–xxx, xxxi, 72, 102
  Christianity based on, 58
  as Christological hermeneutic, 106–13
  education and, 84–88
  Father-led, 102–6, 226
  and friendship, 108
  as reconciliation of Jesus, 113–15
  releasing interest satisfaction, 163
interpersonal oneness elements
  expanding power base for those with inner conflict, 187–88
  listening, 180–82, 192–93
  nuking it, 190–92
  pathway for interest and need, 184–86
  relationship building in reverse, 188–90
interpersonal oneness indicators, 209–16
  avoiding pitfalls to measurement attempts, 217–21
  conversation, 216–17
intimacy, 150
  with Father, 149
inward discipleship, 30–31
Irenaeus, 38, 169
irrationality, 191–92
Isoka, John, 72n32

jazz music, 192
Jeremiah, David, 221–22
Jeremias, Joachim, 104–5, 139, 149, 150
Jerome (saint), 202
Jesus. See also Trinity, xiv, 28, 36, 76–77, 154, 229
  as apothecary, xviii
  call to truth, 106
  on the cross, 151
  dependence on Holy Spirit, 46
  and Father, 45, 103, 107
  friends, 226
  as fulfillment of Abrahamic covenant, 118–22
  as grace, 130
  imitation of, xxxi
  interpersonal oneness as reconciliation of, 113–15
  miracles, 204
  mission, 157
  personhood of, 45–46, 47, 108
  receiving, 199–201
  relationship with humanity, 205
  releasing, 201–2
  role in conditional salvation, 128
  self-emptying, 168–69
  servant leadership lifestyle, 47
  servanthood model, 113
  as Son, as King, 155
  state of self-giving, 49
  suffering, 45
  teaching methods, 84
  wise rule, 171
Jewish community, and *Yahweh*, 118
Jeyachandran, L. T., 94
Judgment Day, 160
justice, 210

*kalam* cosmological argument, xxxii–xxxiiin16
Kanitz, L., 86
Kant, Immanuel, 94, 95
Kärkkäinen, Veli-Matti, 73
Kasper, Walter, 107n14
Keathley, Hampton, IV, 117–18, 120
*kenosis*, 45, 168, 184, 214
  listening and, 194
  reciprocal, 47–51

## Subject Index

kenotic-interest-satisfaction model, 173–77
   example, 174–77
Kierkegaard, Soren, 219
Kierspel, Lars, 199, 200, 205
kingdom of God, xv
kingly office, 171n13
Kissinger, Henry, 166
Kittel, Gerhard, 169n10
knowledge, 212
Kohlberg, Lawrence, 69–70n30
*koinonia*, 99
Krauthammer, Charles, 236
Kruger, C. Baxter, 9, 138
*kubernesis*, 169
Kung, Hans, 169

LaCugna, Catherine Mowry, 32, 197
Lamoureux, P., 86
Larson, Bruce, xii
leadership
   Christlikeness in, 169
   church, 54, 169–73
   facilitating Spirit formation, 191
   mission of, 177
LeBar, Lois E., 81
legalism, 71
Lewis, C.S., xxxii, 201
life, Western view, xxx
lifestyle, 28, 33
   Christian, 25, 70, 218
   servant leadership, 54n64
linear analytical reasoning, 24
listening, 180–82
   biblical view, 182–84
   in Relational Christianity, 167–68
Locke, John, 94
Loder, James E., 75
*Logos*, 38
loneliness, 67
Lord's Prayer, 149
Los Angeles Theology Conference (2014), 97
Lost Son parable, 5–14, 33
   God running, 14
   perspectives on, 8–9
   reunion, 15
   worldview of, 26

love, 20, 77, 112n28, 133, 195, 226, 227
   of Abba, 7
   faith and, 221
   feelings and, 21
   of God, xxiii, 14, 137, 218, 228
   of God, earning, 218
   incarnational way of reflecting divine, 56
   interconnectivity of, 17–22
   as motivation, 63
   of neighbor, 207
   obligations and conditions, 125
   in Old Testament, 3nn1
   oneness, 19
   openness and, 222
   operational or behavioral definition, 212
   recursiveness of, 135–36
   relationships grounded in, 126
   selfless, 184
   self-sacrificing, 201
   Trinitarian communion of, 107
   and Trinity, 135
love ethic, xii
love-based paradigm, xix
Luther, Martin, 76, 125–26

management, abilities valued, 181
Manning, Brennan, 9, 10, 12, 15, 18, 118, 138–39, 153
Martin, Ralph P., 48
*mathetes* (disciple), 84
May, Simon, 3nn1
McFadyen, Alistair I., 67
mechanistic Enlightenment, 36n6
mechanistic individualism, 62, 65, 74
mentorship, 82
metaphors, 77
   in Bible, 61
Migliore, Daniel L., 51, 107, 113, 114
Miller, Samuel, xxvi
Milton, John, 94
ministry, 219
miracles, 46, 204
mirrors, recursion in, 74
mission
   of *Abba* relationship, 155–58
   of Jesus, 157

## Subject Index

mission (cont.)
　of leadership, 177
　of Triune God, 31
modalism, 37n8, 43
Moltmann, Jürgen, 31–32
Montuori, Alfonso, xxvin3
moral reasoning, 69–70n30
Moses, 202–3
Murray, John, 220
"mutual indwelling," 200
Myers, Ben, 228–29

negative emotion, 188
neighbor, love of, 207
new church members, 214–16
New Covenant, 123–24
New Testament, 137
　Greek philosophical backdrop of, 37
　"one another" statements, 212–13, 215
　on Spirit formation, 135
　view of God, 149–54, 160
Newbigin, Lesslie, 31–32, 64, 97n16
Newton, Isaac, 94
Nicea, doctrine of, 97
Nietzsche, Friedrich, 70, 211
*No Future Without Forgiveness* (Tutu), 72
non-being, 226
Norquist, Bruce, 121, 130

Ohannes, Elliott R., 15–16
Old Testament, fatherhood concept, 150
oneness, xxxi
　with God, 195, 223
　interpersonal, xviii
　priority over individualism, 47
"ontological dynamics," 195
ontological hermeneutical approach (onto-hermeneutical), 109
ontology (way of being), 65n20, 197, 216
　I-AM, 202–6
onto-relational category, 40
openness
　as interpersonal oneness marker, 223
　measuring quality, 222–23
optical illusion, 23*f*

optimism, 222
orange, parable of the, 165–66, 167
orthodoxy, 215
ortho-ontology, 198
orthopraxy, 198, 215
otherness, 132
others, believer relationships with, 137
outward discipleship, 32
over/under perspective on culture, 66

Packer, J.I., 96
Palmer, Parker J., 83, 86, 88, 105
Pannenberg, Wolfhart, 30–31, 41n21, 97
parable. See Lost Son parable
parable of the orange, 165–66, 167
paraclete paradigm, 140–42
paradigm, 133
　Abba paradigm, 137–40, 147–48
　based on vision, 133
　of relationships, 145
　servant leadership, 112
　transactional paradigm, 128, 144
　Western, 74
paradigm shifts, xxviii–xxix, xxxiv
parenting, 184–85
*parousia* (return of Christ), 106
past, focus on, 174
pastor, xxviii
　as change agent in revitalization, 175
Paul. See also *letters in Scripture index*, 27, 134, 141, 157, 183, 199, 211, 218, 221
　on *Abba* theme, 153
Pavey, Emma, 195
Pearcey, Nancy, 35
performance-orientation perspective on culture, 67–68
*perichoresis* (mutual indwelling), 40, 82, 95, 100, 142
*Perichoresis* (yacht), 232–35
perichoretic communion, 43
person, 40
　defined, 45, 63, 77n40
　and Trinity, 97n17
　value of, 129
personal dynamic communion, 54–57
personal interests, 172

# Subject Index

personality, 216n11
personhood, xxxi, 37, 44n34, 65n20, 74, 78n41, 172
   of God, 36–44
   human, 52
   interdependence, 72–73
   of Jesus, 45–46, 47, 108
   loss of, 200
   reciprocal communion views, 51
   relational ontology focus, 197
   theology of, 56n71
pessimism, 222
pestle, xvii
Peters, Ted, 216
Peterson, Eugene, 137
*philos*, 112n28
Plato, 22, 153
*pleroma* (fullness), 18n15
Pneumatology, 44–46
Polo-Wood, Chiqui, 60
postmodernism, xxvii
power base, expanding for those with inner conflict, 187–88
pragmatism, Roman, 60
prayer, 15–16, 190, 196
   by Calkin, 13–14
   Gethsemane prayer, 150
   by Jesus, 149
preaching, 76, 128
priestly office, 171n13
priorities
   of thinking self, 229
   worldview and, 26
procedural satisfaction, 174
prodigal son. See Lost Son parable
prolepsis, 216
proleptic opening, 223
promissory covenant, 118
prophetic approach, 171n13, 210, 223
Protestantism, 169–70
Proust, Marcel, xviii
psychological satisfaction, 174
punishment, 60
purpose in life, 113

quantum physics, xxviii

*rachamim* (Hebrew), 12
Rahner, Karl, xxxiin15, 30
reaction, 235
reality, 24, 225
   defining, 3–4
   discovery, 227
   and holism, 22–25
   importance of defining, 91
   nature of, 94–97
   view of, 33
reason, 63
reasoning
   linear analytical, 24
   moral, 69–70n30
receiving Christ, 199–201
reciprocal kenosis, 47–51
recursion, 74
"Recursive Model of Conflict Management" (RMCM), 87
reductionism, 25
Rehfeld, Emmanuel I., 199, 200
relation power, expanding, 187
relational, definition, xi
Relational Christianity, xi, 76
   definition, xii
   listening in, 167–68
relational conflict management, 166
relational connection, xii
   in teaching, 82
relational distance, and friendships, xi
relational interconnection, 143
relational oneness paradigm, 142–45
relational ontology, 197
relational teaching approach, 81–83
relational theology, xii
relational thinking, resistance to, xii
relational ways of being, 83–84
relationships, xxxi
   being as expression of, 199
   building in reverse, 188–90
   in church, 214
   of communion, 43
   developing safe and healthy, 159
   dynamic nature, 187
   Father-Son, 17, 108, 151, 156, 160
   with God, 223
   grounded in love, 126
   holistic interconnectivity of, 22

relationships (*cont.*)
    interconnected in community, 174
    in interest satisfaction, 172
    intimate, xxvii
    listening and, 181, 193–94
    love-based, 88
    maintaining, 201
    ontological hermeneutical approach (onto-hermeneutical), 173
    paradigm of, 145
    self-giving, 163
releasing Christ, 201–2
Rempel, Brent, 110n23, 111n27
renewal, xv
repentance, 15–16
responsibility, 224
revitalization
    achieving, 176–77
    pastor as change agent, 175
revival, 195–98
reward, 60
Richard St. Victor, 135–36
Roman cultural perspective, 62
Roman pragmatism, 60
rule of faith (*regula fidei*), 27
rules, 60
Rush, Myron, 175

salvation, 28, 114, 122, 126
    human responses to, 127
    invitation for gift of, 156
    Jesus' role in conditional, 128
Sanders, Fred, 110
Schaeffer, Francis A., xxix–xxx
Schuller, Robert, 8, 11
    *Self-Esteem: The New Reformation*, 129
Schwöbel, Christoph, 108, 114
scientific theory, xxvn1
Scott, Tim, 156–57
script for listening, 194
Seamands, Stephen, xix
seichel (spiritual perception), 217
self, postmodernist approach, 66
self-actualization approach to Christianity, 68–69
self-emptying, 50
    and filling, 169

self-fulfillment, xii
self-giving relationship, 163
selflessness, 55, 183
self-sacrificing love, 201
self-understanding, Western lack of, xxv
Sellers, R.V., 35n2
semiotics, 109n21
servant leadership lifestyle, 54n64
servant leadership paradigm, 112
servanthood, 113
Shivers, C. Christopher, 33, 36, 45, 46, 50, 51, 52, 53
Silva, Moises, 220
sin, 9–10n5
    destroying power of, 21
sinfulness, 11
Snyder, Howard A., 97
Social Trinitarian thinking, xiii–xiv
Son of God, eternity of, 42–43
sonship, 148, 151, 154, 155, 157
Soulen, R. Kendall, xxxii
speaking, and listening, 182
Spirit of adoption, 138
Spirit-formed believers, 133
Spiritual formation, 68, 133–34, 135, 148
    leadership facilitating, 191
spiritual growth, xii, 69–71
spiritual satisfaction, 174
"*splagchnizomai*" (Greek), 12
Spurgeon, Charles, 202
Stoppard, Tom, 236
stories, 184
strife, 167
substance, 65n20
substance ontology, 65
substantive satisfaction, 174
Suh, Edward, xxxiv
suicide, 17–18
*suntheke* (bilateral) contract, 119
    vs. unilateral, 123–24
Swirsky, Michael, 217
systematic theology, 110n25

Taylor, Charles, 65–66
teaching
    focus of, 128
    models, 82
    relational approach to, 81–83

## Subject Index

Tertullian, 35n2, 65n20
thanksgiving, 127
theological thinking, and holism, 28–32
theology, 37n7
    systematic, 110n25
theophany, 119
Thielicke, Helmut, 9
Thomas Aquinas, 8–9
Thrasher, Andrew, 107, 227
Tinkham, Matthew L., 41
tithing, 70–71
Torrance, James B., xiii, xxxn12, 62, 63, 103, 123–24, 125, 126, 127, 129
Torrance, Thomas F., xiii, xxxiii, 25, 37n7, 38, 39, 40, 41, 43, 44, 49, 93, 96, 130, 141, 144–45, 148
Tozer, A.W., 31n39
transactional paradigm, 126, 128
    detrimental effect, 144
transcendence of eternal purpose, 234, 235
trees, holistic view of, 23
*triadosis*, 53n62
Trinitarian paradigm, transition from Western paradigm, 74
Trinitarian relationship, 157
Trinitarian thinking, xiii–xiv
    influence of, 100
    relational results of, 102
Trinity. See also Father; Holy Spirit; Jesus, xxix, xxxvf, 22, 25, 90, 236
    avoiding heresy with, 228–29
    Christianity and, 93
    closed circle of knowing, 144–45
    doctrine of, 227
    holism of, 32
    and humanity, 45
    and incarnation, 107
    individualism and, xxx
    interpersonal nature, 36
    interpersonal oneness, xxxii
    and love, 135
    oneness of, 36
    personal encounter to discover, 37n7
    practical implications, 97–100
    preincarnate appearance, 119
    relational dynamic, 40
    relational ontology, 77n40
    relationships, 99, 115
    scripture and, 110
    unity of, xxxi, 169
Triune God, xi, 225
    mission of, 31
    qualities, xii
trust, xiv, 175, 187, 223
    by children, 70–71
truth, xxvii, 105
truthfulness, 176f
Tutu, Desmond, *No Future Without Forgiveness*, 72
Twain, Mark, 113

*ubuntu* (African concept), 72–73
understanding, 33
unidimensionality, 25
unilateral covenant (*diatheke*), 118, 126, 139
    vs bilateral, 123–24
upward discipleship, 30

Vanstone, W. H., 168
ventilate, then validate, 188–90
vision, xix
    paradigm based on, 133

Warrington, Keith, 4, 12
way of being, 140, 173
    complaint as, 209–10
    conduct and, 210–11
web, 28
    of discipleship, 32
Western Christianity, cultural view, 61
Western paradigm, Trinitarian paradigm transition to, 74
Western values, 58–59
*what*-ness, 167
*who*-ness, 167
Wiles, Maurice, 95
Willard, Dallas, xxx–xxxi, 4, 21
Winfrey, Oprah, 20
Woodson, Sande K., 82, 88
Word of God. See also Bible, 17, 76n37
    growth stages in relating to, 69–71
    understanding of, 212

works, salvation based on, 128
works covenant, 125
works righteousness, 21
worldview, 33
    biblical (Hebraic), 59
    Christianity, 26
    and understanding of God, 98
Worley, Robert C., 214

Yaffe, Philip, 182
*Yahweh* (*YHWH*), 118, 140, 148, 152–53
Yarnell, Malcom B. III, 110, 111
young adults, church exodus, xxviii

Zee, Len Vander, 135
Ziegler, Geordie W., 130
Zizioulas, John, 32, 37, 38, 44n34, 172n14

# Scripture Index

## OLD TESTAMENT

### Genesis
| | |
|---|---|
| 1:26 | xxix |
| 2:18 | 66 |
| 2:23 | 67 |
| 15 | 118, 121 |
| 15:1–21 | 120n7 |
| 15:17–18 | 119 |
| 17:4–21 | 120n7 |
| 17:7 | 122 |
| 22:15–18 | 120n7 |
| 26:3–5 | 120n7 |
| 26:24 | 120n7 |
| 28:13–15 | 120n7 |
| 35:9–12 | 120n7 |

### Exodus
| | |
|---|---|
| 3:14–15 | 203 |
| 19—24 | 118 |

### Deuteronomy
| | |
|---|---|
| 1:31 | 150 |
| 6:4 | xxix |
| 8:5 | 150 |
| 14:1 | 150 |

### Psalms
| | |
|---|---|
| 2:7 | 155 |
| 22:1 | 104 |
| 23:6 | 17 |
| 23:7 | 223 |
| 27:10 | 158 |

### Proverbs
| | |
|---|---|
| 1:5 | 169n10 |
| 11:24 | 169n10 |
| 23:7 | 26, 71 |
| 24:6 | 169n10 |

### Isaiah
| | |
|---|---|
| 1:2 | 150 |
| 55:8 | 59 |
| 64:6 | 220 |

### Jeremiah
| | |
|---|---|
| 3:19 | 150 |
| 31:35–38 | 123 |

## Zechariah

| | |
|---|---|
| 1:3 | 197 |

## Malachi

| | |
|---|---|
| 1:6 | 150 |
| 3:10 | 71 |
| 4:5–6 | 160 |

# NEW TESTAMENT

## Matthew

| | |
|---|---|
| | 149 |
| 4:21 | 55 |
| 4:23 | 76 |
| 6:9 | 149 |
| 6:10 | 168 |
| 6:25 | 73 |
| 9:6 | 45 |
| 9:35–36 | 12 |
| 10:24 | 84 |
| 11:27 | 142, 144, 154, 155, 156 |
| 11:29 | 45 |
| 11:30 | 134 |
| 12:18 | 107 |
| 17:46 | 159 |
| 18:19–20 | 217 |
| 20:32 | 192 |
| 26:39 | 45 |
| 27:46 | 104–5 |
| 28:18–20 | 31 |
| 28:28 | 14 |

## Mark

| | |
|---|---|
| 2:10–11 | 45 |
| 3:31–35 | 45 |
| 6:34 | 12 |
| 8:31 | 45 |
| 10:18 | 199 |
| 12:31 | 168 |
| 14:36 | 45, 152n15, 154, 155 |
| 15:34 | 104–5, 151, 152n15 |

## Luke

| | |
|---|---|
| | 16 |
| 1:35 | 46 |
| 2:49 | 103 |
| 3:22 | 46 |
| 10:21–22 | 142 |
| 10:22 | 154 |
| 11:1–13 | 45 |
| 11:2 | 156 |
| 14:12 | 113n28 |
| 14:26 | 84 |
| 15 | 26 |
| 15:6 | 113n28 |
| 15:9 | 113n28 |
| 15:11–32 | 5–14 |
| 15:20 | 12, 18, 20 |
| 15:29 | 113n28 |
| 15:31–32 | 9 |
| 22:29 | 156 |
| 22:42 | 45, 107 |
| 23:46 | 103 |

## John

| | |
|---|---|
| | 107, 149, 203, 229 |
| 1:18 | 137 |
| 3:16 | 50, 108, 120n5, 137, 144 |
| 3:16–18 | 11, 31 |
| 3:17 | 13, 114 |
| 4:24 | 51 |
| 5:19 | 157 |
| 5:19–27 | 47, 99, 103 |
| 6:35 | 204 |
| 6:36 | 205 |
| 6:48 | 204 |
| 6:51 | 204 |
| 8:12 | 204 |
| 8:28–29 | 45 |
| 8:34 | 112n28 |
| 10:7 | 204 |
| 10:9 | 204 |
| 10:14 | 204 |
| 10:30 | 108 |
| 11:1 | 113n28 |
| 11:16 | 84 |
| 11:25 | 204 |
| 12:1 | 113n28 |

| | | | |
|---|---|---|---|
| 12:27–28 | 45 | 8:15–16 | 140–41, 186 |
| 12:35 | 73 | 8:16 | 221 |
| 12:50b | 102 | 8:31 | 14 |
| 14:6 | 17, 204 | 8:31–35 | 219 |
| 14:8–79 | 109n21 | 8:34 | 223 |
| 14:9 | 44, 49, 91 | 12 | 184 |
| 14:10 | 103 | 12:4–5 | 27 |
| 14:16 | 141 | 12:5 | 73 |
| 14:16–17 | 82 | 12:10 | 50, 182, 213 |
| 14:20 | 103 | 12:16 | 213 |
| 14:23 | 46, 200 | 12:18 | 213 |
| 14:26 | 31, 141 | 14:1 | 213 |
| 14:28 | 103, 113, 137 | 14:13 | 213 |
| 15:1 | 204 | 15:5 | 213 |
| 15:5 | 204 | 15:7 | 213 |
| 15:12 | 112n28 | | |
| 15:12–15 | 91, 102 | **1 Corinthians** | |
| 15:13 | 113n28 | 1:30 | 223 |
| 15:14–15 | 108, 112n28 | 2:2–16 | 142 |
| 15:15 | 106, 112n28, 226 | 2:9–12 | 145 |
| 15:26 | 141, 200 | 4:15 | 226 |
| 16:7 | 141 | 6:11 | 200 |
| 16:13–14 | 99, 103 | 11:33 | 213 |
| 16:13–15 | 46 | 12 | 54 |
| 17:11–12 | 196 | 12:3 | 157 |
| 17:13 | 15 | 12:12–14 | 32 |
| 17:18 | 31 | 12:12–27 | 82 |
| 17:20–23 | 82 | 12:12–31 | 27 |
| 17:21 | 140 | 12:25 | 213 |
| 17:23 | 105 | 12:28 | 169n10 |
| 17:25–26 | 103, 116, 118 | 13:12 | 112n28, 228 |
| | | 13:13 | 224 |
| **Acts** | | | |
| 1:8 | 31 | **2 Corinthians** | |
| 10:38 | 120n5 | 1:3–7 | 141 |
| 27:11 | 169n10 | 3:3 | 200 |
| | | 3:17 | 51 |
| **Romans** | | 4:4 | 110n21 |
| 4:1–3 | 235–36 | 5:17 | 174 |
| 5:5 | 200 | 9:6–7 | 71 |
| 5:8 | 21 | 10:12 | 217 |
| 8:1–2 | 13, 218 | 11:23 | 141 |
| 8:5 | 151 | 12:10 | 142 |
| 8:9 | 200 | 13:5 | 211, 223 |
| 8:10 | 221 | 13:11 | 55 |
| 8:15 | 138, 145, 152n15, 153, 157 | | |

## Galatians

| | |
|---|---|
| 2:16 | 127n24 |
| 2:16a | 128 |
| 3 | 118 |
| 3:16 | 118 |
| 3:17–22 | 125 |
| 4:2 | 214 |
| 4:6 | 151, 152n15 |
| 5:6 | 221 |
| 5:13 | 213 |
| 5:14 | 135 |
| 5:26 | 213 |
| 6:1 | 55 |
| 6:2 | 135, 214 |
| 6:4 | 211 |

## Ephesians

| | |
|---|---|
| 1:3 | 196 |
| 1:3–10 | 13 |
| 1:4 | 196 |
| 1:5 | 196 |
| 1:13 | 153 |
| 2:6 | 206 |
| 3:1–21 | 4, 12 |
| 3:15 | 105n8 |
| 3:17 | 200, 223 |
| 3:19 | 12, 18, 134, 224 |
| 4:4–5 | 230 |
| 4:12 | 55 |
| 4:16 | 27 |
| 5:2 | 21, 67 |
| 5:32–32 | 223 |

## Philippians

| | |
|---|---|
| 1:11 | 219–20 |
| 2 | 184 |
| 2:1–6 | 49–50 |
| 2:3 | 50 |
| 2:3–4 | 48 |
| 2:4 | 163, 166, 183 |
| 2:5 | 168 |
| 2:5–11 | 48 |
| 2:13 | 220 |

## Colossians

| | |
|---|---|
| 1:15 | 14, 109n21 |
| 1:18 | 27 |
| 1:27 | 68, 224 |
| 1:28 | 68 |
| 2:9–10 | 68 |
| 2:9–11 | 196 |
| 2:12–15 | 218 |
| 3:9 | 214 |
| 3:11–15 | 21 |
| 3:13 | 214 |
| 3:18 | 66 |
| 3:22–24 | 68 |

## 1 Thessalonians

| | |
|---|---|
| 2:7 | 134 |
| 2:8 | 135 |
| 2:12 | 135 |
| 2:20 | 134 |
| 3:5 | 211 |
| 5:21 | 211 |

## 1 Timothy

| | |
|---|---|
| 3:16 | 110n21 |

## Hebrews

| | |
|---|---|
| 1 | 22 |
| 1:3 | 14, 109n21 |
| 2:9 | 45 |
| 2:18 | 141 |
| 4:16 | 206 |
| 4:32 | 214 |
| 6:1–3 | 69, 69n29 |
| 6:13 | 122 |
| 6:17 | 122, 123 |
| 8 | 200 |
| 9:1 | 129 |
| 10:24 | 214 |
| 11 | 235–36 |
| 12:2 | 112n28, 120n5 |
| 13:21 | 55 |

## James

| | |
|---|---|
| 1 | 184 |
| 1:19 | 182–84, 193 |
| 4:10 | 50 |
| 4:11 | 214 |
| 5:16 | 214 |

## 1 Peter

| | |
|---|---|
| 2:9 | 56 |
| 4:9 | 214 |
| 4:11 | 202 |
| 4:20–21 | 201 |
| 5:1–3 | 56 |
| 5:5 | 214 |

## 2 Peter

| | |
|---|---|
| 1:3 | 197 |

## 1 John

| | |
|---|---|
| 1:1–3 | 143 |
| 1:3 | 103 |
| 2:1 | 141 |
| 4:8 | 3 |
| 4:9–10 | 18 |
| 4:12–13 | 207 |
| 4:19 | 18 |
| 5:7 | xxix |
| 20:17 | 18 |

## Revelation

| | |
|---|---|
| 13:8 | 120n5 |
| 18:17 | 169n10 |
| 21:3–5 | 218 |

www.ingramcontent.com/pod-product-compliance
Lightning Source LLC
Chambersburg PA
CBHW050838230426
43667CB00012B/2057